S0-BZR-578

CONTRIBUTING AUTHORS

Robert Bach
Frank D. Bean
Deborah A. Cobb-Clark
Barry Edmonston
Michael Fix
Paul T. Hill
Jason Juffras
B. Lindsay Lowell
Philip L. Martin
Doris Meissner
Demetrios G. Papademetriou
Jeffrey S. Passel
Abby Robyn
Elizabeth Rolph
Martina Shea
Shirley J. Smith
J. Edward Taylor
Wendy Zimmermann

BOARD OF TRUSTEES
Lloyd N. Morrisett
  Chairman
Peter S. Bing
Harold Brown
Solomon J. Buchsbaum
Frank C. Carlucci
Richard P. Cooley
Ann F. Friedlaender
James C. Gaither
Walter J. Humann
Michael M. May
G. G. Michelson
Newton N. Minow
J. Richard Munro
Paul H. O'Neill
John S. Reed
Donald H. Rumsfeld
Donald W. Seldin, M.D.
James A. Thomson
John F. Welch
Charles J. Zwick

The RAND Corporation was chartered in 1948 as a nonprofit insitution to "further and promote scientific, educational, and charitable purposes, all for the public welfare and security of the United States of America." To meet these objectives, RAND conducts rigorous analyses of significant national problems to provide decision-makers and the public with a better understanding of the policy issues involved.

RAND's research is analytic, objective, and interdisciplinary. National security programs focus on the planning, development, acquisition, deployment, support, and protection of military forces, and include international matters that may affect U.S. defense policy and strategy. Domestic programs include civil and criminal justice, education and human resources, health sciences, international economic studies, labor and population, and regulatory policies.

THE PAPER CURTAIN

Employer Sanctions' Implementation, Impact, and Reform

Michael Fix, editor

RAND CORPORATION
Santa Monica, CA

THE URBAN INSTITUTE PRESS
Washington, D.C.

THE URBAN INSTITUTE PRESS
2100 M Street, N.W.
Washington, D.C. 20037

Editorial Advisory Board

William Gorham
Craig G. Coelen
Richard C. Michel
Demetra S. Nightingale

George E. Peterson
Felicity Skidmore
Raymond J. Struyk
B. Katherine Swartz

Copyright © 1991. The RAND Corporation and The Urban Institute. All rights reserved. Except for short quotes, no part of this book may be reproduced or utilized in any form or by any means, electronic or mechanical, including photocopying, recording, or by information storage or retrieval system, without written permission from The Urban Institute Press.

Library of Congress Cataloging in Publication Data

The Paper Curtain: Employer Sanctions' Implementation, Impact, and Reform/ Michael Fix, editor; [contributors] Robert Bach . . . [et al.].

1. Alien labor—United States. 2. Emigration and immigration law—United States. I. Fix, Michael. II. Bach, Robert L.

HD8081.A5P36   1991   91-19906
331.6′2′0973—dc20   CIP

ISBN 0-87766-550-8 (alk. paper)
ISBN 0-87766-549-4 (alk. paper; casebound)

Printed in the United States of America.

9 8 7 6 5 4 3 2 1

Distributed by:
     University Press of America
4720 Boston Way   3 Henrietta Street
Lanham, MD 20706   London   WC2E 8LU   ENGLAND

BOARD OF TRUSTEES
David O. Maxwell
Chairman
Katharine Graham
Vice Chairman
William Gorham
President
Andrew F. Brimmer
James E. Burke
Marcia L. Carsey
Albert V. Casey
John M. Deutch
Richard B. Fisher
George J.W. Goodman
Fernando A. Guerra, M.D.
Ruth Simms Hamilton
Irvine O. Hockaday, Jr.
Michael Kaufman
Ann McLaughlin
Robert S. McNamara
Charles L. Mee, Jr.
Elliot L. Richardson
David A. Stockman
Mortimer B. Zuckerman

LIFE TRUSTEES
Warren E. Buffett
Joseph A. Califano, Jr.
William T. Coleman, Jr.
Anthony Downs
John H. Filer
Joel L. Fleishman
Eugene G. Fubini
Aileen C. Hernandez
Carla A. Hills
Vernon E. Jordan, Jr.
Edward H. Levi
Bayless A. Manning
Stanley Marcus
Arjay Miller
J. Irwin Miller
Franklin D. Murphy
Lois D. Rice
William D. Ruckelshaus
Herbert E. Scarf
Charles L. Schultze
William W. Scranton
Cyrus R. Vance
James Vorenberg

THE URBAN INSTITUTE is a nonprofit policy research and educational organization established in Washington, D.C., in 1968. Its staff investigates the social and economic problems confronting the nation and government policies and programs designed to alleviate such problems. The Institute disseminates significant findings of its research through the publications program of its Press. The Institute has two goals for work in each of its research areas: to help shape thinking about societal problems and efforts to solve them, and to improve government decisions and performance by providing better information and analytic tools.

Through work that ranges from broad conceptual studies to administrative and technical assistance, Institute researchers contribute to the stock of knowledge available to public officials and private individuals and groups concerned with formulating and implementing more efficient and effective government policy.

Conclusions or opinions expressed in Institute publications are those of the authors and do not necessarily reflect the views of other staff members, officers or trustees of the Institute, advisory groups, or any organizations that provide financial support to the Institute.

ACKNOWLEDGMENTS

I would like to thank Frank Bean for helping to guide and shape this volume; Jeff Passel for his helpful review of the final chapter; Wendy Zimmermann for her research support; and Sheila Lopez and Lavonia Proctor for their patient and expert technical assistance.

CONTENTS

Figures

FOREWORD

The passage of laws is a difficult process, especially in areas involving diverse and conflicting interests. Getting political bargains to work is often an exhausting process, one that sometimes fails and sometimes produces outcomes that depart in important respects from the original goals of the participants on all sides. Thus, although it is common for lawmakers, the press, and the public to think that once a law is passed in Congress the job is done, this is not the case. A law, in fact, is only the beginning, only the marching order. But it is frequently a difficult marching order to follow because of the compromises it represents. The conflicting orders embedded in such compromises make laws hard to implement and administer.

The 1986 Immigration Reform and Control Act (IRCA) is a strong example of just this kind of law. It is exceptional, however, in that legislators were well aware that some of the law's components were experimental, might not work as planned, would need to be monitored, and, if the worst developed, might need to be repealed. Because of this, they attached to the law a sunset provision as well as funds and directives to assess how well the law was working to stem the flow of illegal immigrants into the United States.

At the same time that lawmakers were calling for a close evaluation of IRCA, the Ford Foundation, consistent with its ongoing concern with immigration issues, created a new immigration program involving the RAND Corporation and The Urban Institute—the Program for Research on Immigration Policy. Among other things, the Program has sought to understand the impact of IRCA and to assess more broadly the unfolding gatekeeping function of U.S. immigration policies and their demographic, economic, and social effects.

Several conclusions emerge from the chapters in this book. First, the number of undocumented migrants across the southern border appears to be increasing again after a sharp decline following IRCA's enactment. Second, jobs in agriculture appear to have remained a magnet for undocumented migrants, as worker turnover has increased and the number of farm labor contractors who serve as intermediaries between farmers and workers has expanded. Third, the introduction of employer sanctions appears to have increased the incidence of national origin and citizenship discrimination. Fourth, although the generally disciplined and nonconfrontational implementation of employer sanctions succeeded in preserving the legitimacy of the new regulatory scheme, new enforcement missions assigned the Immigration and Naturalization Service and continuing competition within the INS for enforcement resources are threatening the long-term effectiveness of sanctions.

In spite of the problems, however, Congress is unlikely to repeal employer sanctions because of their perceived role in sustaining the essentially liberal, inclusionary immigration policies that distinguish the United States from much of the Western world.

The Urban Institute is frequently in the business of evaluating how things are working. About half of our research is devoted to evaluating government programs. The most common uses of our work are to improve the functioning of programs or to help Congress and the administration assess the worth of those programs. This study is consistent with that mission, assisting Congress in assessing the law's implementation and impacts, the prospects for its reform, and the merits of its repeal. The papers in this volume are a good example of how the social sciences can now be used to assess the efficacy and impacts of our national laws.

William Gorham
President

PREFACE

The papers in this volume address the related issues of the implementation, impacts, and reform of employer sanctions and selected programs authorized by the 1986 Immigration Reform and Control Act (IRCA), which was intended to curb illegal immigration. Four of the chapters (Juffras; Fix and Hill; Rolph and Robyn; and Zimmermann) draw on a common database assembled through a project that examined the implementation of IRCA in eight urban sites. The project was conducted under the aegis of the Program for Research on Immigration Policy, sponsored jointly by the RAND Corporation and The Urban Institute. The chapter addressing IRCA's impact on the flow of undocumented immigrants by Passel, Bean, and Edmonston is adapted from chapters written for a volume on IRCA and undocumented immigration (Bean, Edmonston, and Passel, 1990). The chapter on IRCA's impact on California agriculture by Martin and Taylor is taken from a report prepared for the Program for Research on Immigration Policy. Two other chapters (Papademetriou et al. and Smith and Shea) were written by staff of the Department of Labor's Center for Migration Studies, and were first presented at a conference on the implementation of IRCA convened by the RAND Corporation and The Urban Institute in December 1989. Finally, the chapter by Bach and Meissner was initially written for a small seminar that was jointly sponsored by the Immigration Policy Project of the Carnegie Endowment for International Peace and the Program for Research on Immigration Policy in May 1990; it has subsequently been issued by the Carnegie Endowment (Bach and Meissner, 1990).

References

Bach, Robert, and Doris Meissner. 1990. *Employment and Immigration Reform: Employer Sanctions Four Years Later.* Washington, D.C.: The Carnegie Endowment for International Peace, September.

Bean, Frank D., Barry Edmonston, and Jeffrey S. Passel, eds. 1990. *Undocumented Migration to the United States.* The Urban Institute Press.

Chapter One

EMPLOYER SANCTIONS: AN UNFINISHED AGENDA

Michael Fix

In June 1990, after a long and rancorous debate, the delegates to the NAACP's annual convention voted to urge Congress to repeal the employer sanctions provisions of the 1986 Immigration Reform and Control Act (IRCA). The vote reversed the position that the organization had strongly advocated throughout the debate over IRCA during the 1970s and the 1980s, when NAACP support for employer sanctions had been of great political and symbolic value to the law's proponents.[1]

The NAACP's about-face followed the release of a report by the General Accounting Office (GAO) that found that sanctions had given rise to "widespread discrimination" against foreign-appearing job applicants (GAO, 1990). The report confirmed the results of a number of other widely publicized studies of IRCA's discriminatory effects, transforming the issue of employer sanctions from an immigration matter to a civil rights question. Calls for repealing the sanctions were echoed by such mainstream organizations as the U.S. Chamber of Commerce and the American Bar Association.

At the same time that the controversy over discrimination was taking place, sanctions' critics and proponents were debating the law's success in achieving its central objective: reducing the flow of undocumented immigrants to the U.S. The Immigration and Naturalization Service (INS) claimed the law had had a dramatic impact on reducing the flow (McNary, 1990), while others claimed it had had only a modest effect that was deteriorating over time (see chapters 7, 8, and 9 of this volume). The possibility that IRCA had increased discrimination, while having a diminishing impact on flows, made many wonder whether the costs of sanctions were proving to be worth the price.

Thus, 40 years after Illinois Senator Paul Douglas had first introduced sanctions legislation and four years after IRCA was enacted, many of the basic questions about how the nation should regulate illegal immigration had yet to be put to rest. These included bedrock questions about the ability of sanctions to control illegal immigration, the ethical implications of trading off some discrimination in hiring for reduced illegal immigration, and the privacy interests that might be imperiled by the introduction of a national identity card that all job applicants would have to present to demonstrate their eligibility to work.

THE CHALLENGE OF EMPLOYER SANCTIONS AND IMMIGRATION CONTROL

The 1986 Immigration Reform and Control Act represented the most sweeping change in U.S. immigration law in 34 years. Employer sanctions are one of four major policy innovations contained within IRCA that were intended to reduce the stock and flow of U.S. illegal immigration. The other three were a) substantially increased border enforcement, b) the legalization of undocumented aliens who had continuously resided in the U.S. since 1982 and of selected agricultural workers, and c) the Systematic Alien Verification for Entitlement (SAVE) program, a telephone verification system designed to discourage alien use of public benefits.

Sanctions, however, were thought to be the cornerstone of the law. They would close a loophole in the immigration code by forbidding employers to hire illegal immigrants and allowing the Immigration and Naturalization Service (INS) to penalize violators. Strongly advocated by the influential Select Commission on Immigration and Refugee Policy (SCIRP) in 1981, sanctions were intended to right an asymmetry in American law: while it had been a violation of federal law for undocumented aliens to enter and work in the United States, their employers committed no illegal act by hiring them. Following IRCA's enactment, employers became liable for knowingly hiring undocumented aliens and for failing to conduct mandated verification and record-keeping procedures.

Sanctions' goal of reducing the flow of undocumented migrants was both difficult and ambitious, a goal that their Congressional framers fully expected would take seven to eight years to become a reality (Fix and Hill, 1990, p. 40). In the first place, the demographic, economic, social, and historical forces that lay behind the flow of illegal and legal immigrants to the United States were exceptionally strong (Commission for the Study of International Migration and

Cooperative Economic Development, 1990). These forces included rapid population growth in developing countries (notably Mexico, Latin America, and the Caribbean Basin), widening disparities in income and wealth between the U.S. and these developing nations, historically established migratory patterns, expanding kinship networks, and continuing civil unrest within Latin America. It would clearly be naive to expect a new regime of labor regulation, standing more or less alone, to overcome these forces.[2] Such inherent challenges to sanctions' effectiveness were augmented by the hostile political climate within which sanctions' implementation took place, as IRCA represented a major expansion of federal regulation during a strongly anti-regulatory period.

Further complicating the achievement of IRCA's law enforcement objectives were the nation's deeply-rooted civil liberties norms. Their impact was most obviously felt during debates over the introduction of a national identification card and/or a telephone verification system that would be used by employers to determine a job applicant's work eligibility. The implications for personal privacy of developing a secure identification system remained a constant theme in debates over the reform of the nation's system of immigration controls.

The threat of congressional repeal that hung over the law's implemention during the first three and a half years of its existence also represented a basic challenge to sanctions' potential effectiveness. In response to fears that IRCA would give rise to widespread discrimination, its framers provided for expedited congressional review and the possible repeal of sanctions if the General Accounting Office (GAO) were to find after three years that they had given rise to widespread discrimination. This "sunset" provision led to unusually intensive oversight of the enforcement process and to extreme caution in implementing the sanctions provision. Taken together, the constraints imposed by the hostile anti-regulatory climate and by civil liberties and civil rights concerns would all work to chill efforts to enforce the law vigorously.

The daunting challenges posed by IRCA's basic objective and the political context within which enforcement would take place were compounded by the institutional and resource constraints that faced the law's implementers. Lead responsibility for enforcement was assigned to the Immigration and Naturalization Service (INS), a small and highly decentralized agency within the Department of Justice that had often been criticized for the unfairness, procedural irregularity, and ineffectiveness of its law enforcement activities. Sanctions would put the agency in the position of regulating U.S. firms for the first time, requiring the INS, which had hitherto functioned primarily as a police or paramilitary organization, to transform itself into a mainstream regulatory agency. It would have to grow rapidly in numbers and sophistication—both tough challenges in an era of Gramm-Rudman deficit reduction targets.

The strength of the forces lying behind illegal immigration, coupled with the political, legal, and institutional constraints facing implementation, have all contributed to what most observers view to be sanctions' modest and declining impact on immigrant flows to date.

Several of the authors in this volume (Bach and Meissner; Papademetriou, et al.) counsel patience in coming to final judgment on whether to retain sanctions. They suggest that U.S. policymakers look to the experience of Europe, which they contend holds promise for the eventual success of sanctions in the United States. However, as I argue in the final chapter, the evidence of Western Europe's success in regulating illegal immigration has been, at least by some accounts, a mixed one at best.[3] Moreover, controlling illegal immigration to the United States is more difficult logistically than controlling illegal entry to Europe, owing to the easy access afforded by this country's lengthy land borders. Furthermore, our long history of dependence on illegal foreign labor, our comparatively short history of immigration controls, and our social commitment to civil liberties and anti-discrimination norms all challenge sanctions' effectiveness in the U.S. in ways that differ from Western Europe.

THE PROBLEM OF ILLEGAL IMMIGRATION

The main business of IRCA, as embodied in employer sanctions, increased border enforcement, the legalization programs, and SAVE, was to reduce illegal immigration. As Passel et al. note in chapter 7, meaningful assessments of the volume and impact of undocumented migration must distinguish among several different kinds of entrants. One classification comes from the government, which distinguishes between persons who enter without any sort of legal visa (called "EWIs" because they "enter without inspection") and persons who enter with legal visas but remain beyond the authorized time limit (called "visa overstayers"). Similar to visa overstayers are other foreign-born persons who enter the United States legally but violate the terms of their temporary visas by taking a job. The distinction between EWIs and visa overstayers derives from the fact that almost all EWIs are from Mexico and most visa-overstayers are from non-Mexican countries (Warren, 1990). Much of the illegal immigration to the U.S., especially that originating in Mexico, is circular in character: many who enter illegally do not settle, but go back to Mexico and then return periodically.

Debate Over the "Problem"

The circular character of immigration was largely lost in debates over IRCA, which focused on Border Patrol apprehension data. Advocates often confused flows of illegal migrants, which were large and growing, with stocks of illegal immigrants, which were less large. As a result, there was little agreement on the scale of the problem. The absence of good empirical evidence on the costs and benefits of illegal immigration meant there was some disagreement over whether undocumented migration should be deemed a problem at all.

This indeterminacy complicated efforts to frame a solution and accounted, in part, for the decade-long debate that preceded IRCA's enactment. When the debate began, the scale of the problem was unknown. Like all efforts to gauge inherently clandestine activity, estimates of the number of undocumented aliens varied widely over time, ranging from alarmist claims of 4 to 12 million to more scientifically derived Census Bureau estimates of 2 to 3 million.[4]

LABOR MARKET EFFECTS

But the issue went beyond numbers. There was little consensus over whether illegal immigrants were good or bad for the country, and if they were deemed to be bad, how much of a problem they represented. And here, as in other areas of debate over immigration policy, the principal point of contention was the labor market effects of the new migrants. Did immigrants, both legal and illegal, serve as substitutes for the native labor force, thereby displacing native workers? Or did they serve as complements to the native labor force, filling jobs that would otherwise go begging and keep jobs and industries in America that would otherwise move offshore?

As immigration scholar Wayne Cornelius wrote in 1977:

> Workers cannot be displaced if they are not there, and there is no evidence that disadvantaged native Americans have ever held, at least in recent decades, a significant proportion of the kinds of jobs for which illegals are usually hired, especially in the agricultural sector. (Cornelius, 1977)

At the same time, immigration experts David North and Marion Houstoun were arguing that unchecked illegal immigration would have a number of adverse labor market effects, including:

☐ Depressing the educational and skill level of the labor force;
☐ Depressing labor standards in the secondary sector, which in some cases will create an underground market in illegal wages, hours, and workers;
☐ Displacing low-skill legal resident workers;
☐ Creating a new class of disadvantaged workers, one that will inextricably conjoin national origins and illegal status in the U.S.; and
☐ Inhibiting efforts to improve job satisfaction in the secondary sector (North and Houstoun, 1976).

The lack of strong evidence demonstrating illegal immigration's negative labor market effects led IRCA's principal architect, Senator Alan Simpson (R-WY), to eventually de-emphasize this labor market rationale in his efforts to press for sanctions.[5]

FISCAL IMPACTS

In addition to the labor market effects of the new migrants, their fiscal impacts were also extensively debated. Proponents of immigration control pointed to examples of welfare abuse by the undocumented and argued that their low skill and education levels would lead them to become a welfare-dependent underclass. A survey of apprehended aliens revealed them to have an average of 4.9 years of schooling, compared to 12.4 for American citizens (North and Houstoun, 1976). These perceptions of the undocumented and of immigrants in general were becoming increasingly widely held around the time of IRCA's enactment. A CBS/New York Times poll taken in 1986 revealed that for many, the words "poor" and "welfare" were the first to come to mind in response to the word "immigrant."[6] But other scholars argued that undocumented and recent immigrants not only had a positive labor market impact, but were generally disinclined to use public benefits and contributed more in taxes than they received in benefits.[7]

MORAL CONCERNS

Beyond disagreement over the economic and fiscal rationale for employer sanctions, there was also substantial debate over sanctions' moral legitimacy. Some noted that the predominantly Mexican flow of undocumented immigrants was an integral part of a longstanding, de facto U.S. government policy with regard to Mexico. This policy, embodied in the Bracero program and the Texas Proviso, reflected a national strategy of "bring[ing] them in when they are needed, send[ing] them home when they aren't" (Fogel, 1977). The Bracero program was a "temporary" guest-worker program that responded to labor shortages in agriculture brought about by World War II. The program, which was put in place in 1942 and continued through 1964, involved importing roughly 5 million Mexican workers. Employment of illegal aliens continued, though, despite official indignation. The Texas Proviso was a revision of the immigration laws in 1952 that provided that employers could not be prosecuted for hiring illegal aliens (Congressional Research Service, 1977).

The moral case *for* sanctions was based on the fact that illegal immigration makes a shambles of the visa preference system and mocks the efforts of those who wait patiently abroad to receive permission to enter the U.S. Sanctions' moral authority also derived from the fact that the pre-IRCA system of immigration controls punished only undocumented migrants, leaving employers who benefited from their presence unaffected and undeterred. Furthermore, it was argued that the employers who hired undocumented aliens were not humanitarians but were, in fact, those most likely to be in violation of other labor-related standards governing worker safety, minimum wage, child labor, equal pay, and the like.

Another moral argument for sanctions has been their role in eliminating the exploitation of illegal workers. As Senator Alan Simpson recently remarked,

> The purpose of the bill for me was to avoid exploitation of human beings. It was not a jobs bill; I didn't care about numbers. I cared about the fact that if people were coming to the United States, go to work like dogs, that they ought to have a legal status so they would not be exploited by their fellow man. (Simpson, 1990)

The power of the exploitation argument has been reduced by evidence that illegal aliens are rarely paid less than the minimum wage.

Proponents of sanctions urged their adoption as a means of preventing flows of undocumented migrants from leading to a backlash against legally admitted immigrants and to the adoption of restrictive immigration policies. Hence, IRCA was seen as an effort to "close the back door while keeping the front door open" (Fuchs, 1990) and a prerequisite to retaining the nation's generally liberal, legal immigration policies.

SOCIAL EFFECTS

The social effects of unchecked illegal migration were also the subject of controversy. Some argued that the scale of the flow, coupled with its spatial concentration in a relatively few communities, promised to fragment, disrupt, and impoverish those communities with large immigrant populations and lead to increased tensions. The Senate Judiciary Committee Report accompanying the 1985 version of the Immigration Reform and Control Act offered relevant commentary:

> If immigration is continued at a high level, yet a substantial portion of these new persons and their descendants do not assimilate into the society, they have the potential to create in America a measure of the same social, political and economic problems which exist in the countries from which they have chosen to depart. Furthermore, if language and cultural separatism rise above a certain level, the unity and political stability of the Nation will—in time—be seriously diminished.[8]

EFFECTS ON THE ENVIRONMENT

Some observers tried to focus attention on the environmental and other resource effects of illegal immigration. Former Colorado governor (and current director of the Federation for American Immigration Reform) Richard Lamm has written, "People pollute and too many people living in an area can degrade that area irrevocably. Immigration at high levels exacerbates our resource and environmental problems. It will leave a poorer, more crowded, more divided country for our children" (Lamm and Imhoff, 1985, p. 10).

Critics of this resource depletion argument assert that pollution has declined over the course of the past two decades as population has increased. As two prominent commentators succinctly put it, pollution "is caused by what people do, or do not do, not how many people there are."[9]

THE QUESTION OF "CONTROL"

Finally, proponents of sanctions argued that one effect of illegal immigration was to subvert respect for the power of law. A rigorously enforced regime of employer sanctions would go some distance toward re-establishing control over the nation's borders, and with it the force of our immigration laws. Opponents of the law scoffed at this rationale, arguing that regardless of the level of enforcement, massive non-compliance would result. On this point The Wall Street Journal, a longstanding opponent of immigration controls, editorialized:

The result [of IRCA] is employers turning farms and restaurants into work-easies, running afoul of the law by hiring aliens for jobs no one else will do. Legislation in the face of such overwhelming demand in the marketplace is surely doomed to failure. How much moralizing and how many arrests must we endure in this second period of prohibition?[10]

The Consequences of Disagreement over the "Problem"

Thus, the "problem" of illegal immigration that led to the enactment of IRCA was characterized as several different problems:

—Labor market displacement and wage suppression;
—The fiscal costs associated with service and benefits use and low tax payments;
—Exploitation of undocumented workers;
—Social fragmentation of local communities; and
—The need to re-establish the power of law and the principle of sovereignty.

These differing rationales had clear implications for the groups that would be expected to benefit from IRCA and for the standards used to evaluate the law. For example, if illegal immigrants displace native workers, sanctions' principal beneficiaries would be low-wage, minority workers—especially the foreign-born, who are legally authorized to work (Bean, Telles, and Taylor, 1987). If illegal aliens burden local, state, and federal treasuries by consuming more in benefits and services than they pay in taxes, then sanctions should make taxpayers better off. To the extent that exploitation of undocumented workers is a problem, working illegally needs to be viewed in the same light as child labor or wage and hour violations, and undocumented immigrants should view themselves as gaining the most from this "protective" measure.

These diverse rationales and sets of potential beneficiaries return us to the basic issue addressed by this volume: how should we evaluate a statute as complex and far-reaching as IRCA?

The question of evaluation is particularly salient in the case of IRCA. In the first place, the law provided for the possible repeal of sanctions provisions after only three and a half years of implementation if the GAO found that the law had given rise to "widespread discrimination." As I indicate above, the GAO *has* in fact returned with such a controversial verdict, but the prospects of such a sunset do not appear likely. As a result, the various early evaluations of the law will serve a more conventional purpose of guiding a mid-course correction in the law.

Evaluation will continue to play an unusually important role in shaping the future of IRCA because IRCA appears to have generated what is likely to prove an intolerable type of compliance cost— increased discrimination on the basis of national origin and citizenship status. Because discrimination is an area of special political sensitivity in the society, and because the populations likely to experience IRCA-related discrimination (Hispanics and Asians) have been the fastest growing in the U.S., it is unlikely that sanctions will be retained in their current form unless a) IRCA-related discrimination is significantly reduced or b) sanctions' effectiveness in curbing the flow of undocumented migrants substantially increases. As a result, IRCA and sanctions are likely to continue to be subjected to intense cost-benefit analysis.[11] I will return to this in my conclusion.

IRCA's EMPLOYER SANCTIONS AND ANTI-DISCRIMINATION PROVISIONS

At the time of its enactment, IRCA was an omnibus law, as employer sanctions were packaged with at least six other major provisions. Each represented a political trade that had been added as a way of regulating or mitigating the consequences, first of employer sanctions, and later of one another. The six other provisions are:

—An expansion of existing civil rights laws, barring discrimination in hiring on the basis of national origin or, under certain circumstances, citizenship status;
—A legalization program for individuals who had resided continuously in the U.S. since January 1, 1982;
—A legalization program for individuals who had worked for 90 days or more in agriculture in any of the three years preceding IRCA's enactment (the Special Agricultural Worker program, or SAW); as well as a subsequent legalization program for Replenishment Agricultural Workers (RAW);
—A four billion dollar intergovernmental grants program intended to help state and local governments offset the impact of legalization (the State Legalization Impact Assistance Grant program, or SLIAG);
—Mandatory national adoption of a database and computer-match-

ing program to verify that applicants for certain public benefit programs are citizens or are otherwise eligible for their receipt (the
Systematic Alien Verification for Entitlement program, or SAVE);
and
—Expansion of a program to deport aliens convicted of crimes.

While employer sanctions remained the keystone of the law, the
concerns of those who opposed sanctions found their way into
IRCA's overall structure, driving the inclusion of many of the main
provisions cited above:

□ Concerns on the part of Hispanic and other civil rights organizations led to inclusion of the legalization program to avoid the mass
deportation of millions of undocumented migrants living in the United
States at the time of the law's enactment. The program was supported
by employers who viewed legalization as one means of satisfying
their labor supply needs in a post-IRCA environment.
□ Civil rights groups' concerns about the potential of sanctions to
increase discrimination against lawful job applicants of foreign, especially Latin American, origin led to the enactment of the anti-
discrimination provisions as well as provisions making possible the
repeal of sanctions should they result in "widespread discrimination."
□ Growers' concerns about their future labor supply were met by
the extraordinarily liberal, one-time Special Agricultural Worker program (SAW) and by a Replenishment Agricultural Worker program
(RAW) that would continue to legalize potential farm workers should
SAWs abandon agricultural employment and should the need for
labor persist.

IRCA's employer requirements themselves embodied the trade-offs
and compromises made between sanctions' opponents and advocates, as the discussion below indicates.

Employer Sanctions

The employer sanctions provisions of IRCA prohibit three types of
activity: 1) the knowing hiring of unauthorized aliens; 2) the continued employment of known unauthorized aliens; and 3) the hiring
of any individual without verifying identity and authorization to
work (the law's "paperwork" requirements). The law requires that
all employers verify the authorization to work of employees hired

after November 6, 1986, and maintain records (I-9 forms) indicating that the employee's eligibility was verified. In so doing, the Congress sought to press the vast private administrative apparatus of the nation's employers into service. The strategy was intended to substantially expand the enforcement capacity of the government without incurring immense costs.

Sanctions represent the announcement of a broad, tough, new regulatory regime. This is reflected in the breadth of the law's coverage, as it extends not only to the nation's seven million firms, but also to the employment transactions of individuals.[12] Moreover, the provisions are not limited to full-time employees, but to all situations where an employer/employee relationship has been entered into.[13] Furthermore, to close a loophole that has reduced the effectiveness of similar schemes in some European countries, IRCA expressly makes general contractors equally liable as subcontractors for the knowing hiring of unauthorized aliens (Martin, 1987).

The law requires that applicants for employment attest to the fact that they are authorized to work by signing an "I-9" form. It requires that employers also sign the form, pledging under penalty of perjury that they have examined specified documents to determine the applicants' identify and work eligibility. The burden on employers and applicants imposed by these verification requirements is mitigated somewhat by the fact that many different documents are deemed acceptable to establish work eligibility, and by the fact that employers are required to accept a proferred document if it "reasonably appears on its face to be genuine."[14] At the same time, however, the law makes it a separate offense, punishable by a fine, for an employer to refuse to produce I-9 forms upon the request of an INS or Department of Labor inspector, whether or not those officials have obtained a warrant.[15]

The scope of employers' new liability and the real power of sanctions are best revealed by the law's penalty provisions. IRCA sets out a graduated set of penalties for the knowing hiring of unauthorized workers of $250 to $2,000 per worker for the first violation, $2,000 to $5,000 per worker for the second violation, and $3,000 to $10,000 for the third and subsequent violations. The law also authorizes the INS to issue a "cease-and-desist" order. Violation of the paperwork requirements can result in fines of $100 to $1,000. Unlike violations of the "knowing" or "continuing-to-hire" requirements, the penalty for paperwork violations is not graduated; that is, the range remains the same, regardless of the number of violations.

Significantly, the law also provides for criminal penalties for violators of the employer sanctions provisions who engage in a "pattern or practice" of knowing hires of unauthorized aliens and for those who transport anyone into or within the U.S. with the intention of concealing, harboring, or shielding them from detection in the U.S.[16]

While the breadth of the law's coverage and the potential severity of its penalties cannot be denied, concessions to sanctions' opponents that limit the burden and liabilities it imposes can also be seen in the way the provision was framed.

First, the imposition of heavy penalties that would cumulate with each separate infraction are reserved for "knowing" violations of the law.[17] While "paperwork only" (or technical violations) were contemplated, their dollar value is comparatively low and repeated violations do not lead to escalating fines or to eventual criminal action.[18] The knowledge requirement—coupled with the directive that employers are only responsible for determining if documents are reasonable on their face—restricts employers' liability and limits their compliance burden, while at the same time reducing their incentive to discriminate against foreign-sounding and foreign-looking job applicants.

Another concession to opponents was that sanctions were to be phased in gradually. No enforcement was authorized from the date of enactment through June 1, 1987,[19] and the following calendar year, June 1 to May 31, 1988, was designated as a "citation period."[20] During this year the INS was only to issue a citation for an initial violation. After being cited for a first offense, an employer could be fined for subsequent offenses committed during the period. In short, offenders during this year-long citation period got "one bite at the apple."

INS activities during these two periods were primarily informational in character, as the agency sought to inform employers about their new responsibilities under the law. Full enforcement of the law for all industries other than agriculture began on June 1, 1988. At that time, all detected violations were subject to fine. Full enforcement in agriculture did not begin until December 1, 1988.[21]

To mitigate sanctions' adverse effects on the supply of labor, employers were relieved of any obligation to verify the citizenship status of employees hired before IRCA's enactment on November 6, 1986, and who had worked without interruption for the same employer since that time.[22] However, IRCA does not confer any legal status on these undocumented "grandfathered" workers, who are deportable if they are apprehended.

To appease agricultural employers, the law required for the first time that INS officers have a warrant or consent before they search a farm or outdoor agricultural operation.[23] No other provision of IRCA, with the possible exception of the Special Agricultural Worker program, was as strongly opposed by the INS during congressional deliberations as this new warrant requirement.

Finally, the law provided for intensive scrutiny by the GAO of sanctions' impact to determine, among other things, whether they would lead to "widespread discrimination." Such a finding on the part of the GAO would lead to expedited congressional review and, possibly, the "sunset" of the sanctions provisions. This would occur after the submission of the GAO's annual report following the third full year of the law's implementation.[24]

Anti-Discrimination Provisions

From an employer's perspective, IRCA represents not one but two new regimes of regulation. The law represents a modest expansion of the coverage of U.S. civil rights law to reach discrimination in employment arising in the wake of IRCA's enactment. IRCA makes it unlawful for an employer to discriminate against someone eligible to work in the U.S. on the basis of national origin or citizenship status if he or she is a citizen or what is termed an "intending" citizen. The law creates a new office within the Department of Justice—the Office of Special Counsel for Immigration-Related Unfair Employment Practices—to investigate and pursue charges of discrimination.[25]

The law is intended to complement civil rights protections announced in Title VII of the 1964 Civil Rights Act. It does so in two ways. First, it extends the existing ban on discrimination on the basis of national origin from firms with more than 15 employees to firms with 4 to 14 employees. Second, the law announces for the first time a ban on discrimination in employment on the basis of alienage or citizenship status.

While the provision itself is something of a victory for civil rights organizations and immigrant advocacy groups, Congress mitigated its impact on employers in a number of ways. First, the law's coverage was initially limited to permanent resident aliens, temporary resident aliens, refugees, and asylees who declare themselves to be "intending citizens."[26] Second, unlike Title VII of the 1964 Civil Rights Act, it is restricted to hiring and terminations—and does not reach the "terms and conditions" of employment.[27] Third, the law vests only a limited right of private action in those who believe they have been victims of discrimination. Complaints must be filed with the Office of Special Counsel or the Equal Employment Opportunity Commission.[28] Only if the government decides not to pursue the case can the individual sue the employer directly.[29] Fourth, the law permits employers to select citizens over non-citizens where both are "equally qualified."[30] Finally, unlike IRCA's sanctions provisions, the law exempts employers with fewer than four employees.[31]

A SUMMARY OF THE CHAPTERS IN THIS VOLUME

In the following pages, I summarize the papers in this volume, setting them within the context of the particular type of evaluation questions they answer. The volume is divided into three parts. Part One, consisting of chapters 2 to 5, focuses on the implementation of IRCA. Part Two, encompassing chapters 6 to 8, assesses its impacts. Part Three discusses options for employer sanction reforms.

Part One: The Implementation of IRCA

The four chapters in Part One of this volume address the implementation of IRCA and in so doing focus on assessing the performance of the INS. These chapters were written by participants in the Rand/Urban Institute study that examined IRCA's implementation in eight cities across the U.S.: Chicago, New York, Miami, El Paso, Houston, San Antonio, Los Angeles, and San Jose. All of the cities have large foreign-born populations and significant populations of undocumented immigrants. All but one of the eight cities (San Jose) house prominent INS District offices.

While the focus of all but one of the chapters is IRCA's employer sanctions provisions, other immigration control programs built into IRCA are also discussed. These include increased border control, the expansion of the INS criminal alien program, and the SAVE program.

Each of the chapters focuses on agency performance, and takes as its point of departure an understanding that the INS was an agency that had little prior experience in regulating U.S. firms. INS enforcement branches historically had been chronically undermanned, the agency had grown unusually decentralized, and it was frequently subject to criticism for the arbitrariness of its enforcement activity. In short, expectations of agency performance were low. Hence, in all cases, the assessment of implementation is generally positive, and at worst mixed.

Chapter 2. Chapter 2, "IRCA and the Enforcement Mission of the Immigration and Naturalization Service," by Jason Juffras, sets the institutional context by examining the way in which IRCA affected the enforcement side of the INS. One of the most significant changes that the agency was able to make following IRCA's enactment was to expand its enforcement staff and increase their qualifications and sophistication. New investigative agents were recruited from colleges rather than from the Border Patrol, and a good proportion of the enhanced corps of agency lawyers came from the Department of Justice's honors program. This brought new blood to the agency and set in motion new advancement patterns that could have positive, long-term effects.

Juffras explores in depth a theme that also emerges in the other papers—the diffusion of resources and mission that has character-ized the INS in this post-IRCA period and has detracted from the enforcement of employer sanctions. While IRCA authorized a 70 percent increase in the agency's budget, the lion's share (57%) of new enforcement dollars received by the agency in the first three years of IRCA's implementation went to the politically visible and historically powerful Border Patrol. Sanctions enforcement received only 27 percent of the increased funds. In addition, a substantial share (14%) of new enforcement resources were to go to the agency's criminal alien program—a result of increasing political concerns with drugs and the fact that drugs and immigration were becoming increasingly linked.

Juffras also notes that one result of the infusion of new IRCA-related resources and responsibilities was to blur the formerly dis-tinct roles of the INS's two principal law enforcement branches: the Border Patrol and Investigations. Not only did responsibilities start to overlap as the Border Patrol began to go beyond its traditional "linewatch" function, but the jurisdictional boundaries between In-vestigations and Border Patrol started to blur as Border Patrol offices were opened in interior cities such as Houston and Dallas. These developments were controversial, and as this is written, INS Com-missioner Eugene McNary appears to be working to re-establish the older, comparatively distinct lines of responsibility.

In sum, Juffras finds that IRCA left the INS better staffed, better funded, and better positioned to carry out its new regulatory responsibilities. However, a lack of clear priorities and a diffusion of mission threatened these institutional gains.

Chapter 3. In "Implementing Sanctions: Reports from the Field," Paul Hill and I examine how employer sanctions were implemented by local and regional INS offices during the three years following IRCA's enactment. We evaluate these efforts to implement the law in light of four challenges that the INS faced:

—Establishing and sustaining the legitimacy of sanctions as a regime for regulating business;
—Satisfying the exacting legal requirements that attach to business regulations and generally do not apply to the INS's relations with immigrants;
—Adapting the INS as an organization designed for one purpose (regulating immigration by dealing with individual immigrants) to the very different purpose of regulating, inspecting, and sanctioning employers; and
—Regulating a vast economic process with limited investigative and enforcement resources.

In general we found a low level of enforcement during IRCA's first three years, consistent with Congress's interest in having sanctions phased in gradually and focusing on employer education rather than punishment. But we also found wide variation across sites along a number of important dimensions. First, we found that sanctions remained the highest local enforcement priority in only two of the eight sites: Los Angeles and Chicago. In each of the others it had been supplanted by drug enforcement, removal of criminal aliens, or by prosecution of fraud in the agricultural worker legalization program.

Second, we found wide variation in the practices of the differing districts. In large metropolitan areas such as New York, Chicago, and Los Angeles, local offices took a multi-stage "regulatory" approach to enforcement that emphasized employer education and rights and the analysis of documents as a means of developing cases. Other sites, especially those close to the Mexican border, used a police model in which a raid was initiated early in the investigation and served as the primary way of obtaining evidence.

Third, the targets of enforcement varied across sites. In some, the apprehension and removal of undocumented aliens remained the agency's principal focus. In others, employers had replaced immigrants as primary targets and apprehensions had given way to more sophisticated investigations.

Fourth, the sites varied dramatically in terms of penalties. The average fines assessed ranged from $850 in San Antonio to $45,000 in Chicago. In addition, the number of paperwork-only or technical violations also varied sharply. As of April 1989, the Chicago District office had issued no paperwork-only violations, while more than half of the fines issued in Los Angeles were for technical rather than "knowing" violations.

In sum, we conclude that the agency's low-key approach to implementing sanctions during the first three years successfully averted employer complaints about the new regulatory regime. We also found that the agency stayed within the bounds of administrative law and procedure, winning all of the legal challenges to its enforcement actions it faced during the period (in stark contrast to the INS record in court with regard to legalization). We found that the agency had indeed begun to transform itself from a paramilitary or police organization to a mainstream regulatory agency, and that education efforts concerning sanctions had been intensive and relatively successful. However, these same efforts were significantly less successful with regard to discrimination.

We contend that if the stark differences we observed in penalties and practices across the country are sustained, they could erode the legitimacy built during the program's early years. We also argue that an overreliance on technical violations could trivialize enforcement, again subverting legitimacy. And finally, we conclude that the ephemeral quality of local priorities will diminish the power of the regulatory regime, once businesses and immigrants determine that resources have been shifted and missions changed.

Chapter 4. In "A Window on Immigration Reform," Elizabeth Rolph and Abby Robyn examine the implementation of employer sanctions in Los Angeles, where they monitored IRCA over a two-year period. Los Angeles, located less than 100 miles from the Mexican border, is a critical site for testing the power of IRCA. Not only would the task of controlling illegal immigration in L.A. be especially difficult, but the agency's success would be a significant test of the effectiveness of the new law.

The challenge of implementing sanctions in L.A. would stem from a number of sources. In the first place, the geographical size of the jurisdiction is quite large. Beyond that, the size and diversity of the undocumented population and the degree to which important sectors of the local economy had been dependent upon illegal labor would pose problems for enforcement. If IRCA were strictly enforced, it could have a particularly disruptive effect on the regional economy, and in so doing, undermine whatever political support might exist for immigration control. Here again, the agency faced difficulties because the political culture of the region had been quite tolerant of immigrants. Finally, the sheer number of employers to be covered (over 300,000) was exceptionally large, a problem compounded by the prevalence of small, comparatively disorganized firms that had been the principal source of employment for undocumented immigrants.

Rolph and Robyn find that the Los Angeles office of the INS set and maintained sanctions as the district's top priority. As in the other sites monitored over the course of the project, the general approach to enforcement was conciliatory in character. And like INS district offices in New York and Chicago, in L.A. there was a decisive shift away from police-style law enforcement to the regulatory approach described above.

Interestingly, unlike our other sites, the focus of enforcement in L.A. did not shift so decisively away from immigrants toward employers as the targets of enforcement. In fact, the agency was contemplating focusing increased resources on apprehending and removing illegal aliens who had provided false information in order to obtain jobs, threatening them with criminal penalties should they be caught again. In terms of penalties, the district responded to the broad presence of undocumented aliens in the economy by issuing a large share of fines for technical violations. This predominance of paperwork-only violations derived from three sources. First, it appears agents were responding to quotas for fines imposed on them by their superiors—a controversial approach for law enforcement or regulatory agencies. Second, local INS counsel expressed a strong belief that the law's paperwork requirements were in and of themselves important elements of the law. Not all INS officials shared this view. And third, local INS officials believed that it was more important to "touch a lot of people" in order to make the new regime of regulation felt than it was to bring a few high-profile actions against wanton violators.

An important theme that the authors develop is the divergent interests of the federal government and state and local governments when it comes to IRCA. Despite the fact that both the city of Los Angeles and the state of California have the legal power to assist in enforcement of IRCA's immigration controls, they were "notable for their absence." Indeed, the state legislature expressly forbade the state's employment agency to use state funds to verify documents for employers and the INS. At the same time, the City of Los Angeles had begun to sponsor hiring sites where both legal and illegal workers could make themselves available for day labor, clearly contravening the spirit if not the letter of employer sanctions.

Chapter 5. The fifth chapter in this book, "The SAVE Program: An Early Assessment," by Wendy Zimmermann, examines an important companion provision to IRCA's employer sanctions. SAVE (the Systematic Alien Verification for Entitlement program) was thought by many to represent the most anti-immigrant provision within IRCA. The program mandates that all states verify the immigration status of all non-citizen applicants for six federal benefit programs through an INS database maintained by the Martin Marietta Corporation. SAVE's proponents argued that there were two "pull" factors that accounted for undocumented immigration: jobs and welfare. SAVE was intended to reduce access to, and the appeal of, welfare just as sanctions were to reduce the lure of jobs.

The importance of the provision goes beyond its success in curbing alien use of benefits. In the wake of the GAO report finding "widespread discrimination" linked to IRCA, many thoughtful observers have urged the adoption of a national identity card and/or a telephone verification system in order to reduce employer confusion and the discrimination that results. SAVE would clearly be the prototype for such a system.

It is important to note that while SAVE was authorized by IRCA, and several pilots had been in place for some years prior to IRCA, to date the program is far from universally adopted by federal, state, or local benefits-granting agencies. While this is partly due to the diffusion of missions within the INS, it is also due to indifference and occasional resistance among several federal agencies and a number of state and local bureaucracies.

After analyzing the available evidence, which was surprisingly scant, it would be hard to argue that SAVE has been a major success to date. Savings data are largely absent, and the data that do exist appear to be inflated, exaggerating savings under the program. Indeed, the questionable cost-effectiveness of the program has led Texas—certainly not a state with a liberal political culture when it comes to social welfare programs—to apply for a waiver from the use of this screening program for AFDC, Medicaid, and food stamps.

SAVE's cost-effectiveness to program administrators is determined in part by the completeness and accuracy of the database that is queried whenever an immigrant applies for a benefit. While the database on which the program draws has been improved, Zimmermann found that many refugees and Cuban-Haitians—who are eligible for a wide range of benefits—were not included. This has led to time-consuming and cumbersome verification procedures. Furthermore, key data needed by program administrators to determine eligibility for selected benefits were neither stored nor reported. For example, one piece of omitted data is the date on which an immigrant became authorized to work. This is important because eligibility for benefits is determined by immigration status both at the time the applicant applies for benefits and at the time he or she worked.

The implementation of SAVE, like that of sanctions, reveals the intergovernmental tensions to which IRCA has given rise. IRCA, after all, involves federal immigration officials in the benefits-granting process (formerly the administrative province of state and local governments) at the same time that it enlists state and local welfare officers in the immigration-control process (formerly the exclusive province of the federal government). While the program was designed in a manner that was intended to be deferential to the states, in practice that deference has not been forthcoming. Waivers from participation, which were to reward states with equivalently effective systems, have proven extremely difficult to obtain. As a result, some states (New York, for example) have simply chosen not to participate in the program, flouting the spirit of the law in much the way L.A.'s hiring corners do.

Part Two: Impacts

The second section of the volume addresses the impacts of IRCA and the new immigration controls it established. Obviously, the comparatively short time elapsed from enactment to the time that data had been collected and analyzed means that the programs being investigated were far from mature, and that the impacts identified were susceptible to significant change. That said, however, the results of the papers collected here strongly indicate that, three years after enactment, the law had yet to bring about broad compliance or to stem significantly the tide of undocumented migration to the U.S.

Chapter 6. In their chapter "Employer Compliance with IRCA Paperwork Requirements: A Preliminary Assessment," Shirley J. Smith and Martina Shea examine the degree to which employers have complied with the verification procedures specified by IRCA.[32] They review the results of the 99,000 inspections conducted by the Department of Labor's Employment Standards Administration (ESA) and the INS from October 1987 through June 1989, as well as the results of employer surveys conducted by the GAO. The authors penetrate differences in key definitions, methods of data collection and tabulation, and overall compliance estimates to find what they consider to be generally low levels of compliance with IRCA's verification procedures.

ESA complaint-driven investigations, which constitute roughly 65 percent of all investigations examined, revealed that only 38 percent of employers appeared to be complying with IRCA verification requirements at the time of the first visit. Data from the INS suggest that even with pressure from agents and time to correct paperwork deficiencies, compliance reached only 68 percent by the time the case was closed. Even among larger firms under contract with the federal government—who risk losing federal contracts for violation of labor regulations and have every reason to expect periodic inspections—only a 62 percent compliance rate was achieved.

Other "cuts" at the data reveal higher levels of compliance among some subgroups, such as firms randomly targeted by the INS within the context of its neutral targeting strategy, and lower levels of compliance among others such as firms surveyed by the GAO. Nonetheless, the basic finding of low to modest compliance still holds.

The authors note that paperwork compliance should not be interpreted to mean that firms hire no illegal aliens. Indeed, field research has indicated that it is relatively easy to maintain adequate I-9 records while still hiring undocumented aliens. This leads the authors to conclude:

> When coupled with the continuing high rates of noncompliance observed by the GAO, the INS, and the ESA, "fraudulent" compliance clearly narrows the universe of firms within which sanctions can have their desired effects. In fact, it leaves in question the law's ability to create job opportunities for authorized workers and to foster the labor market adjustments necessary to attract such workers.

Smith and Shea's review of compliance data indicates that:

—Firms in industries with the highest concentrations of aliens are least likely to conduct work authorization checks;
—Firms in states with high concentrations of aliens, especially Texas and California, are more likely to meet IRCA verification requirements;
—Larger firms are more likely to comply than smaller firms; and

—Firms cited in complaints about other types of violations are less likely than other firms to be in compliance with IRCA.

Finally, the authors indicate that only 6 percent of firms found to be non-compliant were eventually fined, and that the fine amounts collected represented less than half of the original amount assessed. This confirms the generally forgiving, conciliatory character of enforcement described in the papers cited above.

Chapter 7. The other chapters in Part Two review the impact of IRCA and employer sanctions on the flow of illegal immigrants to the United States. In their chapter "Assessing the Impact of Employer Sanctions on Undocumented Immigration to the United States," Jeffrey S. Passel, Frank D. Bean, and Barry Edmonston review primary data and recent studies to assess the impact of IRCA on the stock and flow of illegal immigrants to the United States during the three-year period after IRCA was passed. They find the studies and data reviewed to be generally consistent in suggesting a decrease in the flow of illegal immigrants across the U.S.-Mexico border. This effect is due in part to the two legalization programs embedded in IRCA: the Special Agricultural Worker (SAW) program and, to a lesser extent, the general legalization program, available to aliens continuously resident in the U.S. since 1982. These programs removed individuals from the flow by making them part of the legal flow of labor and other migrants across the border, and by allowing these populations to settle permanently in the United States. However, the effect of removing legalized migrants from the illegal flow across the border does not appear to account for all the estimated decline in flows across the border. Thus, sanctions may have had some deterrent effect. But the authors find that this decline in the flow of undocumented migrants began to reverse itself during 1990, as the rate of border apprehensions started to rise significantly.

One unexpected result of IRCA noted by the authors is that women have begun to constitute a larger share of the stock and flow of the undocumented population. They note that this compositional shift may have occurred because IRCA legalized a very large segment of the undocumented male labor force, and because families of formerly undocumented immigrants are migrating to unite with legalized male family members in the U.S. The authors also suggest that IRCA's employer sanctions provisions may be responsible for some of this change, as undocumented women may find it easier than undocumented men to obtain jobs that will not be subject to INS enforcement.

Chapter 8. "Employer Sanctions: A Preliminary Assessment," by Demetrios G. Papademetriou, B. Lindsay Lowell, and Deborah Cobb-Clark evaluates the success of IRCA's employer sanctions provisions. Like the work by Passel et al., this chapter documents a sharp drop-off in apprehensions in the first two years following IRCA's enactment, followed by a recent rise. The authors construct a mathematical model in order to apportion responsibility for the drop between legalization and other IRCA program effects. They find a large share of this decline is attributable to legalization rather than sanctions-related deterrence.

The authors argue that we should view the limited deterrent effect of sanctions to date within the context of the experience of sanctions in Europe. They contend that it takes a long time to establish a new labor standard and that extensive use of illegal workers in the U.S. has a longer history than is the case in Europe. They argue that sustained employer education is required to reinforce the perception that the government assigns a high priority to sanctions, and that sanctions should be pursued as part of a larger effort to enforce other labor laws, as is the practice in Europe. They conclude that no policy will eliminate the pressures for illegal immigration as long as few gains are made in parallel efforts to reduce domestic social and political conflict in immigrant-sending countries.

Chapter 9. In the final chapter in this section of the book, Philip L. Martin and J. Edward Taylor examine the impact of IRCA and its employer sanctions provisions on the use of farm labor contractors and turnover in the agricultural labor force in California from 1985 through 1989.

The authors' results draw on a survey of California farm contractors and a longitudinal study of California Unemployment Insurance data. They conclude that, at least in California, IRCA does not appear to be achieving the goal set for it by its framers: to stabilize and reduce the size of the agricultural labor force. Rather, since employer sanctions have taken effect, the role played by farm labor contractors has grown, and the characteristics of that growth suggest that IRCA has not reduced the flow of new, low-skill immigrant workers into seasonal farm jobs. Martin and Taylor find that the comparative advantage of labor contractors continues to be their ability to recruit new immigrant labor for short-term jobs, not to manage the smaller, more stable, and presumably legal workforce envisioned by IRCA. This finding suggests to Martin and Taylor that employer sanctions may have changed the form of employment for illegal workers in agriculture, but it has not stopped the fact of their employment.

Part Three: Reform Options

The concluding section of the book brings together two essays on possible future directions for the reform of IRCA. The first focuses largely on efforts to eliminate the discrimination to which IRCA has apparently given rise. The second looks not only at the discrimination issue but to sanctions enforcement as well.

Chapter 10. In the chapter "IRCA-Related Discrimination: What Do We Know and What Should We Do?" I distinguish between two broad types of discrimination that have come to light in the wake of IRCA. The first is *confusion* discrimination, where the employer violates the anti-discrimination provisions of IRCA and/or Title VII of the Civil Rights Act in an attempt to comply with what he or she believes to be the the mandate of IRCA. In practice this often means that foreign-appearing job candidates are not hired or are subjected to closer scrutiny than applicants who do not appear foreign. The second type of discrimination is rooted in bias, not confusion. In this case, foreign-appearing job candidates are treated differently because of ethnic stereotypes or animus. Discrimination due to *confusion* is largely attributable to IRCA and, I contend, may be more easily eliminated because it derives from an interest in complying with law rather than evading it. *Bias*-based discrimination is more entrenched, occurs independently of sanctions for the most part, and calls for different remedies, such as strict enforcement of civil rights laws.

The chapter then reviews the principal critiques of the two major studies of IRCA-related discrimination, the GAO's mail survey of employers and The Urban Institute's hiring audit. Principal findings of the GAO report were:

—An estimated 5 percent of employers reported that as a result of IRCA they began a practice of not hiring persons because of their foreign appearance or accent;
—An estimated 8 percent of employers surveyed reported that as a result of IRCA they applied the law's verification system only to foreign-appearing persons; and
—14 percent of employers began a practice of hiring only persons

born in the U.S. or not hiring persons with temporary work eligibility documents.[33]

The most powerful criticism of the GAO was that its finding of "widespread discrimination" was based on the self-reported results of employers who characterized the ways in which their hiring practices had changed since IRCA was enacted. Critics contend that the absence of a pre-IRCA baseline assessment of the prevalence of discrimination against foreign-appearing job applicants is fatal to the finding of IRCA-related widespread discrimination. While these criticisms must be taken seriously, the fact that the GAO undertook not one but two surveys of large samples of employers, and that the agency received results from both that strongly cross-validated one another, has been overlooked. Moreover, the fact that The Urban Institute audit as well as numerous state and local surveys confirmed the existence of significant discrimination against foreign-appearing job applicants also strengthened the study's results.

The chapter then proposes five principal reforms to counteract discrimination due to *confusion*:

□ Revising the I-9 form so that it more closely guides the employer through the hiring process in ways which ensure that he or she complies with *both* IRCA's sanctions *and* its anti-discrimination mandate;

□ Funding a serious national media campaign to increase awareness of the proscription against discriminating on the base of national origin or citizenship;

□ Consolidating the many work authorization documents issued by the INS into two;

□ Charging the GAO with continuing to monitor IRCA's discrimination and other impacts, taking advantage of the baseline established by the prior two reports; and

□ Building in a "sunset" provision of six years from enactment, making the law consistent with a number of other regulatory laws enacted during recent decades.

Chapter 11. The chapter by Robert Bach and Doris Meissner notes that, in the final analysis, IRCA is an immigration-related labor law and not a labor-related immigration law. Accordingly, its success should be judged using the extended timetable necessary to establish a new labor standard. The authors then urge the Congress to adopt a long-term strategy for bolstering immigration enforcement and reducing discrimination, calling for work to begin to determine the feasibility of developing a tamper-proof Social Security card with a photo.

They also note the need for short-term reforms of IRCA that include:

☐ The opening of field offices for the Office of Special Counsel, the branch of the Department of Justice assigned responsibility for administering IRCA's anti-discrimination provisions;

☐ Making the financial penalties for violation of IRCA's anti-discrimination provisions equivalent to those for violating sanctions, thereby eliminating whatever incentives employers might have for "overcomplying" with sanctions; and

☐ Exploring the use of a telephone verification system to determine the eligibility of job applicants coupled with an intensive effort to upgrade the quality of the INS's data systems.

Finally, Bach and Meissner argue for changes in the enforcement of sanctions to ensure that their power is not eviscerated. They urge the cross-designation of Department of Labor inspectors, expanding their powers beyond simply reporting violations to the INS, to initiating prosecutions themselves. They also urge the initiation of several pilot projects that intensively focus enforcement resources on a specific industry, in order to determine what impact such a "full court press" might have on compliance with sanctions.

In the concluding chapter, I update the volume to reflect legislative, administrative, and judicial developments since January 1990 pertinent to sanctions' effectiveness and enforcement. Taking these developments into account, I then revisit the principal arguments for and against the repeal of employer sanctions, and outline what I view to be the limited lessons afforded by the European experience with sanctions.

Notes

1. The House Judiciary Committee Report on The Immigration Reform and Control Act Amendments prominently features the testimony presented to the Immigration Subcommittee by Althea Simmons, Director of the Washington Bureau of the NAACP, who stated in 1985: "The NAACP strongly supports employer sanctions. Our branches across the country, particularly in large cities, report that the undocumented worker impacts the employment of blacks. Many blacks are forced from employment rolls

by the undocumented worker who is hired at a subminimum wage and is at the mercy of the employer." Report on HR 3810, Immigration Control and Legalization Amendments Act of 1986, Report 99-682, 99th Congress, 2nd Session.

2. Looking to the future, though, the growth of these forces might be expected to abate somewhat, depending on the shape of trade relations between the U.S. and Mexico, and a possible reduction in hostilities in Central America that might accompany political change in Nicaragua and Eastern Europe.

3. See Wihtol de Wenden, 1990, which notes that sanctions have generally been weakly enforced in Europe and do not appear to have had a great impact on curbing illegal immigration.

4. Former INS Commissioner Leonard Chapman offered the 4 to 12 million figure (Crewdson, 1983, pp 98–106). The 2 to 3 million figure was offered by Warren and Passel, 1987.

5. Interview by Michael Fix and Paul Hill with Richard Day, Minority Counsel, Senate Immigration Subcommittee, January 26, 1990.

6. New York Times/CBS News, 1986, "Immigration Survey" June 19–23.

7. See Arnold, 1979, who argues that tax payments provided by illegal immigrants may more than offset the costs of providing health care and other social services to undocumented aliens. See also Weintraub and Cardenas, 1984. The authors find that total revenues received from undocumented immigrants exceeded the total costs of providing services.

8. Immigration Reform and Control Act of 1985, Report of the Senate Judiciary Committee 99-132, 99th Cong. 1st Sess. Aug 28, 1985, p. 5.

9. This critique of the resource depletion argument against immigration is found in Wattenberg and Zinmeister, 1989, p. 10.

10. "Simpson-Volstead-Mazzoli." Editorial, *The Wall Street Journal*, July 12, 1987, p. 12.

11. See, for example, H.R. 5572, the IRCA Antidiscrimination Amendments of 1990. These extend for two years the GAO reporting requirements on the impact of employer sanctions. *Interpreter Releases* 67, p. 1067 (September 24, 1990).

12. While IRCA's employer provisions are striking because of the breadth of their coverage, there are two major exemptions from coverage. The first is independent contractors. Following the Internal Revenue Service classification scheme, a contractor's independence will be determined on a case-by-case basis that will take into account whether the contractor works according to his or her "own means and methods" and is "subject to control only as to results." A second potentially important exemption suggested by the regulations is for "contract labor or services." The regulatory language strongly suggests that employees provided by temporary service agencies are the responsibility of the company that pays the employees and not the firm that contracts for their services. *Federal Register*, v. 15, p. 16,221 (1987).

13. Here the implementing regulations appear to have broadened the application of the law to include some employment activities that Congress meant to exempt. The rules exempt only employment in "domestic service in a private home that is sporadic, irregular or intermittent." The rules imply that casual hires for nondomestic tasks (e.g., a painter hired to paint an owner's home) or any casual hire by a commercial establishment (a temporary secretary who works for a single day) are not exempt. 8 C.F.R. Sec. 274a. 1(h).

14. IRCA P.L. 96-603 Sec. 274(A)(b)(1)(A).

15. 3 C.F.R. Sec. 273a.2(b)(2)(ii).

16. IRCA Sec. 112.

17. IRCA Sec. 274 (A)(d)(2)(ii).

18. IRCA Sec. 274 (A)(d)(3).

19. IRCA Sec. 274 (A)(g)(3).

20. IRCA Sec. 274(A)(g)(4).

21. IRCA Sec. 274(A)(g)(5)(A).

22. IRCA Sec. 274(A)(a)(2).

23. IRCA Sec. 116.

24. IRCA Sec. 274A(j)–(n).

25. IRCA Sec. 274B.

26. IRCA Sec. 274(B)(a)(3).

27. IRCA Sec. 274(B)(a)(1).

28. IRCA Sec. 274(B)(b).

29. This contrasts with IRCA's sanctions provisions that allow no private right of action.

30. IRCA Sec. 274(B)(a)(3)(B)(4).

31. IRCA Sec. 274(B)(a)(2)(A).

32. Among other things, IRCA required that each employer and job applicant fill out an I-9 form attesting to the applicant's eligibility to work in the U.S. The law also required that employers examine documents specified by law and regulation to determine the applicant's identity and eligibility to work in the U.S.

33. This would include the 2.5 million persons who qualified for the two major legalization programs, among others.

References

Arnold, Fred. 1979. "Providing Medical Services to Undocumented Immigrants: Costs and Public Policy." *International Migration Review* 13 (Winter): 71.

Bean, Frank D., Edward E. Telles, and B. Lindsay Taylor. 1987. "Undocumented Migration to the United States: Perceptions and Evidence." *Population and Development Review*, vol. 13, no. 4 (Dec.).

Commission for the Study of International Migration and Cooperative Economic Development. 1990. "Unauthorized Migration: An Economic Development Response." Washington, D.C., July.

Congressional Research Service. 1979. "Illegal Aliens: Analysis and Background," House Committee on The Judiciary, 95th Congress, 1st Session, pp. 50–55 (Comm. Print 1977).

Cornelius, Wayne. 1977. "Research Findings." In *Congressional Record*, July 13: H7063, in Staff Report 506-16, The Select Commission on Immigration and Refugee Policy, U.S. Immigration Policy and the National Interest (1981).

Crewdson, John. 1983. *The Tarnished Door: The New Immigrants and The Transformation of America.* New York: Times Books.

Fix, Michael, and Paul T. Hill. 1990. *Enforcing Employer Sanctions: Challenges and Strategies.* Washington, D.C.: The Urban Institute Press.

Fogel, Walter. 1977. "Illegal Alien Workers in the United States." *Industrial Relations,* vol. 16, no. 3 (October): pp. 243–263.

Fuchs, Lawrence H. 1990. *The American Kaleidoscope: Race, Ethnicity, and the Civic Culture.* Hanover, N.H.: Wesleyan University Press.

GAO (U.S. General Accounting Office). 1990. *Immigration Reform, Employer Sanctions and the Question of Discrimination,* GAO/GGD 90-62, March.

Lamm, Richard D., and Gary Imhoff. 1985. *The Immigration Time Bomb: The Fragmenting of America.* New York: E.P. Dutton.

Martin, David A. 1987. Major Issues in Immigration Law. In *Immigration Process and Policy,* eds. Thomas A. Alienikoff and David A. Martin. 1987 Supplement. St. Paul, Minn.: West Publishing Co., pp. 111–115.

McNary, Eugene. 1990. Testimony of INS Commissioner before the Senate Judiciary Committee, April 20, 1990. *Interpreter Releases* 67, p. 464 (April 23).

North, David, and Marion Houstoun. 1976. "The Characteristics and Role of Illegal Aliens in the US Labor Market," S-19 (March) cited in Select Commission on Immigration and Refugee Policy, Id.

Simpson, Alan. 1990. Transcript of Alan K. Simpson's press conference, Senate Radio Press Gallery, March 29, 1990. Cited in Robert L. Bach and Doris Meissner. 1990. *Employment and Immigration Reform: Employer Sanctions Four Years Later.* The Carnegie Endowment for International Peace, September.

Warren, Robert, and Jeffrey S. Passel. 1987. "A Count of the Uncountable: Estimates of Undocumented Aliens Counted in the 1980 United States Census." *Demography* 24 (August): 375–393.

Wattenberg, Ben J., and Karl Zinmeister. 1989. "The Comparative Advantage of The First Universal Nation." The American Enterprise Institute, December.

Weintraub, Sidney, and Gilberto Cardenas. 1984. "The Use of Public Services by Undocumented Aliens in Texas." *LBJ School of Public Affairs, Policy Research Project Report No. 60.* Austin, Texas.

Wihtol de Wenden, Catherine. 1990. "The Absence of Rights: The Position of Illegal Immigrants." In *The Political Rights of Migrant Workers in Western Europe,* ed. Zig Layton-Henry. Berkeley: Sage Publishers.

Part One

IMPLEMENTING EMPLOYER SANCTIONS

Chapter Two

IRCA AND THE ENFORCEMENT MISSION OF THE IMMIGRATION AND NATURALIZATION SERVICE

Jason Juffras

INTRODUCTION

The impact of employer sanctions upon firms and illegal immigrants depended largely on their implementation by the Immigration and Naturalization Service (INS). This chapter examines sanctions implementation in the context of the INS's larger law enforcement mission. It does so 1) to show how the INS determined enforcement priorities and allocated staff and financial resources among competing missions including sanctions, and 2) to trace the indirect but powerful impacts sanctions have had on the INS as an institution.

This chapter will assess how the INS implemented the enforcement provisions of the Immigration Reform and Control Act (IRCA) and how the enforcement side of the INS changed as a result. While people disagree about the mix and extent of policies to enforce the immigration law, most accept the need to deny entry to some people (criminals being the most notable example) while respecting the rights of those here lawfully. Therefore, this paper uses the following standard for evaluating how IRCA affected the INS's enforcement side:

Enforcement of the immigration law should be fair, predictable, and involve minimal disruption to immigrants, businesses, and communities. The INS should avoid harassing the targets of enforcement and respect the rights of people suspected of violating the law.

The analysis draws upon interviews conducted by Urban Institute and Rand Corporation researchers through the joint Program for Research on Immigration Policy. The researchers performed two sets of interviews in 1988 and 1989 with district-level, regional-level, and Washington, D.C.-based INS officials, immigration specialists, and attorneys; employers; trade association and labor union representatives; and state and local officials.

Respondents from all of these categories were interviewed in Chicago, El Paso, Houston, Los Angeles, Miami, New York, San Antonio, and San Jose. Each of these eight sites is home to an INS district office except San Jose, which is a sub-office in the INS's San Francisco district. The sites were selected because they included at least one district office in each of the INS's four regions and they reflected diversity in the local economy and immigrant population.

The Immigration and Naturalization Service

Part of the Department of Justice, the INS is a hybrid of a law enforcement agency and a human services agency. The INS's primary task is to control admission to the United States. The agency's enforcement units bar unauthorized immigrants from entering and expel those who enter unlawfully or violate the terms of their entry. The INS's service units approve qualified applicants for citizenship, legal resident status, and entry visas. Figure 2.1 illustrates the agency's organizational structure.

STRUCTURE

The INS operates through a command structure composed of central, regional, and local offices. The central office sets policy and issues instructions to the field offices, while the four regional offices monitor budgeting, staffing, and policy implementation.[1] The INS's three-tier structure is unique among Justice Department agencies. The Federal Bureau of Investigation (FBI), the Drug Enforcement Administration (DEA), and the Bureau of Prisons have a network of field offices in addition to their headquarters in Washington, D.C., but none has an intermediate structure comparable to the INS's regional offices. Critics have charged that this additional layer makes the INS difficult to manage.

Most of the INS's daily business takes place at the local offices, which have direct contact with immigrants. This pattern is common to agencies in the Justice Department, where cases must be developed and investigated at the "street" level.[2] At the INS, the vast majority of staff work at 33 district offices and 22 Border Patrol sectors. District offices perform all INS tasks except patrolling the land border, which is done by the Border Patrol sectors. In addition to the decentralized nature of the INS, the sheer volume of cases handled daily at the district offices and Border Patrol sectors gives INS local offices considerable discretion and autonomy.

Figure 2.1 IMMIGRATION AND NATURALIZATION SERVICE, 1989

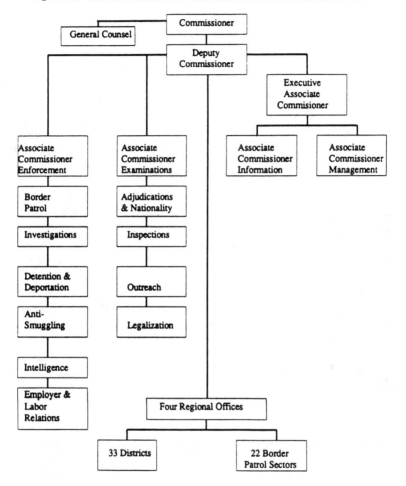

Over the past two decades, the INS has faced growing criticism for its inability to stop illegal immigration to the United States. INS apprehensions of illegal immigrants soared from 139,000 in 1966 to over 1.3 million in 1985, reflecting a large increase in unlawful entries (INS, 1989, p. 109). By 1980, the illegal immigrant population in the United States was estimated to be between 2 and 4 million, and as high as 5 million by the middle of the 1980s.[3] By the late 1970s and early 1980s, polls showed a large majority of the public supporting tougher methods to control illegal immigration, a reaction to the belief that illegal immigrants were taking jobs from Americans and undermining respect for the law.[4] While concern about illegal immigration was broad, it was nevertheless not deep because it was difficult for people to link immigration with specific cases of hardship for American workers. As a result, employer sanctions legislation—first introduced in 1972 and supported by every administration since President Nixon— did not become law until 1986.

By 1981, the problems of the INS led the Select Commission on Immigration and Refugee Policy to describe the INS as "among the most beleaguered agencies in the federal government" (SCIRP, 1981, p. 233). The House Judiciary Committee echoed that sentiment in 1986 when it characterized the INS as "undermanned, ill-equipped, and generally overwhelmed" (U.S. House of Representatives, 1986, p. 63).

CONSTRAINTS

While many have been quick to criticize the INS for its shortcomings, observers have paid less attention to the external constraints upon the agency. Immigration law enforcement is limited by strong international and domestic pressures. Political support for effective administration of the immigration law has often been lacking. As we shall see later in this chapter, these external constraints strongly influenced the INS's implementation of IRCA.

Flows of people into the United States have increased tremendously in the past two decades, making it difficult for the INS to control entry or process people quickly for admission. In 1986 more than 320 million people (many of them citizens returning from travel abroad) entered the U.S., up 40 percent since 1969 (INS, 1989, p. xli). Economic distress and political turmoil abroad have led to sudden and uncontrolled influxes of immigrants, most notably during the Mariel boatlift of 1980, when 130,000 Cubans arrived on the Florida shore.

At home, the concern for civil liberties also hampers INS enforcement of the immigration law. In recent years, the courts have been less willing to grant the INS latitude in stopping, questioning, and searching people, particularly away from the border. Most importantly, during the 1970s the Supreme Court required INS investigators to establish probable cause for searches and seizures.[5]

The value placed on civil liberties leaves the INS politically vulnerable. Polls show that a majority of Americans favor greater control over illegal immigration, but that such support often fades in the face of strict enforcement.[6] In effect, people want the INS to control immigration without disrupting their lives or communties. This attitude made it difficult for the INS to control entry to the United States in the pre-IRCA period, when Congress bowed to business interests and exempted firms from penalties for employing illegal immigrants.

Finally, immigration has been a relatively low priority within the Justice Department. Many observers note that immigration law enforcement—which is mostly civil law enforcement—is simply not as important as the criminal law enforcement tasks of the FBI, DEA, and other Justice units.[7]

The Immigration Reform and Control Act

IRCA gave the INS power to fine employers of illegal immigrants, ending the pattern in which employers could rehire aliens the INS had expelled from the workplace (or the country, for that matter) without any liability. Employer sanctions were often called the "keystone" of IRCA, or in the words of the House Judiciary Committee, "the principal means of . . . curtailing future illegal immigration" (U.S. House of Representatives, 1986, p. 46).

Firms were required to verify the legal status of all new employees by checking documents prescribed by the Attorney General and recording the information on a form called the I-9. IRCA prescribed a set of civil and criminal penalties the INS could impose on violators based on the number and severity of the offenses. In addition, IRCA assigned the INS to educate employers and phase in sanctions over a year-and-a-half, beginning the full implementation of sanctions on June 1, 1988. Congress stressed that the INS should seek voluntary employer compliance, using incentives carefully and avoiding the harassment of business.[8]

While sanctions allowed the INS to increase enforcement in the interior of the United States, that change was matched by a commitment to intensify enforcement along the border. An amendment to IRCA—known as the Moorhead amendment after its chief sponsor, Representative Carlos Moorhead of California—approved during the final floor debate on the House of Representatives, called for a 50 percent increase in staffing of the Border Patrol.

IRCA's enforcement package also required that state agencies use the INS's Systematic Alien Verification for Entitlements (SAVE) database to verify the legal status of all immigrants applying for welfare, Medicaid, unemployment insurance, food stamps, housing assistance, and higher education assistance. INS officials often used the image of a magnet to explain why illegal immigrants came to the United States, with jobs as one pole of the magnet and welfare the other. While sanctions would reduce the pull of jobs, SAVE was needed to reduce the lure of welfare.

To meet the new challenges, IRCA authorized $422 million in extra funds for the INS during fiscal year 1987 and $419 million during fiscal year 1988. These authorizations represented a 70 percent increase in the INS's fiscal year 1987 appropriation of $593 million. The Moorhead amendment stated that as much of the new money as needed should be used to meet the 50 percent target for expanding the Border Patrol.

IRCA attempted to improve the INS's ability to enforce the immigration law through policy changes, not through structural changes. IRCA simply allowed the INS to make employers liable for hiring illegal immigrants, eliminating one of the most important constraints upon immigration enforcement, and promised to increase the agency's resources along the border. Under IRCA, the INS was to be an agent of immigration reform, not the subject of reform itself.

THE INS'S IMPLEMENTATION OF EMPLOYER SANCTIONS: CAREFUL USE OF A NEW ENFORCEMENT TOOL

This section examines IRCA's effects on the enforcement side of the INS, finding that, on balance, employer sanctions improved the INS's capacity for fair and predictable enforcement of the immigration law. However, the impact of employer sanctions on the INS was diluted by a significant growth and diversification of the agency's other law enforcement tasks. By the end of 1989, the growth in the law enforcement mission of the INS left the agency with unclear priorities, weak lines of authority, and a budget deficit. Michael Fix and Paul Hill have examined INS implementation of employer sanctions, finding that the INS did meet the short-term challenges of implementing sanctions (see chapter 3 of this book). By emphasizing employer education, voluntary compliance, and the calibrated use of penalties, the INS established the legitimacy of a new regulatory program. Through employer sanctions, the INS made a partial transformation from a police agency conducting raids and apprehensions to a regulatory agency modifying behavior and incentives.

INS implementation of sanctions has been marred by several problems. Many sanctions cases have been based purely on record-keeping violations, despite the central office's rule that fines should reflect the deliberate hiring or continued employment of illegal immigrants. While the regional and district offices showed allegiance to the broad outlines of central office policy, these field offices differed significantly in enforcement priorities, investigative procedures, and the protections afforded to employers and immigrants. Fix and Hill conclude that the implementation of sanctions has been adequate for a start-up period, but that the INS must strengthen the oversight of sanctions to guarantee the legitimacy of the program (Fix and Hill, 1990).

A detailed discussion of sanctions is beyond the scope of this paper. However, a brief review of how the INS adjusted its personnel policies, investigative procedures, and organizational structure to enforce sanctions is essential in evaluating the larger changes IRCA wrought in the agency.

The careful implementation of employer sanctions largely reflected the constraints Congress imposed upon enforcement. As noted earlier, penalties were phased in gradually with a mandated period of employer education. IRCA also provided a "good faith" defense for employers who checked the necessary documents; required the INS to prove "knowing" violations for larger penalties; and subjected the agency to the stricter legal standards of the Administrative Procedures Act (APA).[9] Finally, IRCA's sunset provision presented the most important incentive for careful enforcement, according to many INS officials.

While sanctions triggered many beneficial changes in the INS, the agency struggled unsuccessfully with the longstanding problem of coordinating policy throughout its diffuse central, regional, and local layers. The INS central office failed to institute strong oversight procedures for sanctions, while the pressure to implement new programs quickly pushed authority to the agency's field offices. This problem in the agency's governance accounted for some of the agency's shortcomings in enforcing sanctions.

Recruitment of Staff

IRCA placed new demands on the INS Investigations Division, the agency's main enforcement unit in the U.S. interior, and the lead unit in implementing sanctions. Before IRCA, INS investigators had specialized in area control, which involved apprehending illegal immigrants in the community or workplace and processing them for deportation. Sanctions required a different set of skills than area control, most importantly the ability to investigate and document business practices, as well as negotiate compliance with employers. The challenge of enforcing the law against businesses with resources to contest INS actions was more difficult than enforcing the law against illegal immigrants.

As the INS expanded its Investigations staff from 875 special agents to over 1500 (INS, 1987, p. 9; INS, 1990, p. 8), it responded to the shift in responsibility by recruiting heavily from outside the agency and stressing communication, writing, and language skills. In the past, most of INS special agents entered the agency through the Border Patrol and then transferred into Investigations. After the passage of IRCA, many INS districts including Los Angeles, Chicago, Houston, and New York exploited the "Outstanding Scholar" program, which allows federal agencies to bypass civil service procedures and hire college graduates with grade-point averages above 3.5.

The infusion of new blood into the Investigations Division reflected an appropriate adaptation to IRCA, as experienced agents trained in raids and apprehensions might be unsuited to regulating employers. Many INS officials, immigration attorneys, and business representatives said that the new agents have helped reorient the INS toward its new regulatory role. One INS regional official commented:

> Sanctions demands in some way a new level of professionalism or
> sophistication. You must be better trained and more sensitive. . . . I
> see that happening, too. We hired 100 special agents in this region as
> a result of IRCA. To a man and a woman, they're excellent.

In the long run, the new recruitment policy for the Investigations Division may have a stronger impact on the agency when this large cohort of special agents begins to assume leadership posts. In the past, management positions in the INS have been dominated by former Border Patrol officers committed to an enforcement policy of raids and apprehensions. The recruitment of agents from different backgrounds, trained to regulate businesses instead of apprehend immigrants, may erode that pattern and broaden the perspectives of agency managers.

The INS also doubled its legal staff from 225 in 1986 to 450 in 1989 (INS, 1987, p. 9; INS, 1990, p. 8), using the Attorney General's honor graduate program to bring promising lawyers into the agency. The expansion of the legal staff was part of a plan to use attorneys to oversee the sanctions process, an important change discussed in more detail below.

Enforcement Procedures

The legislative design of IRCA also impelled the INS to institute procedures that would promote careful implementation and safeguard the tool of sanctions. Consistent with IRCA's intent, the guidelines stressed cooperation with business and protected firms from harassment and heavy-handed enforcement.

The cornerstone of the implementation of sanctions was employer education. Although this role was new to the INS, the agency redirected a large share of its enforcement resources into employer education and began the new assignment with some vigor. The central office required that district offices devote 50 percent of investigative time to employer education between July 1987 and June 1988. To achieve the Commissioner's goal of 1 million education contacts with employers in the year ending June 30, 1988, the INS enlisted staff from Investigations, Detention and Deportation, Anti-Smuggling, and the Border Patrol. Even after the full implementation of sanctions, the INS central office maintained targets for employer education.[10] The central office also required an education visit by INS agents as a precondition to fining an employer. If INS agents found that a firm violating IRCA had not been educated about sanctions, they were to issue a warning letter.[11]

INS policies on employer education were taken seriously at the local level where the employer contacts took place. In all of the sites in this study, the INS offered seminars to employers, and visited "notorious" employers who had relied on illegal immigrants in the past. In El Paso, the INS tried to educate every employer about the new requirements; in San Francisco the district office reported contacting 59,000 out of 250,000 Bay Area employers during the education period.

INS involvement in employer education marked a significant shift toward a regulatory model of enforcement. There was some criticism that the education effort was inadequate, but most trade associations gave the INS decent marks for its education campaign. One restaurant representative expressed a wider sentiment by observing that "Prior to the law, the INS would come in and be belligerent. They are coming in today in a much more conciliatory way."

The INS also signaled a cooperative attitude toward employers in designing investigative procedures. To prevent selective enforcement, the INS mandated that 60 percent of investigations should result from leads, 20 percent from random selection of targeted industries, and 20 percent from random selection of all firms. Businesses were to receive notice three days before the INS inspected their I-9 forms. The central office limited the fining of employers who had not done the verification and record-keeping required by IRCA to instances of "overall refusal to comply" or "egregious" cases. Finally, INS officers were instructed to "pursue settlement strategies when employer is willing to admit violation, promise compliance" (INS, 1988).

Many of the district offices and Border Patrol sectors in this study shared the central office's emphasis on negotiation and voluntary compliance. Some offices continued issuing warning letters after the education period ended, and others allowed employers to fire illegal immigrants without penalty if the firms did not appear to have known of their status. The Chicago district office permitted a candy manufacturer to fire 457 illegal workers without being fined. Referring to a recent INS inspection, one immigration attorney noted, "We called the shots: when, where, why, how, what . . . The attitude and the way we were able to control disruption was 180 degrees different from anything we had ever seen." Overall, the amount of fines levied by the INS has been modest. The most active INS field office, the El Paso Border Patrol sector, has only issued one fine per every two staff months. By the fall of 1989, the INS had issued only 3,500 fines—about 2 fines per agent— and had reduced the average fine by more than half after negotiating with employers (GAO, 1990, p. 88). These patterns in the INS's implementation of sanctions reflect the agency's efforts to use its new enforcement tool judiciously.

Oversight by INS Attorneys

One factor accounting for the agency's measured approach to enforcing sanctions was the oversight role played by agency attorneys. During the 1980s, the INS had shifted attorneys out of routine naturalization and deportation cases into more complex legal work.[12] The central office's requirement that the District Counsel or Border Patrol Sector Counsel approve all employer fines continued that process (many sectors had to create a Counsel position as a result of IRCA). Attorneys were involved in sanctions cases earlier than in other investigations, advising agents how to ask questions, take evidence, and secure subpoenas. The legal staff played a restraining role by sending cases back for more documentation, reducing the penalty, or proposing a settlement. Attorneys helped guarantee the integrity of the process, and by late 1989, the INS had not been defeated in a single appeal of a sanctions case.

Decentralization of Sanctions Policy

While the INS skillfully used its legal staff to provide internal monitoring of sanctions within the district offices and Border Patrol sectors, this close oversight did not extend among INS units. The vertical lines of authority over sanctions—through the central, regional, and local offices—were unclear. At the local level, the independent operations of the district offices and Border Patrol sectors provided a source of further fragmentation. During the post-IRCA period, the INS failed to find an appropriate balance between central authority and local flexibility.

While the INS central office issued guidelines for the implementation of sanctions, it set the parameters broadly and delegated many of the details to the regional and district offices. The central office approved all proposed sanctions cases until April 1988, then turned that authority over to the regional offices. In June 1988, the central office in turn permitted the regions to delegate authority over sanctions to District directors and Border Patrol sector chiefs. The strategy was to empower local office managers to solve problems and respond effectively to differences in the immigrant population and local economy.[13] Although the central office continued to settle important policy questions, its main tool for monitoring sanctions was a numerical target system (called the Priority Management System) for the number of sanctions cases for each region, district office, and Border Patrol sector.[14]

Filtered through four regional offices and interpreted by 33 district offices and 22 Border Patrol sectors, the central office guidelines failed to impart a coherent, nationwide sanctions strategy, despite the widespread emphasis on employer education and voluntary compliance. Even the level of control over sanctions varied sharply throughout the INS: the Eastern and Western regions exerted considerable control, while the Northern and Southern regions delegated more authority to the district offices and sectors.

The Western Region placed the most emphasis on meeting the numerical targets for sanctions cases, monitoring the statistics on a monthly basis. This policy turned numerical targets into quotas, because meeting the targets was connected with pay raises and promotions. To reach the targets, INS agents in the Western Region relied on paperwork fines because these cases were easiest to make, even though the practice contradicted central office policy. One official noted, "They go for the easy ones; there's pressure to do a body count." By March 31, 1989, 53 percent of the sanctions cases in the Western Region were based only on paperwork violations.

The Eastern Region, in contrast, pressed its district offices to develop substantive cases involving "knowing" hires or continued employment of illegal immigrants. The Eastern Region retained the right to review each sanctions case before a fine was issued. The result was that 71 percent of the fines issued in the Eastern Region involved deliberate hiring or continued employment of illegal immigrants.

Overall, there were wide disparities among INS regional and district offices in the number, amount, and type of sanctions cases. The Western and Southern regions had large numbers of small cases; conversely, the Northern and Eastern regions had small numbers of large cases (see table 2.1). In Los Angeles, more than half the sanctions cases were based on paperwork violations alone, whereas all of the cases in Chicago involved substantive violations. As we shall

Table 2.1 INS SANCTIONS CASES BY REGION, AS OF MARCH 31, 1989

Region	Number of fines	Average fine	% of fines "paperwork only"
Eastern	198	$8,176	29
Northern	159	$9,459	26
Southern	832	$2,961	41
Western	380	$3,942	53

Source: Immigration and Naturalization Service.

see later in this chapter, as competing priorities developed, the regions and district offices also attached different degrees of importance to sanctions, further weakening central authority in the INS (see chapter 3 for further discussion of regional disparities).

The fragmentation of authority over sanctions was reinforced at the local level by the role of the Border Patrol in implementing sanctions. The Border Patrol was less involved in sanctions than the Investigations Division: 135 out of 4,000 Border Patrol officers were to be detailed to sanctions, compared to 500 out of 1,500 investigators (INS, 1987b, p. 5).

Still, in places like El Paso and Miami, there were more Border Patrol officers than district office staff assigned to sanctions. The task of coordinating district offices and Border Patrol sectors was made inherently difficult by overlapping boundaries. For example, the San Antonio district includes parts of the Del Rio, Laredo, and McAllen Border Patrol sectors. The involvement of two separate units in sanctions created confusion, competition, and uneven enforcement policies despite the signing of memoranda of understanding to divide the territory.

INS district offices and Border Patrol sectors usually operated independently in enforcing sanctions. One INS district official commented, "Anytime the Border Patrol station encounters an employer sanctions case, they're supposed to give me a call. We haven't received a single call." In another district, where the division of territory was eroding, a district official claimed that the Border Patrol "got a bunch of new agents, expanded their coverage, and now they're involved in activities they have no business being involved in." The sectors typically imposed more fines than the comparable district office and based their cases on raids of local firms instead of I-9 inspections, leaving employers more vulnerable to disruption and unreasonable searches. As shown later in this chapter, the involvement of the Border Patrol in sanctions reflects a mismatch between the flow of resources in the INS and the growth in the agency's enforcement tasks.

Despite the lack of strong central authority, sanctions made immigration law enforcement more fair and predictable, with less disruption to businesses and communities. Employer sanctions subjected the INS to much stronger checks and balances, and the agency adapted its own policies to respect these constraints. Sanctions also strengthened the long-term capacity of the INS for better enforcement in three ways: by strengthening the Investigations and District Counsel staff of the district offices; by using attorneys to provide an internal check on enforcement, creating a model for strong oversight that can be applied in other contexts; and by creating cooperative attitudes toward business as a foundation for enforcement.

A BROADER LAW ENFORCEMENT AGENDA FOR THE INS

While sanctions represented a significant change in INS enforcement practices, the magnitude of the shift was limited by the simultaneous growth of other initiatives. Sanctions became merely one part of a diversified law enforcement portfolio, which affected the implementation of sanctions in two ways. First, the Border Patrol maintained its traditionally strong influence both within and outside the INS, securing a large share of the additional budget and staff during the late 1980s, limiting the resources available to sanctions. Second, political pressures elevated the importance within the INS of criminal alien removal and drug interdiction, further diffusing the resources and the importance attached to sanctions.

The Diffusion of Enforcement Resources

IRCA authorized a 70 percent increase in the INS budget. The promise of an infusion of money set off a competition for resources within the INS, turning IRCA into a broad funding vehicle rather than a narrowly tailored illegal immigration program.

When the INS received $123 million in supplemental enforcement funds for fiscal year 1987 to implement IRCA, it divided the money among four major programs: $70.5 million (57 percent) went for border enforcement; $33.7 million (27 percent) to sanctions; $16.8 million (14 percent) to a new criminal alien removal program; and $2 million (2 percent) to the Systematic Alien Verification for Entitlements (SAVE) (INS, 1987b, pp. 3–7). The most notable aspect of the budget plan was that only one-quarter of the extra money would go to sanctions, IRCA's key new enforcement element.

In seeking additional funds to implement IRCA in fiscal year 1988, the INS requested more money for sanctions, but the pattern was similar. The agency allocated $67.2 million (40 percent) of the extra money for border enforcement; $59.7 million (35 percent) for sanctions; $39.2 million (23 percent) for criminal alien removal; and $3.4 million (2 percent) for SAVE (INS, 1987b, pp. 3–7). As a result, only a share of the new special agents hired after IRCA were detailed to employer sanctions. The El Paso district office added more than 20 special agents after IRCA, but only 8 were assigned to sanctions; the New York district office added more than 70 agents, and assigned only 43 to sanctions.

The first reason why border enforcement received the largest share of the INS supplemental enforcement money was the tension the Moorhead amendment—which set the goal of a 50 percent expansion of the Border Patrol—created between IRCA's enforcement and funding provisions. IRCA's enforcement section (Title I of the law) dealt almost exclusively with sanctions, discrimination, and SAVE. However, the part of IRCA (Section 111) authorizing extra appropriations for the INS set a funding target only for the Border Patrol, giving it a primary claim on INS resources.

The Moorhead amendment, in turn, reflected the political constraints that have shaped immigration policy in the past. The only uniformed arm of the INS, the Border Patrol has long been an elite unit and commands public attention because it performs a visible and demanding task. This visibility has helped the Border Patrol win support largely lacking for other INS units. In 1984, for example, Congress authorized 850 new Border Patrol positions, part of a near doubling of the Patrol from 1,900 to 3,500 officers between 1979 and 1986. Border control topped the Commissioner's list of priorities for 1985 and 1986. This emphasis on the Border Patrol continued after the enactment of IRCA, with the Moorhead amendment serving as a focal point, funneling resources and attention away from sanctions. One Capitol Hill staffer involved in immigration policy observed:

> The Border Patrol is very visible and active; that's why it's a focus of INS budgetary discussions on Capitol Hill. The rest of INS is very behind-the-scenes and bureaucratic. When people think of INS, they think of the men in green at the border. Funding for the Border Patrol is politically valuable for Congressmen from the Southwest because it gives the appearance that they are doing something about illegal aliens.

In justifying the use of IRCA supplemental funds for its criminal alien program, the INS cited Section 701 of IRCA, a sentence stating that the Attorney General should deport criminal aliens from the United States "as expeditiously as possible" (INS, 1987b, p. 3). Section 701—called the MacKay amendment after its sponsor, Representative Buddy MacKay of Florida—was a sleeper, added to IRCA during the debate on the floor of the House of Representatives. No one had expected this provision to be important in the implementation of IRCA.[15]

The MacKay amendment helped turn IRCA into a flexible funding mechanism. The deportation of criminal aliens from the United States had received more attention from the INS since 1983, as public concern about drug trafficking and prison overcrowding added urgency to the issue.[16] In 1986 the INS had been planning a new program, the Alien Criminal Apprehension Program (ACAP), to identify criminal aliens earlier in the justice process so they could be deported.[17] The MacKay amendment tucked ACAP into IRCA, allowing the INS to channel some of the IRCA funds into criminal alien removal.

The Changing Pressures on Immigration Law Enforcement

While the Moorhead amendment reflected a previous institutional pattern of funneling resources toward the Border Patrol, the MacKay amendment signaled a new trend of shifting resources away from illegal immigration into anti-drug and anti-crime policies. The latter trend became more pronounced in 1988 and 1989, when increased funding for the Border Patrol was justified more in terms of fighting drugs than in controlling immigration.[18]

The criminal alien issue had become much more charged in 1986, largely due to a series of critical GAO reports (GAO, 1986a; GAO, 1986b). Most importantly, the GAO found that in New York City the INS was failing to identify and deport criminal aliens. This finding prompted the Senate Appropriations Committee in May 1986 to ask the INS to develop a detailed strategy correcting this problem. In response, in December 1986 the INS announced ACAP.

The criminal alien issue continued to gather momentum. One impetus was the enactment of the Anti-Drug Abuse Act of 1986 only 10 days before IRCA was signed into law. The 1986 drug law expanded INS power to deport aliens convicted of drug offenses and required local law enforcement agencies to notify the INS if they suspected anyone arrested on drug charges of being an illegal immigrant.[19] In December 1986 the INS joined the Justice Department's Organized Crime and Drug Enforcement Task Force, a multi-agency effort to disrupt drug trafficking networks. FBI statistics showing that 20 to 40 percent of people arrested in big cities like Miami, Los Angeles, and Houston were foreign-born focused further attention on criminal aliens (GAO, 1987c, p. 3).

Between 1987 and 1989 public concern about drugs and crime continued to grow,[20] strengthening the new political pressures on the INS. The Anti-Drug Abuse Act of 1988 further expanded the INS role in anti-drug policy, creating a new criminal class of aliens ("aggravated felons") guilty of murder or certain drug or firearms violations. The INS was required to deport these aliens after their jail sentences were finished, and could use expedited procedures to do so. The INS was also directed to help state and local authorities identify alien felons on a round-the-clock basis. Thus, the 1988 drug law deepened INS ties to other law enforcement agencies that could not be easily disregarded. An INS official noted:

> Criminal aliens—there's a lot more that can be done there. . . . We tell these local sheriffs, 'Yeah, I'm going to take criminal aliens.' You turn that tap on, and you'd better have a bucket there to respond—and we don't.

While the growing role of the INS in combating drugs and crime was demanding, the assignment allowed the INS to become a more valued member of the law enforcement community. For the first time, the INS received supplemental drug funding in 1988 and 1989. The 1988 drug law authorized $52.4 million for the INS, including funds for the Border Patrol to add 435 officers and buy equipment for drug enforcement. In the 1989 legislation, the INS received $16.9 million in extra money for drug enforcement. When the budget increases for IRCA ended in the late 1980s, the supplemental drug funding gave the agency its only claim on discretionary funds. The 1989 drug bill, for example, provided 84 percent of the $20.2 million increase in the INS's Congressional appropriation for FY 1990 (INS, 1990, pp. 7–8).

In contrast to the persistent pressure on the INS to do more to combat drugs and crime, concern about illegal immigration faded once the battle over IRCA's passage receded from the headlines. The number of illegal aliens apprehended by the Border Patrol dropped from a record 1.7 million in FY 1986 to less than 1 million in FY 1988 (INS, 1989, p. 128), diffusing some of the unease about illegal immigration.

As noted in the introduction, public support for IRCA was broad but shallow, while opposition to the law was more concentrated. This pattern continued after the passage of IRCA. Opponents of employer sanctions continued to monitor the law and lobby for repeal, while many supporters of sanctions turned their attention to other issues.[21] In big cities with large immigrant populations like Chicago, Houston, Los Angeles, and New York, coalitions formed to monitor the implementation of IRCA and the law's impact on discrimination.

The intense scrutiny of sanctions, the constraints upon enforcement, and the growth of fraudulent documents enabling illegal immigrants to evade the law caused some INS managers to downgrade the importance of sanctions. One INS regional official argued that "We're as effective now as we're going to be [in enforcing sanctions] as long as Congress doesn't move on a secure [tamper-proof] work authorization card."

Congress and the administration also paid less attention to sanctions over time, as the anti-drug effort drove policy and budget decisions relating to the Justice Department. U.S. Attorney offices in our study sites were too overwhelmed—typically with drug cases—to prosecute criminal violations of IRCA, even though the INS loaned its own lawyers to serve as Special Assistant U.S. Attorneys handling immigration matters. Similarly, the Administrative Law Judges (from the Department of Labor) assigned to hear appeals of sanctions were often too busy to handle IRCA violations, and frequently pressed the INS and the employers to reach settlements on their own.

A More Versatile Law Enforcement Agency

The simultaneous introduction of major programs targeted at employers, criminal aliens, and drug smugglers leaves the INS a larger, more complex, and more versatile law enforcement agency as it enters the 1990s. An analysis of budget and staffing patterns reveals that increases in resources available to combat illegal immigration have been modest, that enforcement resources are now more diffused across a number of tasks, and that organizational missions have blurred as the Border Patrol has assumed investigative tasks.

Congress and the President did provide the INS with a substantial increase in enforcement resources after the passage of IRCA, as promised in the legislation. The enforcement budget grew by 85 percent, from $290 million in 1986 to $536 million in 1990, while the enforcement staff rose by 38 percent from 5,800 to over 8,000. Figures 2.2 and 2.3 show that the growth in budget and staff was almost proportionately shared among the five main enforcement units.[22] While the Investigations staff grew fastest on a percentage basis—increasing its budget by 126 percent and its staff by 75 percent—the Border Patrol received more money and staff in absolute terms, claiming 46 percent of the increased enforcement funds between 1986 and 1990.

Although INS enforcement units benefited from funding and staffing increases, they were trying to do much more than before. The strain on the Investigations Division was particularly acute because the unit's personnel growth only brought it back to 1978 levels, when

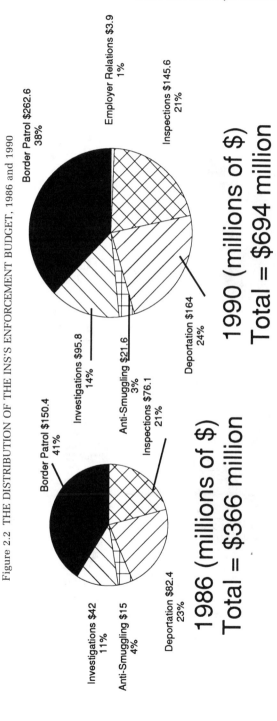

Figure 2.2 THE DISTRIBUTION OF THE INS'S ENFORCEMENT BUDGET, 1986 and 1990

Border Patrol $262.6
38%

Employer Relations $3.9
1%

Inspections $145.6
21%

Deportation $164
24%

1990 (millions of $)
Total = $694 million

Border Patrol $150.4
41%

Investigations $95.8
14%

Anti-Smuggling $21.6
3%

Inspections $76.1
21%

Investigations $42
11%

Anti-Smuggling $15
4%

Deportation $82.4
23%

1986 (millions of $)
Total = $366 million

Source: INS budget documents.
Pies are proportional to budgets.

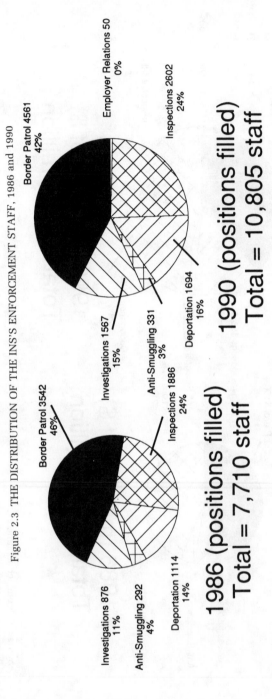

Figure 2.3 THE DISTRIBUTION OF THE INS'S ENFORCEMENT STAFF, 1986 and 1990

Border Patrol 4561
42%

Employer Relations 50
0%

Inspections 2602
24%

Investigations 1567
15%

Anti-Smuggling 331
3%

Deportation 1694
16%

1990 (positions filled)
Total = 10,805 staff

Border Patrol 3542
46%

Investigations 876
11%

Anti-Smuggling 292
4%

Deportation 1114
14%

Inspections 1886
24%

1986 (positions filled)
Total = 7,710 staff

Source: INS budget documents.
Pies are proportional to size of enforcement staff.

sanctions and the Alien Criminal Apprehension Program did not exist.[23] The division of Investigations resources among three major responsibilities—criminal aliens, sanctions, and fraud—is reflected in figure 2.4 showing the allocation of agent hours in the eight district offices in our study. In four of the eight sites, sanctions accounted for less than one-third of investigative time.

The growth of the criminal alien removal program was rapid during the post-IRCA period, and enabled the INS to strengthen its anti-drug efforts. The number of aliens deported for violating the narcotics laws more than quadrupled between 1986 and 1988. During that same period, the share of aliens deported for narcotics violations increased from 4 percent of all deportations to 17 percent.[24]

In addition to the major programs targeted at employers, criminal aliens, and drug smugglers, the INS interior enforcement staff was also involved in marketing the SAVE program to state agencies and explaining IRCA's anti-discrimination requirements to employers (see chapter 5 for an extended discussion of SAVE). In an attempt to help employers adjust to IRCA's effects on the labor supply, the INS also developed a Legally Authorized Worker program to encourage firms needing workers to recruit from public employment agencies. These activities reflect how, in the post-IRCA period, the INS became immersed in a wide range of issues related to immigration, and how INS agents had to become proficient in a far wider range of tasks than area control. One result is that some tasks have suffered. For example, many INS officials said that the challenge of educating employers about sanctions was causing education about anti-discrimination to be neglected.

Changes in the Border Patrol also reflected the growth of the INS law enforcement mission and the agency's struggle to juggle new tasks. In July 1986, the Border Patrol joined Operation Alliance—a federal, state, and local effort to control the flow of drugs, firearms, and illegal immigrants across the border—as the lead agency in interdicting drugs along the border between ports of entry. The Border Patrol began detailing officers to local schools for drug education in 1988 and also set up its own criminal alien task forces.

The Border Patrol's growing role in drug interdiction was partly due to the increased flow of drugs across the Mexican border. Interdiction programs during the 1980s induced drug smugglers to change their air supply routes from Colombia to the eastern coast of Florida, to land routes through Mexico (The White House, 1989, pp. 73, 74, 79). As a result, the estimated value of narcotics seizures by the Border Patrol rose from $162 million in 1986 to $701 million in

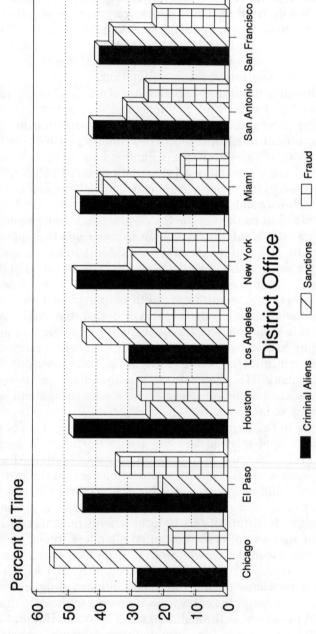

Figure 2.4 THE ALLOCATION OF INVESTIGATIVE TIME BY 8 INS DISTRICT OFFICES, FY 1989

Source: Immigration and Naturalization Service, sanctions totals include employer education.

1988 (INS, 1989, p. 128). The Border Patrol claimed responsibility for 60 percent of marijuana seizures along the Southern land border and 50 percent of cocaine seizures (Nelson, 1988).

While drug interdiction often accompanies alien apprehension, the Border Patrol's participation in anti-drug task forces diverted officers from guarding the border, as did the Patrol's participation in sanctions. Total officers devoted to line watch (the patrolling of the border) increased by 7 percent (from 2.4 million to 2.6 million) between 1986 and 1989, despite the INS's focus on increasing the Border Patrol. Overall, line watch dropped as a total percentage of Border Patrol officer hours from 42 percent in 1986 to 38 percent in 1989.[25] The agency's failure to substantially increase line watch hours reflects how IRCA's mandate to devote more resources to the control of illegal immigration was not fulfilled when the Border Patrol broadened its mission.

As the INS enforcement agenda expanded during the late 1980s, the division of labor in the agency became blurred. Both the Investigations Division and the Border Patrol were involved in sanctions, employer education, and criminal alien removal, reflecting a mismatch between resources and responsibilities. As shown above, the INS continued to concentrate resources in the politically dominant Border Patrol between 1986 and 1990, despite the substantial growth in interior investigative programs. The INS then had to divert Border Patrol officers into new tasks, duplicating the work of its interior enforcement units. "There are no resources in Investigations," said one regional official in 1989. "The only resources this agency has are in green uniforms [of Border Patrol officers]."

STRAINS ON THE ENFORCEMENT SIDE OF THE INS

By 1989 the rapid and somewhat haphazard growth of the INS law enforcement mission was clearly straining the agency. Rapid growth generated confusion about agency priorities and sent the agency into a budget crisis.

Unclear Priorities and Weak Management

The enforcement priorities of INS district offices varied significantly by 1989. Often the differences did not reflect deliberate specialization so much as the personal preferences of regional and local office managers. By 1989 Chicago and Los Angeles were the only district offices in our sample that still identified sanctions as their most important enforcement priority. New York, Miami, and San Antonio regarded criminal alien removal as the most important program. Houston had stopped developing new sanctions cases so it could spend more time investigating fraud in the Special Agricultural Workers (SAW) legalization program, despite the disapproval of the regional office.

This statement by an INS regional official attests to the confusion about enforcement priorities:

> It really is becoming increasingly difficult to know what you're work- ing on because there's so much you should be working on. We're like a cat on a hot tin roof.

Without more effective control from the central office, the gradual drift in enforcement policy away from sanctions toward criminal alien removal and drug interdiction is likely to continue. In March 1990, the GAO concluded that sanctions had caused "widespread" discrimination. Although Congress declined to repeal sanctions, the link to discrimination will probably encourage INS managers to downgrade sanctions as a priority. In addition, the Immigration Act of 1990 further expanded the definition of aggravated felony and streamlined deportation procedures for alien felons, reflecting the continuing pressures on the INS to deport more criminal aliens. The President's drug control strategy envisions a continuing role for the Border Patrol in drug interdiction, which will be facilitated by the broad arrest powers granted INS officers in the Immigration Act of 1990 (The White House, 1989, pp. 72, 77–79).

The Budget Crisis

The best reflection of how the INS failed to relate enforcement means and ends was the severe budget crisis of 1989. The first strain on the INS budget arose from a weekly flow into South Texas of 2,000 Central Americans seeking asylum. In response, the INS detailed examiners to South Texas to review asylum applications, posted additional Border Patrol officers to the area, and set up detention centers to keep the Central Americans from fleeing into the interior. By the time these policies reduced the flow of people into South Texas, the project had cost the INS $27 million.[26]

The second cause for the budget crisis was a central office decision in mid-1988 to hire 500 more Border Patrol officers to approach the goal of the Moorhead amendment. Due to the time necessary to train officers and to high attrition, the INS was far from the target of 5,400 Border Patrol officers. The INS believed that it could pay for the new officers through the supplemental funding in the 1988 drug bill, which was pending at the time.

At that point, the cleaver of the Gramm-Rudman-Hollings deficit reduction law fell on the INS. Because Congress did not pass the drug bill until late in the legislative session, it had already committed most of the funds available in 1989 according to the budget law guidelines. As a result, many agencies saw their allotments from the 1988 drug bill slashed. The INS received only $26.2 million—half of the $52.4 million authorized under the law—leaving the agency short of money to pay for the Border Patrol expansion.

Together with the South Texas crisis, the Border Patrol expansion left the INS with a $50 million deficit. The INS was forced to shift funds from other accounts to the Border Patrol and also impose an agency-wide hiring freeze in early 1989 to eliminate the deficit.[27]

The overhiring for the Border Patrol reflected poor management by the agency. In a time of persistently large federal budget deficits, the INS would be unable to secure large funding increases year after year. The deficit caused cutbacks throughout the agency, including a reduction of enforcement of employer sanctions in New Mexico; of the Border Patrol sector in El Paso, Texas; and of special agent positions in Miami and San Antonio.

CHALLENGES FOR THE ENFORCEMENT SIDE OF THE INS IN THE 1990s

The INS budget crisis of 1989 was a powerful signal that the agency would have to lower its sights and set enforcement priorities more clearly during the 1990s. The large budget increases of the late 1980s are clearly over, as extra funds for the INS were shrinking by 1989 and 1990.[28] Dismayed by the disarray in the INS, Congress and the administration have stressed better management and organization as watchwords for the agency over the next several years.[29]

Listed below are several of the most important challenges for Congress, the administration, and the INS as they try to make immigration law enforcement more focused and effective. Eugene McNary, the new INS Commissioner who took over in late 1989, has already started shifting the agency in some of the directions described below, announcing a reorganization that would reduce the policy role of the regional offices and end the Border Patrol's involvement in enforcing sanctions. This plan was being reviewed by the Justice Department, Office of Management and Budget, and Congress as of this writing.[30]

1. Centralize authority in the INS and return the regional offices to their previous role as operational support areas in budget and personnel. The role of the regional offices in overseeing sanctions and setting enforcement priorities created two managerial layers in the INS and fostered the creation of personal fiefdoms within the agency. The central office should be more involved in setting enforcement priorities and overseeing investigative techniques in INS field offices.

2. Delineate the responsibilities of the Investigations Division and the Border Patrol more clearly. The Border Patrol should not duplicate the Investigations Division's roles in enforcing sanctions, educating employers, or removing criminal aliens from the United States. If more agents are needed for these functions, they should be added to the interior enforcement staff instead of detailed from the Border Patrol. The present situation is not only duplicative but also inefficient, as Border Patrol officers are better trained in monitoring and apprehending illegal immigrants than in regulating employers. The INS should also strongly consider reorganizing its local office structure to house Border Patrol and Investigations staff under one authority.

3. Ensure that policies to control illegal immigration are not neglected in the rush to expand criminal alien and anti-drug programs. After working for more than a decade to enact employer sanctions, Congress and the INS should not give up on sanctions after four years, particularly if anti-discrimination and employee verification strategies can be improved.

4. Continue the successful recruitment and oversight policies that have strengthened the Investigations and Counsel staffs in the INS. Both the Investigations and District Counsel staffs have been strengthened by attempts to infuse them with new blood from the outside. The attempt to bring in special agents from outside the INS is particularly appropriate since enforcement tasks have grown so rapidly. The greater involvement of the legal staff in overseeing enforcement policy should also be continued.

Notes

1. While both the central and regional offices perform management and oversight functions, the division of labor has frequently been discussed, disputed, and changed.

During the Carter Administration, for example, regional commissioners initially did not have line authority to supervise programs. In 1979, the line authority of regional commissioners to supervise and direct local office operations was restored. See U.S. House of Representatives, Committee on Government Operations, 1980.

2. According to the General Accounting Office, 75 percent of Department of Justice staff work in field offices. See U.S. General Accounting Office, 1986a.

3. Demographers Jeffrey Passel and Karen Woodrow used 1980 Census data to develop a "lower-bound" estimate that there were 2.1 million illegal immigrants in the United States in 1980. See Passel and Woodrow, 1984. If 50 percent of illegal immigrants were uncounted in the Census, the total population would have been 4 million. In testimony before the House Subcommittee on Census and Population in 1985, Passel estimated that the illegal immigrant population had grown to between 3 and 5 million by the mid-1980s.

4. For example, 72 percent of the public agreed that penalties should be imposed on businesses hiring illegal immigrants in a 1977 Gallup poll. This percentage increased to 79 percent when Gallup conducted the same poll in 1983. A May 1982 Merit survey found that 84 percent of the public was concerned about illegal immigration to the United States. See Harwood, 1986.

5. For further discussion of court decisions affecting INS enforcement, see Morris, 1985, pp. 115–119.

6. Edwin Harwood has described this paradox as the public's "statute of liberty" syndrome (1985, p. 74). Throughout the years, well-publicized enforcement efforts by the INS have angered community groups and led cities like Chicago, New York, and Los Angeles to pass resolutions preventing city agencies, including the police, from cooperating with the INS.

7. Morris, 1985, pp. 91–92, has echoed a common theme by referring to the INS as a "weak" agency within the Department of Justice, citing the fact that the INS Commissioner does not report directly to the Attorney General as evidence of the low status of the INS within the Justice Department.

8. For example, IRCA states that in determining penalties, "due consideration shall be given to the size of the business of the employer being charged, the good faith of the employer, the seriousness of the violation, whether or not the individual was an unauthorized alien, and the history of previous violations" (Section 101 of IRCA).

9. Previously, enforcement had operated under the rules of immigration law, not administrative law as governed by the APA. This change gave employers who challenge sanctions cases before an Administrative Law Judge stronger rights to cross-examination, discovery, and other protections than aliens challenging cases before an Immigration Judge. For further discussion of this distinction, see Fix and Hill, 1990, pp. 51–53.

10. For the year July 1, 1988, to June 30, 1989, the INS set a goal of 500,000 employer education contacts. INS district offices were required to devote 25 percent of their time to employer education.

11. This summary of INS guidelines for sanctions is based on a memo from the Office of the Commissioner entitled "Employer Sanctions Policy After June 1, 1988."

12. See the discussion of changes in the INS legal staff in INS, 1986, pp. 56–58.

13. As INS Commissioner Alan Nelson noted in his memo spelling out employer sanctions policy after June 1, 1988, to the INS field offices, "These decisions . . . pursue my management philosophy of maximum field involvement and control."

14. The targets set under the Priority Management system were quite detailed and were monitored quarterly. For example, the Eastern Region's targets for sanctions enforcement during fiscal year 1989 included presenting 10 sanctions cases for crim-

inal prosecution, issuing 100 fines, targeting 3 smuggling organizations, conducting 1,500 random inspections of businesses, conducting 1,500 inspections of businesses in targeted industries, and educating 177,000 employers about sanctions. Each region had a similar set of targets. In turn, the regions assigned goals to the district offices and Border Patrol sectors to make sure that the overall goal would be reached.

15. Legislative histories of IRCA include little or no discussion of criminal alien removal or the MacKay amendment. See, for example, Montweiler, 1987. Montweiler's 65-page description of IRCA contains one sentence (p. 87) describing the criminal alien provisions of IRCA.

16. The criminal alien issue was formally identified as an INS priority in 1983. Because the INS can deport only a small percentage of apprehended aliens, the agency decided to concentrate more resources on deporting criminals. See the INS description of investigative priorities in INS, 1989, p. 19.

17. ACAP was designed to identify "chokepoints" in the criminal justice system— arrest or arraignment, for example—where the INS could identify criminal aliens and begin deportation proceedings. ACAP also directed that the INS would cooperate with local law enforcement officials in both "proactive" (working with police units to identify criminal aliens on the streets) and "reactive" (identifying aliens already in criminal justice proceedings) measures to remove criminal aliens from the United States.

18. In language that would have been surprising three years earlier, the Senate Appropriations Committee noted in its 1989 report on funding for the INS that "The Committee recommendation provides for . . . necessary enhancements to maintain a high level of border patrol staffing along the Southwest border of the United States. The Committee continues to be concerned with the trafficking of drugs across our borders and strongly supports the efforts of the border patrol in interdicting large quantities of illegal drugs between ports of entry and at border patrol traffic checkpoints." See U.S. Senate, 1989, pp. 47–48.

19. The drug law of 1986 broadened INS power to exclude and deport aliens possessing, selling, or smuggling drugs by expanding the definition of illegal or "controllable" substances under the Immigration and Nationality Act. Previously, drug violations under the Immigration and Nationality Act only applied to narcotic drugs and marijuana. Section 1751 of the Anti-Drug Abuse Act broadened the definition of controllable substances to include synthetic drugs such as LSD, PCP, and other "designer" drugs. The law also specified that a state, federal, or foreign narcotics violation can render an alien excludable or deportable.

20. A Gallup Poll reported that by September 1989, 63 percent of Americans cited drugs as the nation's top problem, up from 11 percent in April 1987. See the *Gallup Report: Political, Social and Economic Trends*, no. 289 (Oct. 1989), pp. 4–6; and no. 260 (May 1987), p. 6.

21. One of the few groups pressing for strict enforcement of sanctions was the Federation of Americans for Immigration Reform (FAIR), which published a "Rogues' Gallery" column listing firms that had been fined. FAIR newsletters frequently reported on the implementation of sanctions.

22. Although the Intelligence Division reports to the Associate Commissioner for Enforcement, it is listed in the INS budget classification under "Immigration Support" instead of enforcement. This analysis uses the budget classification.

23. The Investigations staff had been steadily reduced since 1978, when it was cut from 1377 positions to 1,052. This reduction reflected the viewpoint that it was more efficient to concentrate resources on the Border Patrol than let illegal immigrants enter the country and establish roots in the interior. In 1982, the number of Investigations positions was again reduced, from 1,052 to 649, although 121 positions were subsequently restored.

24. These calculations were made using data provided in INS, 1989, p. 119.

25. These calculations were made using INS data cited by Bean et al., 1990, table 3.

26. This figure was cited by Justice Department officials and was also reported in *Interpreter Releases: Report and Analysis of Immigration and Nationality Law*, 66, no. 28 (July 24, 1989).

27. The INS resorted to some creative—but cynical—methods to cover the costs of the South Texas crisis, shifting user fee funds intended to provide better services to immigrants. With the approval of the Department of Justice and congressional Appropriations Committees, the INS defined the South Texas detail as an adjudications effort (even though most of the funds were spent on detention and Border Patrol details). The INS was thus able to use funds from a newly created Examinations Fee Account (funded by immigrants' application fees) to pay for the South Texas detail. One administrator claimed that the INS Adjudications Division was "systematically looted" in this transaction. See *Interpreter Releases*, per note 26.

28. INS budget data show that the agency's yearly expenditures from Congressional appropriations were projected to increase by only 4.3 percent between fiscal years 1989 and 1991. See INS, 1989b, p. 5, and INS, 1990, p. 6.

29. The opening salvo in the recent drive to improve INS management came shortly after the Bush administration took office, when the Justice Department's Management Division issued a scathing audit of the INS. Criticizing the lack of adequate accounting systems, spotty review of applications for immigration benefits, and competition among units, the audit concluded that "Increasing resources alone will not correct these problems." See U.S. Department of Justice, 1989, p. i.

30. See the discussion in *Interpreter Releases: Report and Analysis of Immigration and Nationality Law*, 67, no. 21 (May 25, 1990): pp. 605–607 and vol. 67, no. 26 (July 16, 1990): pp. 745–748.

References

Bean, Frank, Thomas Espenshade, Michael White, and Robert Dymowski. 1990. "Post-IRCA Changes in the Volume and Composition of Undocumented Migration to the United States: An Assessment Based on Apprehensions Data," Urban Institute Program for Research on Immigration Policy Paper PRIP UI-6, January.

Fix, Michael, and Paul T. Hill. 1990. *Enforcing Employer Sanctions: Challenges and Sanctions*. Washington, D.C.: The RAND Corporation and The Urban Institute Press, May.

GAO (U.S. General Accounting Office). 1990. "Immigration Reform: Employer Sanctions and the Question of Discrimination." Washington, D.C.: U.S. Government Printing Office.

_____. 1987. "Criminal Aliens: INS' Law Enforcement Activities." Washington, D.C.: U.S. Government Printing Office.

_____. 1986a. *Justice Department: Improved Management Processes Would Enhance Justice's Operations*. Washington, D.C.: U.S. Government Printing Office, p. 18.

_____. 1986b. "Criminal Aliens: INS' Investigative Efforts in the New York City Area." Washington, D.C.: U.S. Government Printing Office, March.

_____. 1986c. "Criminal Aliens: INS' Detention and Deportation Activities in the New York City Area." Washington, D.C.: U.S. Government Printing Office, December.

Harwood, Edwin. 1986. In Liberty's Shadow: Illegal Aliens and Immigration Law Enforcement. Stanford, CA: Stanford University Press.

_____. 1985. "How Should We Enforce Immigration Laws?" In Clamor at the Gates: The New American Immigration, Nathan Glazer, ed. San Francisco: The Institute for Contemporary Studies, p. 74.

INS (U.S. Immigration and Naturalization Service). 1990. "Fiscal Year 1991 Authorization and Budget Request for the Congress," January.

_____. 1989a. Statistical Yearbook of the Immigration and Naturalization Service, 1988. Washington, D.C.: U.S. Government Printing Office, p. 109.

_____. 1989b. "FY 1990 Budget Authorization and Request for the Congress," January.

_____. 1988. "Employer Sanctions Policy After June 1, 1988." Memo.

_____. 1987a. "Fiscal Year 1988 Authorization and Budget Request for the Congress," January.

_____. 1987b. "1987 Supplemental/1988 Amendment for Immigration Reform and Control Act of 1986," January.

_____. 1986. "Fiscal Year 1987 Authorization and Budget Request to the Congress," February.

Montweiler, Nancy Humel. 1987. The Immigration Reform Law of 1986. Washington, D.C.: The Bureau of National Affairs, Inc.

Morris, Milton. 1985. Immigration: The Beleaguered Bureaucracy. Washington, D.C.: The Brookings Institution.

Nelson, Alan. 1988. Testimony of INS Commissioner before the Subcommittee on Commerce, Justice, State, the Judiciary, and Related Agencies, U.S. Senate, April 20.

Passel, Jeffrey, and Karen Woodrow. 1984. "Geographic Distribution of Undocumented Immigrants: Estimates of Undocumented Aliens Counted in the 1980 Census by State." In International Migration Review, Fall, pp. 642–671.

SCIRP (the Select Commission on Immigration and Refugee Policy). 1981. "U.S. Immigration Policy and the National Interest", Washington, D.C.: U.S. Government Printing Office.

The White House. 1989. "National Drug Control Strategy." Washington, D.C.: U.S. Government Printing Office.

U.S. Department of Justice, Justice Management Division. 1989. "Special Audit of the Immigration and Naturalization Service." February.

U.S. House of Representatives, Committee on the Judiciary. 1986. "Immigration Control and Legalization Amendments Act of 1986," Report 99-682, Part 1. Washington, D.C.: U.S. Government Printing Office.

U.S. Senate Committee on Appropriations. 1989. "Departments of Commerce, Justice, and State, the Judiciary, and Related Agencies Appropriations Bill, 1990," Report 101-144. Washington, D.C.: U.S. Government Printing Office.

U.S. House of Representatives, Committee on Government Operations. 1980. "Immigration Service Regional Offices Reflect Mismanagement," House Report 96-821. Washington, D.C.: U.S. Government Printing Office.

Chapter Three

IMPLEMENTING SANCTIONS: REPORTS FROM THE FIELD

Michael Fix and Paul Hill

In this chapter we report the results of a two-year study by the RAND Corporation and The Urban Institute of the implementation of IRCA's employer sanctions provisions. The strategies, process, and results documented here are based on extensive interviewing conducted between February 1988 and November 1989 in Washington, D.C., in the four regional offices of the INS, and in four state capitals and eight localities.

The chapter has four goals. First, we attempt to identify the principal implementation challenges that sanctions posed for the lead enforcement agency, the INS. Second, we describe sanctions' implementation at the regional and local level, where Congressional intentions and national policy pronouncements were translated into concrete enforcement actions and priorities. Third, we assess that performance in light of Congress's expectations and the challenges identified above. And fourth, we identify the challenges that must be met if sanctions are to have the effect that Congress intended.

IMPLEMENTATION CHALLENGES

As INS officials set out to implement IRCA, they faced the problem of how to administer a vast new regulatory program under intense political scrutiny. They faced four basic challenges:

□ Establishing and sustaining the legitimacy of sanctions as a regime for regulating business;

□ Satisfying exacting legal requirements that attach to business regulation and generally apply with less power to the U.S. government's relations with immigrants;

□ Adapting the INS as an organization accustomed to dealing with

individual immigrants to one capable of educating, regulating, inspecting, and sanctioning businesses; and

☐ Regulating a vast economic process with limited investigative and
enforcement resources.

Establishing and Sustaining Legitimacy

IRCA imposed burdens on all employers, requiring that they keep
new records and submit to inspections, and depriving some of traditional sources of labor. This broad expansion of regulatory authority was enacted in a pro-business, anti-regulatory era, with
implementation ultimately overseen by presidents who had been
closely identified with the movement to deregulate industry. Moreover, sanctions regulated an action (employment of illegal aliens)
that many people considered morally neutral rather than reprehen-
sible.[1] Sanctions enforcement, therefore, lacked a strong constituency. Unlike anti-discrimination or environmental laws, only a few
interest groups (the Federation for American Immigration Reform
and several labor unions) saw themselves as direct beneficiaries of
enforcement. And unlike enforcement of securities or criminal statutes, enforcement of employer sanctions generates few political re-
wards.[2]

While the political advantages of strong enforcement were few,
the potential liabilities were many. Clumsy or overzealous enforcement could create a backlash from powerful business groups, which
might in turn create pressure for the repeal or weakening of sanctions.
Thus, the question of legitimacy became paramount for the implementers of employer sanctions. The INS, which had long sought an
employer sanctions law to complement its traditional alien apprehension functions, had a strong institutional interest in protecting
sanctions from political attack. And the INS's own institutional reputation depended on its performance in implementing sanctions. Its
past relationships with business focused on forcible removal of undocumented workers, and were thus often confrontational (Crewdson, 1983, pp. 113–141). Even businesses that had not dealt directly
with the INS knew that it had been broadly criticized for unscru-
pulous enforcement practices in other contexts. Thus, the INS had
to expect to operate under intense and sometimes skeptical scrutiny
from Congress, the General Accounting Office (GAO), the press, the
immigration bar, the human rights community, business, and even
the private research community.

The challenge of legitimacy required consistently applying clear

standards and avoiding complaints of selective enforcement or set-
tling old scores. Legitimacy required that the INS mitigate employer
time and cost burdens, take responsibility for employer education,
help employers who wanted to stop depending on illegal immigrant
employees, and emphasize negotiated compliance rather than penalties.

Finally, sanctions implementation would be judged in part in terms
of its effect on other IRCA goals and programs, especially legalization
and anti-discrimination. With regards to the former, enforcement
would have to be managed in a way that did not frighten eligible
aliens from applying under the legalization program. At minimum,
this meant that the profile of the enforcement effort should be kept
low and that actions would have to take place well away from the
legalization centers. With regards to discrimination, enforcement
strategies would have to accommodate the often conflicting goal of
reducing employer discrimination against foreign-appearing job candidates.

Satisfying Unfamiliar Legal Requirements

IRCA's implementers faced the challenge of conforming their enforcement of sanctions to the requirements of U.S. constitutional,
criminal, and administrative laws, which would constrain any effort
to regulate U.S. firms and citizens. These mandates make more rigorous demands of government actions than those embedded in U.S.
immigration laws, which traditionally accord fewer protections to
those challenging INS action.

The distinctiveness of immigration law lies in the fact that it represents the terms set by the state for entry exclusion and citizenship.
Therefore, it regulates the rights and entitlements of aliens who, by
definition, "lack full membership in the moral and political communities that create and sustain our system of justice" (Schuck,
1984). IRCA's employer requirements, by contrast, create obligations
for individuals and entities who do hold full membership in the
nation's moral and political community and are, thus, entitled to
full protections of the system of justice. The INS could expect that
the rights extended to employers would likely be fully exercised. At
the same time, it had no reason to expect the level of judicial deference that had historically characterized court review of actions
against immigrants.[3] These higher legal standards would influence
the initiation, conduct, and resolution of enforcement actions.

Three of the most demanding legal challenges faced by sanctions' implementers are contained in IRCA itself. First, the law specifies that hearings that contest charges brought under IRCA's sanctions and non-discrimination provisions will be conducted according to the dictates of the Administrative Procedure Act (APA).[4] In practice, this means that administrative hearings resemble trial-type actions brought in the federal courts, which are governed by federal evidentiary rules and the Federal Rules of Civil Procedure, and accord extensive procedural rights to defendants. This is in contrast to the informal practices and procedures that govern in most immigration proceedings and in the IRCA legalization program.[5] Compliance with the APA requires that the INS meet the same standards as other federal agencies seeking civil penalties under federal regulatory statutes. It means that the entire enforcement process—targeting, investigations, evidence gathering, and formulation of charges—must anticipate challenges at trial.

Second, IRCA imposes for the first time a requirement that INS agents have a warrant or consent before they conduct an open field or ranch check.[6] Hence Congress, responding to pressures from agricultural employers, extended them protections that exceed those required under the Fourth Amendment of the Constitution.[7]

Third, IRCA emphasizes penalizing employers who can be shown to have knowingly hired an undocumented alien.[8] This requirement imposes a difficult burden of proof on the INS, making enforcement frequently rely on employers' admissions or on the testimony of undocumented workers. In the latter case, the INS must balance its responsibility for removing illegal aliens from the United States against the need to keep them available to provide evidence against their employers. In this way, IRCA creates for the INS more difficult problems of proof than most federal agencies typically face.

The enforcement process must also conform to generally applicable legal norms, most notably the body of Fourth Amendment case law pertaining to search and seizure, and associated warrant requirements that have been so influential in civil and criminal law.

Finally, IRCA's implementers need to keep the enforcement process itself out of harm's way. Federal agencies implementing IRCA are subject to the Equal Access to Justice Act, under which private parties can recover fees and expenses when a government-initiated legal action is determined not to be "substantially justified."[9] Thus, inept or abusive enforcement practices can lead to claims for damages filed against the INS and its staff.

Together, these legal and procedural constraints pose a number of challenges. The INS needed to carefully control early litigation to avoid setting precedents that would erode rather than strengthen the regulatory regime. This argued against leaving much discretion to field investigators, at least during the early phases of implementation. Furthermore, given complications introduced by IRCA's exemptions regarding employment of independent contractors and the likely restructuring of businesses to escape liability, INS agents and attorneys needed to understand business, agency, and contracts law.

Adapting the INS to Serve a New Purpose

Sanctions enforcement required fundamental changes in the INS's operating style. Agents had to go beyond the normal daily activity of apprehending undocumented aliens and develop the investigative skills needed to examine complex personnel and financial records. This, in turn, required that the INS establish new procedures, recruit and train staff in new techniques, and change its incentive structure to reflect new responsibilities and political expectations.

In addition, the INS had to adapt an organization designed to foster local initiative and innovation to one that required substantial standardization of policy and procedure. Sanctions policy had to be made and implemented within the framework of the INS's decentralized structure. The agency had historically delegated significant discretion, both in policymaking and operations, to its 4 regional, 33 district, and 22 Border Patrol sector offices. This raised the possibility that national implementation strategies, carefully constructed to meet legitimacy and legality imperatives, could be undone by independent local action. Furthermore, sanctions enforcement required that the Border Patrol and Investigations divisions act in a more coordinated manner, especially in those urban areas where they share a common jurisdiction.

Mounting an Effective Enforcement Process with Limited "Investigative Resources"

Because many undocumented immigrants are employed by small, informally organized firms, and because Congress wanted to avoid imposing burdens inequitably, employer sanctions apply to all hiring transactions. As a result, the law's prohibitions and verification requirements extend not only to the nation's seven million firms, but to all individuals entering into employer-employee relationships. Regulation that reaches individual conduct is rare in U.S. administrative and regulatory law.[10] Regulatory schemes with such broad coverage raise questions about the feasibility of law enforcement. As Schuck has written:

> Other things being equal, the more numerous the firms, people or processes that must be regulated, the less likely it is that regulation will be effective. . . . If scarce regulatory resources are to be spread over a large number of entities, inspection and monitoring become sporadic, thereby diminishing the credibility of regulatory sanctions. . . . The number of entities may be so great as to make it difficult or impractical for the regulatory agency even to identify, much less regulate them all. (Schuck, 1979, p. 712)

Given the scale of the regulatory enterprise, it is clear that the INS had to use its limited enforcement resources efficiently. This required a strategic use of information and manpower in order to obtain voluntary compliance. It also meant that the agency had to coordinate the efforts of enforcement staff outside the INS who had been enlisted in the sanctions implementation effort, including the Department of Labor's inspection staff and lawyers in U.S. Attorneys' offices.

To some extent, the INS's response to the scale of the mission it confronted was compromised by the proliferation of major new enforcement responsibilities the agency took on during the same period when it was gearing up to implement IRCA and employer sanctions. These included enforcement of the 1986 Immigration Marriage Fraud Amendments, the Anti-Drug Abuse Acts of 1986 and 1988, and participation in the Organized Crime and Drug Enforcement Task Force. Competing missions claimed staff hours that could be devoted to sanctions and crowded out the publicity campaigns dedicated to legalization, sanctions, and IRCA's non-discrimination provisions. The agency's record of incompetence in carrying out its traditional missions raised questions about its ability to succeed at a variety of challenging new assignments.

Mitigating the problems posed by scale and resources was the fact that a relatively small proportion of U.S. firms depended on undocumented employees, and that some of them opted to comply voluntarily with the law. As one commentator has written:

> Enforcement, happily, is not the sole means of assuring compliance with regulatory directives. Businesses obey regulations for a host of reasons—moral or intellectual commitment to underlying regulatory objectives, belief in the fairness of procedures that produced the regulations, pressure from peers, competitors, customers or employees, conformity with a law-abiding self-image—in addition to fear of detection and punishment. (Diver, 1980)

REPORTS FROM THE FIELD

In this section of the chapter we review the local and regional implementation of IRCA's employer requirements in light of the challenges identified above. The findings are based on extensive interviewing in eight cities with large immigrant populations. Because we conducted interviews under promise of confidentiality, no respondents are identified by name. We use quotes from the interviews whenever they illustrate a key point.

Five important generalizations emerge from our data.

1. *In the communities we visited, the numbers of investigations conducted were low relative to the numbers of employers.* While INS Investigations units have been enlarged, INS Investigations staff size—which had declined between the mid-1970s and mid-1980s—only returned to the number of agents in place in the mid-1970s. Furthermore, the inexperience of new staff members and competing responsibilities claimed many available resources, thus limiting the effort devoted to sanctions enforcement.

2. *The INS was circumspect in dealing with most employers and avoided generating broad public opposition to sanctions enforcement.* Individual employers were investigated and penalized, but actions were not so widespread or arbitrary as to cause the business community to oppose the sanctions program.

3. *The enforcement effort—and the burden of coping with inspections and fines—fell on small firms owned by ethnics.* These firms are also the most likely to be dependent on immigrant labor.

4. *Local INS offices differed with respect to the priority attached to sanctions enforcement, procedures followed, characteristics of firms targeted for enforcement, and numbers and types of fines imposed.* Regarding priorities, some INS local offices saw sanctions as their top enforcement priority, while others focused instead on the pursuit of criminal aliens or drug-related crimes. In terms of practices and procedures, some INS offices dealt with employers through a standard regulatory investigative process, starting with an analysis of business records; other offices made employer sanctions an extension of the traditional INS alien apprehension process, raiding business premises to remove undocumented aliens and investigating firms identified by apprehended aliens as their employers. Some INS offices made employers the primary targets of sanctions enforcement; others used sanctions enforcement as a way to identify undoc-

umented workers for deportation.

Localities also varied in their relative emphasis on fines for paperwork and substantive violations. Criminal sanctions were seldom sought, in part because U.S. Attorneys' offices were busy prosecuting more sensational and dangerous crimes.

5. *Poor coordination between INS Investigations and Border Patrol officers led to different treatment of similar firms within the same geographic area.* INS Border Patrol and Investigations staffs were found to be applying different targeting, investigations, and penalty strategies within the same jurisdiction.

We begin our analysis of sanctions implementation with a brief discussion of the communities we visited, their economic and political contexts, and the resources and staffing local INS offices are able to devote to sanctions enforcement. We then analyze the local enforcement process in terms of goals and priorities, targeting of employers for investigations, and penalties proposed and levied.

The Communities

The eight communities we visited—Los Angeles, San Jose, Houston, San Antonio, El Paso, Miami, New York City, and Chicago—differed dramatically in size, economic and demographic composition, and political climate. The INS establishments in those communities are also highly varied due to differences in proximity to the border and to the local importance of drug and alien smuggling activities.

Size. Variation in the population size and geographic scope of the communities covered by the INS create very different problems for enforcement. Communities with the largest populations also contain vast numbers of business establishments, presenting a daunting challenge to any inspections program. The INS New York District contains over 500,000 business establishments, and Los Angeles contains more than 325,000. The El Paso District, in contrast, covers fewer than 20,000 business establishments.[11]

Some of the districts with relatively few establishments, however, cover very large territories. The San Antonio District Office sprawls over much of central and southern Texas, reaching from Austin to Corpus Christi, covering 78 counties and 3,000 square miles.

Political Climate. Each of the three largest cities in our sample (Chicago, Los Angeles, and New York) has adopted official or unofficial policies of noncooperation with the INS in the reporting of city residents who are undocumented.[12] Each tacitly or expressly encourages the provision of city services to undocumented residents where not otherwise prohibited by law, and each had been an important actor in litigation to include undocumented immigrants in the 1990 Census.[13] In contrast, many other city governments in our study resemble Houston's, which has been less active in pro-immigrant causes.

The institutionalization of immigrant-serving organizations was an important factor in determining the local political climate. Mature, legally sophisticated organizations scrutinized IRCA implementation closely in Chicago, New York, and Los Angeles.[14] Houston and San Antonio, in contrast, had fewer and less powerful immigrant advocacy organizations.

Traditional INS Missions. INS offices in the different sites had different histories and strong prior commitments to specific tasks. In New York, for example, the defining INS mission has been to ensure that persons arriving from abroad at the city's airports are processed quickly and efficiently. In Miami, the continuing fight against drugs from South and Central America has dominated the INS's attention for several years. In San Jose, due to the proximity of San Quentin prison, the traditional emphasis has been on deportation of criminal aliens.

Proximity to the Border. Immigrant apprehension is inevitably a major enterprise in border cities and it affects the character of all INS activities there. The constitutional protections accorded individuals to be free from unreasonable searches and seizures without "probable cause" have less power at the border.[15] Hence, law enforcement tends to be less deferential to constitutional and procedural norms at the border than elsewhere. Furthermore, because of the relatively low cost of removing apprehended aliens from border cities to their source countries, the focus of INS activity tends to be on arrest and deportation of illegal aliens. In interior cities such as Chicago, stronger constitutional protections apply, the costs of deportation are significantly higher, and alien removal is not the dominant priority.

Proximity to the border also influences the degree to which foreign-born populations are settled and have become part of the fabric of the local community. There are obvious differences between recent border-crossers in El Paso and a Polish family that has found its way to an Eastern European enclave in Chicago.

Enforcement Resources

Initially, following IRCA's enactment, new resources flowed to INS local offices, staff size grew rapidly, and internal growth was supplemented by the involvement of other federal agencies in the enforcement process. However, the impact of increased INS resources and staffing on sanctions enforcement was limited or complicated by emerging budget issues, by the number of competing missions assigned to INS enforcement staff, and by the problem of mobilizing several major initiatives simultaneously.

Growth in Local INS Staffing. Sanctions implementation at the local level falls to four branches: Investigations, the Border Patrol, the district and sector counsels' offices, and the newly formed Employer and Labor Relations (ELR) branch. Each of these branches grew significantly at the local level following IRCA's enactment in 1986. In Chicago, for example, the size of the Investigations staff increased from 47 to 86 between 1986 and 1989. In Los Angeles the size of the district's Investigations staff rose from 35 in 1985 to 152 in 1989, an increase of more than 400 percent.

As table 3.1 shows, in 1989 staff allocations resulted in uneven coverage of different jurisdictions. The Los Angeles District Office assigned two staff members to sanctions enforcement per 10,000 local employers; the El Paso District Office assigned eight per 10,000 employers, and the El Paso Border Patrol deployed an additional ten agents per 10,000 employers. In San Jose, our one site where the INS office was only a branch of a distant district office, sanctions enforcement was staffed at a rate of less than one person per 10,000 employers. In general, communities not served by district offices had far fewer investigators than did district office cities.

IRCA also had a substantial impact on the size of the Border Patrol. The El Paso Border Patrol sector, for example, added 200 agent positions to bring its authorized force to 800. The Border Patrol assigned a smaller proportion of its staff to sanctions enforcement than did Investigations. (In the Western Region, for example, only eight percent of Border Patrol staff time was allocated to sanctions.) However, the total force was so large that the number of Border Patrol agents assigned to sanctions may have been higher in a particular district than the number of Investigations agents. For example, in 1989, ten Border Patrol agents had sanctions responsibilities within the El Paso District, compared to eight district Investigations agents.

Table 3.1 STAFFING INS EMPLOYER SANCTIONS[a]

Site	Enforcement staff	Sanctions staff	% Sanctions staff	Sanctions staff per 10,000 employers[b]
Los Angeles	152	70	46	2.2
Chicago	86	35	41	2.0
Miami	48	18	38	2.0
San Antonio	36	13	36	4.6
Houston	48	18	31	2.3
New York	156	43	27	0.9
El Paso	39	8	21	8.0
El Paso BP	800	10[c]	4	30.0

a. Data reporting the number of enforcement staff for individual districts is drawn from an unpublished INS document, *Investigtions Program: Full-time Permanent Authorized Positions & Staffing Report*, as of March 31, 1989. Data on the number of employer sanctions staff on duty were drawn from the second wave of field interviews by study staff conducted during June 1989.

b. Source: U.S. Bureau of the Census, *County Business Patterns, 1986*, Selected States, U.S. Government Printing Office, Washington, D.C., 1988. See Table 2: Counties— Employees, Payroll and Establishments by Industry: 1986.

c. The figure reflects the number of El Paso Border Patrol staff assigned the same approximate jurisdiction as the El Paso District Office investigating staff.

INS district counsels' offices also grew rapidly as they were transformed from offices with skeletal staffs to full legal departments. In San Antonio, for example, the district counsel's office grew from four to eleven attorneys. The number of attorneys in El Paso doubled from four to eight; in Houston, the counsel's staff grew from one attorney in 1983 to ten in 1989.

Finally, virtually all district and sector offices assigned one to two persons to carry out employer education and serve as ELR officers. The growth in resources did not translate directly into increased enforcement of employer sanctions. This was due to two factors: a proliferation of new enforcement responsibilities and the competition for resources to which it gave rise; and deployment and management problems associated with rapid growth.

Competing New Missions. To some extent, the staffing of sanctions at the district level reflected choices being made among the number of competing missions that have been assigned to the INS's enforcement personnel in recent years. These include a movement into criminal law enforcement and the removal of criminal aliens from the U.S.,[16] participation in the Organized Crime and Drug Enforcement Task Force (OCDETF),[17] new responsibilities under the Immigration Marriage Fraud Amendments of 1986, and anti-fraud activities, some of which are IRCA-related.[18]

As we indicate above, this proliferation of responsibilities assigned to INS enforcement staff subordinated sanctions to one among several competing missions.

At the district level, the competition had direct implications for the size of the sanctions enforcement staff. Two factors appeared to drive the proportion of enforcement staff dedicated to sanctions: the priority assigned to criminal law enforcement and fraud, and the number of businesses to be regulated.

In addition to reducing the manpower available for sanctions enforcement, this competition for resources led to leadership losses and a "brain drain," as the most experienced investigators gravitated to higher prestige activities such as drug law enforcement that were more glamorous and offered more career mobility. In particular, the INS's participation in the OCDETF attracted many of its most accomplished agents.

Rapid Growth. The rapid scale-up in Investigations and Border Patrol personnel in the wake of IRCA's enactment inevitably raised problems. Though newly hired agents are much more likely than older INS staff to hold college degrees, they are inexperienced. In 1988 and 1989 virtually all the members of one unit of the Los Angeles employer sanctions staff were new recruits. Managers were reluctant to assign them difficult investigations or sensitive criminal harboring and transporting cases. As an official in another locality noted, "they [the new recruits] cannot understand, much less enforce, the law."

This inexperience may be aggravated by other factors. For example, high turnover in Border Patrol employer sanctions units in the Western Region was slowing the enforcement effort.[19] Furthermore, the large number of new recruits, coupled with the INS budget crisis, have made it difficult to find space for new agents at the government's training academy in Glynco, Georgia.

The Enforcement Process

Local Priorities. INS officials in all sites welcomed employer sanctions as an important new weapon for immigration control. Many INS respondents in our fall 1988 interviews said employer sanctions were their number one priority. However, by summer 1989, many

Table 3.2 SITE ENFORCEMENT PRIORITIES: JUNE 1989

Site[a]	Priority
New York	criminal alien
El Paso	alien apprehension
Houston	SAWs fraud
Miami	criminal alien
San Antonio	criminal alien
Chicago	employer sanctions
Los Angeles	employer sanctions

a. Refers only to INS district offices.

indicated that employer sanctions had declined as a local enforcement priority. This development was partly due to the fact that the INS was trying to balance competing enforcement responsibilities.

Characterizing a complex agency's priorities is difficult, because every official has his or her own version. But we have made aggregate judgments by considering the diverse sources of information available.

In Houston, for example, the INS Investigations branch had virtually shut down its enforcement of sanctions in order to devote available resources to Special Agricultural Worker (SAW) fraud investigations. Houston's decision reflected a mix of considerations: a local commitment to investigating and prosecuting SAW applicants suspected of fraud, a severe budget crunch, and an abiding skepticism over the INS's ability to serve as a regulatory agency for U.S. business. As one senior agency official stated:

> Sanctions is an albatross for the INS. It affects citizens more than aliens; and it should have been placed with the Department of Labor. The INS doesn't have the background in employer communities. We're juveniles in this thing.

Exercise of Caution. While district offices differed in the priority assigned sanctions, there was general agreement over the need for enforcement to proceed cautiously and to some extent deferentially with regard to the business community. Officials frequently noted to us that arbitrary, high-profile enforcement of the law could lead to a congressional repeal of the sanctions provisions. The near constant presence of auditors from the GAO further emphasized the need for INS staff to consider the fairness and legitimacy of the enforcement approach.

The incentives for INS managers and agents to implement the law in a cautious and creditable manner stemmed from more than sanctions' value as a potentially powerful tool for deterring illegal immigration. As one INS attorney stated, "If sanctions is sunset, we lose jobs and money. The incentive here is not just idealistic."

In some jurisdictions these concerns with legitimacy had a powerful impact on sanctions enforcement. This was felt most strongly in Chicago, where members of the immigration bar, longstanding antagonists of the INS, noted the INS's businesslike approach to sanctions enforcement. When first interviewed, immigration bar members characterized INS agents as "an instant-gratification crew" that would wreak havoc when turned loose on sanctions enforcement. By the second wave of interviews, their assessment had shifted. In the words of one attorney, "The attitude and the way we were able to control disruption (during an I-9 inspection) was 180 degrees different from anything we'd ever seen."

While this was the predominant response of immigration attorneys and employers interviewed, it was not the universal view. For example, others noted, "They [INS agents] used to have a hammer. Now they have a sledge hammer." And, "They [INS agents] used to be cowboys chasing people. Now they're cowboys chasing paper."

Other immigration attorneys were simply waiting for intensive enforcement to begin. "The human rights community is interested in how sanctions is being enforced, but there isn't enough activity for us to get involved."

Despite INS-wide interest in preserving sanctions during the three-year probation period during which its implementation and outcomes would be under close GAO scrutiny, divergent approaches to enforcement were adopted in different cities. This diversity is reflected in strategies for targeting employers, investigations, and penalizing violators.

Targeting Employers for Investigation

At the local level, we observed the tensions that exist between achieving legitimacy goals and generating impressive enforcement statistics. We also observed the INS's difficulties in expanding its enforcement effort by deputizing the Department of Labor's Wage and Hour (W&H) inspectors.

Use of the General Administrative Plan (GAP). Random, neutral targeting has been broadly adopted if not accepted. The random targeting plan is directly modeled on the Occupational Safety and Health Administration's two-track system for random targeting of employers. One set of employers is drawn randomly from a list of all U.S. firms (this list is called the General Administration Plan, or GAP). A second set of employers is drawn at random from lists of firms in local industries that have traditionally employed large numbers of undocumented aliens. (The latter is called the Special Emphasis Plan, or SEP list). All the local INS agencies we visited except one were implementing the GAP and the SEP.

Although most of the agencies were meeting their GAP quotas, many reported that the share of staff time devoted to GAP cases was closer to 25 percent than to the 40 percent anticipated by INS central office planners. Some local offices purposely limited GAP inspections because they appeared unproductive. Few GAP inspections identified violations that led to enforcement actions,[20] and many targeted extremely small employers who rarely hired anyone (e.g., the frequently cited dentist with his lifelong secretary/technician). In other cases, officials believed that it was enough to advertise the existence of an inspection program and that it was unnecessary to devote major resources to it.

These views reflected a widespread skepticism among local INS staff about GAP's importance and cost effectiveness. In Chicago, agents informed us that they counted calls to closed businesses as completed GAP visits. In Los Angeles, GAP visits were used to train inexperienced staff; in San Antonio, Border Patrol agents were not doing GAP inspections at all.

A minority of our respondents valued random targeting as a means of avoiding charges of selective enforcement, identifying trends in noncompliance, and alerting employers in all industries that they must comply with IRCA. One New York official stated, "If all we did was lead-driven inspections, a whole segment of industry would never see immigration inspectors."

Labor Certifications. Some INS district offices were using Department of Labor records of petitions for labor certification as key elements of their targeting strategy. These petitions, filed by employers, ask permission to hire an alien worker for a hard-to-fill specialist position. In theory, these positions are empty because qualified U.S. residents cannot be found to fill them and the requested alien employee will enter the U.S. only after certification is granted. In fact, many such workers are in the U.S. illegally and working for the employer at the time certification is requested. When the INS receives a petition, it may target the employer for investigation, suspecting that the immigrant is already working for the employer filing the petition.

If the agent's suspicion is borne out, the existence of a petition virtually proves the government's contention of a knowing hire. The simplicity of the resulting enforcement action is attractive for INS offices that have limited investigative resources but need to generate a designated number of enforcement actions. In Miami, for example, labor certificate applications were among that district's chief targeting methods, a development stemming from the high priority given to drug-related crime and the corresponding need to conserve enforcement resources.

Some immigration attorneys claim that the process has the look and feel of entrapment and that it harms employers making good-faith efforts to comply with the law. Some claim that it violates the employer's and the alien's constitutional rights to due process and protection from self-incrimination.

Department of Labor (DOL) Referrals. Referrals based on DOL Wage and Hour inspectors' reviews of I-9 forms (the forms filled out by employers and job applicants attesting to their eligibility to work) are routinely received at INS offices. In many cases, however, they help expand an already large backlog of leads, tips, and complaints. DOL referrals were virtually ignored in some INS offices. As one agent stated, "DOL picks up paperwork violations, and we don't do paperwork violations." In Houston, for example, when the district office received a report of apparent or clear I-9 noncompliance from DOL, investigators followed up with a letter to the suspected employer informing him or her of IRCA's requirements and the fact that the business had been identified as a possible violator. According to enforcement staff, there was no follow-up even if there was no response, a result that was attributed to budget constraints. Of our eight sites, DOL referrals appeared to be regularly pursued only in El Paso and Los Angeles.

Investigations

As with targeting, there was a sharp division among local INS offices in how they carried out sanctions investigations. Some approached enforcement as a regulatory function and emphasized the use of records in the development of a case. Others focused more on the apprehension of undocumented workers, relied more heavily on raids and street arrests, and used traditional INS enforcement techniques.

Initiation. The sites differed in the way an investigation was triggered. According to guidelines to the field from INS Headquarters, employers were to be targeted through the GAP, through complaints, or through DOL referrals (INS, 1988). That was the case in New York, Chicago, and Los Angeles. However, other methods were often used in sites closer to the border, with many leads coming from INS-initiated street encounters with aliens or apprehensions. In fact, in one Border Patrol office it was standard operating procedure for the agents to spend their mornings apprehending aliens and their afternoons pursuing enforcement actions against those aliens' employers. In sum, we observed substantial variation in the degree to which IRCA has led the INS to abandon an alien-focused police model that depends on stops and arrests in favor of the new employer-focused regulatory model that depends on investigation and documents.

Dealing with the Employer. Once agents made contact with the employer, INS offices adopted one of two strategies. Under what might be termed "the regulatory model" of immigration control, the INS made several visits to a work site, starting with an education visit and proceeding through a careful review of the employer's I-9s. Raids or fines came only after the employer had notice of his deficiencies and had been given opportunities to resolve them.

"The police model" in place in other jurisdictions, especially on the border, proceeded in a more summary fashion. A tip or apprehension led to a raid rather than an education visit or an I-9 inspection. The I-9s were reviewed only after the apprehension of undocumented aliens, and did not serve as the engine of the enforcement process but simply as an additional piece of evidence to be marshalled against the employer. Under this model, enforcement looks less like a regulatory law enforcement proceeding than like an old-style INS raid involving entry, arrest, and deportation.

INS offices in cities near the Mexican border were the most likely to rely on the police model. In El Paso, for example, a lead was received and followed by surveillance of the business and, in turn, a raid. Only following a raid and the apprehension of undocumented aliens was a three-day notice of inspection typically provided the employer. With minor variations, this sequence of events also resembled the enforcement process described to us by the Houston District Office.

In Chicago, New York, and Los Angeles, the process conformed more closely to the regulatory model. In New York, for example, an investigation started with an education visit. Observations made during the course of an education visit might lead the agent to schedule an inspection to review the employer's I-9s. Following review of the

I-9s, a notice of results of inspection letter was sent or delivered. A follow-up inspection was then made and if the employer remained out of compliance with the law, he was served with a Notice of Intent to Fine. On the face of it, this is a rather forgiving process because it provides the employer with at least three opportunities to "get the hint" and come into compliance.

But even this rather liberal path could be a barbed one. For example, education visits were not always conducted exclusively for the employer's edification. Some INS offices treated education as the immediate precursor to enforcement, saying "When we find an employer with an illegal alien, first we educate him, and then we return three days later to seize his records and pick up any illegal aliens he has on site." Or, as another enforcement official stated, "When we make an appointment for an education visit, we don't tell them that we are going to be setting them up. If we did, they would go on an Oliver North shredding party."

Different INS branches in the same city (i.e., the Border Patrol and Investigations) often took different approaches to enforcement. This was partly due to different enforcement styles and coordination problems. For example, in Miami, San Antonio, and Houston, Border Patrol and Investigations enforcement efforts were not coordinated. There was no rational division of the territory and no systematic referral process for leads, much less common targeting, fine, or settlement standards. Moreover, relations between enforcement staff seemed antagonistic at times. In one site, for example, despite the existence of a memorandum of understanding assigning the Border Patrol lead enforcement responsibility in rural areas and Investigations the lead in urban areas, Investigations staff complained that the Border Patrol "was walking all over Investigations agents here."

As one district office supervisor in another city noted,

> We're beside ourself about the Border Patrol presence [in the
> city]. . . . We want a good relationship with the employers. . . . They
> [the Border Patrol] aren't used to attorneys or the Fourth Amendment
> or any kind of restraints.

Another, concerned about the possibility that employers would complain about double jeopardy, said, "I'm worried we're going to get gangbanging complaints. . . . If we get overzealous, we could screw up the law."

Focus on Alien Apprehension. Our eight sites also varied in whether the primary focus of enforcement was on changing the employer's hiring practices or apprehending aliens.

The INS Chicago District Office has focused its effort on employers. As a result, unauthorized alien workers were not apprehended when they were found in the work place. Instead, the employer was given notice of the fact that he was employing unauthorized aliens, and the workers were given voluntary departure notices while the inspectors were on the job site. The burden of firing the workers then fell to the employer, who knew that an INS agent would soon return to check to see if they continued to be employed. According to one senior district official, undocumented immigrants were not "apprehended or removed—they are simply dislocated."

Other sites did not adopt an employer focus. In Houston, for example, the investigations process typically began with a raid. Statements were taken from those apprehended, and aliens were deported unless they were also involved in a criminal matter.

Los Angeles initially adopted an employer focus for its investigations, but our interviews in summer 1989 suggested that some features of an alien-focused approach were being adopted. District officials stated that they planned to target prosecutions against undocumented immigrants, charging those who had given employers fraudulent documents with felonious false attestation. The INS would reduce the charge to a misdemeanor, but the alien would be deported and placed on notice that he would be prosecuted for a felony upon reentry. The program would be widely publicized and used as a way to discourage unauthorized aliens from seeking employment.

Penalties

Criminal Prosecutions of Employers. As noted earlier, IRCA supplements the INS's civil enforcement powers by providing for the criminal prosecution of employers. The grounds for such prosecutions are two: a pattern and practice of knowingly hiring unauthorized aliens, and intentionally harboring and transporting undocumented immigrants.

One INS official enthusiastically described the usefulness of the harboring provisions in the following terms:

> It [the harboring provisions of IRCA] is a beautiful statute and the best result of the law. It is a sleeper; it's wonderful. We can indict on harboring and seize the vehicle. We can cut the administrative stuff and go right to jail. It will have a major effect on enforcement. We don't have to educate employers about harboring the way we do about sanctions.

Despite this enthusiasm and the latent power of the criminal provisions, only half the INS offices in our eight sites (Houston, San Antonio, Chicago, and Los Angeles) claimed to have brought any criminal sanctions cases.

The most vigorous use of criminal sanctions was in San Antonio. The first four criminal prosecutions against employers took place during the citation period that ran from June 1, 1987 to June 1, 1988. According to local staff, criminal actions were brought against employers as a way of getting around constraints on civil sanctions during this period.

By our second wave of fieldwork in summer 1989, San Antonio appeared to be moving away from use of criminal sanctions. Local INS officials informed us that the district was no longer seizing vehicles because the U.S. Attorney did not want to prosecute violators, in part because requirements of the 1988 Anti-Drug Abuse Act complicate the seizures. Furthermore, we were told that both INS regional and central offices applied pressure on the district to start making civil sanctions cases and to abandon the criminal-focused efforts.

There have been other inhibitions to the broad use of criminal sanctions. The most powerful has been the resistance of U.S. Attorneys. Respondents in New York, Miami, Chicago, Los Angeles, and San Antonio all reported that U.S. Attorneys had rejected criminal cases presented to them. While U.S. Attorneys might be promoting the legitimacy of sanctions enforcement by rejecting poorly prepared or politically questionable cases, it is likely that their rejection of these cases reflected the fact that their calendars were filled with more pressing criminal matters, such as high-profile drug or organized crime cases.

Other factors inhibiting the use of criminal sanctions were the inexperience of INS enforcement staff and the fact that criminal cases are expensive to prosecute.

Most criminal prosecutions that did take place relied on IRCA's harboring and transporting provisions, as employers were rarely charged with pattern and practice violations. This is probably due to the newness of the law and the fact that INS investigators seldom conduct follow-up investigations of employers cited for violations.[21]

Criminal sanctions, then, most notably harboring and transporting, were used to circumvent the constraints placed on enforcement during the sanctions citation period. Indeed, the appeal of criminal sanctions to enforcement personnel was due in part to the fact that they do not require such procedural niceties as a previous educational visit, a three-day inspection notice, or review of I-9 forms to make a case against an employer.

Civil Penalties. The usual penalties IRCA was expected to generate were civil fines. National and local INS offices have accordingly built their processes of investigation and penalty determination around civil actions. After analyzing data about civil penalty actions in our eight sites and on a national basis we found that:

□ The INS proposed a small number of civil fines, relative to the number of establishments covered by employer sanctions and to the number of investigations conducted;

□ Patterns of civil penalties varied widely among INS regions and from district to district within regions in terms of the numbers of fines proposed, the aggregate amounts of fines imposed, the average size of fines, the proportions of fines that cite knowing substantive violations (relative to the proportion that cite only paperwork violations), and the numbers of fines per investigative person-year;

□ Regional differences were due in part to the different enforcement problems encountered in different parts of the country and in part to regional and local differences in policy and procedure.

Average Fine Amounts. The average fine proposed against alleged violators varied widely across INS districts and Border Patrol sectors (see table 3.3). The lowest average notice of intent to fine (or NIF, which represents the penalty assessed vs. the penalty collected) was $850—proposed by the San Antonio District Office—and the highest average was $45,545—proposed by the Chicago District Office.

Table 3.3 AVERAGE FINES (AS OF MARCH 31, 1989)

Site	No. of NIFs	NIFs/ 100,000 employers	Amount NIFs	Average NIFs
Chicago	11	6.1	$501,000	$45,545
New York	53	10.8	610,075	11,511
El Paso District	21	210.0	139,550	6,645
Miami	22	23.0	118,475	5,385
Los Angeles	67	20.6	298,700	4,458
Pembroke Pines BP	53	57.0	210,700	3,975
El Paso BP	99	990.0	386,130	3,900
Houston	53	67.1	204,850	3,865
Laredo BP	48	171.1	138,850	2,892
San Antonio	57	203.6	48,550	850

The highest average fines in our sample of sites were assessed by the Northern and Eastern regions. Based on nationwide data, nine out of the ten INS offices assessing the highest average fines were in those regions. Average NIFs through March 1989 were $9,459 for the Northern Region and $8,176 for the Eastern, but only $3,942 for the Western and $2,060 for the Southern Region.

Differences within regions were comparably striking. Within the Northern Region, for example, the average fines for major cities ranged from $45,545 in Chicago to $1,333 in Cleveland. This difference in the amount of NIFs reflected differences in strategy. At one level, it revealed a district office policy of reserving penalties for employers who had committed major violations, rather than pursuing enforcement against employers whose violations were less egregious. At another level, however, it revealed differences in the mechanics of negotiating and reporting fines. Cleveland negotiated final fine amounts before it issued an NIF. In Chicago the district office set its NIFs at high levels and then negotiated them down. A review by the GAO of 300 sanctions cases brought by different INS offices showed that overall the INS reduces the amount of the initial fine by an average of 59 percent.[22]

Even within one city, there were major differences in fines proposed by the INS district office and by the Border Patrol. In El Paso, for example, where the Border Patrol and the district office Investigations staff worked together more closely than in any of the other sites we examined, average NIFs assessed were $3,900 for the Border Patrol and $6,645 for Investigations. This 70 percent difference paled in comparison to the nearly fourfold difference between the San Antonio District Office ($2,983) and the Laredo Border Patrol sector ($852), which cover much the same area.

Paperwork-Only Violations. We saw substantial variation across the country in the willingness of local INS enforcement offices to fine employers for technical, paperwork-only violations. In most sites, the majority of NIFs were based on substantive, knowing violations. But Los Angeles and El Paso emphasized paperwork violations (see table 3.4).[23] Los Angeles is an exceptionally important district, since it has the highest number of immigrants, immigrant-dependent employers, and enforcement agents of any city in the country.

These data reflect differences in local implementation. In Los Angeles, an employer's failure to verify the eligibility of a job applicant was considered grounds for a penalty; prosecution of paperwork violations was an element of Los Angeles's strategy for creating wide-

Table 3.4 SHARE OF NIFs THAT DO NOT CITE A KNOWING VIOLATION
(AS OF MARCH 31, 1989)

Site	No. of NIFs	% Paperwork only	% Fines paperwork only
Los Angeles	67	51	55
El Paso	21	43	59
Pem Pines BP	53	30	20
El Paso BP	21	23	12
New York	53	21	20
Laredo BP	48	15	5
San Antonio	57	12	16
Miami	22	5	5
Houston	53	2	0
Chicago	11	0	0

spread voluntary compliance. In Chicago, there was less weight placed on the quantity of violations cited and far more on bringing enforcement actions against major violators. Furthermore, there was a general district and regional policy against citing technical violations except in rare instances. Hence, it is not surprising that the INS's average fine in Chicago was the highest in the nation and that during the period documented, it cited no paperwork-only violations. As one district official stated, "IRCA was about deterring illegal immigration, not filling out forms."

Again, regional data provide a good but imperfect predictor of the likelihood that a local enforcement office would cite paperwork-only violations. Nine of the ten local INS offices that cited the largest share of technical violations during 1988 and 1989 were in the Western and Southern regions.

The difficulty of proving a knowing violation may drive local INS offices to cite only paperwork violations even when an unauthorized worker is apprehended. In New York, for example, we were told, "In the future, it may be that in lieu of making a knowing case, we may go for paperwork violations because they are easier."

Numbers of Fines. The number of fines served in our sites was not large relative to the number of employers covered by IRCA. Only the El Paso Border Patrol had approached 100 NIFs by March 31, 1989.

The numbers of fines served also varied by region. Of the ten local INS offices with the highest numbers of NIFs served as of March 31, 1989, nine are in the Southern and the Western regions.

Differences in the number of fines proposed are tied to the fact that agents in the Southern and Western regions proposed more fines per person-year than agents in the Northern and Eastern regions. For example, as of March 31, 1989, the El Paso Border Patrol had issued 5.3 NIFs per agent-year, roughly ten times the number issued by the Investigations staff of the Chicago District Office. Yet the amount of fines assessed per agent-year by the two organizations was roughly the same: $23,000 (El Paso Border Patrol) vs. $25,000 (Chicago District Office).

Plainly, we are capturing differing strategies of enforcement—assessing large fines against a few egregious violators versus smaller fines against larger numbers of employers. In Chicago, for example, we were told "You're not going to find numbers in this district; you're going to find quality." In contrast, a Western regional official told us: "In the Western Region and in Texas, we need to touch as many people as possible to let them know we're serious."

These differences may reflect adaptations to the enforcement problems faced by the different regions. Undocumented immigrants comprise a large proportion of the labor force of many western and southern cities, and they work in a large range of industries. Many of their employers are themselves immigrant entrepreneurs on the margins of the economy. Enforcement officials in the North and the East may operate on the assumption that immigrants in eastern and northern cities are less numerous and may be more concentrated.[24] Thus, to influence employers' hiring patterns, enforcers in the West and South may believe they need to create a widespread fear of enforcement, whereas enforcers in the East and North may seek to maximize their influence by imposing large penalties on representative members of the few immigrant-dependent industries.

Chicago's strategy at the beginning of sanctions implementation—pursuing only knowing hires and exacting large fines—may have increased the INS's bargaining leverage. A large candy manufacturer, found to be employing over 400 undocumented workers, fired all unauthorized employees within two days of receiving notice of their status. No further enforcement action was needed or taken.

Another important factor affecting the number of fines is the quota system established by individual regions and districts. Such quotas are facts of life in the INS. As one senior administrator told us:

They are written right into the work plans. Obviously, I disagree with that. The stats are written right into your performance evaluation. The ratings relate directly to pay . . . and these depend directly on meeting your numbers.

In the Western Region, where some members of the immigration bar charged that quotas were supplemented with monetary bonuses for sanctions enforcement, we found that INS staff had issued large numbers of NIFs. Such "productivity" incentives could discourage staff from making refined calculations of employers' bad faith or likely future compliance. This could threaten the legitimacy of the enforcement effort and undermine the Congress's express intent that:

> The Immigration and Naturalization Service . . . target its enforcement resources on repeat offenders and that the size of the employer shall be a factor in the allocation of such resources.[25]

On the other hand, relatively high numbers of fines do influence local employers' calculation of their own likelihood of being inspected or penalized.

In the final analysis, however, despite regional quotas and other staff incentives for high numbers of fines, during the period covered by our study—June 1, 1988 through June 1, 1989—the number of enforcement actions taken against employers across the country was generally low. Even in El Paso, where NIFs were most frequently served, the Border Patrol issued one fine for every two months of agent service. In Chicago, that rate fell to one NIF for every two years of agent service. Plainly, INS enforcement activity could not be characterized as hyperactive.

Employer Targets of Enforcement. Again, there was substantial variation among the eight sites. In New York, Los Angeles, and especially Chicago, employers charged with violations represented a wide range of industries, including a proportional share of large, formally organized companies.

In the other sites, virtually all enforcement actions were against small, ethnic-owned businesses. This targeting of enforcement meant that many firms cited for violations were small businesses that lack the legal and organizational resources needed to fight government enforcement actions. At the same time, however, they were likely to be those most inclined to hire undocumented workers. A large share of the defendants in these cases were ethnic restaurant owners— such a large share that INS officials in some districts worried about the possibility of lawsuits for selective enforcement.

SUMMARY AND CONCLUSIONS

Approaches to implementation varied widely in our sites in terms of whether the local enforcement process involved conducting multiple visits to give employers an opportunity to come into compliance or took a more summary and often punitive approach; whether aliens or employers served as primary enforcement targets; and the degree to which criminal penalties were pursued against employers who had hired unauthorized workers. At the same time, penalties for violators varied in terms of the size of fines assessed, the character of violations singled out for punishment (i.e., the emphasis placed on technical versus substantive violations), the number of fines issued, and the targets of sanctions.

Divergent implementation practices may be partially explained by the fact that the INS assigned responsibility to two largely independent branches—Inspections and the Border Patrol—and by the INS's tradition of decentralized policymaking at the region and district levels. Variation also resulted from limited central oversight. Furthermore, given the traditional autonomy of the regions and districts, nominal national policies (e.g., that paperwork-only violations be "egregious") were often subject to widely different interpretation in the field. Indeed, the national office did not conduct the kind of rigorous oversight of sanctions implementation adopted by the Eastern regional office. There, a standing panel of attorneys and officials reviewed all proposed enforcement actions to ensure their consistency with regional and national policy.

The strength of local INS leadership also drove variation. Some local officials took a strong position in shaping enforcement. In Chicago, for example, the District director articulated a clear enforcement strategy, consistent with the regulatory model described above, that appears to have been internalized by the enforcement staff. In sites where local leaders took a more hands-off approach, decision-making fell to field staff. In those places, implementation emphasized traditional enforcement approaches and targets.

In a few areas, however, we noted important ways in which local enforcement practices appeared to converge. Neutral targeting strategies have been broadly adopted (although the share of manpower dedicated to them differed, as did the level of commitment to their success), and district and sector counsel exerted considerable authority in the enforcement process, making a final determination of the legality of all NIFs. Finally, two possible enforcement tactics were absent. There was a general abandonment of mass apprehensions as a strategy of immigration law enforcement and, with one exception, households were excluded from the focus of sanctions enforcement.

Conclusions

In assessing sanctions' implementation we need to take into account several basic characteristics of the INS. Prior to IRCA, the INS had little experience directly regulating U.S. employers. Furthermore, over the years its enforcement branches had been chronically undermanned; it had grown unusually decentralized; and it had historically been subject to criticism for the arbitrariness of its enforcement activity. All raised concerns about the legitimacy and effectiveness of enforcement, and tempered expectations.

Over the first three years, the INS made substantial progress toward meeting the implementation challenges posed by legitimacy, legality, organizational adaptation, and resource scarcity. At the national level, where general policies and practices were developed, and at the local and regional levels, where policies were put into operation and at times modified in application, IRCA's implementers made the following progress:

1. *They headed off any fundamental challenge by the regulated community to the legitimacy of a potentially controversial and burdensome regulatory regime.* Though individual employers complained about local tactics, the larger employment community did not organize to oppose the policy or its implementation. To some extent this lack of opposition was accomplished by means of low levels of enforcement activity and by concentrating enforcement on disorganized and undercapitalized firms. While these firms were the most likely to employ illegal aliens, they would not prove strong opponents. Credit for the political success of sanctions implementation should be claimed in part by the Congress itself, which foresaw the need for a transition period and for extensive employer education. However, substantial confusion remained regarding compliance with the complex documentation requirements established by the law and, in general, education efforts regarding the law's non-discrimination provisions proved inadequate.

2. *IRCA's implementers generally operated within the boundaries of administrative law, which to a greater degree than immigration*

law emphasizes the rights of the regulated over the powers of the regulators. Though many unresolved legal issues remained, the INS avoided legal reversals that would cripple future implementation. This success in court was in stark contrast to the INS's dismal record in overcoming legal challenges to the standards and practices adopted in the legalization program. It reflected the INS General Counsel Office's early efforts to anticipate problems, standardize procedures, and require that lawyers authorize all NIFs, as well, perhaps, as a reluctance to tackle "hard" cases.

3. *IRCA's implementers, especially INS officials in the largest cities, began to adapt the agency's culture and operations to the exacting demands of a program that regulates U.S. citizens.* However, this conversion from a paramilitary and police agency to one that is also a regulatory and educational organization remained incomplete, as traditional targeting and enforcement approaches were retained in many local agencies, most notably those within border communities.

4. *IRCA's implementers made progress in adapting to the vast scope of a regulatory program that covers all U.S. employers,* finding ways to inform millions of employers about their obligations, and creating a broad awareness of the existence of the new law. The INS succeeded in expanding the size and capability of the staff responsible for employer sanctions implementation. Though hiring was slowed by budget crises and manpower was often diverted to other tasks, in general, recruits to enforcement and legal positions were of high quality, and the INS's enforcement capability was increased.

FUTURE ISSUES AND POTENTIAL PROBLEMS

Despite the initial successes, INS officials were and, to a significant degree, still are faced with several basic implementation issues that could threaten the future political, legal, and administrative stability of the employer sanctions program.

First, inconsistencies in policy and tactics among different areas of the country and between Border Patrol and INS district office investigators could create serious inequities in the treatment of employers, as similarly situated employers in one INS jurisdiction are treated differently from their counterparts in others. In the long run these inconsistencies could also stimulate internal migration of immigrant-dependent businesses and alien workers. Furthermore, the prevalence of paperwork-only violations and the use of fine quotas raise the age-old legitimacy issue: Is program administration following the letter rather than the spirit of the law? Does it engender respect for the law or contempt for its enforcers? Furthermore, extreme levels of variation across regions and districts give rise to abiding questions of consistency and fairness. Inconsistencies are tolerable, perhaps even desirable, in the short run as ways of developing, testing, and refining approaches to enforcement, but they can destroy legitimacy in the long run if they serve no strategic purpose and alienate the regulated community.

Second, a low level of enforcement activity could lead many employers to discount the possibility that violations will be detected and punished, thus weakening the deterrent effect of employer sanctions. At the program's inception, publicity about the new law and uncertainty among businesses about the INS's strategy provided the agency's enforcement efforts with great leverage. That leverage could decline sharply if businesses learn to calculate their chances of being inspected or penalized.

Third, arbitrary use of criminal sanctions under both pattern and practice and harboring and transporting provisions—e.g., charging first-time violators with pattern and practice violations—could lead to crippling legal challenges.

Fourth, failure to develop strong investigative capabilities will limit the INS's effectiveness in dealing with the most heavily immigrant-dependent employers. In many cities, the most immigrant-dependent firms are small and mobile and are in industries with low barriers to entry. Enforcement can reach them only if investigators have good systems for tracking and monitoring the proprietors. In the short run, it has been possible to reach some of these firms through apprehended aliens, but in the long run such an undisciplined and haphazard approach would prove inadequate. Furthermore, fraud and other evasion techniques can be expected to grow more sophisticated as enforcement is stepped up, and could require the introduction of comparably sophisticated investigative techniques to defeat them.

Notes

1. Three years after IRCA's enactment, some local governments are still helping undocumented aliens find jobs. See, for example, "Los Angeles Project Aids Illegal Aliens, in Challenge to U.S.," *The New York Times*, October 26, 1989, p. 1.

2. This was not the case with regard to the enforcement of IRCA's anti-discrimination

provisions, where powerful interest groups like the Mexican-American Legal Defense and Education Fund (MALDEF) and La Raza did view their constituents as being protected by vigorous enforcement.

3. While Schuck notes that judicial deference to congressional and administrative action in immigration policy has begun to break down, for almost a century the courts' deference to the political branch and to administrative expertise was striking, especially when viewed alongside other areas of public law where that deference was often more rhetorical than real (Schuck, 1989, pp. 14–17).

4. Title 8 USC Sec. 1324a(e)(3)(B) requires that in an employer sanctions case, "the hearing shall be conducted in accordance with the requirements of 5 USC 554."

5. These procedures have been broadly challenged. See, for example, Haitian Refugee Center, Inc. v. Nelson, 872 F. 2d 1555 (11th Cir. 1989), holding, among other things, that legalization offices had to make available translators in Spanish and Haitian Creole, that applicants had to be afforded the opportunity to present witnesses at their interviews, and that the interviewers had to "particularize the evidence offered, testimony taken, credibility determinations, and any other relevant information" on the worksheets prepared following the interview that recommended approval or denial of the legalization application. Interpreter Releases 66, p. 745 (July 10, 1989).

6. INA Sec. 287(e); (a)(3) provides that an immigration officer may not enter the premises of a farm or other outdoor agricultural operation for the purpose of interrogating a person believed to be an alien regarding his right to be in the United States, absent the consent of the owner or a properly executed warrant.

7. In Oliver vs. United States 466 S. Ct. 170 (1984) the Supreme Court affirmed that warrantless searches in open fields did not violate the Fourth Amendment's ban on unreasonable searches and seizures.

8. This knowledge requirement also serves to distinguish IRCA from most other regulatory regimes, which do not require knowledge to make out a substantive violation of the statute. Two exceptions are the Walsh-Healy Act of June 30, 1936 (41 USCA Secs. 35-45) barring the knowing employment of male children under age 16 by an agency or instrumentality of the U.S. in the manufacture of supplies and equipment exceeding $10,000. The 1972 Consumer Product Safety Act (15 USC Sec. 2051 et. seq.) bars the manufacture, distribution, or sale of hazardous products and makes parties "knowingly" in violation of the Act subject to civil penalties.

9. 5 USC 504 (1985).

10. For example, the Occupational Safety and Health Act of 1970, P.L. 91-596, restricts coverage to firm-level behavior.

11. U.S. Bureau of the Census. 1988. County Business Patterns 1986, Selected States. Washington, D.C.: U.S. Government Printing Office. See especially Table 2: Countries—Employees, Payroll and Establishments by Industry, 1986.

12. Cf. Executive Order 85-1, Office of Chicago Mayor Harold Washington, March 7, 1985; New York City Executive Order 1245, August 7, 1989. The City of Los Angeles has recently implemented an employment program that purposefully makes available employment opportunities to undocumented residents. See The New York Times, October 26, 1989, p. A1.

13. See The City of New York, et al., v. U.S. Department of Commerce, et al. 88 Civ. 3474 (JMcL).

14. For example, the Mexican-American Legal Defense and Education Fund filed an amicus brief on behalf of the employer in USA vs. New El Rey Sausage Company, U.S. Department of Justice, Executive Office for Immigration Review, Office of the Chief Administration Hearing Officer, Case No. 88100080.

15. See Almeida-Sanchez v. U.S. 413 U.S. 266 (1973), holding that neither probable

cause nor reasonable suspicion is required for general searches at the border or the functional equivalent of the border.

16. The criminal alien sections of District Investigations staffs typically address narcotics cases involving immigrants and deportation of convicted criminals from state, local, and federal prisons.

17. OCDETF commits a share of Investigations staff to participate in an interagency drug enforcement task force directed by the Justice Department.

18. The fraud sections of District Investigations staff address legalization-related fraud, public benefit fraud, marriage fraud, and the manufacture and distribution of fraudulent documents.

19. Turnover appears to be due, in part, to union regulations, which do not allow field agents to remain in sanctions enforcement for more than 12 months.

20. The only exception was in El Paso, where 10 percent of GAP inspections led to enforcement actions. However, of all our sites, El Paso was the one in which the INS was most willing to charge employers with technical, paperwork-only violations.

21. However, a limited number of pattern and practice prosecutions that did not build on prior successful prosecutions under IRCA have been brought to court. One, *United States of America v. DAVCO FOOD, INC.*, was filed in federal court in the Eastern District of Virginia in July 1988. The complaint charged the defendant with 13 cases of knowing hire and/or continuing employment violations from November 6, 1986 through May 31, 1988. Significantly, the suit was not the result of the accumulation of separately cited violations over time.

22. Conversation with Alan Stapleton, General Government Division, General Accounting Office, November 14, 1989.

23. The number of complaints that cite only paperwork violations is an imperfect gauge of the share of identified violations that are technical alone—i.e, where no undocumented aliens are found to be working on the premises but where the employer has failed to fill out I-9s or has filled them out improperly. In some instances, the NIF may cite only paperwork violations because the challenges of proving a substantive violation, e.g., a knowing hire, are unlikely to be met. In those cases, the agency may include only paperwork violations in the NIF. In short, these figures tend to *overstate* paperwork-only violations.

24. See Chiswick, 1988, which finds that undocumented immigrants in Chicago are widely distributed across the spectrum of low-wage industries despite pockets of concentration in selected industries.

25. Conference Report No. 99-1000, 99th Cong. 2nd Sess. 86.

References

Chiswick, Barry. 1988. *Illegal Aliens, Their Employment and Employers.* Kalamazoo, Michigan: W. E. Upjohn.

Crewdson, John. 1983. *The Tarnished Door: The New Immigrants and the Transformation of America.* New York: Times Books.

Diver, Colin S. 1980. "A Theory of Regulatory Enforcement." *Public Policy*, no. 28, p. 297.

INS (U.S. Immigration and Naturalization Service). 1988. *Field Manual for Employer Sanctions*, INS Publication No. M-278. U.S. Department of Justice.

Schuck, Peter. 1984. "The Transformation of Immigration Law." Columbia Law Review 84, p. 1.

_____. 1979. "Regulation: Asking the Right Questions." *The National Journal*, April 28.

Chapter Four

LOS ANGELES: A WINDOW ON EMPLOYER SANCTIONS

Elizabeth Rolph and Abby Robyn

No city in the United States was more important to the implementation of IRCA than Los Angeles. Not only did it house the largest foreign-born population, its undocumented population was broadly acknowledged to be the largest in the country. These facts had important implications for the relative dependence of the local economy on the foreign-born and the undocumented, for the political climate within which IRCA's implementation would have to take place, and for the scope of the enforcement mission.

Because of Los Angeles' centrality to IRCA's success or failure, RAND and The Urban Institute established an ongoing monitoring project in Los Angeles in 1988 and 1989, which was part of the larger implementation study being conducted by the two organizations during that period. This chapter reports the results of that project's investigation of local enforcement of employer sanctions.

LOS ANGELES: THE IMPLEMENTATION CONTEXT

Local conditions play a major role in determining the difficulty of the implementation task and, indeed, what implementation strategies will be successful. Because of its size and location, its industrial structure, and the size and economic significance of its immigrant population, Los Angeles presents a particularly difficult context for developing an effective enforcement process and maintaining political support for such a program.

Geography

In size and geography, Los Angeles presents special enforcement problems. It is home to over 14 million inhabitants. Its Consolidated

Metropolitan Statistical Area (CMSA) is composed of five large counties encompassing 34,000 square miles—a very large area to monitor—and it leads the nation with 1.2 million manufacturing jobs, more than twice as many as second-place Chicago. It is a major transportation hub and, more important, it is just 100 miles north of the Mexican border, making it by far the most accessible urban area able to absorb large infusions of unskilled labor.

Labor and Employment Markets

Demographics suggest that Los Angeles relies heavily on immigrant labor, and, by inference, undocumented labor. Most immigrants to the state have arrived in the last two decades. Between 1970 and 1980, over 2 million immigrants are estimated to have entered the state, 1.5 million of them illegally.[1] Estimates for 1980 to 1990 are higher, because immigration into California and the illegal flow across the southern border both increased substantially during this decade. Hispanics account for about half of the total increase and Asians account for about one-third (Muller and Espenshade, 1985, p. 42).

Many of these immigrants have located in the Los Angeles area, where they account for a dramatically increasing share of the population and where they have assumed a significant role in the local economy. Like the Midwest's "rust bowl," Los Angeles has lost much of its manufacturing base, which traditionally depended upon blue collar, unionized labor. Unlike its Midwestern counterparts, however, the Los Angeles economy added 225,000 new jobs—25 percent of the national total—during those same years, and, as table 4.1 indicates, over half of them went to recent immigrants (Soja, Heskin, and Cenzatti, 1985, p. 16).

As table 4.2 shows, immigrants accounted for differing shares of employment growth across economic sectors, and in several sectors they have replaced native workers.

Furthermore, immigrant labor (and undocumented workers) has concentrated in particular industries in Los Angeles. By 1980 immigrants accounted for well over 50 percent of the workers in several manufacturing industries (table 4.3). For example, the garment industry, which is traditionally dependent upon foreign-born employees, has undergone rapid growth in recent years. Nearly 15 percent of new manufacturing jobs in Los Angeles are in the apparel industry, and some estimate that as many as 80 percent of the workers in that industry are undocumented. Certain service industries such as restaurants, hotels, landscaping, and janitorial are similarly dependent.

Table 4.1 IMMIGRATION TRENDS IN THE LOS ANGELES STANDARD
METROPOLITAN STATISTICAL AREA, 1970 AND 1980

	1970	1980
Foreign born as % of population	11.2	22.3
Recent immigrants as % of all recent immigrants in U.S.	11.6	17.1
% of recent immigrants arriving within 0–10 years	42.0	57.0
1970–1980 immigrants as % of 1970–1980 labor force growth	—	65.0

Source: *General Social and Economic Characteristics, United States Summary and Statement Summaries.* U.S. Census of Population, 1980, Table 99.
Freeman, Richard B. ed., *Summary Report Immigration, Trade, and The Labor Market,* National Bureau of Economic Research, 1988.

Table 4.2 IMMIGRATION SHARE OF NET EMPLOYMENT GROWTH IN LOS
ANGELES COUNTY, SELECTED INDUSTRIES, 1970–1980
(in thousands)

	Total employment growth	Employment of immigrants arriving between 1970 and 1980	Net replacement (total growth minus sum of immigrants)
Manufacturing	113.2	168.3	− 55.1
Eating and drinking establishments	52.1	29.0	23.1
Other retail	32.1	42.8	− 10.7
Personal services	− 7.4	24.4	− 31.8
Business services	64.4	23.1	41.3
Other services	213.0	61.7	151.3
All other	177.8	94.3	83.5
Total	645.2	443.6	201.6

Source: Muller and Espenshade, 1985, p. 59, taken from U.S. Bureau of the Census, *Census of Publication*, Vol. 1, *Characteristics of the Population*, Chapter C: "General Social and Economical Characteristics," Part 6, California, PC80-1-C6, July 1983, Chapter D, "Detailed Population Characteristics," Part 6, California, PC80-1-D6, November 1983.

Table 4.3 IMMIGRATION SHARE OF MANUFACTURING EMPLOYMENT IN LOS
ANGELES COUNTY, 1980

	Total employment (thousands)	Immigrant share of employment (%)	Immigrant share of workers[a]
Food	42.8	44.4	54.8
Textiles	11.1	57.3	73.7
Apparel	76.1	74.6	89.4
Lumber and wool	10.4	48.8	59.2
Furniture and fixtures	33.5	59.4	73.6
Metals	90.4	33.8	38.2
Machinery	181.3	27.6	31.3
Transportation equipment	184.5	16.6	21.4
Other sectors	254.0	32.1	34.4
All manufacturing	884.1	33.9	39.9

Source: Tabulation by The Urban Institute of the 1980 Census Public Use Microdata
Sample, as found in Muller and Espenshade, 1985, p. 58. Figures are rounded.
a. Based on production worker/nonproduction worker distribution in Los Angeles
industries as reported in the 1977 Census of Manufacturers.

Janitorial services and some of the construction trades have shifted
almost entirely from native to foreign-born employees within the last
20 years.

These data indicate that, minimally, industries currently heavily
dependent on undocumented labor will be disrupted if employer
requirements are enforced effectively. At the extreme, those employers will be unable to replace workers at competitive rates and
will fail, leading to broader economic dislocations and growing political opposition to the program.

Table 4.4 documents the fact that firms in immigrant-dependent
industries are very difficult targets of education and enforcement.
They are often small and numerous and therefore difficult to monitor.
Moreover, small employers are probably the least able to get information about the new law or to provide an orderly hiring process
that will accommodate I-9 requirements. The high rate of new business formation in Los Angeles further aggravates the problem. New
businesses register at the rate of about 25,000 per month.[2] Although
many of these enterprises may not actually employ- workers, many
do, and these new firms place demands on the Immigration and
Naturalization Service (INS) for an extensive and continuous education effort.

Table 4.4 BUSINESS AND EMPLOYMENT PATTERNS IN IMMIGRANT-
DEPENDENT INDUSTRIES, LOS ANGELES CSMA, 1980

	Number of establishments	% with < 50 employees
Landscaping services	1621	97.1
Building contractors	4964	96.9
Food preparation	962	71.1
Textile mill products	296	76.0
Apparel	3262	86.0
Furniture and fixtures	1149	76.8
Hotels, lodging	1973	90.5
Personal services	8096	98.4
Building services (janitorial)	1870	94.5
Eating, drinking	17517	91.3
Automative services (no repair)	713	97.6
Electrical	761	68.7
Miscellaneous manufacturing	1196	89.7

Source: County Business Patterns, U.S. Department of Commerce, 1984.

Political Environment

The INS enforcement program is not likely to receive substantial local political support in Los Angeles. The public does not typically view undocumented aliens or their employers as criminals or the employment of undocumented workers as harmful to society. Immigrant workers are often sought after by Los Angeles employers, many of whom consider them hardworking and reliable. Moreover, residents currently perceive immigrants as a positive addition to the labor pool. As one 1988 poll reported, almost 75 percent of California respondents agreed that the growing numbers of Hispanics and Asians in California would provide "increasing numbers of people anxious to work hard" and "needed labor for new jobs" (The Field Institute, 1988). Even though the AFL-CIO supported the passage of IRCA, some important unions now evidence growing reservations about IRCA and the very concept of closed borders. Although not advocating civil disobedience, the Los Angeles Archdiocese has enunciated a policy for undocumented persons that "includes support for expansion of legalization, a commitment to change the employer sanctions of the immigration law, safe haven for displaced persons, and the development of poorer countries" (Mahoney, 1989). Moreover, several local churches provide sanctuary to undocumented aliens.

Not only is the political climate of Los Angeles reasonably tolerant of immigrants, immigrants enjoy an unusual political voice in the community. Several immigrant rights advocacy organizations are headquartered in the city, including the Coalition for Humane Immigrant Rights of Los Angeles (CHIRLA) and the Mexican-American Legal Defense and Education Fund (MALDEF). These groups have been strong and consistent opponents of IRCA, principally because they oppose the employer requirements. Their location makes them ready participants in state and local immigration policymaking and vigorous watchdogs over INS district activities.

In sum, Los Angeles has characteristics that make the design and application of an effective INS enforcement program very difficult. Enforcement must cover a broad geographical area that is dense with small employers. The large undocumented population is likely to be employed in industries dominated by these small employers. Moreover, because undocumented workers are concentrated in some industries, any effective enforcement program is likely to result in significant economic dislocations, undermining political support for the program.

INS CAPACITIES AND INCENTIVES TO ENFORCE IRCA

The law places the difficult job of enforcement squarely on the shoulders of the INS, with only a peripheral role assigned to the Department of Labor (DOL). The latter, in the course of other routine inspections, reviews I-9 forms and reports irregularities to the INS for further investigation. Thus, the institutional environment for enforcement is reasonably uncomplicated. The quality of the enforcement effort rests, for the most part, on the resources, organizational capacities, personnel, and adaptability of the INS—an agency from which little was expected and which, in the early phases of implementation, pleasantly surprised many.

Organization

The INS has an unusually complex and decentralized structure (see chapter 2). Its central office and four regional offices establish broad policy and oversee performance. The district and Border Patrol offices share responsibility for the work, with the Border Patrol assuming principal responsibility for enforcement activities centered at the borders, at ports of entry, and in rural areas, and the district

offices assuming responsibility in urban areas. Because the Los Angeles district is predominantly urban, the Border Patrol plays only
a small enforcement role at its rural periphery.

Decentralization implies the importance of personal leadership at
the local level, and, indeed, local personalities have done much to
shape local implementation of employer requirements. During the
period observed, the Los Angeles district director, the district counsel, and the assistant district director for investigations were all experienced administrators. The district director had held that post for
many years. The assistant district director returned to the Los Angeles district office in May 1987 after serving as assistant commissioner at the regional level, where he developed enforcement
implementation plans for the entire region, including Los Angeles.
The district counsel came to Los Angeles in May 1988 after serving
as district counsel in Phoenix for four years.

Budget

Although all INS offices complain of resource shortages, the Los
Angeles district is, perhaps, more affected than most. Congress initially failed to match its massive regulatory mandate with commen-
surate appropriations. Although the INS received a major supplemental
appropriation for enforcement in 1987, the money was not immediately appropriated, and only 26 percent was ultimately allocated
to investigations units for enforcement of employer requirements.
The Border Patrol and the INS program to remove criminal aliens
from the country received the lion's share (Fix and Hill, 1990, p. 54).

Within the INS, the central office allocates money to the regions
by major activity or program (Investigations, District Counsel), and
regional offices, in turn, divide it among their district offices, also
by activity area. The central office did not use a publicized allocation
formula. Rather, allocation depended largely on politics and nego-
tiations between regional and central office personnel and not on
more objective measures of workload. The Western Region, which
was burdened with a rapidly growing workload, did not win a commensurately increasing share of money. Among the district offices
of the region, however, the Los Angeles Investigations unit and District Counsel's office were reputed to be successful competitors.

Staff

Budget translates quite directly into staff. An effective IRCA enforcement staff must be adequate in size, trained to investigate and build

strong cases, attuned to working with a citizen population, and located in reach of its target.

Although the Los Angeles district office greatly expanded its enforcement staff, that staff was still very small compared to the area's employer population of 335,000. Because the INS did not actually receive its budget augmentations until 1988, the district was slow to increase its staff. However, once the money began flowing from Washington, both Investigations and the District Counsel's staff were increased. Staff positions in Investigations grew from 92 to 168 between June, 1986 and 1989—an increase of more than 50 percent. The increase in agents employed was an even more dramatic 134 percent, increasing from 50 to 165 during that period. Similarly, the District Counsel's office gained 10 staff attorney positions, four clerical positions, and one supervisory position, in part because the workload of that office could also be expected to increase substantially with the introduction of the IRCA cases.

Developing a seasoned investigations staff has long been a problem for the district office, because starting salaries are low and cost of living in Los Angeles is high.[3] The passage of IRCA did much to enhance the image of the service and to bolster its morale, both of which facilitated recruiting. However, recruiting continued to be hampered by a cumbersome recruitment process, which required that applicants take and pass government examinations and then await a security clearance. By the time the district was in a position to make job offers, applicants had often accepted other jobs. Retention also continued to be a problem, with newly trained agents frequently attracted to higher-paying local law enforcement jobs.

During the period of our study, all but five Investigations agents were quartered in the service's downtown office, substantially curtailing their access to the employers located in the outskirts of the city. These areas are rapidly growing and are home to large immigrant communities.

IMPLEMENTATION AND EFFECTS OF THE EMPLOYER REQUIREMENTS PROVISIONS IN IRCA

In this section we explore in some detail how the INS in Los Angeles has implemented the employer requirements set forth in IRCA, with what effect, and why implementation has proceeded along the course that it has. The questions governing our exploration are:

□ Is the INS developing the capacity to implement a strong program?
□ Is the INS building a comprehensive and effective process that includes education, monitoring, and sanctions?
□ Is the INS systematically building supportive case law?
□ Is the INS garnering political support for employer requirements?

Building the Capacity

Although regulation of employers was new to the INS, policing behavior was not. The service already had a well-established enforcement infrastructure and considerable enforcement responsibility. Thus, it had to integrate its new IRCA mandate into a preexisting structure and set of responsibilities.

SETTING PRIORITIES

IRCA added a number of enforcement activities to the already full INS platter. These included drug control, deportation of criminal aliens, managing fraud, especially in the SAW legalization program, and employer sanctions. In a study of eight important district offices, only two—Chicago and Los Angeles—gave high priority to enforcing IRCA's employer sanctions and maintained that commitment through the period of the study.[4] As the Los Angeles assistant district director commented, "It is the only hope to control illegal immigration."

The L.A. district's commitment was perhaps best reflected in its staffing assignments. During the period of our study, 55 percent of its 165 agents were assigned to IRCA-related employer activities, compared to an average of about 35 percent in the Western Region. At the same time, the District gave its interior apprehensions program, which before IRCA was the chief avenue for controlling illegal immigration, lowest priority among its investigative responsibilities. Only 15 agents were assigned to interior apprehensions, compared with the full roster of about 50 agents assigned to the job in 1986. These 15 agents also conducted employer surveys and performed other apprehension activities as well.

Some sources suggest that the District's decision to scale back its interior apprehensions effort was born of practical necessity rather than strategic policy choice. Existing detention facilities were already overflowing, and without more detention space the district was forced to allow those apprehended to depart voluntarily or release them on their own recognizance. In short, it was not worth spending money to apprehend aliens who would just be returned to the streets.

Not all traditional enforcement efforts, however, gave way to the employer sanctions program. The INS Investigations unit is also responsible for controlling counterfeit documents and fraud and deporting criminal aliens, neither of which are functions the District can easily ignore. New demands by employers for documentation dramatically increased the traffic in fraudulent work documents, clearly threatening the employer sanctions program. At the same time, Los Angeles City and County incarcerate a large number of criminals, perhaps as many as 15 percent of whom are illegal aliens.[5] INS agents are responsible for screening the jailed population, identifying those who are undocumented or no longer qualify for residency, and deporting them immediately upon their release.[6] Given the local context, and despite of the emphasis given to fraud control at the regional level, the District therefore gave more attention to its labor intensive criminal alien responsibilities, assigning 45 agents to that program compared to the 25 it assigns to its fraud unit.

The District Counsel's office shared a commitment to enforcement of employer sanctions but it also had to choose among competing programs. At the outset, that office assigned a smaller fraction of its staff to employer sanctions because the legal caseload was still relatively small, and deportation work—its other main job—consumed considerable attorney time.

STRATEGY

The Los Angeles office formally espoused an enforcement strategy that is entirely consistent with the measured regulatory approach advocated by the Congress. The strategy entails the application of staged enforcement. Every employer is entitled to education, therefore, all first-time violators are educated. Second-time violators receive moderate sanctions, and any further violations draw the full arsenal of sanctions, including penalties from the IRS and the DOL. The District adopted this strategy at the outset of the program, and it continued to guide enforcement through the three years of this study. The staged approach is cautious and conciliatory, but will take many years to reach maturity—the point at which severe sanctions predominate.

Consistent with the District's policy of slowly increasing pressure on employers who violate the law while at the same time building solid relations with the broader employer community, the District Counsel was very reluctant to pursue anything but strong, well-developed cases. That office wanted cases that would win, "so charges will be taken seriously and employers cannot accuse us of pillaging." Furthermore, the Counsel noted that "poor cases may make poor case law," an important consequence of any case brought to trial within the context of a new statute.

However, the tension between conciliation and punishment does creep in. An important component of enforcement strategy is targeting. How should one choose employers to inspect? Possible criteria might include size of firm, level of immigrant employment in the industry, whether undocumented workers appear to be replacing documented workers in the industry, current information suggesting that the employer is now violating the law, or random selection. Of these criteria, 1) randomness, 2) a high proportion of immigrant labor in the industry, and 3) current information play a role in targeting strategy. As we described above, the INS central office required that all districts draw at least 40 percent of their inspections at random from lists of all employers and of employers in immigrant-intensive industries, with the remaining employers identified through leads or tips from other agencies or individuals. This mixed strategy satisfies the demand that an enforcement strategy be fair, with a neutral target component. Random selection also warns employers that the law applies to *everyone*, encouraging more widespread compliance. On the other hand, the most direct path to those who violate the law is through leads, a much more efficient targeting mechanism. As we discuss below, there was considerable tension within the Los Angeles District over whether to target employers at random or to concentrate more on leads. Over time, many districts including Los Angeles allowed lead-based investigations to become an increasing share of the total, despite central office policy.

That same debate carries over to the sanctions phase of the program. Although some districts prefer to emphasize complex cases that target the more serious and willful offender, Los Angeles District leaders believed compliance was better encouraged through the pursuit of larger numbers of smaller, straightforward cases.

Although employers were the focus of attention, the District also considered how best to control the growing tide of counterfeit documents. The concept under consideration at the time of our study was to target the immigrant using counterfeit documents, pressing well-publicized and severe felony charges against repeat offenders, a reemergence of the adversarial motif. At the same time, the District and the rest of the INS were pressing hard for the adoption of some form of national work card.

Los Angeles chose to pursue conciliation for several reasons. First,

District leaders believed this strategy would work. Moreover, it was consistent with their new view of themselves as professional investigators, akin to IRS and FBI agents. However, no explanation would be complete without attention to IRCA's sunset provision, a subtext of implementation in Los Angeles. Although no one announced that the District was tailoring its enforcement programs to minimize the possibility that the employer requirements would be sunsetted, when asked, most acknowledged that strategy and practice certainly had been developed with an eye toward protecting the program. To do this, enforcement must not threaten employers to the point that they overrespond by adopting discriminatory employment practices. Nor must employers feel compelled to organize and seek statutory revisions. Some people suggested that to preserve the program, the District intentionally adopted a "go-slow" approach, allowing the program to become firmly rooted and the sunset deadline to pass before assuming a more active posture.

Personnel and Training

Recruitment and training policies have a profound effect on an agency's capacity and work style. Sensitive to this fact, the District made significant changes in its recruitment and training practices to attract agents who would be compatible with its enforcement strategy. The rapidly expanding Investigations unit, for the first time, recruited not from the ranks of the Border Patrol, but from the pool of college graduates. To explain this change, the assistant district director observed that training can substitute for experience and that the law is new, demanding a new set of skills, particularly the ability to write well and document cases. He noted, "We need professional investigations with complete, persuasive reports. Everything must be documented." Although the central office urged districts to hire at least 50 percent of their new staff from the college pool, Los Angeles aimed for 90 percent.

Inevitably, changes in hiring strategy delayed the time when the Los Angeles Investigations team could be at full strength and, quite probably, altered the flavor of their approach. New recruits had to be found, trained, and then given some "on-the-job" seasoning before assuming their full share of responsibility. And recruits "from the street" (as they call agents who do not come from the Border Patrol) would be much less comfortable confronting employers and conducting floor sweeps than agents trained in the Border Patrol.

The Regulatory Process in Los Angeles

The regulatory process comprises three distinct activities: education, monitoring, and the application of sanctions.

The Education of Los Angeles Employers

The INS central office emphasized education from the outset, and despite the fact that reaching the employers of Los Angeles presents a Herculean task, the District gave the effort strong support. The central office required that at least 50 percent of the hours spent on employer sanctions be spent on education, effective through June 1988. It also required that no employer be sanctioned without first receiving an educational visit. Los Angeles more than complied. In the early days of IRCA, the Investigations unit had only 35 to 50 agents. More than half of them were assigned to employer education, and agents were also borrowed from other activities while new positions were being filled.

The education program consisted of two tasks—outreach and employer visits. The outreach program was the first to be launched. As early as December 1986, the INS organized a seminar on IRCA employer sanctions, inviting representatives from a broad cross section of the city, including trade association representatives, attorneys, and personnel directors of major corporations. Over the next 18 months, the District continued a very active outreach program, making frequent presentations at conventions and trade association functions, as well as holding regular meetings with some trade associations and the local law bar.

The District's program of direct employer visits was harder and riskier than the outreach effort, because traditionally such direct INS contacts had been confrontational. The District firmly believed that to build voluntary compliance it would have to inform employers without threatening them. Thus, it built an education agenda in which agents "identified" areas of the city with concentrations of businesses and went door to door, passing out the INS employer handbook, explaining the employer requirements, and answering questions. To completely dissociate these visits from enforcement actions, agents did not ask to see I-9s or to visit firms' work areas. After some months, the District began targeting the smaller and the new firms for educational visits, because these were the two classes of firms most often found to be ignorant of the law's provisions.

In an urban area the size of Los Angeles, where over 90 percent of businesses employ fewer than 50 workers, directly touching a large fraction of employers is not a realistic target, given current INS resources. Of the approximately 335,000 business establishments in the District, the INS reports having made educational visits to some 56,000 (about 17 percent) between November 1986 and June 1988.[7] They also report contacting an additional 25,000 individuals and firms through other channels during that same period.

The transition from education to full enforcement was, by design, incremental. Congress mandated a 12-month period, June 1987 through May 1988, during which education would continue and sanctions could be applied only against repeat offenders. During this time, the Los Angeles District continued to emphasize education and to work slowly into enforcement, developing its investigative format but using it primarily for education.

Groups outside the District office also committed time and resources to local employer education. The central office mailed seven million employers nationwide an employer handbook describing the rationale underlying IRCA, explaining what was required of employers, and providing copies of the I-9 and copies of the more frequently encountered work authorization documents. The DOL, as mandated by IRCA, apprised employers of their obligations and checked I-9 forms when visiting firms on DOL-related business. And finally, a host of organizations in the private sector, especially attorneys and trade associations, undertook educational efforts, sometimes without but most often with the assistance of the INS. These other efforts contributed greatly to District efforts to educate employers. In fact, they may have been the employers' primary source of information.

Education no longer commands a central position in the District's regulatory program. After June 1988, it was turned over to the two-man Employer Labor Relations unit and to agents as they conducted enforcement activities. Similarly, after shifting program emphasis to enforcement, the INS did not encourage continuing outreach efforts by trade associations and other groups. Considering the extremely high rate of new business formation in Los Angeles and the turnover rate of firms' personnel managers, compliance with the law may decline unless the INS institutionalizes a larger, permanent educational program. The GAO, in fact, reports that understanding of the IRCA I-9 requirement and hiring restrictions dropped by about 30 percent between 1988 and 1989 among the nation's employers (GAO, 1990, p. 61).

THE EFFECTS OF THE DISTRICT EDUCATION PROGRAM

To measure employers' understanding of the law, we conducted interviews with a sample of 18 employers.[8] Of our respondents, slightly over half had a very good understanding of the terms of the law; seven had a poor understanding. Of those seven, five knew that the law's purpose was to prevent employers from hiring undocumented workers; they vaguely understood they had an obligation to check some documentation, but they knew nothing of the requirement to fill out I-9s. Said one construction firm representative who knew a good deal about other IRCA provisions, including fine details, "If you don't hire illegal aliens, you don't need to fill out any forms."

As expected, the well-informed firms tend to be the larger ones, those with over 50 employees, and these firms tend to get their information from trade associations and the INS. The poorly informed firms tend to be smaller and more decentralized, particularly those providing janitorial and construction services. These firms, by contrast, tend to get their information from the media.

Our respondents and trade association and union representatives reported that one provision caused considerable confusion even among reasonably knowledgeable firms. This was the grandfather clause, which relieved employers of the obligation to verify documents for workers already in their employ at the time IRCA was passed. Not uncommonly, employers requested documents of their current workforce, as they instituted routine verification procedures, and they dismissed workers who lacked proper documents. Although not illegal, such action was not necessary.

Although our survey was extremely small and clearly not representative of firms hiring aliens, it is interesting to note that our results are quite consistent with those obtained in two other surveys of Los Angeles employers, one of larger firms (over 400 employees) in the garment industry that predominantly hire Asians, and one of a similar group that hire Hispanics (Cheng and Azores-Gunther, 1988). Firms in both groups understood the IRCA requirements; over half had received their information from the INS and the rest from attorneys.

These responses suggest that the INS mailing and the District's outreach program have been reasonably successful in reaching larger firms that are organizationally equipped to digest and institutionalize the more detailed information that comes to them. Smaller firms are very often not so equipped.

They also do not readily share business information with one another, and their source of information—the media—has not proved adequate. In fact, the "grapevine" in the Hispanic undocumented community is far superior to that in the small employer community. In a survey of the former, 95 percent of the respondents understood the employer requirements provisions of IRCA (Cornelius, 1989, p. 5).

ENFORCEMENT OF IRCA'S EMPLOYER SANCTIONS

Before discussing enforcement in Los Angeles, it is important to note that the INS central office established a priority management system to encourage a serious enforcement effort in the region.[9] Under the system, regions set district performance standards or "numerical thresholds" for a number of actions that were identified as proxies for "good performance." These included 1) number of General Administrative Plan (GAP) inspections; 2) number of notices of intent to fine (NIFs) issued; 3) number of investigations targeting serious violations; 4) number of criminal prosecutions; 5) number of criminal convictions; and 6) number of apprehensions at the workplace. Commissioner Harold Ezell of the Western Region is reputed to have taken these targets very seriously. This explains why they drove numerous local enforcement decisions.

The Monitoring Process. The Western Region established a multistage model regulatory enforcement process that consisted of several contacts and contrasted sharply with the traditional INS police model. First, an agent advised the employer that the agent would visit the firm. Then, typically within a week, the agent visited the firm to explain IRCA's requirements, and review the employer's procedures. The agent returned to the District office with the I-9s (or a sample of I-9s, if the firm was large) and corroborating payroll information to check the validity of the documents listed on the I-9s against a central INS database, and to determine whether I-9s exist for all new employees. If the employer refused to supply documents to the agent, the INS issued a subpoena or warrant. The agent then drafted a written report identifying any irregularities and submits that report to the employer. After a week or two, the agent returned to ensure that undocumented workers had been replaced and that the paperwork was in order. Only then, if the employer remained out of compliance, could the investigating agent resort to a floor survey.

The District supported this model, and in most cases, agents appeared to be following it quite closely.[10] Similarly, in most cases employers appeared to be supplying documents voluntarily. However, individual agents do exercise considerable discretion in the field, and we had a few reports of agents who asked to survey the factory working area or, more often, asked for a broader array of documents on their first visit. But typically, agents conducted floor sweeps or surveys only in instances of more serious violations, averaging less than one per month out of an active caseload of 150 to 175 cases.

Because enforcement requires direct contact between agents and employers, the effort cannot be magnified through intermediaries as can education. During the period of our study only a small fraction of Los Angeles employers actually received compliance visits from District agents. The District reports that it conducted approximately 2,220 compliance inspections by October 1989, visiting about 7 percent of the employer population.[11]

To better serve program and bureaucratic needs, the District adjusted its initial targeting strategy. Although District agents still met central office requirements by quickly conducting a minimal number of GAP visits, the GAP lists supplied an increasingly small proportion of total visits conducted in the District. Agents found that the lists often waste investigative time because they contained firms that moved or closed. Moreover, these randomly selected cases resulted in very few violations when compared with those for which they had leads.[12] Their only value, reported one senior member of the investigative team, is as a training ground for new employees. By 1989, about 20 percent of the District's caseload was drawn from the GAP list, whereas about 80 percent was drawn from the pool of leads, most of which came from the community or from visa petitions requiring DOL certification. Furthermore, outside observers also note that firms with a history of hiring undocumented workers appeared to be the most frequent objects of these visits.

Although there was no explicit policy regarding the targeting of firms by size or type, there did appear to be patterns. The District did not generally enforce employer sanctions among household employers. To facilitate their investigations, agents tended to focus on firms with central concentrations of employees. These included restaurants and garment or furniture manufacturing sites rather than construction or janitorial firms, whose employees are spread among several sites. Agents also continued to concentrate on small- to medium-sized firms. Although the District did not have a policy of targeting small firms, most firms visited employed fewer than 50 workers. Such firms were more likely targets because they constitute more than 90 percent of the firms in the area, were more likely to be out of compliance, and were more likely to be targeted through leads.

The INS "numerical thresholds" also affected which employers may be targeted for enforcement action. The Western Region was expected to open and review at least 1,200 cases in 1989 and to issue at least 250 NIFs. As the largest district within the region, Los Angeles was assigned a large share of these quotas. Consequently, District agents targeted cases with a high probability of yielding a violation even if that violation was relatively minor. For example, agents would examine labor certification requests and then work backward to the employer on the assumption that the employee in question was already working illegally. As one observer noted, "It's like shooting fish in a barrel."[13] By all accounts, the "numerical thresholds" loomed large in the targeting decisions of the investigations unit.

In sum, monitoring compliance, like educational visits, did not directly touch a substantial proportion of the employers in the Los Angeles area. The realities of implementing the law also prompted the District to shift somewhat from its original targeting principles. On the other hand, its enforcement process continued to be consistent with its goal of forging a new conciliatory rather than confrontational relationship with local employers. Employers' perceptions of the service's reach—the truly important measure when striving for voluntary compliance—will be examined below.

The Sanctions Process. The final step in the enforcement process is applying sanctions to those few Los Angeles employers violating IRCA's provisions. In June 1988, on the eve of full enforcement, Commissioner Nelson emphasized that the substantive violation of "knowingly hiring or continuing to employ" undocumented workers was to be the focus of enforcement action (GAO, 1990, p. 89). He identified four situations suggestive of "knowingly hiring" in which sanctions should be applied:

☐ Failure to complete I-9s for all workers after an educational visit;
☐ Discovery of unrecorded workers in the workplace when the INS cannot prove that undocumented workers were "knowingly" hired;
☐ A paperwork fine as a result of a plea agreement;
☐ Other egregious but undefined factors.

These rules, which were entirely consistent with the Los Angeles strategy of conciliation and staged enforcement, guided the District in its application of sanctions.

The District Counsel's office is the agent for applying sanctions under IRCA, and it has acquired new authority to shape investigative activities to insure that practices are consistent with the demands of defining IRCA in the courts and of regulating the behavior of U.S. citizens. The District Counsel assumes control of a case once the investigation is complete and fully documented, and a penalty is proposed and justified by the investigation team. The District Counsel's office reviews the charges and the proposed penalty, asks for more information as necessary, and often limits the charges to those that can be pursued with certain success, reducing the fines commensurately. This process frequently lasts several weeks, at which time the employer is issued an NIF. The District Counsel's consistently conservative posture in applying sanctions was clearly a source of some tension between that office and the investigative staff.

In addition to its responsibilities for applying sanctions, the District Counsel's office played some role in revising investigative practices and educating investigative staff in proper information gathering techniques, as well as in other areas important in building trial-worthy cases.

The types of violations, the penalty levels, and the number of cases receiving sanctions during the first 18 months of the program all seem entirely consistent with, although not necessarily a product of, the District's three-staged strategy. By October 1989, the Los Angeles District had filed 165 NIFs. The district issued only 6 to 8 NIFs per month in the months following the education period, but increased that number to 15 to 20 NIFs per month by the end of the first enforcement year. On the other hand, average fines, usually ranging between $3,000 and $5,000 per NIF, did not increase during this period. The vast majority of the counts were for "egregious" paperwork violations, although a majority of NIFs contained at least one substantive violation—usually "continuing to employ [an undocumented alien]."[14] The most common paperwork violation tended to be the scattered absence of I-9s that "coincidentally" match undocumented workers on the floor. Employers apparently hoped that investigators would not compare I-9s with other documents or that the missing documents would not be noticed. The District pursued only two criminal charges during this period. Small- and medium-sized service firms, especially hotels, restaurants, and garment makers, tended to dominate the group of employers receiving NIFs. The increasing number of NIFs being issued seems to reflect a number of factors including 1) the emphasis on NIFs in the priority management system; 2) the growing numbers of trained enforcement staff;

3) the changing emphasis from education to enforcement; 4) experience with the new program; and 5) the District's staged approach.

Table 4.5 compares the enforcement record in Los Angeles with that in two other urban districts.

Los Angeles has been criticized for issuing large numbers of paperwork violations (more than any other city in our national study). However, as the assistant regional commissioner pointed out with some feeling, agents typically issued paperwork violations when there was every reason to believe that the employer was guilty of "knowingly hiring" an undocumented employee, but that more serious offense was difficult to prove.[15] Furthermore, he argued that failure to verify documents and complete the I-9 is a serious violation; believing that documents will be checked is the only deterrent to illegal immigration. Thus, "paperwork violations" may, in fact, be more than they initially seem. Finally, the District noted that the U.S. Attorney's office insisted that the district office attempt administrative remedies for "pattern and practice" cases before it would press criminal charges.

Of the employers who received NIFs between June 1988 and February 1989, only 12 had requested hearings. However, many were within their 30-day filing period and could still exercise that option. None who had filed had yet come to hearing, and 24 had received final orders in which the fines of 9 had been reduced, usually by just a small amount. Observers sense that these data accurately represent the process. They say that at least 50 percent of employers simply paid their fines, and most who requested a hearing pled guilty and negotiated before the hearing date to avoid the high costs of the hearing. This behavior is common in any litigation.

In addition to punishing offenders and deterring potential offenders, the sanctions process also uses the courts to define ambiguous areas in the law. At the time of the study, the District Counsel had pursued only one such case to appeal. It centered on the issue of defining the employer's obligation to ascertain the legal status of

Table 4.5 CHICAGO, NEW YORK, AND LOS ANGELES ENFORCEMENT
ACTIONS THROUGH MARCH 31, 1989

	Chicago	New York	Los Angeles
No. of NIFs	11	53	67
% paperwork violations	0	21	51
Average fine	$45,500	$11,500	$4,500

Source: Fix and Hill, 1990.

workers, and the District prevailed. As further evidence of the Counsel's determination to build strong cases, the INS had not lost a single case heard before an administrative law judge during the first three years of IRCA implementation, a remarkable record.

The U.S. Attorney's office is responsible for pressing criminal charges, including fraud and false attestation, and for enforcing the orders handed down by administrative law judges in hearings. This office tends to be interested primarily in dramatic, high-impact jury cases, and therefore was unwilling to pursue "run of the mill" IRCA cases, typically fraud cases. However, the District Counsel did plan at some future date to have two of his new staff attorneys assist the U.S. Attorney's office in handling INS cases that the District wants to bring to trial as misdemeanors.

EFFECTS OF THE L.A. DISTRICT ENFORCEMENT PROGRAM

Our information on employers' experiences with and perceptions of early enforcement is ambiguous. Among the employers we interviewed, 8 out of 18 had been visited by the INS or DOL, but only a few of the remaining 10 had direct knowledge of any firm that had been visited.[16] The comparable Cheng and Azores-Gunter (1988) study of large firms hiring Asians, however, found that only one out of their 13 respondents had been audited. (They did not comment upon educational visits.)

Other sources suggest the employer community did not believe itself to have been hard hit by INS enforcement actions. One early newspaper headline read: "EMPLOYERS WONDER: INS, WHERE IS THY STING?" The article reported that garment industry leaders were surprised that their industry had not yet "felt the sting of the massive federal enforcement effort against employers. . . ." (Hernandez and Braun, 1988). Trade association and union leaders in target industries continued to report that their industries had not been much affected by INS enforcement action, and other knowledgeable sources observed that sanctions were failing because there was no highly visible enforcement in the Los Angeles area.

Although L.A. District officials emphasized the role of media coverage in accomplishing their compliance goals, a review of both the major English and Spanish language newspapers indicates that coverage was spotty at best. The Los Angeles District's cautious enforcement program did not have media appeal, except when there was an occasional dramatic raid. Instead, INS officials drew remarkable press coverage for their legalization program.

In spite of seemingly weak exposure to enforcement activity, Los

Angeles employers—even those who were not in compliance—said they expected enforcement action. In our employer survey, 13 of the 18 respondents said they expected an INS or DOL visit. Similarly, in the study of employers of Asian workers, although only 1 had experienced an enforcement action, 7 of 13 respondents said they expected a visit and most believed the INS could force compliance (Cheng and Azores-Gunther, 1988, p. 9). Neither survey probed further to uncover what other forces might be shaping employers' perceptions of the likelihood of a visit or how detrimental they believed a visit would be.

How painful employers expected the consequences of noncompliance to be is another matter. We found that those familiar with the law also had some sense of IRCA's fine structure and knew its upper limits. Our small- and medium-sized employers agreed that the highest allowable fines would be very hard on most businesses. On the other hand, few had any direct or indirect exposure to any business that had been sanctioned.

COMPLIANCE WITH EMPLOYER SANCTIONS IN LOS ANGELES

The purpose of an education and enforcement program is to promote compliance with the requirements of the law. Thus, to assess the quality of the INS enforcement program in Los Angeles, we must examine employer compliance rates in the area.

Our survey responses tend to mirror those reported by the GAO. Fifty percent of the Los Angeles employers we surveyed described themselves as in reasonably full compliance. All completed I-9s, although some did not have systems to flag employees whose documents expire. Of these 9 employers, 3 carefully screened documents for fraud. Another one-third, those who did not know the law, *believed themselves* to be more or less in compliance because they checked the documents of most or many applicants, although they may not routinely have filled out I-9 forms. Only 3 described themselves as making no effort to comply. The rate of compliance was much higher in larger firms than in smaller firms; compliance was also higher in firms with an office-based hiring routine. In small firms and those with decentralized hiring and work characteristics, for example, construction and janitorial services, complying with any type of paperwork requirements is very difficult. The institutional mechanisms do not exist.

Local employers were not much disturbed by IRCA for several reasons. The abundance of newly legalized immigrants (both pre-1982 immigrants and the large pool of agricultural workers), the availability of counterfeit documents, and the fact that smaller firms were often not in full compliance combined to minimize the effects of IRCA on employers. Moreover, employers apparently did not expect that situation to change soon.

However, because IRCA had not yet measurably affected the labor market and the costs to most employers of complying remained relatively low, we could not predict future compliance in an environment where these costs may be higher.

Documentation: The Linchpin of IRCA

Employer compliance is a hollow exercise if employers verify fraudulent or counterfeit documents, and tolerance of the program will be short-lived if those entitled to work in the United States find themselves denied employment because their documents are confusing or replacements for lost documentation are not readily available. The twin problems of counterfeit and confusing documents, especially the former problem, pervaded the implementation environment in Los Angeles and challenged the concept underlying IRCA.

COUNTERFEIT AND FRAUDULENT DOCUMENTS

IRCA requires that employers verify the identity and work eligibility of new hires by examining documents the applicant presents. Checking documents specified by the INS serves as an affirmative defense against sanctions. Thus, the law states and the Congress clearly intended that employers be responsible for checking documents, not that they be responsible for hiring truly documented workers. Furthermore, neither IRCA nor the legislative debate suggests that employers should be able to distinguish counterfeit from genuine documents. If counterfeit documents are readily available and employers make no effort to distinguish the fake from the genuine, employer sanctions cannot be expected to substantially affect the flow of illegal immigration.

Few people familiar with the workings of IRCA in Los Angeles would speculate on the prevalence of illegal documentation. Most employers, when asked what proportion of their hires have probably submitted counterfeit or fraudulent documents, simply shrugged, and the INS had no way to gauge the proportion. The INS reports that 39 percent of the undocumented workers they identified in their early inspection visits presented the employer with invalid documents to satisfy I-9 requirements (GAO, 1988). Wayne Cornelius reports similar findings, noting that 41 percent of a sample of Mexican immigrants working in the United States in 1987 to 1988 had obtained employment using counterfeit or fraudulent documents. Similarly, 25 percent of a group of migrants who had recently returned to Mexico reported having used such documents to get employment on their most recent trip to the United States (Cornelius, 1989, p. 8). But both sets of data come from information gathered early in the IRCA implementation process when the market for counterfeit documents may have been less well-developed. Counterfeit documents are currently very readily available. At the time of our study, they were so abundant, in fact, that the price had been falling steadily, and a packet containing identification and work documents of reasonable quality could be had for $35 in Los Angeles. The false documents most commonly acquired were Social Security cards and INS alien registration cards.

Because of its commitment to the IRCA employer enforcement program and its responsibility for criminal aliens, the Los Angeles District had little manpower to devote to fraud control. Moreover, some in the INS office believed that policing the availability of counterfeit documents was perhaps hopeless.[17] As one member of the Los Angeles District office responded, "Oh yes, the fraud unit has been very successful, but I'm not sure they have had much of an effect."

Given the inability of the INS to control the availability of counterfeit documents and the typical unwillingness of employers to push beyond the letter of the law, presenting false documents stood as the simplest of tools to neutralize the effectiveness of IRCA. Many contend that the only effective response to this threat is the introduction of a national work card that would be hard to counterfeit. Commissioner Harold Ezell stated in 1989, "We are as effective now as we're going to be as long as Congress doesn't move to secure a work authorization card."

Surprisingly, not only the INS but also many of the employers we interviewed would welcome the introduction of one national work card to be used by the entire population. Our employer respondents, five of whom volunteered that the program needed such a national work card even though it would reduce their opportunities to circumvent the law, said the card would be worth it to them because it would make verification simple. However, introduction of a national card to be carried by citizens as well as resident aliens would be costly, and there has long been resistance in the United States to any type of personal registration. Thus, forging the necessary consensus for such a move will not be easy.

The success of IRCA also requires that those entitled to work in the United States have ready access to documents and that employers accept such documents. On both counts, residents in Los Angeles, like those in other parts of the country, encountered difficulty. The INS did not have the record-keeping capability or the personnel to provide duplicate documents to people (especially to those naturalized a number of years ago) in a timely fashion when theirs are lost. Similarly, a wide variety of documents provide individuals with work authorization, and local observers reported that employers unfamiliar with many of them would sometimes deny employment to their holders.[18]

Complementary State and Local Activities

Consistent with their traditional posture, state and local governments declined to play a complementary role in the enforcement of IRCA provisions. Responsibilities associated with immigration have traditionally rested firmly with the federal government. Because immigration issues may be politically charged, especially in areas with large immigrant populations, state and local governments have been quite content with that allocation of authority. IRCA did little to shift this balance, although in a minor provision it did explicitly permit states to facilitate verification.

IRCA expressly permits state employment agencies to verify the identity and work authorization documents of job applicants they place. Once verified by the state, employees would not have to present documentation again to their employers. California's Employment Development Department (EDD), a state agency that provides job placement services, moved quickly to institute a document verification program. The department expected such a program to serve its small business constituency, make its labor pool more attractive, and assist in the launching of IRCA.

EDD had hardly launched its verification program when legislative opposition boiled to the surface. Liberal legislators, pressed by a number of the state's advocacy groups, argued that it was not the state's business to help enforce or implement IRCA and that certification cards were the first step toward national identity cards. After a stormy debate, the legislature forced EDD to discontinue its program by forbidding use of department appropriations for that purpose. Observers believe that legislative opposition was the product of heavy lobbying by immigrant advocacy groups, which generally oppose employer sanctions.

Consistent with their historic posture, local governments and police departments usually managed to avoid any role in enforcing IRCA provisions. The one exception was in communities where the "street corner" labor market had gotten out of hand. After the passage of IRCA, the Los Angeles area saw a rapid growth in the number of men, most of whom were undocumented, who sought day work at several informally designated pick-up corners throughout the region.[19] As the number of laborers grew, so did the number of citizen complaints of improper behavior. In most instances, police ignored these sites until they became a political problem, and then they moved to discourage use of the site. However, a few jurisdictions, including the City of Los Angeles, tried to solve the problem by setting up city-run hiring sites. In some sites the city checked documents, thereby screening for the prospective employer; in others, including Los Angeles, the city denied any responsibility for ascertaining the status of individuals using the facility.[20] Although unhappy with this position, the INS did not immediately respond with a policy for dealing with "official" sites that failed to screen laborers.

Effectiveness of IRCA in Reducing Illegal Immigration

According to IRCA's logic, if jobs are no longer available to those in the United States illegally, illegal immigration will decline and eventually undocumented residents will leave. Although there has been considerable recent effort to determine the degree to which IRCA may be affecting the flow of illegal immigration into the country, the evidence is mixed and has not engendered a consensus in the research community.[21] However, there is evidence that IRCA has created the impression in the minds of some prospective illegal immigrants that jobs will be harder to find. Sixty-two percent of the respondents in a private 1989 survey of randomly selected Mexican towns reported that IRCA had discouraged them from going to the United States.[22] The results of an earlier study of three rural Mexican villages by the Center for U.S.-Mexican Studies at the University of California at San Diego support this finding, reporting that 39 percent of their respondents who had previously crossed illegally to the United States decided against another trip because of IRCA. Seventeen percent of those who had not been before decided against the trip.[23] Because Los Angeles is the primary job market for prospective Mexican immigrants, perceptions in Mexico are likely to be driven by experiences in Los Angeles.

Beyond these national data, there is little firm information to address the question of whether, in Los Angeles, the employer sanctions program is shrinking job opportunities for those who have immigrated illegally. The Los Angeles District office noted two indications that employment opportunities were shrinking: the increasing numbers of day laborers at pick-up points and the increasing number of self-employed street vendors. These two categories of workers indeed expanded between 1986 and 1989, but they were still small compared to the total pool of immigrant labor. Moreover, it is difficult to prove that IRCA was responsible for either trend.[24] Although employers reported considerable compliance with IRCA requirements, we have no data on the number of jobs removed from the reach of the undocumented or on the number of jobs filled by applicants using counterfeit or fraudulent documents.

In sum, our examination of the first three years of employer sanctions uncovers both predictable early outcomes and surprises. The undocumented population in Los Angeles, indeed, worked to circumvent IRCA requirements, but principally through counterfeit documents. Employers themselves proved reasonably compliant, considering what the law demanded of them. And despite the fact that there is little evidence suggesting that employer sanctions turned the tide of illegal immigration, the INS did, contrary to early predictions, develop an adequate institutional infrastructure and enforcement process, capable of giving the program a permanent place in the federal government's arsenal of regulatory programs.

FINDINGS

Before succumbing to the temptation to draw firm conclusions from our analysis of the first three years of IRCA implementation in Los Angeles, it is important to emphasize that the program had by no means reached a mature and stable state. Many employers remained ill-informed. District Investigation units were just reaching full, trained strength. The staged enforcement strategy adopted by the Los Angeles District had not yet led to the imposition of stiff penalties for noncompliance. Compliance did not demand sacrifice from many employers. Although we can draw some conclusions regarding the INS approach and the responses of the employer and undocumented populations, the behavior and strategies of all remained fluid, offering considerable potential for adaptation to changing circumstances.

Below are the key findings from our study:

Undocumented immigrants in Los Angeles were effectively circumventing the intent of the law through the use of counterfeit and fraudulent documents. As expected, the undocumented population found ways to circumvent the law. What was not anticipated was the ease with which that became possible. The market for credible counterfeit documents developed rapidly into an effective method of neutralizing the law. Little short of a major change in the verification system seems capable of halting their use.

The INS Los Angeles District office was building a sound program structure. A close study of INS program-building activities indicates that the Los Angeles District office was systematically building a sound, balanced regulatory program. It committed substantial resources to its employer sanctions program, considering that its resources were severely limited and that it had other enforcement obligations. The District office provided program balance, effectively structuring processes to accomplish the three regulatory tasks of education, monitoring, and sanctions. The District, as well as the central office, reflected an awareness of the importance of building supportive case law to buttress its regulatory agenda, selecting cases with thought and discipline.

The INS Los Angeles District office developed a strategy and enforcement tactics that were entirely consistent with the need to husband political support for the program. The Los Angeles District office moved into its new regulatory arena with caution and diplomacy. Rather than pursuing a punitive strategy, the District chose conciliation. It introduced sanctions through a staged policy. It continued education beyond the mandated period. INS staff were accessible, and investigative leaders emphasized the importance of developing good working relationships with the employer community. The INS has long wanted some regulatory hold over employers. IRCA offers that hold, and the INS was mindful of the possibility of losing it if its enforcement program engendered a political backlash. Finally, the reach of the independent Border Patrol did not extend much into the Los Angeles District, leaving district enforcement policy unchallenged by a differing approach.

The INS District office proved to be unexpectedly adaptable and able in this new endeavor. The District was successful in developing an unexpectedly strong enforcement framework for two reasons. INS investigative leaders welcomed the opportunity to shed the role of "cop" and assumed the mantle of "investigator"—a professional, who is responsible for working with employers, pursuing complex cases, and participating in litigation. They built an employer sanctions enforcement staff in that more professional image. Second, decentralization allowed the District Counsel and the assistant district director for investigations to build the enforcement program as they chose and to reject efforts to reintroduce more aggressive, adversarial tactics.

Los Angeles employers were more compliant with IRCA provisions than might be expected. Because undocumented labor plays such a significant role in the local economy, we expected compliance with IRCA requirements to be low in the absence of a strong and pervasive enforcement effort. Although enforcement cannot be characterized as strong and pervasive, compliance rates among the small sample of employers we interviewed nonetheless exceeded 50 percent. Apparently, the legalization programs (the agricultural program and the regular program), in combination with widespread use of counterfeit documents by undocumented workers, enabled many employers to comply with IRCA without suffering labor dislocations.

Early employer compliance rates do not predict future rates. Employer compliance is extremely sensitive to a variety of influences, many of which are subject to future change. Compliance may decline as INS education efforts decline, or if cheap, legal labor becomes scarce, and it may increase if enforcement becomes harsher.

Efforts to improve compliance through more visible, punitive sanctions risk generating a political backlash, especially in Los Angeles. Because a substantial segment of the Los Angeles economy depends on cheap immigrant labor and because the community has generally accepted its undocumented workforce, an escalation in sanctions is likely to create economic dislocations in service of a goal not strongly shared by the community. However, attitudes and, thus, tolerance of dislocations could change with the perception of some crisis related to uncontrolled immigration, permitting much more severe enforcement practices under the IRCA umbrella.

State and local governments did not contribute to INS enforcement efforts. Local political units have traditionally remained aloof from immigration policy, and IRCA did nothing to change that.

CONCLUSION

Although IRCA seems to have had some effect, cautious enforcement and the availability of counterfeit documents precluded a dramatic reduction in employment opportunities for undocumented workers in Los Angeles. These early results by no means signify that employer sanctions have failed. On the contrary, Los Angeles was building a viable regulatory mechanism with the infrastructure, policies, and experience to regulate a citizen population. It was building it cautiously, allowing the INS to preserve its authority for some future date, when situations and political attitudes may change sufficiently to empower the program with more resources, a solution to its documentation problem, and popular tolerance of the inevitable dislocations following more serious enforcement.

The lesson of the Los Angeles experience is that the INS can build an employer sanctions program and that the practice of employer regulation, when conducted appropriately, is acceptable even in a community as dependent on immigrant labor as Los Angeles.

Notes

1. See Muller and Espenshade, 1985, pp. 38–39. These numbers represent flows into the state and would be higher if immigrants already residing in California were included. The numbers are based on estimates from the 1970 and 1980 censuses corrected for the authors' estimates of those not counted who are assumed to be largely undocumented.

2. Data from *New Business Listings for 1989*, private communication.

3. The salary of an investigations agent started at $16,000, which is almost 50 percent less than salaries for similar positions with the Los Angeles Sheriff or Police Department.

4. Some other districts, after an initial period of strong commitment to the employer sanctions program, shifted priorities. For example, by the third year of the program, Houston had shifted a major share of its IRCA resources to investigating fraud in the amnesty applications of SAWs. See Fix and Hill, 1990, pp. 67–68.

5. Informal communication from the Los Angeles District office of the INS.

6. The new emphasis on deporting undocumented criminal aliens is a direct result of another IRCA provision, the MacKay Amendment, which requires the INS to remove criminal aliens from the United States expeditiously (see chapter 2 of this work, pp. 47–48.

7. We base our estimate of the number of business establishments in the District as reported by the Department of Commerce in 1985. These data are based on firms paying FICA at that time (U.S. Department of Commerce, 1984). Seventeen percent is considerably higher than the 3 percent of businesses the GAO reports have received visits nationwide (GAO, 1988b). Given the relative concentration of employers and the intensity of the District's educational effort, one is not surprised by the high percentage in Los Angeles. However, the District's definition of a "visit" includes very brief encounters in which agents simply drop off material at business establishments. This may help explain some of the difference.

8. We attempted to find a representative sample of firms from industries that tend to hire immigrants by drawing them from the Yellow Pages. However, difficulties finding willing respondents from this pool resulted in some self-selection and forced us to use trade association lists and referrals to gain access to some of the respondents. Consequently, our group is almost certainly biased toward the complying and the better-informed firms. We report these results because they still give a good flavor of the situation in Los Angeles.

9. This policy was introduced by Commissioner Alan C. Nelson and rescinded when he left office in September 1989. Our discussion deals with the period during which targets played a significant role in determining enforcement practices.

10. As a testament to decentralization in the INS, neighboring San Diego district continued to pursue the police model of routinely conducting confrontational floor sweeps to apprehend undocumented workers as an introduction to its inspection process.

11. Again, this estimate is based on *County Business Patterns* data from the U.S. Department of Commerce (1984). These data do not include many employers of domestic help and others who do not pay FICA. Thus, our estimates err on the high side.

12. As of our first interviews in February 1989, only one GAP inspection had led to an NIF.

13. However, some argue that these apparently "minor" infractions are, in fact, more significant, since the jobs may have been created for the alien in question, and since this type of lead offers almost the only avenue to undocumented skilled or semi-skilled immigrants.

14. "Egregious" paperwork violations include failure to fill out an I-9 form, failure to present the form to the agent requesting it, or failure to fill out Section 2, the employer review and verification.

15. The GAO has examined sanctions case files and confirmed that paperwork violations are typically not pressed if they do not relate to the presence of undocumented workers. Los Angeles Regional Office, private communication, June, 1989.

16. Among the firms visited, several had offices in other locations as well as Los Angeles and the visit occurred at another site. We have counted these as visits, since they served to heighten the firms' awareness of the program and to shape their perceptions regarding the likelihood of a visit in Los Angeles.

17. The INS has a particularly difficult time uncovering the sources of the forgeries. The agency apprehended its first producer in May 1990 in Los Angeles.

18. The INS reported that it was about to improve this situation by replacing existing documents with two hard-to-duplicate work authorization cards for immigrants. A national work authorization card for all residents eligible to work would also address this problem.

19. Estimates of the proportion of day laborers who are undocumented range from 20 to 80 percent ("Los Angeles Project Aids Illegal Aliens, in Challenge to U.S.," *The New York Times*, October 25, 1989, part B, p. 9). The INS sets the number at about two-thirds, leaving one-third who are documented and eligible to work.

20. This position was also taken by the Glendale City Council, which set up a hiring site at a local church. Prospective laborers very quickly overwhelmed the facility's capacity and the site has been closed, although the city is looking for a new, larger location. There is concern that the Los Angeles sites will suffer the same fate.

21. For a summary of the findings of seven studies that bear on this question, see GAO, 1990, pp. 103–106.

22. This was a survey conducted for The Los Angeles Times by Belden and Russonello Research and Communications of Washington, D.C.

23. These results are presented in GAO, 1990, p. 104. This survey was conducted between July 1988 and January 1989.

24. Other explanations are certainly as plausible. For example, these workers may come from new areas of Mexico and lack the networks that others have had to find them jobs.

References

Cheng, Lucie, and Tania Azores-Gunther. 1988. "Impacts of the 1986 Immigration Reform and Control Act on Asian Workers and Their Employers: A Final Report." Center for Pacific Rim Studies and Asian American Studies Center., University of California, Los Angeles, December.

Cornelius, Wayne A. 1989. "Impacts of the 1986 U.S. Immigration Law on Emigration from Rural Mexican Sending Communities." Population and Development Review, Vol. 15, No. 4, December.

The Field Institute. 1988. California Opinion Index. Fresno, Ca. July.

Fix, Michael, and Paul T. Hill. 1990. Enforcing Employer Sanctions: Challenges and Strategies. The RAND Coporation, JRI-04, and The Urban Institute, Report 90-6, May.

GAO (U.S. Government Accounting Office). 1990. Immigration Reform: Employer Sanctions and the Question of Discrimination. GAO/GGD-902D62. Washington, D.C., March.

_____. 1988a. Immigration Reform. GAO/GGD-89-16. Washington, D.C., November.

_____. 1988b. Immigration Control: A New Role for the Social Security Card. GAO/HRD-88-4. Washington, D.C., March.

Hernandez, Marita, and Stephen Braun. 1988. "Employers Wonder: INS, Where Is Thy Sting?" The Los Angeles Times, November 8, Part II, p. 1.

Mahoney, Roger. 1989. "Welcoming Immigrants and Entertaining Angels." The Los Angeles Times, January 15, part V, pp. 3 and 6.

Muller, Thomas, and Thomas J. Espenshade. 1985. The Fourth Wave, The Urban Institute Press, Washington, D.C.

Soja, Edward W., Allan D. Heskin, and Marco Cenzatti. 1985. Los Angeles Through the Kaleidoscope of Urban Restructuring. UCLA Graduate School of Architecture and Planning.

U.S. Department of Commerce. 1984. County Business Patterns. U.S. Department of Commerce, Office of Business Economics.

Chapter Five

THE SAVE PROGRAM: AN EARLY ASSESSMENT

Wendy Zimmermann

The 1986 Immigration Reform and Control Act (IRCA) reflects both inclusionary and exclusionary impulses in American immigration policy. On the one hand, the law contains the largest legalization program in recent history. On the other hand, it introduces a major new regime of employment regulation—employer sanctions—intended to discourage illegal immigration to the United States.

INTRODUCTION

No element of IRCA better reflects the law's exclusionary character than the provision that mandates national adoption of the Systematic Alien Verification for Entitlements or SAVE program. This provision requires that state agencies administering six federally funded benefit programs verify the immigration status of non-citizen applicants for benefits through an automated database developed by the Immigration and Naturalization Service (INS). The program's primary objective is to ensure that unauthorized (i.e., illegal) immigrants do not receive federal benefits. The sponsor of the provision, former Senator Paula Hawkins of Florida, has stated:

> The principle that underlies my amendment is simple: a person who has broken U.S. immigration laws and entered the country illegally should not have access to U.S. government benefits that are paid for by U.S. taxpayers.[1]

The story of SAVE is relevant to a broader discussion of IRCA and sanctions implementation in a number of ways. First, like sanctions, SAVE addresses the problem of illegal immigration by providing a disincentive to further entry of undocumented immigrants. Indeed, SAVE was often presented by INS personnel as only one element of a comprehensive effort (with sanctions and enhanced border controls) to deter illegal immigration.

Second, like sanctions, SAVE expands immigration policy and the jurisdiction of the INS far beyond its historic bounds. In the case of sanctions, the INS has found itself regulating the nation's employers and the hiring process. In the case of SAVE, the INS has found itself involved in the operation of the social welfare system and in the relationship between state and local governments and the clients of these welfare systems.

As a result, SAVE and sanctions have both led to tensions among the many parties involved in their operation, and their implementation has been slowed to some degree by a continuing search for legitimacy. Consequently, both have enjoyed limited success to date, at best.

Finally, SAVE represents an important test of a technology that was thought to be important to sanctions' future. SAVE's proponents believed that the technology it tested—automated verification of immigration status—would be used by employers and would therefore make sanctions more effective by reducing fraud and discrimination.

Debate over SAVE reveals the mixed imagery attached to undocumented immigrants during debate over IRCA. The undocumented immigrant was presented as a low-wage worker who demanded little in terms of benefits or working conditions and whose participation in the labor force displaced American workers or reduced wage levels. The other anti-immigrant image presented was that of an increasingly welfare-dependent population, fraudulently obtaining a range of public benefits.

Proponents of SAVE joined these opposing images by using the symbol of a horseshoe magnet when describing the two principal "pull factors" leading to illegal immigration to the United States: one pole of the magnet is jobs, the other is public benefits. Employer sanctions, IRCA's cornerstone and principal policy innovation, would reduce the power of the jobs magnet; SAVE would limit the draw of public benefits.

The development of this automated verification system should not be seen within the context of immigration policy alone. It should also be viewed within the framework of broader trends toward automated verification in welfare policy. These trends were introduced in the early 1980s in federal and state benefits programs in order to counteract fraud and reduce welfare expenditures (Greenberg and Wolf, 1986).

Viewed in this context, SAVE's basic design responds to some of the privacy and technological concerns of civil liberties and immigrant advocates who worried that computer errors would deprive individuals of important benefits to which they were entitled. For example, SAVE places the burden on the government agency, not the individual, to demonstrate that the applicant is ineligible for benefits. Furthermore, IRCA holds that the applicant will be considered "presumptively eligible" for benefits during the period when his or her immigration status is being determined.

SAVE must also be seen within the context of federalism, and specifically the use of federal mandates, as IRCA requires that all states participate in SAVE. Again, SAVE's lawmakers responded to state concerns over costs and intrusiveness by including a provision for waivers and a guarantee of full federal reimbursement.

As indicated above, SAVE's significance goes beyond its current, narrow application. While SAVE was designed to verify the immigration status of applicants for federally funded public benefits, its potential use extends to other areas, most notably verifying the immigration status of job applicants. This potential role for SAVE takes on added importance in light of the General Accounting Office's (GAO) finding that the employer sanctions provision of IRCA has caused a "widespread pattern of discrimination" (GAO, 1990). One frequently advocated approach to reducing discrimination is to simplify the employer's efforts to verify an applicant's work eligibility by creating an automated verification system such as SAVE.[2] Under this system the employer would call up a database that would provide him or her with information on a job applicant's employment eligibility. The purpose of this system would be to eliminate much of the confusion surrounding current efforts to check documents.

Focus of Study

Fieldwork for this report was conducted in New York, Miami, Chicago, San Antonio, Houston, El Paso, Los Angeles, and San Jose. Since policy decisions on implementing SAVE were made on the federal and state levels, the report will also focus on SAVE implementation issues in the states in which those eight cities are located. However, examination of certain issues requires a broader perspective, and will include discussion of problems related to the program in other states. Because it is early in the implementation process, it is difficult to draw conclusions on the ultimate cost-effectiveness of SAVE and on the long-term impacts of the program. This chapter will therefore focus on the issues that have arisen in the initial stages of implementation, and will highlight potential future issues. Finally, as indicated above, the implications of using an automated verification system such as SAVE for employment eligibility verification will be discussed in light of the debate over employer sanctions and ways to reduce discrimination.

BACKGROUND AND LEGISLATIVE HISTORY

While advocates of SAVE saw it as an inexpensive verification system that would deter undocumented immigration and save the government billions of dollars, critics saw it as a nationally mandated system with a faulty database that was not cost-effective and could keep eligible applicants from receiving benefits. True to the general balancing trend in IRCA, the critics' arguments led legislators to include in the provision protections for benefit applicants.

Proponents of the Provision

The INS was the key institutional advocate for including SAVE in IRCA. Alan Nelson, former Commissioner of the INS and the driving force behind SAVE, advocated it as a means of keeping undocumented immigrants from receiving public assistance, while saving federal dollars. In 1985, officials at the INS stated that SAVE would save the federal government 11 billion dollars a year (Purtell, 1986). This figure was contested, however, by states who had implemented pilot programs, leading the agency to reduce its savings estimate. In August 1986 Commissioner Nelson said,

> Successful implementation of SAVE is expected to result in an estimated federal-state cost avoidance of nearly 3 billion dollars annually, and act as a strong deterrent to illegal immigration to the United States. (Nelson, 1986)

These projected savings were based on the assumption that undocumented immigrants receive federal benefits at the same rate as other groups (Conner, 1982; Lamm and Imhoff, 1985), an assumption questioned by the program's opponents.

SAVE was introduced as an amendment to IRCA on the Senate floor by Senator Paula Hawkins (R-FL) in September 1985. Like Nelson, Hawkins saw SAVE as a companion to the employer sanctions provision that would deter undocumented immigration.

Proponents of SAVE saw it as a way to better enforce existing restrictions on benefit eligibility by strengthening existing verification systems or creating verification systems where none existed. Prior to IRCA, undocumented immigrants were already prohibited from receiving federal benefits under specific laws applicable to each of the benefit programs.[3] Most state agencies were also required to verify the immigration status of applicants for benefits. However, proponents of the SAVE program believed that these laws were not being enforced. A House Judiciary Committee Report from July 1986 states,

> Congress, by law, has specifically disqualified undocumented and nonimmigrant aliens from certain of these programs. Regrettably, Federal, state and local agencies have not taken adequate steps to enforce these prohibitions. The INS believes that significant numbers of ineligible aliens are receiving assistance and that a verification procedure for alien applicants will result in a considerable cost saving for the Federal Government. (U.S. House of Representatives, 1986)

SAVE provided a mechanism for uniformly enforcing these prohibitions across all states for all major federally funded benefit programs.

Advocates also claimed that SAVE would not be a costly system to implement for state and local governments, or for the federal government. Since the costs of implementing SAVE were to be fully reimbursed by the federal government, states would incur no costs. It was believed that the greatest expense would be start-up costs, such as installing a computer system or touch-tone telephones to gain access to the SAVE database. After initial set up, costs would be minimal and the savings from the program would outweigh the start-up costs.

In addition to generating savings at little cost, SAVE was also seen as a political trade-off for IRCA's generous and inclusionary legalization programs, in which undocumented immigrants who had been in the United States for at least five years and agricultural workers who had worked for at least 90 days could legalize their status. Individuals legalized under these programs were not eligible for most federal benefits for five years from the date of achieving legal temporary residency. SAVE would provide a verification system to ensure that those individuals becoming legalized under IRCA would not in fact receive the benefits for which they had been deemed ineligible.

Opposition to SAVE

Opposition to SAVE cut across the political spectrum, coming from immigrant advocacy groups, the American Civil Liberties Union (ACLU), the Department of Health and Human Services, and even from within the Reagan administration. Three concerns dominated: 1) the cost-effectiveness of the system for all states, 2) the quality of the INS database, and 3) privacy issues. In its final form, the provision took into account each of these concerns.

Cost-Effectiveness. Since SAVE's purpose is to keep undocumented immigrants from receiving federally funded benefits for which they are not eligible, cost-effectiveness depends largely on the extent to which undocumented immigrants apply for those benefits. Studies documenting comparatively low welfare participation rates by both documented and undocumented immigrants suggested to critics of SAVE that the program would not be cost-effective. A study conducted by Marta Tienda and Leif Jensen found that "immigrants were, other things equal, considerably less likely than natives to become welfare recipients" (Tienda and Jensen, 1986). A study by Thomas Muller and Thomas Espenshade confirmed this view. The authors found that "Los Angeles County spent an average of $437 per Mexican immigrant household in 1980, compared with $492 per household for all households in the county" (Muller and Espenshade, 1985, p. 137). One study that differentiates between documented and undocumented immigrants found that the taxes paid to the state of Texas by undocumented immigrants exceed the costs to the state to provide those same individuals with public services (Weintraub and Cardenas, 1984). Other researchers have found that undocumented immigrants use public services at an even lower rate than documented immigrants (North, 1983; Heer, 1990). Based on these and other studies, critics felt that SAVE would not be cost-effective and would create increased labor for state agencies without resulting in significant savings.

Another issue related to the law's cost-effectiveness is implementing SAVE in states with small immigrant and undocumented immigrant populations. According to figures from the 1980 Census, 80.8 percent of all undocumented immigrants live in five states: Texas, California, Florida, New York, and Illinois (Passel and Woodrow, 1984).

Critics also argued that many states already had effective verification systems in place and that changing to a new one would generate unnecessary costs and few benefits.

Two provisions were included in SAVE that were designed to overcome concerns about SAVE's cost-effectiveness and respond to a government-wide interest in federalism and the deference to the states it implied. First, state agencies were to be reimbursed by their federal counterparts for 100 percent of the costs of operating and implementing SAVE. Second, to allay concerns over SAVE's mandatory nature, the Education and Labor Committee of the U.S. House of Representatives introduced amendments providing for the program Secretaries to issue waivers under certain circumstances (U.S. House of Representatives, 1986b, p. 15). As finally enacted, this waiver provision permitted the Secretaries of the federal departments to waive participation in SAVE for the entire department or for specific states or localities if an equally cost-effective system was in place, or if the costs of SAVE exceeded the projected savings.

Quality of INS Database. The quality of the INS database is another concern that has remained an issue throughout SAVE's implementation. Senator Alan Simpson (R-WY) opposed the program, questioning, "whether the technology is actually efficient [sic] at this time to avoid mistaken denials of assistance benefits."[4] In addition, the House Judiciary Committee stated in its July 1986 report that the Committee had concerns "related to perceived inadequacies of the INS' data base and the potential misuse of the information available through the verification procedure" (U.S. House of Representatives, 1986a, p. 67).

The requirement that all records be checked manually as well as automatically before an applicant for benefits is denied on the basis of immigration status is a response to fears that the database would provide inadequate or incorrect information. Manual or secondary verification, included largely as a result of Representative Barney Frank's (D-MA) efforts, ensures that no denials are based solely on the information received from the SAVE database. According to the law, public agencies must wait for a response from the INS after conducting manual verification before terminating benefits based on immigration status. Thus, all applicants are presumptively eligible for the benefit for which they are applying until manual verification of their immigration status is obtained from the INS. The law also provides for a fair hearing process in the event of a denial of benefits. To protect the states from responsibility for errors in the database, the law stipulates that states are not liable for any errors committed in determining eligibility in compliance with SAVE.

Privacy Issues. Confidentiality issues were a primary concern of opponents, since SAVE moves information on immigration status, previously available only to the INS, closer to the public sphere by making it available to state and local benefits-issuing agencies. Opponents were concerned that information on immigrants obtained by the INS through SAVE would be used by the INS for enforcement and deportation purposes.

Fears that SAVE information would be used for purposes other than determining benefits eligibility arose from earlier INS use of SAVE information for enforcement purposes. During the influx of Cubans and Haitians to southern Florida after 1980, the INS had issued work authorizations uniformly to Cuban and Haitian entrants. In 1984 the INS revoked the authorizations without advance notice. At that time the Florida Department of Labor and Employment Security was conducting a SAVE pilot. Those Cuban and Haitian entrants who applied for unemployment compensation were verified through SAVE. The INS followed up information obtained through this process to contact the individuals and revoke their work authorizations.

A lawsuit arose from the incident, *Agustin v. Harrison*,[5] which resulted in the INS agreeing not to use SAVE data for this enforcement purpose.[6] This lawsuit led to IRCA prohibiting the INS from using information gained through SAVE for administrative immigration enforcement (i.e., deportation). However, the law stipulates that if any information obtained through SAVE indicates criminal misuse of documents, the INS may investigate for fraud. The law also mandates that the verification system "protect the individual's privacy to the maximum degree possible."[7]

In sum, nearly every concern raised regarding the system was met with a legislative response. Cost concerns resulted in 100 percent reimbursement for states by federal agencies. Federalism and cost-effectiveness concerns resulted in the inclusion of the waiver provision. Privacy concerns were met with the requirement that no information gained through SAVE could be used for purposes of administrative enforcement. Concerns over the quality of the database that might result in unfair denials of benefits led to the manual verification requirement and the rule that applicants were presumptively eligible for benefits until their immigration status was verified. However, the extent to which these provisions provided adequate protection to those individuals and agencies affected by SAVE would depend on the way in which the law was implemented.

THE SAVE SYSTEM

The SAVE provision requires states to verify the immigration status of non-citizen applicants for six federally funded benefit programs. These benefit programs are Aid to Families with Dependent Children (AFDC), Medicaid, food stamps, unemployment compensation, federal housing programs, and Title IV educational assistance programs.[8] The federal agencies that administer these programs are, respectively, the Department of Health and Human Services, the Department of Agriculture, the Department of Labor, the Department of Housing and Urban Development, and the Department of Education.

Section 121 of IRCA states that all applicants for the designated benefits must sign a form declaring under law that they are either a U.S. citizen or a non-citizen in a legal immigration status. If the applicant declares U.S. citizenship, he/she is not verified through SAVE and continues with the standard benefit application process. If the applicant declares legal non-citizen status, he/she must present documentation proving legal status, which is then verified through SAVE.

The law also states that if the non-citizen applies without sufficient documentation, participating agencies must provide the applicant with a reasonable opportunity to submit evidence indicating his/her legal immigration status. The agency may not delay, deny, reduce, or terminate eligibility on the basis of the applicant's immigration status until a reasonable opportunity to present documentation has been provided.

SAVE is made up of two verification procedures. Primary, or automated, verification of immigration status involves transmitting information to and receiving data back from an automated database, the Alien Status Verification Index (ASVI). Secondary, or manual, verification involves copying an applicant's documents and forwarding them to the district level of the INS where other databases and hard copy files are reviewed.

The Alien Status Verification Index (ASVI) database contains files on over 23.5 million immigrants and was created solely for the SAVE system. It is a "read only" database; its data cannot be altered directly. It is a subset of a larger INS database, the Central Index System (CIS), which can be updated and altered by over 8,500 INS employees throughout the United States.[9] An updated version of this subset of CIS, or ASVI, is sent every two weeks to the Martin Marietta Corporation in Orlando, Florida, where the ASVI database is maintained.[10]

PILOTS AND PRE-EXISTING PROGRAMS

Unlike IRCA's other major programs—legalization, employer sanctions, and State Legalization Impact Assistance Grants (SLIAG)—the SAVE program could draw on the experience of a number of pilot tests that predated the law's enactment, as well as the experience of a number of states that had institutionalized SAVE or programs similar to it. It is important to bear in mind that IRCA did not create the SAVE program. Rather, the law mandated its national adoption. Prior to the passage of IRCA, six states had formal agreements with the INS to use SAVE: Idaho, Montana, Illinois, Florida, Indiana, and Colorado, as well as Puerto Rico and the Virgin Islands. A number of states had conducted SAVE pilots, but the cost-effectiveness data on these programs vary greatly according to which agency, the state or the INS, is reporting it.

A Colorado SAVE pilot program in unemployment compensation found that in fiscal year 1985, only 17 of a total of 147,000 noncitizen applicants for AFDC or food stamps were ineligible for such benefits. The state estimated savings from the program at approximately $3,000 and costs at approximately $10,500 (U.S. House of Representatives, 1986a). The INS estimated savings for approximately the same period at $426,060 (U.S. House of Representatives, 1986c).

Florida's SAVE pilot program for unemployment compensation began in 1984. Florida found the participation rate of ineligible aliens in unemployment compensation was 0.2 percent, and the savings did not exceed the costs of implementing the program (U.S. House of Representatives, 1986d). The INS claimed that between October 1985 and March 1986, savings from the Florida SAVE program for AFDC, unemployment compensation, and food stamps amounted to $3,688,633 (U.S. House of Representatives, 1986c).

The New York Department of Labor conducted a three-month pilot project in 1985 during which it found that .04 percent of the alien unemployment compensation claims were overpaid. It estimated these overpayments at $51,722, but did not estimate costs of the verification process. As a result of the pilot, the N.Y. Department of Labor did not favor implementing the program. The INS found that between October 1985 and March 1986, the New York SAVE program for AFDC, unemployment compensation, and Medicaid generated total savings of $925,157.

The Illinois Department of Employment Security got favorable results from its pilot, begun in 1984. Its estimated maximum savings in 1984 for unemployment compensation was $53 million. This figure, however, is inflated since savings were estimated by calculating average weekly benefits for the maximum possible receipt period for each individual denied.

The Illinois state welfare office, the Illinois Department of Public Aid (IDPA), also conducted a SAVE pilot program, finding that .07 percent of all applicants for AFDC and Medicaid were denied benefits due to SAVE. IDPA found this number of denials too small to make the system cost-effective.

Despite the meager results reported by the above state agencies, the INS maintained that SAVE was cost-effective. The INS Annual Report for fiscal year 1986 stated:

> The SAVE Program identified 49,817 unentitled aliens resulting in a savings of $101 million to the administering agencies. . . . SAVE is recognized as a cost-effective means of preserving the integrity of entitlement programs. . . (INS, 1987, p. 5)

EARLY EVIDENCE OF SAVE'S COST-EFFECTIVENESS

The cost-effectiveness of SAVE is difficult to measure at this stage of implementation for a number of reasons. First, implementation has not yet begun, or has only recently begun, in a number of states. Second, the data that have been collected on savings are not always accurate and reliable. Third, gauging incremental savings from SAVE is difficult because of difficulties in estimating the savings from agencies' previous verification systems.

Problems in Reporting Cost-Effectiveness

SAVE's cost-effectiveness, of central concern during the debate to include SAVE in IRCA, is difficult to measure because of the scarcity of cost-benefit analyses that have been conducted by state or federal agencies implementing SAVE or by the INS. While the pre-passage debate over SAVE focused largely on the costs and savings of the program, since its implementation surprisingly little accurate and systematic tracking of costs and savings has been conducted. Although agencies issuing unemployment compensation have kept track of costs and estimated savings, these figures may be inflated and do not accurately reflect denials due solely to SAVE. For the AFDC, Medicaid, and food stamp programs, only the Texas Department of Human Services has conducted a cost-benefit analysis, and its results have been questioned by the federal agencies involved. Numerous public agency respondents from the other states said that they were not planning on conducting cost-benefit analyses, because they were not required to do so by law and doing so would add unnecessary labor.

Only the General Accounting Office (GAO) was required by law to report on the implementation of SAVE, but these reports did not include an analysis of cost-effectiveness.[11] Although IRCA required each federal agency responsible for administering the programs to report to Congress by April 1, 1988 on whether the verification system was cost-effective, none of the federal agencies was mandated to record cost-effectiveness after the date of required implementation, October 1, 1988.[12]

Delayed implementation has also contributed to the lack of cost-benefit analyses. For many agencies, it is simply too early in the implementation process to determine cost-effectiveness. Although according to the law SAVE was to be implemented in full by all states on October 1, 1988, many agencies have yet to implement the system. Some agencies have not yet implemented because they are awaiting waiver decisions, or have only recently received the decision. Other state agencies that administer AFDC and Medicaid have delayed implementation because of a lack of regulations from the Department of Health and Human Services. One respondent said, "We've been waiting for implementing regulations for over two years, but they're [HHS] still breathing down our back to implement."

OVERSTATED SAVINGS IN UNEMPLOYMENT COMPENSATION

In each of the five states in which we conducted fieldwork, agencies administering unemployment compensation kept track of estimated savings. Only in Texas were savings tracked for AFDC, Medicaid, and food stamps.[13] This discrepancy can be attributed to SAVE's better established history in verifying status for unemployment compensation and to the Department of Labor's administration of the SAVE program. Since agencies issuing unemployment compensation have been using SAVE longer than the other agencies, they are more familiar with the program.

The cost-benefit analyses conducted by the agencies issuing unemployment compensation produced data that tend to overstate savings. For example, the Florida Department of Labor and Employment Security estimated that from October 1985 through September 1988, $1.17 million in unemployment compensation payments were denied to 790 individuals disqualified because of immigration status. This dollar figure was calculated according to average benefits paid to all individuals in one year. However, most recent immigrants earn less than the average income and therefore would receive lower unemployment compensation payments than the average individual (Tienda and Jensen, 1986). Thus, the figures are inflated by estimating savings according to the average recipient, not the average immigrant recipient of benefits.

In addition, the number of individuals denied benefits may be inflated because it includes individuals who were ineligible for the benefit for other reasons. For example, an applicant for unemployment compensation who was denied the benefit because of immigration status would also have been denied if his status had not been verified because he/she had not worked enough hours to earn compensation, or because the wages he/she earned were ineligible according to the program's criteria. Hence, an unknown number of individuals included in those denied unemployment compensation because of immigration status would have been denied the benefit for other reasons. This too would inflate the amount of potential savings.

According to several respondents, much of the savings in unemployment compensation is temporary. The estimated savings figures include payments to individuals who were in a legal immigration status at the time they applied for benefits but who had been in an illegal or ineligible status at the time they earned some or all of the wages for which they were collecting compensation. Many of these individuals have obtained legal status under the IRCA legalization provisions. Hence, the savings attributed to SAVE are transitory, since these individuals will eventually be eligible for unemployment compensation benefits. As one agency respondent said, "In theory, SAVE won't be necessary after a couple of years because so many of these guys are legal now. They were just out of status [in an illegal immigration status] when they accrued their compensation."

Claims for the overall cost-effectiveness of SAVE were further thrown into doubt when the Texas Department of Human Services applied for a waiver from the program. The request was based on cost-benefit analyses that found that the costs of implementing SAVE exceeded the savings generated by the program for AFDC, Medicaid, and food stamps. The state agency's letter to the Department of Health and Human Services and to the Department of Agriculture stated,

> For Food Stamps the ratio for 1989 is 1 to .48, or that for each dollar spent on SAVE, a maximum of 48 cents could be recovered. The Food Stamp ratio for 1990 is 1 to .45. The AFDC ratios for 1989 and 1990 are 1 to .66 and 1 to .62 respectively. In all situations, more money would be spent in recovering the benefits in error than could possibly be recovered.[14]

However, HHS claims that these data are not significant because they are based on a sample of cases not statistically large enough to prove cost-ineffectiveness. For this reason, Texas was issued a conditional waiver for participation in SAVE for AFDC and Medicaid.[15]

Another reason that SAVE's cost-effectiveness may be exaggerated is because the INS credits the program with savings that are generated by independent INS investigations and not by SAVE. That is, if an INS investigator apprehends someone who also happens to have been illegally receiving benefits, any estimated savings are attributed to the SAVE program.

These reporting practices led numerous public agency respondents to argue that savings were often inflated by both agency and INS estimates. One public agency respondent said, the "INS is publicly misrepresenting the importance and usefulness of the SAVE database to Florida."

Commenting on the lack of data on SAVE's cost-effectiveness, an official from the INS Northern region stated:

> With regard to the cost-effectiveness of SAVE, our field offices doing secondary verification used to have data on the type of benefit denied and were reporting that through the record system. That reporting requirement has been deleted. The federal oversight agencies were going to monitor the effectiveness of SAVE. The state people were concerned that they were going to have to do 5 or 6 separate reports to federal agencies; they wanted one report. They aren't doing the monitoring. So we're going to be in the unenviable position of not having data to show how good it is.

Critics and supporters of the system lack evidence to support arguments in favor of either retaining or modifying the system. Furthermore, in considering using SAVE for purposes such as employment verification, the absence of data will make careful review more difficult.

SAVE's deterrent effect is impossible to measure, as there is no way to quantify savings from individuals with counterfeit documentation who learn of the existence of an automated verification system, or who apply for a benefit and see that their documentation will be checked, so subsequently retract their application.[16] The INS estimates that this deterrent effect is responsible for a large proportion of the savings. While it is true that SAVE may have had a deterrent effect on ineligible immigrants applying for benefits, its magnitude should take into account incremental savings. Where documents were being verified using pre-existing state or local systems prior to SAVE, ineligible applicants may also have been deterred.

Another issue in assessing cost-effectiveness is the "citizenship loophole," or the possibility that an applicant will claim U.S. citizenship in order to bypass the verification system altogether. Since SAVE only verifies the status of non-citizen applicants, any applicant who declares U.S. citizenship circumvents the system. It is possible for an undocumented or ineligible immigrant to falsely claim U.S. citizenship and successfully apply for a benefit. As one INS respondent stated, "Everybody will tell you that the biggest problem with SAVE is that all you have to do to get around it is make a false claim of citizenship."

Estimating Incremental Savings

In analyzing SAVE's effectiveness it is important not only to examine the quality of the SAVE verification system, but to compare SAVE's effectiveness with that of an agency's previously existing verification system. Prior to IRCA, all states were required to verify the immigration status of applicants for most federally funded benefits. While most states did not have both automated and manual verification systems, nearly all had some kind of verification process in place. In California, for example, caseworkers not only checked for documents, some were trained to detect fraudulent documents. In Los Angeles, caseworkers issuing AFDC and Medicaid examined documents under a black light to detect fraud (The Urban Institute, 1988, p. 50). When an applicant's documents were questionable, or when an applicant did not present identification, he/she was referred to the local INS office.

A food stamps administrator responded, "Our system that we had before was just as good. Before, we just checked the documents ourselves, and if they were questionable then we contacted the INS."

The Special Case of Unemployment Compensation

Officials from state employment security offices, although not always enthusiastic about SAVE, were consistently more optimistic about its effectiveness than were officials from agencies administering AFDC, Medicaid, and food stamps. For example, an administrator of Medicaid and AFDC in Texas said, "Most of us familiar with SAVE know it's not cost-effective and our major concern was cost-effectiveness. But we're still required to do it." At the same time, administrators of unemployment compensation in Texas reported identifiable savings of nearly $36,000 in a two-month period in San Antonio.

These responses from the field are consistent with the GAO study that reported on expected benefits from SAVE. The March 1989 GAO report found that "state UC [unemployment compensation] program offices expected the greatest benefits from using SAVE" (GAO, 1989). That study showed that nearly 55 percent of the unemployment compensation programs that were using SAVE expected the system to either greatly or somewhat improve their verification efforts, and 17 percent expected little or no improvement. For food stamps, AFDC, Medicaid, and adult assistance programs, only 23 percent expected somewhat or great improvement and 49 percent expected little or no improvement.

One possible explanation for the greater savings in unemployment compensation is greater use of that public service by undocumented immigrants. David North found that despite an overall below average usage of income-transfer or benefit programs, "the unemployment insurance utilization rates for the small group in California were above the national norm" (North, 1983). Thus, if undocumented immigrants use unemployment compensation at a higher rate than they use other public services, the Department of Labor stands to benefit more from SAVE than do other federal agencies. In fact, higher use of this benefit may reflect the fact that undocumented immigrants had previously worked in covered employment, often under a false social security number. Thus, the "savings" to the unemployment compensation fund may come from workers who had been working, albeit illegally, and contributing to the fund for some time.

PROBLEMS WITH THE DATABASE

One obstacle to the successful implementation of SAVE is the ASVI data base. The 1989 Justice Department Audit of the INS found inaccurate data in the Central Index, from which ASVI is drawn:

> Our review of 84 adjustments of status cases from the Dallas Regional Service Center and the San Francisco District Office revealed that 17.4 percent of the data are missing or incorrect. (U.S. Justice Department, 1989, p. 26)

Although the database has improved over the past few years, there are still missing and inaccurate data. The central problems with ASVI are the omission of certain classes of immigrants from the database, such as refugees, and the lack of key information in the automated responses received by the agencies. These problems result in an increased number of manual verifications, which include copying the document presented by the applicant and mailing it with the document verification request form to the local INS office. While the INS is verifying the document, the applicant is presumptively eligible to continue receiving the benefit. Since this aspect of SAVE is the most costly and time-consuming, these problems affect SAVE's cost-effectiveness.

In states with large numbers of refugees, including Florida and Illinois, gaps in the database are causing benefits issuing agencies to initiate a high percentage of manual verifications, also decreasing cost-effectiveness. For example, refugees and Cuban-Haitian entrants who have recently entered the United States are often missing from the ASVI database. Since these individuals are often eligible for AFDC, Medicaid, and food stamps, agencies are having to conduct a large number of manual verifications. According to an INS official, to resolve this problem some refugees will soon be added to the database when their application for refugee status is approved, *prior to* entering the United States. Other immigrants who are not on the database but who may be eligible for certain benefits are those considered PRUCOL, "permanently residing under color of law."[17] This status is not officially recognized by the INS and many of these individuals do not have alien registration numbers. Their eligibility for various public benefits, however, has been recognized by the courts. For these reasons, there are no plans to enter them onto the database and those applicants must undergo manual verification. Therefore, states with large numbers of individuals who fall into this category incur costs associated with conducting manual verifications.

Public agency respondents also claimed that there were key elements not included in the response from ASVI that are necessary in order to determine benefits eligibility. The class of admission code, which denotes an individual's immigration status, e.g., refugee, asylee, or legal permanent resident, is one of the most important elements in the ASVI response.[18] This information is often missing from the response received by the agency because it was not entered into the database when the individual's record was created. This omission is possible because the class of admission code is not a required element in the Central Index System, the larger INS database from which the ASVI database is taken. Thus, when an immigration official creates a record on an immigrant in the Central Index, the class of admission may not be included in the data file because it is optional. In these instances the public agencies must institute manual verification in order to verify immigration status, again limiting cost-effectiveness.

Another element missing from ASVI affects only applications for unemployment compensation. While the ASVI response includes a statement of work authorization, it does not contain the date on which the individual received that work authorization, needed for determination of unemployment compensation eligibility. Thus, when an immigrant applies for unemployment compensation and he/she is verified through SAVE, the response to the agency may indicate that the individual is authorized to work at the time of application. However, it does not indicate if the individual was authorized when he/she worked and accrued the unemployment compensation. The agency then has to institute manual verification to determine if the applicant was authorized for employment at the time that he/she actually worked, and not just at the time of application.

Most public agency representatives agree that the ASVI database has improved since the start of SAVE implementation in 1988. While the percentage of manual or secondary verifications has not decreased significantly (approximately 15 percent of automated verifications require manual verification), the manual verification component of SAVE provides the INS with a mechanism for updating the database. As immigration status verifiers process requests for manual verification from public agencies, they also update the database.

An INS internal study on manual verification that sampled 50 percent of the file control offices in the first nine months of 1989 found that during that time period, 6,879 files were updated as a result of manual verifications. If this figure is representative of the updating that occurs at all INS file control offices at all times, approximately 26,000 files would have been updated as a result of the SAVE program from October 1988 to March 1990. Improving the INS database has become a top priority for the INS, and SAVE provides a systematic way for the INS to do so. Nonetheless, 26,000 updated files has only a limited impact on a database with over 23 million files.

The problems with the ASVI database are of central importance to the quality of the verification system. Cost-effectiveness of SAVE depends largely on a high percentage of automated verifications that do not require manual verification. The more complete the ASVI database, the more cost-effective SAVE becomes.

SLIAG REIMBURSEMENT

Another way in which SAVE is being used represents a intersection with the State Legalization Impact Assistance Grant (SLIAG) provision of IRCA. The ASVI database is used to keep track of costs incurred by immigrants legalizing their status through IRCA's general legalization program. This cost documentation system (CDS) assists states in claiming costs reimbursable by the federal government. Twenty-four states, including California, Florida, New York, Texas, and Illinois, have recently begun to use ASVI for tracking costs reimbursable with SLIAG funds.

This cost documentation system was developed by the Department of Health and Human Services in conjunction with the INS and Martin Marietta. It matches the state agency's client tape of individuals who have used services with the ASVI database to determine the number of eligible legal aliens (ELAs) who have received those benefits reimbursable under SLIAG and the cost per ELA. The tapes are sent to Martin Marietta, where records are matched by Alien Registration number (A-number) and by social security number. A-numbers that begin with 90 are generally, but not always, legalization applicants. If the A-number or social security number of an individual on the agency's tape appears in the ASVI database, the status code is checked. If this code indicates that the individual is an ELA, then the estimated dollar amount associated with the individual is recorded. The agencies provide Martin Marietta with a cost per user. This way Martin Marietta sends the agency back the estimated dollar amounts spent on legalizing aliens.

However, the same problems that exist in ASVI and affect the verification of eligibility for benefits also affect the accuracy of the cost documentation system. Not all individuals who have applied for or achieved legalization are in the ASVI database. The delays in processing those applications affect the speed with which those individuals are entered into the Central Index. A New York State agency official said that there is a fear of undercount, where the cost documentation system would count fewer ELAs than are actually using the service because of the incompleteness of the database.

It is ironic that SAVE, which was developed to reduce federal expenditures, should be turned to by the states as a way to secure federal reimbursement for their own spending on legalizing aliens.

USE OF SAVE TO VERIFY EMPLOYMENT ELIGIBILITY

In March 1990, the GAO released its third annual report on IRCA's employer sanctions provisions. The principal finding of the report— that IRCA has given rise to "a widespread pattern of discrimination"—has led some to propose an automated verification system like SAVE as a means of reducing employment discrimination. Indeed, proposals for conducting demonstration projects on automated verification have been introduced in Congress. Senator Alan Simpson (R-WY) has introduced a bill that, in his words:

> requires the Attorney General and the Secretary of Health and Human Services to conduct demonstration projects to determine whether a computerized call-in worker verification system would be the most effective means of determining whether someone is authorized to be employed in the United States.[19]

IRCA also provides for the development of a telephone verification pilot to determine work eligibility.[20] The INS has planned to implement such a pilot using the SAVE database, in which employers would verify the immigration status of newly hired employees. The pilot program, which will involve nine employers, is scheduled to begin once an executive order is issued giving the INS authority over the implementation of the project.[21]

The telephone verification pilot as planned by the INS would operate almost identically to the way in which SAVE is used for verifying eligibility for benefits. As in the SAVE program, employees would have to sign a declaration form swearing that they were either citizens or non-citizens legally eligible to work. This kind of system would therefore only verify the work eligibility of non-citizen employees.

After hiring an applicant, the employer would gain access to the ASVI database using a touch-tone telephone or a point-of-sale device (such as those used for credit card sales), and then enter the A-number of the non-citizen employee. The employer would then receive information such as the name of the employee, a verification number, and an employment eligibility statement. The employer would compare the document submitted by the employee with the information received from ASVI, and if any discrepancies existed between the two, he/she would institute manual verification. The employer would also initiate manual verification if the ASVI response indicated to "institute secondary verification."

If an applicant had to undergo secondary, or manual verification, the employer would be required to wait until a response was received from the INS before taking any action based on immigration status. Just as agencies must continue issuing benefits, the employer could not delay, deny, or terminate employment on the basis of immigration status until receiving a response from the INS.

Supporters of an automated database for employment verification argue that if an employer could verify an employee's documents and be confident that the employee was in fact in a legal immigration status, the employer would be less likely to discriminate against foreign-looking or sounding individuals who might be illegal. Under current law, employers are not required to verify the authenticity of documents presented by employees, and if they comply with the law in good faith, they are not held responsible for having accepted fraudulent documents. If they suspect a document to be false, they may contact the INS and verify the document.

Problems

While it is true that automated verification of employment eligibility may give employers increased confidence in the documents they receive from employees, this type of verification system, as currently planned in the telephone verification pilot, may not reduce discrimination, and could in fact cause discrimination for a number of reasons. First, it is a requirement of the pilot that the employer only conduct the verification after the employee has been hired. However, the possibility exists for an employer to use the verification system before hiring an applicant as a screening mechanism for certain foreign-looking or sounding individuals. If the automated response does not come back affirmative, the employer may choose not to hire that applicant based only on the information received from the database, which, as previously discussed, is not completely accurate or complete.

Second, the absence of an audit mechanism to monitor whom the employers verify also leaves open opportunities for discrimination. No system has been planned to ensure that employers verify every non-citizen they hire, as is required in the pilot. Thus, an employer could verify only those he/she suspects are illegal. In addition, although the law requires that employers not take any action against an employee until the results of the manual verification have been received, no audit system is planned to ensure that employers follow these regulations.

Third, as planned, the program would cost employers a small fee per verification, giving the employer incentive to not hire an applicant whom he/she would have to pay to verify. If only non-citizens will be verified through the system, it will be less expensive for employers to hire citizens. This pilot could therefore result in discrimination against all non-citizens.

Since about 15 percent of automated verifications require the more expensive process of manual verification, a national employment eligibility system such as this would result in high costs for the INS, which conducts the manual searches.

Another potential problem with this type of verification system is that the same citizenship loophole that exists in SAVE for verification of benefits eligibility would exist when using a SAVE-like system for verification of employment eligibility. Undocumented immigrants could claim to be citizens and show only, for example, a fraudulent social security card and driver's license. They would then bypass the automated verification system altogether, just as non-citizen applicants currently can, under penalty of perjury, by swearing to be a U.S. citizen when applying for benefits. The prevalence of fraudulent social security cards and driver's licenses would cause this loophole to severely limit the effectiveness of such a verification system.

A system that uses the ASVI database is limited to verifying only those people with A-numbers. Therefore, this verification system could not be used to verify the employment eligibility status of all employees, citizens and non-citizens. To verify the documents of citizen employees, another automated system, such as one in which social security numbers were verified, would have to be used in conjunction with the SAVE-like verification system. Another possibility would be to verify all employees or applicants with a social security number verification system. However, these other systems of verification would raise a new set of issues requiring further examination.

CONCLUSIONS AND ISSUES FOR THE FUTURE

Although it is early in the SAVE implementation process, certain issues have arisen that raise questions about the program's effectiveness, its impacts, and the potential for using such a system for employment verification. Cost-effectiveness was a central concern to legislators in the debate before the passage of IRCA. Because it is difficult to monitor the effectiveness of sanctions in deterring illegal immigration, it is both difficult and expensive to monitor the effectiveness of SAVE. Consequently, little systematic evaluation of the costs and savings from the program has been done either by the INS or by federal or state agencies. Where cost-benefit analyses have been conducted, there are problems with the data that tend to inflate savings and make conclusions regarding cost-effectiveness difficult.

Overall, the program that has claimed the greatest success from SAVE is the Department of Labor's unemployment compensation program. Most respondents from agencies administering AFDC, Food Stamps, and Medicaid expressed less satisfaction with SAVE, and preliminary data indicate that costs may exceed savings for those programs. As state agencies progress in the implementation process and more data become available, it is possible that requests for waivers from agencies administering these programs could increase in the future.

The issuing of waivers to state agencies has raised questions about the role of the states in implementing a federal program and about the effects of national immigration policy on federal-state dynamics. The recent issuing of "conditional waivers," requiring states to implement SAVE and compare its effectiveness to the current verification system, is an example of an unanticipated provision that tends to defeat the federalism goals of SAVE's framers. In addition, the waiver issue highlights the increased interaction among the INS, the Department of Health and Human Services, and other federal agencies implementing SAVE. Immigration officers have become more involved in the benefits issuing process, while public agency workers have become more involved in immigration status verification and the effort to combat fraud.

SAVE has also had impacts on the INS and on other federal agencies that may not have been anticipated when implementation began. SAVE has provided the INS with a systematic way to collect information on fraudulent documents and potentially enhance enforcement of other immigration laws, such as deportation. The SAVE database, ASVI, is also being used by states to track costs related to IRCA's legalization programs that are reimbursable through SLIAG, ironically bringing costs rather then savings to the federal government.

The GAO finding that employer sanctions caused a widespread pattern of discrimination has sparked debate over how to create a secure system for verifying employment eligibility. As a result, automated verification of immigration status, clearly not limited to the area of benefits eligibility, has gained renewed interest on the part of lawmakers. The issues that have arisen in examining the implementation of SAVE shed light on the implications of using an automated verification system like SAVE in employment. While automatically verifying employment eligibility may increase employers' confidence in those documents that are verified, "false negatives" could result in expensive or manual searches or improper denials of employment. At the same time, if employers verify only foreign-sounding and -looking job candidates, such a practice could itself be construed as discriminatory.

Notes

1. *Congressional Record*, S.11414, September 13, 1985.

2. "Employer Sanctions Improvements Amendments of 1990," S.2446, April 5, 1990. See also chapter 11 of this volume, and Stein, 1990.

3. For the law on housing assistance, see Pub. Law No. 96-399; 42 U.S.C. Sect. 1436a. For unemployment compensation, see 1976 Amendments to the Internal Revenue Code. For Aid to Families with Dependent Children (AFDC), see 45 C.F.R. sect. 233.50; 42 U.S.C. Sect 602(a)(33). For Medicaid, see Pub. Law No. 99-509, codified at 42 U.S.C. Sect. 1396a. For food stamps, see 7 C.F.R. Sect. 273.4(d).
Other categories of immigrants may be ineligible for federal benefits depending on the administering agency's definition of the term "permanently residing under color of law" (PRUCOL). Immigrant categories that fall under PRUCOL include individuals who have filed for adjustment of status, individuals granted a stay of deportation, and individuals for whom an immediate relative petition has been filed or approved. Nonimmigrants, such as tourists who are admitted on a temporary basis, are also prohibited from receiving federal benefits.

4. *Congressional Record*, S.11414, September 13, 1985.

5. No. 86-0882-CIV-Marcus (S.D. Fla. September 29, 1986).

6. *Interpreter Releases*, December 8, 1986, Washington, D.C.: Federal Publications Inc., p. 1142.

7. Immigration Reform and Control Act of 1986, Section 121.

8. Programs administered by the Social Security Administration, such as Supplemental Security Income (SSI), were not included in the legislation because the INS believed that the existing system used by the Social Security Administration, which involved working closely with the INS, was sufficiently effective.

9. Aliens included in the larger Central Index but excluded from the ASVI data base include, for example, individuals with border crossing cards and those apprehended along the Mexican border.

10. Martin Marietta was awarded the contract to operate the SAVE system in 1987. The INS received an 85 percent discount from Martin Marietta, partly in anticipation of the additional potential uses for the database, such as employment verification.

11. The first report issued in September 1987 examined only the effectiveness of the automated component of SAVE in three states that had conducted pilots. The GAO concluded that in the majority of cases SAVE provided a timely response and was identifying immigrants in an illegal status. However, it also found that there was considerable room for improving the accuracy and reliability of the SAVE database. See GAO, 1987.

12. The Department of Health and Human Services reported that savings achieved by implementing SAVE would generally exceed the costs of the program. See HHS, 1988.

The Department of Agriculture issued its report in March 1988 and found that both costs and savings associated with SAVE were small, but that costs could be expected to exceed savings. See The Urban Institute, 1988.

13. The Texas Department of Human Services conducted its savings analysis in order to apply for a waiver from the federal agency.

14. Letter from Ron Lindsey, Texas Department of Human Services, to Norma Goldberg, Family Support Administration, HHS, December 7, 1989.

15. Conditional waivers require the state to compare its existing verification system with the SAVE system for a six month test period. As a result, the state will have to implement the system in order to conduct cost-benefit analyses and prove that its existing systems are equally or more cost-effective than SAVE. HHS issued conditional waivers to six states as well as New York and Texas for AFDC and Medicaid.

16. Concerns were also voiced about undocumented immigrants being deterred from receiving benefits for which they are actually eligible. This is particularly true in cities with specific policies making it unlawful to deny certain benefits to an individual based on his immigration status. In 1985, New York City Mayor Ed Koch passed a directive requiring all city agencies to provide city-funded services to residents regardless of immigration status.

17. See second paragraph of note 3.

18. The GAO's June 1989 report on the alien verification system database found that the class of admission code, or the indicator of immigration status, was missing in about 20 percent of the 648 records sampled from the ASVI database. In addition, the GAO analyzed 296 hard-copy records at the three largest file control offices. The class of admission code was missing from 17 percent of those records and of those that had codes, 11 percent were incorrect. See GAO, 1989b.

19. *Congressional Record*, S.4272, April 5, 1990. "Employer Sanctions Improvements Amendments of 1990, S.2446, April 5, 1990.

20. IRCA 1986, Section 274A(d).

21. IRCA authorizes the President to oversee the development of demonstration projects to evaluate the effectiveness and security of the employment verification system (Section 274A(d)). Implementation of the telephone verification pilot is pending while that authority is redelegated from the President to the Attorney General of the Justice Department. The development of this verification system falls under a separate provision of IRCA which authorizes the President to undertake demonstration projects to test more secure systems of determining employment eligibility. IRCA, Section 274A(d).

References

Conner, Roger. 1982. *Breaking Down the Barriers: The Changing Relationship Between Illegal Immigration and Welfare.* Washington, D.C.: Federation for American Immigration Reform, September.

GAO (U.S. General Accounting Office). 1990. "Immigration Reform: Employer Sanctions and the Question of Discrimination." Washington, D.C.: author, March.

————. 1989a. "Federal Programs Show Progress in Implementing Alien Verification Systems." Washington, D.C.: author.

————. 1989b. "Immigration Reform: Alien Verification System Data Base Problems and Corrective Actions." Washington, D.C.: author, June.

————. 1987. "Immigration Reform: Systematic Alien Verification System Could Be Improved." Washington, D.C.: author, September.

Greenberg, David, and Douglas Wolf. 1986. *Using Computers to Combat Welfare Fraud,* New York: The Greenwood Press.

HHS (Department of Health and Human Services). 1988. "Evaluation of the Costs and Effectiveness of the Systematic Alien Verification for Entitlements (SAVE) System for Verifying the Immigration Status of Applicants and Recipients of Aid to Families with Dependent Children and Medicaid," May.

Heer, David M. 1990. *Undocumented Mexicans in the United States.* New York: Cambridge University Press.

INS (U.S. Immigration and Naturalization Service). 1987. "Immigration and Naturalization Service Annual Report, Fiscal Year 1986." Washington, D.C.: Immigration and Naturalization Service.

Lamm, Governor Richard D., and Gary Imhoff. 1985. *The Immigration Time Bomb: The Fragmenting of America.* New York: E.P. Dutton.

Muller, Thomas, and Thomas J. Espenshade. 1985. *The Fourth Wave: California's Newest Immigrants.* Washington, D.C.: Urban Institute Press.

Nelson, Alan. 1986. "Impact of an Alien Verification System on Assisted Housing Programs." Joint Hearing on H.R. 3810, Serial No. 99-100, August 6.

North, David S. 1983. "Impact of Legal, Illegal, and Refugee Migrations on U.S. Social Service Programs." In *U.S. Immigration and Refugee Policy: Global and Domestic Issues*, ed. Mary M. Kritz. Lexington, MA: D.C. Heath and Company.

Passel, Jeff, and Karen Woodrow. 1984. "Geographic Distribution of Undocumented Immigrants: Estimates of Undocumented Aliens Counted in the 1980 Census by State." *International Migration Review*, vol. 18, no. 3, pp. 642–671.

Purtell, Daniel. 1986. Testimony on the Immigration Control & Legalization Amendments Act of 1985 (H.R. 3810) before the House Committee on Ways & Means, July 22.

Stein, Daniel A. 1990. Testimony before the Committee on the Judiciary's Subcommittee on Immigration, Refugees, and International Law, June 27.

Tienda, Marta, and Leif Jensen. 1986. "Immigration and Public Assistance Participation: Dispelling the Myth of Dependency." *Social Science Research*, 15, pp. 372–400.

The Urban Institute. 1988. "Evaluation of the Costs and Effectiveness of the Systematic Alien Verification for Entitlements (SAVE) System for Verifying the Immigration Status of Food Stamp Program Applicants." The Urban Institute, March.

U.S. Justice Department. 1989. *Audit Report: Special Audit of the Immigration and Naturalization Service*, February.

U.S. House of Representatives, Judiciary Committee. 1986a. "Immigration Control and Legalization Amendments Act of 1986." Report 99-682, Part 1, July 16.

U.S. House of Representatives, Committee on Education and Labor. 1986b. "Immigration Control and Legalization Amendments Act of 1986," Report 99-682, Part 2, August 5.

U.S. House of Representatives, Judiciary Committee. 1986c. "Immigration and Naturalization Service, Oversight Hearing." Serial No. 92, March 13.

U.S. House of Representatives. 1986d. "Impact of an Alien Verification System on Assisted Housing Programs," Joint Hearing on H.R. 3810, Serial No. 99-100, August 6.

Weintraub, Sidney, and Gilberto Cardenas. 1984. "The Use of Public Services by Undocumented Aliens in Texas: A Study of State Costs and Revenues." Lyndon B. Johnson School of Public Affairs, Policy Research Project Report, no. 60.

Part Two

ASSESSING SANCTIONS' IMPACTS

Chapter Six

EMPLOYER COMPLIANCE WITH IRCA PAPERWORK REQUIREMENTS: A PRELIMINARY ASSESSMENT

Shirley J. Smith and Martina Shea

The Immigration Reform and Control Act (IRCA) of 1986 attempts to deny unauthorized workers access to employment in the United States. It does so by requiring that all employers request, examine, and record specific documents verifying each new employee's right to work in this country.

Three separate federal agencies have collected data on employer compliance with this regulation: the General Accounting Office (GAO); the Department of Justice's Immigration and Naturalization Service (INS); and the Department of Labor's Employment Standards Administration (ESA). Their findings on compliance with IRCA regulations differ substantially, causing a comparability problem across data sources. In this chapter we will address the reasons for the discrepancy in an attempt to develop a more cohesive view of employer compliance.

DATA SOURCES

Below is a discussion of how employer compliance has been monitored since the implementation of IRCA by the three different government agencies tasked with this effort.

The 1988 GAO Employer Survey

IRCA requires that the GAO monitor and report to Congress progress in implementing the employer sanctions provisions.[1] The GAO has conducted two nationwide surveys of employers exploring the effectiveness of employer education programs, the level of employer burden imposed by the new law, the degree of compliance with IRCA's paperwork requirement, and evidence on whether or not the new law has fostered a pattern of discriminatory hiring practices detrimental to U.S. citizens or others eligible for work in this country. At the time of this study, results of the second survey, conducted in 1989, had not yet become available; hence our discussion rests on the 1987/1988 survey's findings.

That study was based on a stratified random sample of 5,998 employers drawn from a list of more than six million firms nationwide.[2] Firms in five key states and five industries of "high alien concentration" were oversampled.[3] Grouped together, these provide a basis for comparing the attitudes and actions of employers in these states and industries with those of employers in all other "low alien" states and industries.[4] The survey was conducted shortly after the INS had completed its summer 1987 mailing of employer handbooks, and after the federal government had begun its systematic monitoring of compliance. Questionaires were mailed out between November 1987 and the spring of 1988, with a close-off date of April 1988.[5]

In analyzing compliance with the requirement that employers fill out I-9 forms for all employees hired since November 1, 1986, GAO included in its estimate only employers who indicated familiarity with IRCA regulations, had hired new workers since those regulations went into effect, and were thus in a position to actively comply with the law. Compliance behavior was rated as follows. If an employer reported having completed at least as many I-9s as were required for the number of employees hired since November 1, 1986, he was viewed as being "in compliance." Those who had hired one or more employees during this same interval without completing **any** I-9 forms were designated "noncompliant." Firms that had completed one or more I-9s, but too few for the number of new employees hired, were rated as "partially compliant."[6]

The Official Monitoring and Enforcement Systems: INS and ESA

The administrative records of the INS and the Department of Labor's Employment Standards Administration (ESA) provide an ongoing perspective on compliance behavior since the fall of 1987 when monitoring began. An understanding of the institutional constraints behind these monitoring systems helps to clarify differences in resulting compliance findings.

IRCA gave both the INS and the ESA statutory responsibilities for the implementation of employer sanctions provisions. However, only the INS was given responsibility for the enforcement of those provisions. The ESA assumed a major share of the monitoring function, in conjunction with its enforcement of labor laws. Hence, at present both the INS and the ESA collect information on employer compliance.

The decision to share monitoring responsibilities evolved out of practical considerations. Prior to IRCA, there had been a clear delineation between immigration and labor law. IRCA for the first time introduced labor market controls to bolster U.S. immigration law. Although the INS continues to enforce that law, it does not have the necessary field infrastructure to handle this tremendous oversight function alone.[7]

The ESA has a compliance staff of approximately 1,600 investigators, visiting about 60,000 firms annually to enforce various labor laws. The two agencies, therefore, have arrived at an operational agreement under which ESA investigators assess the employment verification practices of all firms they visit and forward their findings to the INS. Distributing the monitoring function in this manner has certainly increased the field visibility of federal investigators—one of the arrangement's chief aims. In the 21-month period starting in October 1987, ESA reviewed or attempted to review the records of about 75,100 firms,[8] as compared to fewer than 22,000 reviewed by the INS (INS, 1989a).

THE COMPLIANCE CONCEPT

As regulatory enforcement agencies, both INS and ESA adopt a legal definition of compliance as the "absence of violation." Thus firms that have hired no new employees since November 6, 1986 are legally (albeit "passively") compliant. This definition is both consistent with the law and appropriate for enforcement purposes. However, it may have inflated compliance rates in the early months of implementation.[9] Firms that have checked workers' documents incompletely or inconsistently (GAO's "partially compliant" group) are rated "noncompliant" under this legal definition.

Since ESA has no authority to enforce IRCA regulations, its role is solely that of a monitoring agency. ESA compliance staff primarily visit businesses believed to be in violation of major labor laws, such as the Fair Labor Standards Act (FLSA).[10] During the ESA investigator's first visit to a firm, he or she is required to determine whether the firm maintains proof that it has checked the work-authorizing documents of each person hired since November 6, 1986. The resulting compliance rating is then forwarded to enforcement personnel at INS.

There is no ESA follow-up of noncompliant cases. Because the agency is not charged with enforcing IRCA, the Department of Labor (DOL) has no programmatic rationale for monitoring improvements in I-9 compliance. Indeed, the data generated at first visit address the issue of greatest interest to many observers:[11] the extent of voluntary cooperation and the nature of paperwork shortcomings in high-risk firms.

By contrast, the underlying objective of INS investigations is to exclude unauthorized workers from the workplace. An INS citation for noncompliance sets in motion several enforcement mechanisms. All involve considerable INS paperwork and are resource-intensive. To minimize unnecessary costs, INS agents are encouraged to suggest possible improvements and allow time for these suggestions to be implemented before issuing citations or fines. Only firms that continue to ignore warnings are rated noncompliant, and then only when the case closes—after two or more INS visits. By that time, the firm and its new employees have had ample opportunity to gather and record all necessary documents.

THE MIX OF FIRMS INSPECTED

Both the INS and the DOL handle a mix of lead- (or complaint-) driven and directed investigations.[12] Within each monitoring system, most of the firms inspected have come to the respective agency's attention either through allegations of violation or because of a high statistical probability that they may be violating labor or immigration laws. Despite this similarity, differences in the geographic and industrial allocation of agency resources lead to differences in the mix of firms from which the INS and ESA obtain compliance data.

About 80 percent of INS investigations center on industries believed to be at high risk of violating immigration law. The INS focuses its greatest effort at points of alien entry along the border and in large metropolitan areas. More than 60 percent of all INS investigations occur in the South and West, where Mexican nationals are known to concentrate (see table 6.1). During the first three quarters of FY 1989, the four states making up the INS's Western Region (California, Arizona, Nevada, and Hawaii) accounted for nearly as many INS investigations as did the 34 states making up their Eastern and Northern regions combined.

In contrast, ESA investigations are more broadly dispersed, and firms in the remaining 46 states, as represented in the INS Eastern, Northern, and Southern regions, contribute more heavily to overall ESA compliance rates.

Both agencies appear to conduct more investigations in the service

Table 6.1 GEOGRAPHIC DISTRIBUTION OF INS AND ESA I-9 INSPECTIONS

| | I-9 Inspections Oct. 1, 1988 through June 30, 1989 | | | | Regional ratio of ESA to INS inspections |
| | ESA | | INS | | |
	Number	Percent	Number	Percent	
Total	34,716	100.0	10,095	100.0	3.4
East	9,585	27.6	2,028	20.1	4.7
North	10,572	30.5	1,824	18.1	5.8
South	11,266	32.5	3,271	32.4	3.4
West	3,293	9.5	2,972	29.4	1.1

Notes: This table shows INS regional designations with ESA's regional areas regrouped to these boundary specifications. See appendix A (p. 192) for boundary specifications.

sector than in other industrial sectors (see figure 6.1).[13] About 74 percent of INS investigations take place within the service-producing sector, broadly defined. However, because the major laws enforced by the ESA Wage and Hour Division span all industries without regard for workforce characteristics, the overall ESA investigation profile is industrially more diverse. It includes proportionately more firms in heavy industry (i.e., mining and durable goods manufacturing), construction, and agriculture, and thus more closely resembles the larger labor market.[14]

EXISTING DATA SYSTEMS

As a result of IRCA, both employers and government programs have had to adapt their record-keeping systems to the new requirements. There are no data on compliance during the initial educational and warning periods immediately following the implementation of IRCA. The official record begins in the fall of 1987, when both INS and ESA began to tabulate their compliance findings. The manner in which they do so is largely the outgrowth of previously established reporting procedures within each agency.

INS Data System. Because of the INS's institutional preoccupation with enforcement, data about many basic field operations have not yet been automated to facilitate policy analysis (Morris, 1985; National Academy of Sciences, 1985). Consequently, most enforcement data are still processed manually. The material reaching the national office varies both in content and coverage, limiting the agency's ability to readily identify and respond to emerging patterns.

Demands to increase field visibility both geographically and in-

Figure 6.1 INDUSTRIAL DISTRIBUTION OF INS AND ESA I-9 INSPECTIONS

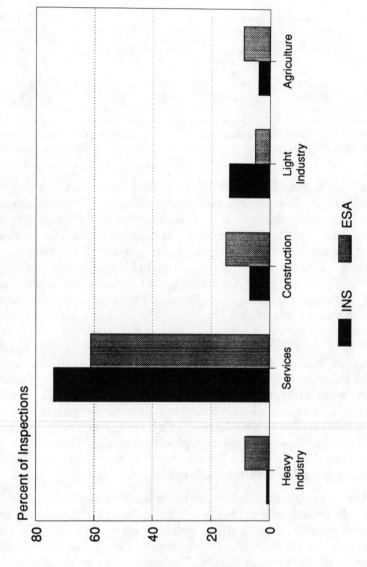

dustrially, as well as to provide IRCA enforcement information, have motivated the INS to develop a more systematic method of operation and data collection. Its newly implemented General Administrative Plan (GAP) is an important element in this program. At present, about 60 percent of INS I-9 activity still centers on lead-driven investigations. However, the remaining 40 percent of inspections are targeted by the GAP (INS, 1989a). These cases are evenly distributed between two parallel GAP programs: a *General Compliance Inspection*, directed at a random sample of firms from all industries; and the *Special Emphasis Section*, targeting the five Standard Industrial Classification (SIC) codes of industries known to be the heaviest past users of undocumented workers within a given locality. Although the GAP has enhanced INS field coverage, it does not yet include an automated information system to facilitate the disaggregated analysis of program outcomes.

ESA Data System. Within ESA, both the Wage and Hour Division (WHD) and the Office of Federal Contract Compliance Programs (OFCCP) had already developed comprehensive management information systems when the agency began monitoring employer compliance with IRCA regulations. Thus, from the outset, WHD and OFCCP automated their I-9 findings; WHD actually appended these findings to each case record in its data system. The resulting data are a rich source of information on employer compliance by firm size, location, SIC code, and other key attributes, including the firm's behavior with respect to other key labor laws. Although employer compliance findings are often summarized in three categories (apparent compliance, apparent noncompliance, and undetermined compliance), the case file also includes a detailed justification for the particular rating shown (see table 6.2 below).

As noted earlier, ESA compliance ratings are normally recorded during the initial visit to the firm. The Wage and Hour Division resolves or "conciliates" many complaints over the telephone, obviating the need for an on-site visit. Because this eliminates the opportunity to inspect I-9 records, ESA I-9 findings reflect only those cases that result in on-site investigations.

ENFORCEMENT ACTIVITIES

Before examining the available information on employer compliance from these many sources, it is important to consider the nature of

Table 6.2 DETAILED COMPLIANCE RATINGS, ESA I-9 INSPECTIONS

| | I-9 Inspections | | |
	Total	Wage/Hour Division	OFCCP
Total I-9 Inspections	75,067	64,886	10,181
Percent	100.0	100.0	100.0
Apparently Compliant	37.8	34.1	61.1
Apparently Noncompliant	49.0	50.9	36.7
Nonexistent Records	28.6	32.3	5.1
Incomplete Records	19.7	18.1	29.9
Other Noncompliant	0.7	0.6	1.6
Undetermined Compliance	13.2	15.0	2.3
Records Elsewhere	7.0	7.9	1.3
No Advance Notice	4.6	5.3	0.2
Suspect Documents	0.1	0.1	0.1
Other	1.5	1.7	0.7

Note: Data pertain to investigations opened on or after October 1, 1987 and closed by July 7, 1989.

the enforcement process. This process is intended to convince firms of the necessity of meeting IRCA paperwork requirements. Thus, patterns of compliance can be expected to vary with patterns of actual enforcement.

The administrative records of the INS and the ESA provide information on the likelihood of a firm being visited for I-9 inspection, of its being found in violation when visited, and of its being fined if found in violation.

Visibility of Inspection and Enforcement Programs

The combined annual outreach of INS and ESA on-site I-9 inspection programs is less than one percent of the nation's approximately seven million employers. The roughly 99,000 I-9 inspections completed by the two agencies between September 1, 1987 and June 30, 1989 resulted in about 45,000 firms receiving noncompliant ratings (INS, 1989a; ESA, 1989). Because as a function of its broader labor market mandate, ESA had a larger field infrastructure than that of the INS, more than four out of five of the noncompliant ratings were registered by ESA. However, since ESA has no authority to levy fines for violation, its findings were then forwarded to the INS field offices.

The INS's enforcement resources are limited. Hence, INS field officers decide which noncompliant leads to pursue and how vigorously to pursue them. Field offices make their enforcement presence known in a number of ways: by the number of firms inspected, the share of inspected firms that are issued warnings or citations, the number of fines levied and types of legal charges brought against employers, their willingness to negotiate the amount of the fines (avoiding protracted and costly legal proceedings), and the intensity with which they pursue collection of those fines. There are no nationwide INS guidelines regarding the mix of enforcement mechanisms to be used. Furthermore, fines are still not automatic for those found in violation. In fact, although

> as of June 1, 1988, the Service was no longer under a legislative requirement to issue citations [i.e., warnings], . . . in order to maintain balance and flexibility in enforcement, the Service adopted policies permitting issuance of [such] warnings for first violations in appropriate circumstances. (INS, 1989b)

Because the dual-agency scheme for inspecting I-9 paperwork focuses more resources on monitoring than on enforcement, relatively few ESA reports of noncompliance actually culminate in legal action by INS.[15] During the first nine months of fiscal year 1989, ESA forwarded records of 17,435 "apparently noncompliant" firms to INS for follow-up. During the same period, the INS handled only 3,436 such cases, many of which had come to their attention through other sources. Of these, 1,863 led to the assessment of a fine. Only 1,189 final order fines were collected.[16]

Although it may not be obvious to individual firms, their risk of being sanctioned, even if violations were detected, has been small: about six percent of total noncompliant ratings resulted in final order fines. Furthermore, the amount collected has been usually less than half that originally assessed: an average of $1,994 as compared with $5,091.

Patterns of Enforcement

The INS national office has given individual regional and field offices considerable flexibility to plan and implement the sanctions program, in order to deal with the specific labor market problems they confront. The limited data available suggest that this practice leads to considerable regional and industrial variation in enforcement (INS, 1989a; Schumer, 1989). Judging by the number of INS investigations conducted and the number of fines assessed, INS enforcement efforts are greatest in the INS Southern Region (see figure 6.2). The smaller number of fines levied in other regions, however, carry with them stiffer monetary penalties.

Figure 6.2 IRCA ENFORCEMENT ACTIVITIES BY REGION

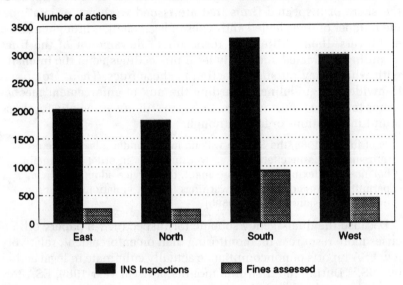

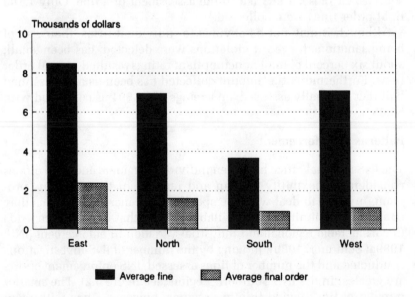

October 1988 - June 1989

Figure 6.3 IRCA ENFORCEMENT ACTIVITIES BY INDUSTRY

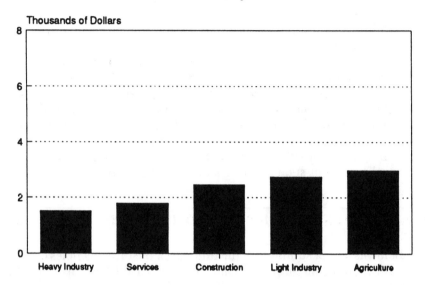

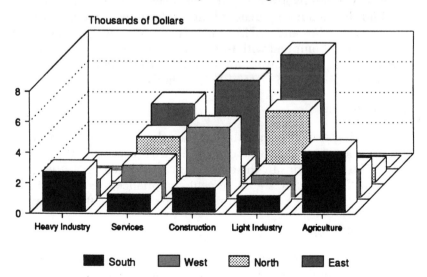

October 1988 - June 1989

The actual collection of fines varies substantially by industry (see figure 6.3). Overall final orders are stiffest in agriculture, where the average fine is about twice as high as that in heavy industry. However, this average fine in agriculture is less than half that collected within light industry in the North. There is no consistent pattern to final order fines in any single industry, nationwide (see figure 6.3).

The existing data systems do not allow us to observe how these variations in the elements of enforcement affect employer behavior. A statistical model of compliance incorporating 1) INS data on the number of inspections, citations, and final order fines (as well as the characteristics of firms sanctioned), and 2) ESA compliance data by detailed industry and locality might be highly informative. But the near absence of sub-national INS enforcement statistics makes the development of such a model currently impossible.

PATTERNS OF EMPLOYER COMPLIANCE: THE FINDINGS

Below is a brief summary of the findings of the three agencies charged with monitoring employer compliance with IRCA's paperwork requirements.

GAO Findings

The GAO employer survey, taken between fall 1987 and spring 1988, found that about 50 percent of the 1.9 million employers who were aware of the law and had hired at least one employee since November 6, 1986 had complied with I-9 paperwork requirements (GAO, 1988). Another 12 percent were found to be partially compliant, while 38 percent appeared to be totally noncompliant.

INS Findings

According to INS administrative records, between October 1, 1987 and June 30, 1989, 68 percent of all INS-inspected firms had met their I-9 obligations by the time their cases closed (INS, 1989a). This overall figure reflects a 69 percent compliance rate during the first 12 months and a 66 percent rate in the remaining 9-month period.

ESA Findings

The Employment Standards Administration reports that during the same 21-month interval, 38 percent of all ESA-inspected firms had properly completed the appropriate paperwork so that it was on file at the outset of their investigations (ESA, 1989).[17]

The ESA internal monthly reports show this rate to vary considerably by region, from less than one-third of the cases handled through the Atlanta regional office to nearly half of those handled in the San Francisco region. By this accounting, firms in the high-immigrant Southwest appear to be most diligently recording their workers' employment eligibility verification documents.

Monthly ESA tabulations also pinpoint the types of actual and suspected violations encountered in the field (see table 6.2). About 29 percent of all firms visited by ESA investigators have nonexistent records (a problem particularly common among firms investigated by the Wage and Hour Division). Another 20 percent either had too few I-9s on file or had the appropriate number, some of which were not properly or completely filled in (a type of violation encountered most frequently by OFCCP investigators).[18] During the period in question, seven percent of all firms claimed to have I-9s on file elsewhere,[19] while about five percent denied ESA investigators access to their files because of inadequate advance notice.[20] These latter two groups made up the bulk of the indeterminate category.

Further Examination of GAO, INS, and ESA Data

The three agencies' estimates appear to vary systematically by location, size of firm, and reason for investigation.[21]

INDUSTRY

INS data do not permit an assessment of compliance levels of industry. However, findings from both GAO and ESA Wage and Hour Division data are consistent with the view that the industries GAO regarded as most reliant on alien labor have also been most remiss in keeping I-9 records (see figure 6.4).[22]

ESA Wage and Hour Division SIC data allow a more detailed look at specific industries. Table 6.3 shows the compliance rates observed in major and selected smaller industries nationwide. Below-average compliance rates are found in construction, mining, retail trade, and agriculture.[23] Apart from mining, these are all known to be sites of heavy immigrant concentration.

Looking at detailed industries strengthens the conclusion that compliance rates are lowest in high-alien activities. They are exceptionally low in private household services, eating and drinking es-

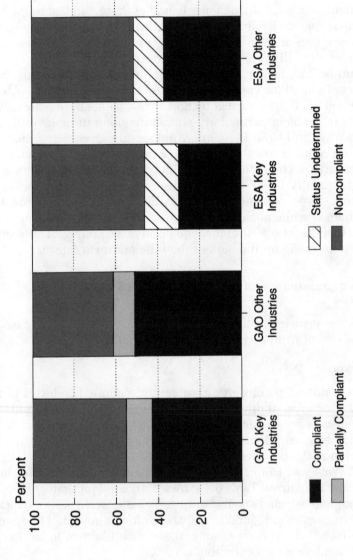

Figure 6.4 GAO AND ESA/WHD COMPLIANCE FINDINGS BY INDUSTRY

Table 6.3 ESA FINDINGS REGARDING COMPLIANCE STATUS BY INDUSTRY
(Percent Distribution)

		Apparent compliance status		Status
	Total	Compliant	Non-compliant	undetermined
WHD Total	100.0	34.1	51.0	14.9
MAJOR INDUSTRY				
Agriculture	100.0	33.0	45.9	21.1
Mining	100.0	30.9	55.3	13.8
Construction	100.0	27.5	58.1	14.5
Manufacturing				
Nondurable	100.0	37.6	50.1	12.3
Durable	100.0	41.8	49.3	8.8
Transportation, Public Utilities	100.0	35.8	50.7	13.4
Trade				
Wholesale	100.0	40.2	47.0	12.8
Retail	100.0	31.0	53.2	15.8
Finance, Insurance,				
Real Estate	100.0	42.9	42.1	15.0
Services	100.0	37.0	49.9	13.1
Public Administration	100.0	49.9	33.4	16.7
Other	100.0	42.1	38.9	19.0
SELECTED DETAILED INDUSTRIES				
Food and Kindred Products	100.0	38.6	46.9	14.5
Apparel, Other Textile Products	100.0	26.4	54.0	19.6
Furniture, Fixtures	100.0	39.9	54.8	5.3
Eating, Drinking Places	100.0	29.6	55.7	14.7
Hotels, Other Lodging	100.0	34.8	52.8	12.4
Personal Services	100.0	29.0	55.5	15.5
Business Services	100.0	35.4	49.4	15.2
Private Household Services	100.0	15.8	65.8	18.4

tablishments, personal services, and the manufacture of apparel and textiles.

LOCATION

The GAO survey suggests that firms in low-alien states are somewhat less likely to be in compliance than those in high-alien states: 49 versus 51 percent. The difference, however, is not statistically significant. Nonetheless, the ESA combined program data point to a similar conclusion. Employers are more likely to examine and properly record employees' documents in the states of California, Texas, and New York than they are elsewhere. The average compliance rates in immigrant-heavy California and Texas are among the highest in the nation (see figure 6.5).

FIRM SIZE

Large firms are much more likely than smaller firms to meet IRCA's paperwork requirements. The INS does not tabulate compliance data by size of firm. However, the GAO survey shows firms with fewer than 10 employees having a compliance rate of only 35 percent, compared with 93 percent in firms employing more than 500 workers (see figure 6.6). ESA combined program investigations reveal a similar pattern. The share with an indeterminate ESA rating also clearly diminishes with firm size.

Although the low compliance rates of smaller firms could be due to a higher concentration of illegal workers in such firms, other factors may also contribute. For instance, the larger the firm, the more likely it is to have legal counsel and organized personnel structures, both of which facilitate learning about and complying more readily with IRCA requirements.

REASON FOR INVESTIGATION

The INS and the ESA data both indicate that noncompliance with IRCA requirements is higher in firms against which other types of complaints have been registered. ESA data show that thirty-two percent of the firms undergoing complaint-driven investigations and thirty-seven percent of those undergoing directed investigations have met their paperwork obligations. The comparable figures from the INS are fifty-four and eighty-seven percent, respectively.

THE SOURCES OF DIVERGENCE IN OVERALL RATES

Although the GAO, INS, and ESA data are in agreement about certain basic patterns of employer compliance, their estimates of overall compliance are markedly different. The combined program ESA data yield an overall compliance rate of 38 percent; GAO survey data set the figure at 50 percent; INS data show it to be 68 percent. To reconcile these findings we must first recognize the sources of this divergence.

Method of Data Collection

In surveys such as that conducted by the GAO, employers have an opportunity to place their own behavior in its most favorable light.[24]

Figure 6.5 ESA COMPLIANCE FINDINGS BY STATE

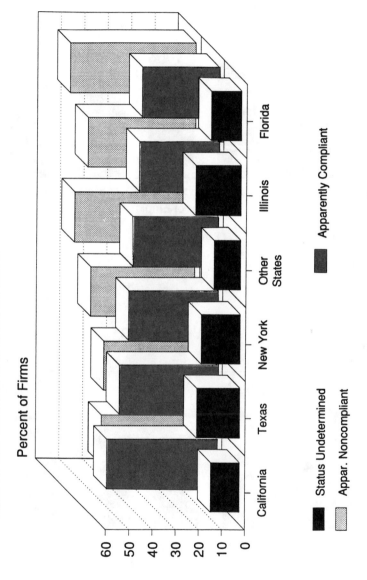

Percent of Firms

California   Texas   New York   Other States   Illinois   Florida

Status Undetermined

Appar. Noncompliant

Apparently Compliant

October 1, 1987 - June 30, 1989

Figure 6.6 GAO AND ESA COMPLIANCE FINDINGS BY SIZE OF FIRM

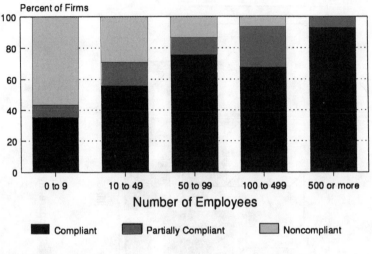

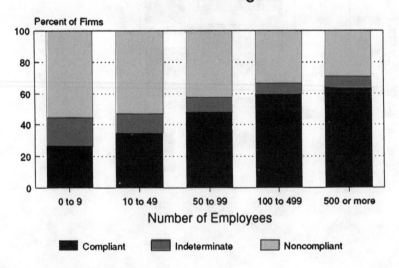

Hence, all else being equal, surveys might indicate somewhat higher compliance rates than other methods of data collection.

Universe from Which the Information Is Drawn

The GAO compliance rate was based on a stratified random sample of U.S. firms. ESA and INS data are both derived primarily from firms being scrutinized for regulatory violations.[25] Other things being equal, focusing on probable violators should bias compliance rates downward.

The Subset of Employers for Which Compliance Rates Are Calculated

Different institutional mandates have caused the GAO, ESA, and INS to focus their attention on somewhat different concepts of compliance. The effect of conceptual differences on outcome, even within a single data set, can be illustrated with GAO microdata.

The GAO compliance rate discussed above (and denoted GAO1 below) differs in several respects from that used elsewhere. While the regulatory agencies are concerned with strict *legal* compliance, GAO analysts were interested in the level of *potential* compliance, given adequate information. Thus respondents who were unfamiliar with IRCA were omitted from the base of the GAO1 index. In light of the GAO's reporting responsibilities, this exclusion was clearly appropriate. However, the question addressed by the GAO1 index is markedly different from that which ESA and INS figures purport to answer. From the legal standpoint, ignorance is no excuse: if firms failed to verify their new employees' right to work, both ESA and INS would classify them as in violation.

Respondents who claimed to be unaware of IRCA were asked to skip part of the GAO survey, including a question concerning the number of I-9 forms completed. This prevents closer examination of the paperwork practices of the 22 percent of employers who claimed ignorance of IRCA. Nonetheless, a partial reconciliation of concepts is possible. Assuming that none of these firms would have prepared I-9 forms for any persons hired during the relevant interval, we can reclassify those with new hires as legally noncompliant. Including these additional employers widens the base from 1.9 to 2.3 million employers nationwide, and thus reduces overall compliance. This adjustment of the GAO index (designated GAO2) narrows the GAO-ESA compliance gap from 13 to 5 percentage points.

The GAO1 index differs from the INS and ESA compliance indices in yet another important respect. Both ESA and INS defined compliance as the absence of violation, and therefore classified employers with no new hires since November 6, 1986 as compliant.[26] However, GAO chose not to classify them as compliant, since these firms' intent to comply had not been tested in a real hiring situation. At the time of the survey (autumn 1987 to spring 1988), 37 percent of employers in GAO's survey had yet to make their first hiring decision under IRCA. Recalculating the original index to include employers with no new employees in the base and regard them as compliant (GAO3), increases the overall GAO compliance rate from 50 to 72 percent. As illustrated in figure 6.7, these passively compliant employers then account for more than half of all compliant employers.

A final index, GAO4, combines the features of the two intermediate indices just described: employers who have hired new workers but were unaware of their new legal requirements under IRCA are treated as noncompliant, while those with no new employees are classified as compliant. Given these adjustments, the same GAO survey data suggest that in the spring of 1988, 64 percent of employers were compliant with paperwork requirements.

Figure 6.8 depicts the change in compliance levels associated with each such adjustment to the index base. It shows the index to be highly sensitive to specification.

Stage of Investigation at Which Compliance Is Determined

Although a large share of both ESA and INS cases are prompted by complaints, the compliance rate of ESA-inspected firms (38 percent) is markedly below that of firms visited by the INS (68 percent). A major reason for this difference is that firms that ESA would classify as noncompliant have had an opportunity to reclassify themselves as compliant when processed through the INS monitoring system. Here, the difference in the timing of the compliance assessment, mentioned earlier, is crucial. Firms investigated by ESA are given just a three-day notice prior to I-9 inspection during which to correct paperwork deficiencies. Those inspected by the INS have both time and official guidance in correcting such defects. Thus, the two agencies' estimates report compliance at different points in the inspection cycle.

To obtain more consistent readings on employer compliance, the INS and ESA would have to inspect the I-9 forms and report their findings at the same point in the inspection process. INS inspectors

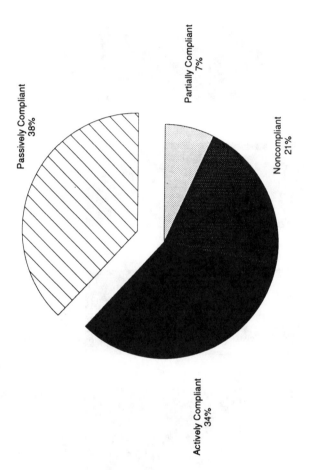

Figure 6.7 PASSIVELY COMPLIANT EMPLOYERS

Passively Compliant
38%

Partially Compliant
7%

Noncompliant
21%

Actively Compliant
34%

GAO 1988 Survey data

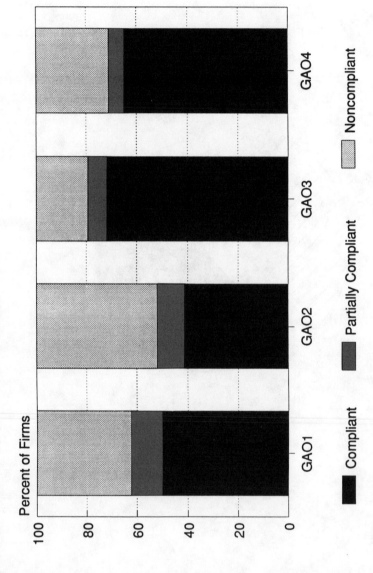

Figure 6.8 COMPARISON OF DIFFERENT GAO COMPLIANCE INDICES

have only recently begun collecting some additional compliance information during their initial visit. Until this information becomes available, the two agencies' distinct measures are best used to discern lower and upper bounds of cooperation in firms whose employment practices have come under scrutiny.

Index Classification

The timing factor contributes to still another bias. Resolution of "undetermined" ratings affects the number and content of compliance categories which, in turn, strongly affect estimated compliance levels. From a legal standpoint, only two such classifications exist: in compliance or out of compliance. Because INS enforcement officers make this determination in order to close out each case, their data adhere to this clear two-way break.

ESA investigators are also mindful of the legal definition, but with no opportunity to resolve their indeterminate cases, report them as such to the INS. Thus, official ESA statistics rest on a three-way classification. If all indeterminate readings were followed through to resolution, each would be reclassified as compliant or noncompliant, and both of these categories would probably expand. However, because ESA has no follow-up responsibilities, this resolution is not achieved within their data system. As a result, it is misleading to draw conclusions on the basis of the ESA "apparent compliance" rate without regard to the 13 percent of cases that are unresolved. Reconciliation of estimates requires that these firms be removed from the base of the ESA compliance rate.

The particular three-way classification introduced by the GAO1 index obscures comparisons in other ways. The GAO scheme subdivides the legally noncompliant classification into partially compliant—i.e., firms with some I-9 records, but less than the appropriate number—and totally noncompliant firms. Although not normally displayed this way, ESA statistics can be regrouped in a similar fashion. However, the ESA "partially compliant" category will include not only firms with an inadequate number of I-9s (i.e., the GAO "partially compliant") but also those that failed to record an adequate amount of information on these forms.[27]

It is easiest to reconcile the ESA, GAO, and INS estimates of total noncompliance. As seen in table 6.4 and figure 6.9, about 38 percent of the firms covered by the GAO survey had **no** I-9 records for their new employees. Adjusted ESA statistics place this share at 33 percent. At case closing, INS still found 32 percent to be in violation.

Table 6.4 RECONCILIATION OF GAO, ESA, AND INS COMPLIANCE FINDINGS
(Percent Distribution)

	Total	Compliance	Noncompliance		Status undetermined
			Total	Partial	
GAO Survey Findings	100	50	38[a]	12[b]	—
Total ESA Inspections					
Original Classification	100	38	29[a]	20[c]	13
Adjusted Classification[d]	100	44	33[a]	23[c]	—
Total INS Findings	100	68	32	—	—

a. Denotes no I-9 records on file.
b. Denotes insufficient number of I-9s on file for number of persons hired; some I-9s on file.
c. Denotes either inadequate number of I-9s or inadequate amount of information on existing records; some I-9s on file.
d. Undetermined cases removed from base of rate.
Note: GAO data, spring 1988; ESA data, September 1987 through June 1989; INS data October 1987 through June 1989.

Adjusted figures show that between 44 and 50 percent of the firms contacted met initial ESA or GAO standards for paperwork compliance. An additional 12 to 23 percent were keeping I-9 records, but did not do so fully and consistently, and were thus legally in violation.

Juxtaposing these figures with INS findings, it appears that when confronted with such paperwork shortcomings, most firms must have been able to resolve them to the INS inspector's satisfaction.

THE UNRESOLVED ISSUE

A firm's compliance with verification regulations can translate into labor market impact only through its effect on individual workers. None of the existing employer compliance indices measures the share of the workforce that is employed by genuinely compliant firms.

Both the GAO survey and the ESA data contain information on the number employed in each firm. It is possible to approximate the share of all workers in the firms contacted that held jobs with nominally compliant employers. We estimate that the 50 percent of em-

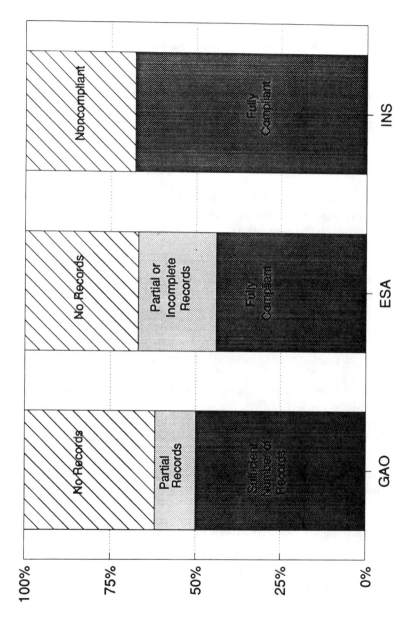

Figure 6.9 RECONCILIATION OF COMPLIANCE ESTIMATES

ployers whom GAO deemed in compliance employ 67 percent of all U.S. workers.[28]

The ESA estimate of workforce coverage in compliant firms is lower than that of GAO. Nonetheless, even in the sample of firms under Labor Department scrutiny, slightly more than half of the total employment count is estimated to be found in apparently compliant firms.

However, by focusing solely on employer compliance rates, a more important issue is overlooked. Because these rates pertain to compliance with the letter of the law, they leave the more basic question of compliance *with the intent of the law* unresolved.

Exclusion of Unauthorized Workers from the Workplace

As noted initially, IRCA was intended to curb illegal employment by requiring employers to screen new employees for employment authorization. None of the data systems discussed above addresses the degree to which this intent of the law is being met.[29] A firm's technical noncompliance with the letter of the law does not necessarily indicate that it employs unauthorized workers. In fact, paperwork violations are most widespread in the regions of lowest alien concentration. In such areas it may suggest that firms are still unclear about what the law requires, either because these localities have been given lower priority in the IRCA educational campaign, or because the local public media have taken little interest in the immigration issue.

By the same token, paperwork compliance cannot be interpreted as evidence that the firm hires no illegal aliens. Preliminary field research indicates that it is both possible and relatively easy to maintain acceptable I-9 records while still hiring illegals:

> ... after two years of phased-in enforcement ... the law has had no dramatic impact on the California labor markets in which undocumented immigrants from Mexico typically participate. ... The only real change for most of these employers is a new paperwork burden. ... In our study, we found that 93 percent of the employers were doing the required paperwork. (Cornelius, 1988, p. 25)

Bach and Brill report similar preliminary findings from several industrial case studies funded by the Department of Labor and undertaken in areas of high immigrant concentration. When coupled with the continuing high rates of noncompliance observed by GAO, INS, and ESA, "fraudulent" compliance clearly narrows the universe of firms within which employer sanctions can have their desired effects. In fact, it leaves in question the law's ability to create job opportunities for authorized workers and to foster the labor market adjustments necessary to attract such workers.

CONCLUSIONS

There is currently no mechanism to ensure that noncompliant firms are sanctioned, and very few of the firms that are assessed a fine actually pay the amount initially levied. Responsibility for monitoring employers' record-keeping in connection with IRCA is shared by two agencies: the INS and the Department of Labor's Employment Standards Administration. Actual enforcement, through the imposition of employer sanctions, rests solely with the INS. Hence the resources allocated to detection of I-9 violations far exceed those available for the resolution of such violations.

As yet we can say little about the size and characteristics of the IRCA-compliant business community. The distribution of monitoring responsibilities across agencies has complicated the analysis of how well employers are meeting their I-9 paperwork obligations. The federal government obtains information on employer compliance from a variety of sources, the most important of which are: periodic surveys of employers' self-reported performance; the results of ESA on-site investigations prior to intervention; and the results of INS on-site inspection after intervention. Because the purpose of data collection in each of the information-gathering agencies differs, so too do key definitions, methods of data collection and tabulation, and overall compliance estimates.

The existing data systems each monitor a different segment of the economy. None is completely representative, nor do any two fully agree on what constitutes compliance. Manipulation of GAO survey data reveals that definitional subtleties can alter the compliance rate by as much as 31 percent within a single data set.

However, the various compliance estimates do give bounds to the discussion of employer cooperation with the letter of IRCA. The findings of ESA complaint-driven investigations probably establish a lower bound regarding the share of employers now voluntarily fulfilling their I-9 paperwork obligations. Among employers cited in WHD complaints (about other possible labor law violations), about 37 percent of those with an I-9 rating appeared to be complying with these IRCA regulations at first visit. The INS inspections data suggest that with pressure from INS agents and time to correct paperwork deficiencies, this figure can be raised to about 54 percent. Although a noticeable improvement, this still means that almost half of the firms accused of violating other labor laws are also violating IRCA regulations.

The upper bound of probable cooperation is suggested by two data sets: the ESA/OFCCP inspections data for firms under contract to the U.S. government, and the INS data resulting from directed inspections. Firms scrutinized by OFCCP risk losing their federal contracts for violating labor regulations. The expectation of compliance reviews makes it prudent for such firms to meet all necessary requirements. Yet, even with this strong incentive to comply, only sixty-two percent appear to have done so successfully.

A more optimistic upper bound is suggested by the INS General Administrative Plan, which found that 86 percent of the firms sampled for directed visits were compliant. A substantial portion of the gap between 62 and 86 percent is probably traceable to minor violations of the type that rank the firm as noncompliant in ESA inspections, but might have been resolved after the INS closed the case and recorded its own rating.

The adjusted GAO4 index suggests that approximately a year after the implementation of IRCA, roughly two-thirds of all firms may have been technically compliant.[30] However, removing firms that had not yet hired any new employees during the relevant period (as in GAO2) would reduce this figure to about 41 percent. The GAO1 index shows that, when given the opportunity to rate their own performance one year after the law went into effect, half of the employers who were familiar with IRCA and had made hiring decisions stated that they had filled out an I-9 form for each new worker.

Finally, on-site compliance ratings by ESA show that as many as one-third of the firms that have filled out I-9 forms remain technically noncompliant because this paperwork is incomplete.

Despite differences in levels observed, GAO, INS, and ESA data systems reinforce one another in finding systematic variation by industry, location, size of firm, and reason for investigation. In particular, they indicate that:

☐ Firms in the industries of highest alien concentration are least likely to conduct work authorization checks;
☐ Firms in high-alien states are somewhat more likely than firms in other states to meet this IRCA requirement. Based on detailed compliance information available through ESA, the high-immigrant states

of California and Texas appear to have some of the highest overall compliance rates in the nation;

□ Larger firms are more likely to comply than smaller firms; and

□ Firms cited in complaints about other types of violations are less likely than other firms to be in compliance with IRCA.

While official compliance statistics help focus the discussion on IRCA's likely effects, they do not address the fundamental issue: employers' intent to avoid hiring unauthorized workers. Failure to comply with I-9 regulations does not appear to vary systematically with the presence of unauthorized workers. Noncompliance is widespread in certain sectors with high levels of immigrants, but is also widespread in sectors where immigrants are seldom found. Likewise, high rates of paperwork compliance are observed both in sectors of high and low immigrant involvement. Hence federal statistics on paperwork compliance leave unanswered the question of whether IRCA has impeded illegal workers' access to employment in the United States.

Notes

1. Three such reports are required from the GAO, each due annually on November 6, the anniversary of IRCA's signature into law. (See GAO, 1987 and GAO, 1988.)

2. The actual sampling was done by a private marketing research firm. Internal Revenue Service data indicate that there are about seven million U.S. employers.

3. The states were those with the largest alien populations: California, Florida, Texas, New York, and Illinois. The industries were those generally thought to employ the largest number of aliens: construction, agriculture, food processing, apparel, and hotels and restaurants.

4. The sampling procedure intended to provide 95 percent certainty that the outcomes would not have differed by more than 10 percent if another sample had been chosen. However, a significant number of employers identified their industry differently than anticipated by the marketing firm that drew the sample. This "inter-strata migration" led to a response rate of more than 100 percent for the low-alien industries. Consequently, survey results pertaining to individual industries became less reliable than anticipated at the onset. Because the survey was anonymous, the researchers were unable to match specific questionnaires with the strata they were selected to represent. As a result, the number of valid findings in some of the 36 cells was too small to project the findings to the whole universe of employers, given existing weights. Weighting the data to extend the results to the whole employer population would have reduced the level of confidence below that intended. For these reasons, this discussion takes place at a higher level of aggregation than originally intended.

5. Respondents were guaranteed anonymity to assure a high response rate and honest

answers. The response rate was 78 percent, for a projected universe of approximately 4.2 million employers.

6. These firms were technically in violation, and therefore legally noncompliant.

7. The INS now has about 400 field officers handling I-9 investigations.

8. In the initial seven months of this period, October 1987 to April 1988, most of the ESA caseload involved investigations begun before the I-9 inspection program was in place. The monthly number of I-9 reviews increased substantially thereafter. In total, about 8,700 of the ESA-inspected firms did not give access to their files, either because of lack of advance notice (3,400) or because those records were maintained elsewhere (5,300).

9. As the number of firms with new employees increases, any failure to fulfill paperwork requirements necessarily exerts a downward pressure on total compliance statistics. Because 37 percent of all respondents to the GAO survey had not employed any new workers since November 6, 1986, GAO analysts chose to exclude this group from the base of their compliance rate. Had it been included, the overall GAO compliance rate for the firms surveyed in 1987/88 would have risen from 50 to 72 percent.

10. There are two major programs within ESA with employment eligibility verification responsibilities: the Wage and Hour Division (WHD) and the Office of Federal Contract Compliance Programs (OFCCP). About 88 percent of ESA investigations are handled by the WHD and 12 percent by OFFCP. Approximately 80 percent of WHD investigations pertain to possible violations of FLSA. The remainder of the WHD investigations concern federal contracts, as covered by the Davis-Bacon Act (construction), the McNamara-O'Hara Service Contract (services), and Walsh-Healey Public Contracts Act (manufacture of furnishing supplies or equipment), and possible violations of the Migrant Seasonal Agricultural Worker Protection Act and other farm labor protective statutes. OFCCP enforces Executive Order 11246, section 503 of the Rehabilitation Act of 1973, and Section 2012 of the Vietnam Era Veterans' Readjustment Assistance Act of 1974, to assure non-discrimination and affirmative action by government contractors and subcontractors in hiring, employment, and advancement of minorities, women, veterans, and disabled workers. Approximately 18 percent of OFCCP's compliance actions are the result of complaints. The balance are scheduled compliance reviews or investigations of randomly selected contract establishments.

11. Each firm is given a three-day notice prior to the inspection, but may agree to an inspection without such notice. Although those with minor violations may thus have an opportunity to clean up their records before this rating is made, the rating in most cases probably reflects the status of records prior to intervention.

12. INS "leads" derive from a number of sources, including employees within the inspected firm, other individuals or firms within the community, and the records of noncompliant firms forwarded to INS by ESA. ESA "complaint-driven" inspections derive largely from the complaints of employees within the firm. About 40 percent of INS inspections are "directed," i.e., initiated through random or quasi-random sampling. About 48 percent of the ESA on-site investigations are also directed, in connection with various labor regulations. One-third of these firms are reviewed by OFCCP to confirm that they are meeting the terms of their Federal contracts.

13. The industrial detail maintained in the INS records is quite limited and not readily comparable with the Standard Industrial Classification code maintained by ESA. Evidence cited above is based on combining industries for rough comparability. Industries included in the service-producing sector are transportation and public utilities, wholesale and retail trade, finance, insurance and real estate, services, and public administration.

14. Even within the ESA data, compliance patterns differ with the particular mix of firms visited. The ESA I-9 inspection data from OFCCP depict firms undergoing

scheduled compliance reviews regarding contracts they hold with the federal government. As a group, these firms are both larger and more vulnerable to the consequences of noncompliance than are firms inspected by the Wage and Hour Division. Not surprisingly, a greater share of this group appears to be meeting IRCA paperwork requirements.

15. There is no established mechanism for checking the outcome of cases forwarded from one agency to the other.

16. Fines are subject to appeal and are often reduced or dismissed. As a result, the term "final order fine" is used to denote fines that are actually collected.

17. The rate has been constant at about this level since June 1988. Looking only at the cases for which a clear determination could be made, this figure increases to 44 percent.

18. These firms might also be regarded as "partially compliant," although not necessarily in the sense measured by the GAO index.

19. Employers who manage one of many outlets for a centrally managed business are not required to maintain I-9 paperwork on the premises. When an employee is hired through the U.S. Employment Service (USES), the I-9 paperwork may consist of a letter from the USES certifying that the I-9 requirements have been met.

20. Investigators are legally required to give a three-day notice prior to inspection.

21. The GAO results have been evaluated using a standard t-test, and are significant at the five percent level unless otherwise specified.

22. The OFCCP caseload includes firms that are much more strictly monitored, and thus much more likely to comply. Because their weight within the ESA caseload is not proportionate to the weight of such firms in the national economy, and their inclusion distorts this relationship for certain specific industries, we have excluded them from figure 6.4 and table 6.3. Their inclusion would dampen, but not substantially alter, these findings.

23. The nature of real or suspected violations is by no means uniform across industries. In certain industries (e.g., public administration, finance, insurance and real estate, retail trade, agriculture, and construction) many firms report maintaining their personnel records elsewhere. In others (e.g., mining and construction) the problem of nonexistent records is widespread. Agricultural enterprises are frequently visited without prior notice. Hence, a disproportionate share of these enterprises have refused access to their files. This makes it particularly difficult to analyze employer behavior in the agricultural sector.

24. The GAO attempted to check the validity of respondents' answers by sending specially coded survey forms to 200 employers previously visited by the INS. Ninety percent of those answered correctly that they had been visited and the remaining 10 percent replied that they did not know.

25. Both data sets include directed as well as complaint-driven cases. However, with the exception of ESA/OFCCP, even the directed cases are usually located in industries believed to include a disproportionate share of likely violators.

26. Legally, at the outset of the new law—on November 6, 1986—all firms were compliant. Only after hiring a new worker without completing the required I-9 paperwork could they shift into the noncompliant category.

27. GAO survey analysts were forced to assume that any I-9 on file must be complete, and that a firm with the appropriate number of such records was therefore compliant with the law. ESA compliance officers check not only for the number of records, but for their content. As a result of this conceptual discrepency, the two agencies' definitions of "compliance" also differ slightly.

28. The percentage of employees working for compliant employers is calculated from

the number of total employees in compliant firms and the number of total employees in all firms for whom compliance was rated under GAO1. Caution should be used in interpreting this result. The problem of inter-strata migration, discussed in note 4 above, resulted in biased estimates of employer compliance. An attempt to translate employer compliance into worker coverage (by applying respondents' weights to employees) might magnify this problem, because the average employer has more than one employee.

29. A related issue is the question of whether, in complying with the IRCA paperwork requirements, firms might screen applicants for employment eligibility in a discriminatory fashion on the basis of the applicant's ethnicity or national origin.

30. Based on 3,735 directed visits during the first three quarters of FY 1989.

References

Bach, Robert, and Howard Brill. 1989. "Shifting the Burden: The Impacts of IRCA on U.S. Labor Markets." Unpublished Interim Report to the Division of Immigration Policy and Research, U.S. Department of Labor, November.

Cornelius, Wayne A. 1988. "Los Migrantes de la Crisis: The Changing Profile of Mexican Labor Migration to California in the 1980s." Paper presented at the conference on Population and Work in Regional Settings, El Colegio de Michoacan, Zamora, Mexico, November.

ESA (Employment Standards Administration). 1989. "Summary of ESA-91's by Region, Combined OFCCP and Wage Hour." Unpublished Statistics, U.S. Department of Labor, July 26.

GAO (U.S. General Accounting Office). 1988. "Immigration Reform: Status of Implementing Employer Sanctions after Second Year." GAO/GGD-89-16. Washington, D.C.: U.S. General Accounting Office.

———. 1987. "Immigration Reform: Status of Implementing Employer Sanctions after One Year." GAO/GGD-88-14. Washington, D.C.: U.S. General Accounting Office.

INS (U.S. Immigration and Naturalization Service). 1989a. "Employer Operations Activity Report." Activity Report, Investigations Division, July.

———. 1989b. "INS Response to 'Review of the Implementation of the Immigration Reform and Control Act of 1986' Issued by the Office of Congressman Charles E. Schumer." Unpublished memo, May 17.

Morris, M.D. 1985. *Immigration: The Beleaguered Bureaucracy.* Washington, D.C.: The Brookings Institution.

National Academy of Sciences. 1985. *Immigration Statistics: A Story of Neglect.* Washington, D.C.: National Academy Press.

Schumer, C.E. 1989. "A Review of the Implementation of the Immigration

Reform and Control Act of 1986". A Report by the Office of Congressman Charles E. Schumer, Congress of the United States, House of Representative, Washington, D.C., March.

Appendix A: COMPARISON OF INS AND DOL REGIONAL BOUNDARIES

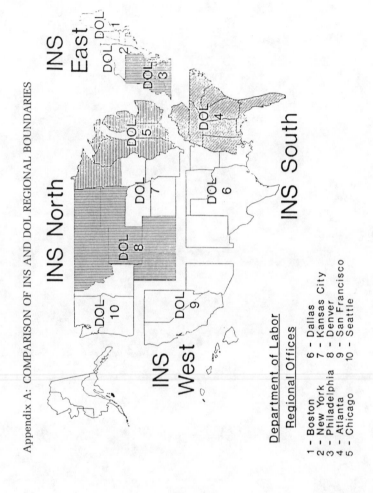

Department of Labor
Regional Offices

1 – Boston   6 – Dallas
2 – New York   7 – Kansas City
3 – Philadelphia   8 – Denver
4 – Atlanta   9 – San Francisco
5 – Chicago   10 – Seattle

ASSESSING THE IMPACT OF EMPLOYER SANCTIONS ON UNDOCUMENTED IMMIGRATION TO THE UNITED STATES

Jeffrey S. Passel, Frank D. Bean, and Barry Edmonston

The Immigration Reform and Control Act (IRCA) of 1986, the first major change in immigration law in a generation, was designed principally to decrease the flow of undocumented immigrants to the United States. IRCA included two provisions that, it was thought, would work together to reduce the flow of undocumented immigrants. First, increased Border Patrol enforcement would diminish the chance for successful entry to the United States. Second, effective employer sanctions would discourage employers from hiring undocumented workers, and hence reduce the demand for these workers (the so-called "jobs magnet"). A reduction in illegal immigration through the success of IRCA's provisions would represent a dramatic shift in the nature of immigration to the United States as it has evolved over the last several decades.

INTRODUCTION

Starting in the mid-1960s, patterns of immigration to the United States began to change in three important ways (Bean, Vernez, and Keely, 1989). The first change involved increases in legal immigration brought about by the passage of the 1965 Amendments to the Immigration and Nationality Act of 1952. These 1965 amendments abolished the national origins quotas that had been in operation since the early 1920s, thus opening up immigration from many countries that had been excluded for decades. By broadening the range of immigration sources and by giving priority to family reunification as a basis for immigrant admission, the amendments eventually led to levels of immigration that, by historical standards, were quite high. For example, average annual legal immigration increased steadily from about 250,000 per year in the 1950s to nearly 600,000 per year in the 1980s. These current levels had been surpassed only in the peak immigration years early in the twentieth century.

The second major change consisted of a shift in the national origin composition of immigration. During the 1950s, nearly 70 percent of immigrants came from European countries or Canada. This figure dropped to about 20 percent during the 1970s and then to about 15 percent during the 1980s. The percentage coming from Asian, Latin American, or Caribbean countries increased from about 30 percent during the 1950s to about 75 percent during the 1970s, and then to over 80 percent during the 1980s (U.S. Immigration and Naturalization Service, 1989). The shift toward Asia has been particularly marked as these immigrants accounted for about 6 percent of legal immigration in the 1950s, but about 45 percent in the 1980s. The Hispanic and Asian components in the recent immigration flows have also included sizeable numbers of refugees from Cuba and Southeast Asia, persons who subsequently have changed their status to that of permanent resident alien. Thus, immigrants not only have become more numerous than at any time in decades, they have also become more visible (Bean, Telles and Lowell, 1987; Bean and Sullivan, 1985).

The third important shift involved an increase in illegal immigration. After the end, in 1964, of the agreement under which the United States and Mexico operated the Bracero Program for temporary workers in agriculture, illegal immigration began to rise. In particular, illegal labor migrants from Mexico came in increasing numbers. Visa overstayers, i.e., persons who entered the country legally and then stayed beyond the expiration dates of their visas, also increased. Partly in response to these trends, the Select Commission on Immigration and Refugee Policy was established in 1981 and given a mandate to study all aspects of U.S. immigration policy. The Commission concluded in its final report that "one issue has emerged as most pressing—that of undocumented/illegal immigration" (U.S. Select Commission on Immigration and Refugee Policy, 1981, p. 35). This perception also came to be shared by the general public. For example, 87 percent of the respondents to a Southern California survey in the early 1980s thought that "the illegal immigration situation" was currently either "somewhat serious" or "very serious" (Muller and Espenshade, 1985, p. 201).

All of these changes contributed to a movement to reform U.S. immigration policy. To many lawmakers and citizens during the late 1970s and the early 1980s, the country seemed to have "lost control of its borders" and the costs of immigration appeared increasingly to outweigh the benefits. Even worse to some observers, the nation's immigration policies appeared ineffective in preventing illegal entry to the country at the same time that tens of thousands of legal petitioners were waiting to obtain entry visas. These concerns combined to create a strong push to curtail illegal immigration, but without a broad consensus about effective methods for doing so. After several false starts reflecting continuing debate and controversy over immigration policy, Congress passed the Immigration Reform and Control Act in October of 1986, and the legislation was signed into law the following month.

The litmus test by which IRCA will be judged is the extent to which future flows of illegal immigrants to the United States are reduced. As indicated by the numbers of people involved, IRCA's legalization programs have been quite successful, enrolling 1.8 million and 1.3 million applications in the regular and SAWs legalization programs, respectively (González Baker and Bean, 1990). But determining whether employer sanctions and Border Patrol enforcement have changed the flow of illegal immigrants coming to the country is a more difficult matter.

The purpose of this chapter is to review and assess the evidence on this issue. The question of the size of the illegal population in the United States and its changes during the 1980s is obviously a topic of considerable public policy significance (e.g., see Bean, Vernez, and Keely, 1989; Passel, 1986). Issues pertaining to the size, growth and impact of the illegal population in the United States were debated vociferously before the enactment of IRCA (Bean, Telles, and Lowell, 1987). They will continue to be important policy issues for years to come, if for no other reason than it is impossible to evaluate the degree to which employer sanctions have been successful without knowing the extent to which the flow of undocumented immigrants coming to the United States and the numbers of illegals residing permanently in the country has changed in the years after the passage of the legislation.

TYPES OF UNDOCUMENTED IMMIGRANTS

Meaningful assessments of the volume and impact of undocumented migration must distinguish among several different kinds of entrants. One classification comes from the government, which makes a distinction between 1) persons who enter without any sort of legal visa (called "EWIs" because they "enter without inspection") and 2) visa overstayers. Similar to visa overstayers are other foreign-born persons who enter the United States legally but violate the terms of their temporary visas by taking a job (for example, persons who hold tourist visas but work). The distinction between EWIs and visa overstayers derives from the fact that almost all EWIs are from Mexico and most visa-overstayers are from non-Mexican countries (Warren, 1990). In addition, some estimation techniques are particularly applicable to one group or the other. The distinction does not provide much insight, however, into two important dimensions of variation that are important for understanding the results of studies of the size and impact of the undocumented population. These dimensions are the degree of commitment to living in the United States and legal status.

Degree of Commitment to Living in the United States

Undocumented migrants come to the United States with varying degrees of commitment to reside in the country. Those intending to stay permanently are often called "settlers," and those intending to return to their countries of origin, "sojourners" (Chavez, 1988). In the case of undocumented Mexicans and Canadians, some observers would add still a third category — "commuters," or persons who "do not actually live in the United States, but rather cross the U.S.-Mexican or U.S.-Canadian borders on a daily or almost daily basis to work in the United States" (Passel, 1986, p. 183). This typology should be kept in mind when attempting to sort through the evidence on illegal immigration, particularly the evidence relating to labor migration from Mexico. The distinctions are also quite relevant to discussions of *stocks* (or populations) of undocumented aliens versus *flows* across the border (Bean, Vernez, and Keely, 1989).

Although it is common to think of sojourners as consisting of Mexican undocumented immigrants, there are also sojourners from other countries, as well as sojourners who are legal immigrants. Indeed, the high rates of emigration from the United States by legal immigrants from Caribbean countries (Warren and Kraly, 1985) suggest that many are actually sojourners. Sojourners from countries other than Mexico and Canada probably have longer durations of residence in the United States.

The distinction between sojourners and settlers is often a matter of degree. Massey and others have documented that migration between Mexico and the United States is a process occurring over a period of time, rather than a single event (Massey et al., 1987; Portes and Bach, 1985). Many individuals start as sojourners. Over time, as their ties to the United States become stronger and those to Mexico weaker, they extend their stays in this country to the point where they consider their residence to be the United States.

IRCA may have changed this settlement process in several ways. IRCA has converted a large segment of the sojourner population into settlers through the Special Agricultural Worker (SAW) legalization program (Bean, Vernez, and Keely, 1989). On the other hand, many formerly undocumented immigrants, having now been legalized, will travel to Mexico more frequently. Some proportion of this settled population may, however, ultimately return to Mexico and become sojourners or commuters as a result of the legislation.

Legal Status

The groups of aliens legalized under IRCA, as conceived of in the law, correspond to the "settler" and "sojourner" ideal types. Those granted legal status under the general legalization program should be settlers since legalization required at least five years continuous residence in the United States. SAWs, on the other hand, were generally conceived as sojourners who returned to the United States every year to participate in seasonal agricultural activities. However, large numbers of the persons legalized as SAWs apparently do not fit the ideal type envisioned in IRCA. Half or more of the SAW legalizations appear to have been gained fraudulently (Martin and Taylor, 1990). Some of the fraudulent cases are persons who did indeed work in agriculture, but not long enough to meet IRCA's requirements; others may not have previously been in the United States at all. Finally, some of the SAW legalizations are persons who chose the SAW program as a less complicated route to legal status than the general legalization program. It is undoubtedly the case, however, that a significant number of SAWs were settlers. In addition, even the SAWs who were really sojourners are entitled to settle in the United States once approved under the terms of IRCA. At this point, the proportion of the SAW population that has settled in the United States is not known.

ASSESSMENTS OF UNDOCUMENTED MIGRATION

Undocumented immigrants fall into all three categories — settlers, sojourners, and commuters. Lack of clear demarcation between the settler and sojourner-commuter categories is partly responsible for the exaggerated numbers sometimes used to describe the size of this population (Bean, Telles, and Lowell, 1987; Passel, 1986). Large flows of sojourners or commuters across the U.S.-Mexico border (as suggested by INS apprehensions) have been interpreted by many observers as indicating growth in the settled undocumented population that is as large as the labor migration flows. However, empirical work over the last decade has failed to find evidence for annual growth of 1 million or more persons in the undocumented population, as would be implied by annual INS apprehensions exceeding this amount (Warren and Passel, 1987).

It is particularly important to distinguish between "stocks" and "flows" when considering undocumented immigration to the United States. The former term refers to the number of illegal aliens residing in the country at a particular point in time. The latter term refers to the number entering (or exiting) the country within a particular time interval. The failure to distinguish these has contributed to confusion about the size of this population. Stated differently, because the number of illegal migrants (especially Mexicans) coming into the country has often appeared to be quite high, observers have sometimes assumed the number residing here was equally high. This view overlooks the fact that the majority of illegal migrants, particularly Mexicans, return to their country of origin. In short, commuters and sojourners have often been mistaken for settlers.

One useful way to think about efforts to estimate illegal immigration is according to whether they measure the "stock" or "flow" of illegal aliens, or both. It is also useful to distinguish among efforts that estimate Mexican or non-Mexican illegal immigration, or both. The reason these distinctions are important is that estimating these different segments of illegal stocks and flows requires different data sources. And different data sources are not equally useful for estimating number of Mexicans and non-Mexican stocks and flows. Current Population Survey (CPS) data, for example, are more useful for estimating the number of Mexican immigrants than the number of immigrants from other countries because the latter are spread over so many different countries of origin that the individual country estimates are unreliable (Woodrow and Passel, 1990). Apprehensions data, when used to assess changes in flows, yield particularly valuable information only on Mexican flows because the vast majority of apprehensions are of Mexicans (Bean et al., 1990).

Estimates of stocks and flows from individual non-Mexican countries must thus rely on other data sources. Fortunately, illegal aliens from non-Mexican countries differ from Mexicans in some important ways, making this possible. Illegal aliens from other countries appear largely to come to the United States initially through legal channels and then overstay their visas. Data on visa overstayers thus provide one way to estimate changes in illegal flows involving persons from particular countries other than Mexico. CPS data are also useful for assessing overall non-Mexican stocks and flows although, as noted, the sample size in these surveys is not large enough to yield reliable information for individual non-Mexican countries.

We review below the results of recent studies using various sources of data to tackle the problem of estimating whether IRCA and employer sanctions have had an impact on illegal immigration to the United States. Most data are from the United States, although some were collected in Mexico, the single most important source country for illegal immigration to the United States. Examining Mexican as well as U.S. data is particularly important to round out the picture of changing patterns of illegal immigration. IRCA could have the effect of reducing both the "stock" of illegal Mexicans in the country (through legalization) and the "flow" coming into the country (through the creation of disincentives for sojourners already in the country to continue going back and forth) without deterring the initiation of new migration. Looking at what is going on in Mexico helps to shed light on such questions.

Flows of Migrants Across the U.S.-Mexico Border

The largest flow of temporary and permanent migrants into the United States occurs across the border with Mexico. The flow of people back and forth across this border is immense in scale—more than 200 million crossings occur through ports of entry every year (INS, 1989). Of course, most of these crossings do not represent net immigration into (or out of) the United States; rather, they represent shoppers, tourists, or commuters crossing for trips of short duration.

Another large flow across the U.S.-Mexico border consists of temporary labor migrants. This flow, which consists principally of EWIs, is the one that INS taps into with Border Patrol apprehensions. The temporary nature of the labor migration should be apparent from the composition of the flow—about 80 to 90 percent of the apprehensions are adult Mexican males. If all the Mexican males apprehended over the last 10 to 20 years actually represented permanent migrants to the United States, the adult population of Mexico would now be overwhelmingly female and, conversely, the Mexican-born population of the United States would be overwhelmingly male. Neither of these situations has occurred. The close relationship of apprehensions with seasonal labor demands in the United States further reinforces the view that this is a temporary flow of labor (Bean et al., 1990)

RELATIONSHIP BETWEEN INS APPREHENSIONS AND MIGRATION FLOWS

Most journalistic references to INS apprehensions of illegal entrants along the U.S.-Mexico border make the simplistic assumption that there is a direct relationship between the number of illegal immigrants and the number of INS apprehensions. Both the popular and official interpretations of the apprehensions data make a further assumption that there are more illegal immigrants than apprehensions. This assumption is usually stated as "for every one that gets caught, X get away," where "X" is most often two or three.

These interpretations of apprehensions data fail on a number of accounts. First, they fail to distinguish between settlers and sojourners. Clearly, empirical studies of the size of the undocumented population in the United States do not offer support for the proposition that the INS apprehensions (or those who "got away") represent net additions of illegal settlers to the U.S. population. Second, they fail to take into account the fact that the count of apprehensions includes many repeaters, i.e., individuals who are apprehended more than once on each trip to the United States plus other individuals who make multiple trips to the United States. Third, they assume that the "got-away ratio" is independent of the level of INS effort put into apprehending aliens and the resources (personnel and materiel) available to the Border Patrol.

What the apprehensions actually represent, in the most basic terms, is the portion of the migratory flow across the U.S.-Mexico border that is intercepted by the INS. Simply multiplying apprehensions by a "got-away" ratio is inappropriate for estimating flows across the border, because apprehended individuals tend to make additional attempts to enter the United States until they are successful. As a result, if the probability of apprehension increases, apprehensions increase at a faster rate because multiple apprehensions of the same individuals also increase. In other words, there is a relationship between the number of successful border crossers and the number of apprehensions, but it is not necessarily a one-to-one relationship.

Careful attention to the probability of apprehension is necessary in order to understand the changing relationship between the number of apprehensions and the number of border crossers. Two broad conditions affect the probability of apprehension: INS effort and the "skill" of the crossers. If INS devotes more personnel to patrolling the border or makes technological improvements in detection technology, the probability of apprehension should increase. Sensible analysis of INS apprehension data, therefore, needs to take into account changes in Border Patrol enforcement efforts, as measured by such factors as man-hours worked, budget, and technological improvements. On the other hand, if the crossers become more skillful at eluding detection (e.g., by learning from previous apprehensions or by using smugglers, called "coyotes"), the probability of apprehension should decrease. Such changes in the probability of apprehension also affect the reported apprehensions.

REVIEW OF RESEARCH RESULTS

Several recent studies have used time series methods to analyze apprehensions data as an indicator of illegal migration into the United States across the southern border. One group of studies has been conducted by researchers working at The Urban Institute (Bean et al., 1990; Espenshade, 1990; Espenshade, White, and Bean, 1990; White, Bean and Espenshade, 1990). These studies conceptualize apprehensions as a product of the size of the population at risk of being apprehended (i.e., the people crossing the border illegally) times the probability of apprehension. They further model the number of border crossers as a function of the size of the Mexican population likely to migrate and the propensity to migrate. The propensity to migrate is modeled with economic factors, seasonal factors, and factors related to IRCA. With the exception of Espenshade's (1990) study, these inquiries do not directly estimate the probability of apprehension. Rather, they include INS effort in terms of linewatch hours or non-linewatch hours (depending upon which type of apprehension is being modeled), and they include border patrol budgetary resources in their model as indicators of the probability of apprehension. The economic variables included in the model use national ratios of wages and unemployment rates. Ratios specific to certain areas in Mexico and the southwestern United States might be better indicators of the factors affecting migration, but such ratios are not generally available. The final results of their analyses are estimates of the number of apprehensions averted as a result of IRCA, i.e., the number of additional apprehensions that would have occurred in the absence of IRCA.

The research of Espenshade (1990) includes the same variables to represent the population at risk of migrating and the propensity to migrate. The contribution of Espenshade's research is that it explicitly converts apprehensions into estimated border crossings using an estimate of the probability of apprehension derived from the proportion of all apprehensions that are multiple apprehensions. This result is then an estimate of the change in border crossings brought about by IRCA, rather than the change in apprehensions.

Another study was conducted by researchers working at the RAND Corporation (Crane et al., 1990). The models used in the RAND research include linewatch hours (as a measure of INS effort), seasonal effects, and a time trend to represent the increasing size of the population of potential migrants in Mexico. The research also attempts to convert the estimate of change in apprehensions into an estimate of the change in number and proportion of border crossings due to IRCA. This approach supplies a range of plausible values for various populations and proportions in an analytical model of the border crossing and apprehension process.

In spite of the problems of apprehensions data, some consistent findings emerge from the above research studies. First and foremost, there has been a clear reduction in the flow of undocumented immigrants across the U.S.-Mexico border in the post-IRCA period. Furthermore, this reduction has occurred in the presence of increased INS effort, indicated by more linewatch hours and upgraded equipment. The current research also suggests that a significant portion of the reduction in apprehensions is attributable to the legalization of large numbers of Mexicans in the general legalization and SAW programs.

Second, the studies are broadly consistent in how much of the reduction can be attributed to IRCA. Espenshade estimates reductions of 30 and 44 percent in border crossings for fiscal years 1987 and 1988, respectively, that can be attributed to IRCA. The Bean et al. (1990) study, which reports the most complete data for the post-IRCA period, estimates a 47 percent decline in apprehensions between November 1986 and September 1989 below the level that would have been anticipated in the absence of IRCA. For the same period, the models used by Crane et al. lead to 21 to 32 percent estimates of the decline in apprehensions.

Bean et al. (1990) further partition the decline and find that about half of the decrease in apprehensions was attributable to SAW legalizations, i.e., the removal of SAWs from the labor stream subject to potential apprehension. The remainder of the decline is due to other IRCA effects. In other words, about one-fourth of the decline of apprehensions between late 1986 and 1989 was due to IRCA effects other than SAW legalization. They found no significant impact of the general legalization program on apprehensions, and none should be expected since this group is made up of settlers who would contribute very little to the apprehensions. (This point is corroborated by John Bjerke of the INS through personal communication in 1990, who reports that about two-thirds of a sample of legalized aliens interviewed reported that they had made no trips out of the United States since 1982.) Although not directly comparable, the work of Crane et al. points in the same direction.

Other research addresses the effect of IRCA on the magnitude of immigration across the U.S.-Mexico border less directly than the apprehensions studies. One recent study (Bustamante, 1990) reports the results of a data collection project that has been following the number and kind of undocumented persons crossing the border at one of its highest traffic points—Canyon Zapata just outside Tijuana, Mexico, about 20 miles south of San Diego. This research suffers from some of the same limitations as the analyses of apprehensions data—for example, the lack of any measure of successful entry to the United States, the inclusion of the same individual more than once (crossings versus entries), and the failure to distinguish settlers from sojourners. In addition, the Canyon Zapata data do not have a pre-IRCA baseline for comparison. Lack of baseline data means that a strong statistical test cannot be made of Canyon Zapata trends, as affected by IRCA. Nonetheless, Bustamente's data show a clear decline in border crossers in the post-IRCA period; the numbers of crossers in late 1988 fall significantly below the corresponding figures for late 1986, immediately after the passage of IRCA.

Other Mexican data is reported by Cornelius (1989; 1990), who draws upon 946 interviews conducted in 1988–1989 in three communities in the Mexican states of Jalisco, Michoacan, and Zacatecas—states that have traditionally sent migrants to the United States. Cornelius examines how IRCA has affected perceptions of the U.S. labor market, the propensity to migrate, settlement patterns in the United States, and the economies of migrant families and their home communities. He finds evidence that is consistent with the idea that IRCA may have had a small deterrent effect on undocumented immigration. About 83 percent of the surveyed undocumented immigrants and would-be immigrants thought that IRCA had made getting a job in the United States harder. Furthermore, about 20 percent of potential immigrants who thought of going to the United States gave an IRCA-related reason for not making the trip. Cornelius notes, however, that this small effect may be more than offset by new undocumented immigrants, notably wives and children of newly legalized aliens, leaving Mexico to join family members in the United States.

Not all research supports the position that IRCA has had a small, but demonstratable, deterrent effect. Massey et al. (1990) find no evidence that IRCA has lowered the probability of first-time undocumented migration to the United States from communities in Mexico. Nor did they find that the costs or difficulty of illegal entry had increased. However, Massey et al. characterize their results as "preliminary" because of the small number of communities involved, the very small number of cases examined, and the necessity of extrapolating from the past.

Crane et al. (1990) also attempt to find evidence of a decline in the stock and flow of undocumented workers resulting from employer sanctions, by examining the change over time in wages of dishwashers and car washers in cities with significant undocumented populations and those without. Their analysis requires a number of assumptions about the relationship of wages to undocumented labor supply, plus the assumption that their results are in fact due to (unobserved) fluctuations in the presence of undocumented workers. A problem with their results, however, is that their approach does not fully take into account the possibility of a preexisting oversupply of available labor or that wage levels might be supported by a minimum wage. In the former case, for example, even if IRCA did reduce the labor supply in these occupations, one would not expect to find an effect on wages. None of the effects they isolate is large. Overall, they conclude that they can find little evidence of an IRCA-related effect on undocumented workers in these occupations.

The Stock of Undocumented Immigrants and Additions to the Permanent Resident Population

Woodrow and Passel (1990) examined 1980 Census data and a series of CPS data sources from the 1980s (including the June 1988 CPS) in order to estimate the size of the illegal population included in these data sources and its change over time. These researchers make use of a methodology that involves subtracting an estimate of the legally resident foreign-born population from the census or survey estimate of the foreign-born population in order to obtain an indication of the size of the undocumented component. They also examine changes during the 1980s in the size of this component. Their results are directly relevant to assessing the effect of IRCA on the stock of undocumented immigrants living in the United States.

REDUCTION IN STOCK BUT NOT IN OVERALL FLOW

Woodrow and Passel find that IRCA had definitely reduced the undocumented population of the United States to the point where the total number in 1988 may have been smaller than the number in the country in 1980 (estimated by Passel, 1986, to be in the range of 2.5 to 3.5 million). However, the evidence from their analyses is that the reduction is due entirely to the legalization of formerly illegal residents; that is, they do not find evidence consistent with the idea that IRCA's employer sanctions have led to net outmigration of undocumented residents. In addition, they do not find evidence for a decrease in the overall net flow of illegal migrants, although some of their results suggest the possibility of a decline in the flow of undocumented immigrants from Mexico. This latter point supports the evidence reported above from the apprehensions data regarding flows across the U.S.-Mexico border. This result leaves open the question of whether IRCA's effects on Mexican flows are unique because of the predominance of Mexicans in the legalization programs, the special character of southwest regional economies in the United States and their labor demands, the long shared border with Mexico, and the geographic concentration of Mexican immigrants in the United States.

SHIFT IN COMPOSITION

The CPS data also show a definite shift in the composition of the undocumented population living in the United States. As a result of the legalization programs, the proportion of the undocumented population that is Mexican has declined, possibly to the point where a majority of undocumented residents in 1988 may be from countries other than Mexico. More than three-quarters of the Mexican-born population living in the United States consists of legal residents, according to the CPS. Before the passage of IRCA, less than 40 percent were legal residents. This shift is one of the most significant changes wrought by IRCA and is likely to have ramifications for the composition and magnitude of future legal immigration flows for some time because of the delayed effects of family reunification policies.

INCREASE IN PROPORTION OF WOMEN

Another change found in the CPS-based estimates of the undocumented population is the greatly increased proportion of women in

this population. Apparently only 20 to 40 percent of the undocumented population included in the 1988 CPS are men. In the 1980
Census estimates, the corresponding figure was 55 percent. The decreased proportion of men is the result of the disproportionately
male population that was legalized, particularly in the SAW program.
In addition, there is some evidence to suggest that post-IRCA flows
of undocumented female immigrants are increasing. Bean et al. (1990)
also report that apprehensions of Mexican women and children (and
of non-Mexicans) increased in 1988 and 1989, a time when apprehensions of Mexican males were decreasing dramatically. Cornelius
(1990) also finds some evidence for augmented undocumented flows
of families (i.e., women and children) who are leaving Mexico to
join the newly legalized aliens in the United States. Finally, Bustamante's (1990) photographs from Canyon Zapata show higher percentages of women in the flows for 1987 and 1988 than in the 1986
flows.

VISA OVERSTAYERS

Warren (1990) has developed estimates of visa overstayers in the
United States, including data for two years before and after the passage of IRCA. His research represents the first successful attempt to
estimate the number of visa overstayers, an important but largely
unstudied component of illegal migration to the United States. For
fiscal years 1985–1988, Warren estimates 217,000 to 255,000 new
visa overstays per year, with some evidence of a modest increase
during this period. After allowing for "old" visa overstayers who
depart the country or become legal residents, Warren generates provisional estimates of net overstays for fiscal 1988 (only). He finds
that the net addition of visa overstayers is 174,000, almost one-third
below the total estimated overstayers of 255,000. The relationship
of net to gross overstayers that Warren finds for 1988 should be
typical of earlier years also.

Warren's estimates of net visa overstays are broadly consistent with
the CPS and Census-based estimates of undocumented immigration.
His estimate of 174,000 net visa overstayers per year includes about
126,000 per year from countries other than Mexico. Because most
non-Mexican undocumented immigrants are probably visa overstayers, it is appropriate to compare Warren's estimates with the CPS-
based estimates of average annual changes in the undocumented
population of roughly 100,000 to 180,000 for countries other than
Mexico. Warren's estimates for 1988 fall in the middle of this range.
In addition, tabulations of overstayers by region of origin are also

broadly consistent with the CPS data, as Europe and Canada show lower levels in both data sets and Latin America, higher levels. Exact agreement between the two data sets should not be expected, given the sampling variability of the CPS estimates and the residual nature of both sets of estimates.

Warren finds a slight increase between 1985 and 1988 in the number of annual apparent overstays. On its face, this finding suggests no impact of IRCA on the flow of illegal immigrants who enter through this route. However, to some extent, this finding is due to increases in the number of nonimmigrant visa grants during the same time period. When examined in terms of the number of overstayers per nonimmigrant entry, the same data show a decline in the rate of overstays. However, because the estimates of visa overstayers are derived by taking the difference of two numbers that are very large compared with the number of apparent overstayers, the resulting estimates are sensitive to rather small errors in the data and assumptions. (The CPS-based estimates of the undocumented population have this same property.) Thus, even though the annual estimates appear to be robust in terms of their overall magnitude and geographic composition, the trend over time could be different from what is shown in Warren's paper.

CONCLUSION

A considerable body of evidence has emerged to gauge the impact of IRCA on the stock and flow of illegal immigrants to the United States during the three-year period after the legislation was passed. Several of the studies whose results are reported here were based on data collected before or just after the beginning of INS enforcement of employer sanctions, which were phased in only gradually. Thus, the full force of deterrent effects of the legislation may not yet have emerged by the time of observation for some of these studies. Consequently, only very large and immediate effects are likely to be detectable.

The studies are generally consistent in suggesting at least a short-term decrease in the flow of illegal migrants across the U.S.-Mexico border. However, it is difficult to ascribe this decline to effects of employer sanctions. A large proportion of the decrease is due to the effects of the legalization programs. The SAW legalization program, to a great extent, and the general legalization program, to a lesser extent, removed individuals from the illegal flow in two ways. It did so first, by making them part of the legal flow of labor and other migrants across the border, and second, by allowing them to settle permanently in the United States. The effect of removing legalized migrants from the illegal flow across the border does not appear to account for all of the estimated decline in flows across the U.S.-Mexico border, however. Thus, IRCA's employer sanctions may have had some deterrent effect.

As a result of IRCA, the proportion of the undocumented population and undocumented flow that is from Mexico is smaller than it was before IRCA. In addition, a larger proportion of the post-IRCA undocumented population is female, especially for Mexican migrants. This compositional shift occurred because IRCA legalized a very large proportion of the undocumented Mexican and undocumented male labor force. There is also some evidence that the composition of the undocumented flow has changed because families of formerly undocumented immigrants are migrating to join the legalized men in the United States. Some men who were legalized under IRCA provisions already had spouses and children in the United States, even though their family members may not have qualified for legalization. Many other men who received legal immigrant status had family members living in Mexico; these men often united their families in the United States by moving (usually illegally) their wives and children to the United States.

IRCA's employer sanctions provisions may have brought about some of this compositional shift because female illegal migrants may have some advantages over males in locating jobs less subject to the enforcement of employer sanctions. Employer sanctions have particularly targeted industrial and larger manufacturing firms that might have illegal aliens. These establishments tend to have predominantly male workers and, thus, sanctions are thought to have a stronger effect in discouraging employment opportunities for illegal male aliens than for illegal female immigrants. One consequence of these patterns and other IRCA provisions may be an alteration of the migration process so that there are more settlers and fewer sojourners than before the enactment of IRCA. More data are needed, however, before this conjecture can be confirmed.

The INS has instituted a policy of not deporting illegal aliens who are immediate relatives of aliens legalized under IRCA (González Baker, 1990). Although the number of such relatives is not known, they may constitute a significant fraction of the remaining undocumented population. If so, the number of *deportable* aliens actually residing in the United States may now be even smaller than the estimates from the CPS and other sources suggest.

Whether the changes observed in the undocumented population through 1988–1989 continue into the future is a key question in determining the success of IRCA in controlling illegal immigration. Ultimately, an important factor will be the ability of INS to obtain sufficient budgetary resources to enforce the provisions of IRCA (Fix and Hill, 1990). Some recent data suggest that undocumented migrant flows continue to evolve in the post-IRCA period.

INS apprehensions are higher in fiscal 1990 than they were a year earlier, but the evidence pointing to higher underlying flows remains contradictory after taking INS effort into account. (See table 7.1.) For the last three months of 1989 (October to December of FY 1990), Mexican border apprehensions were 40 percent higher than the corresponding period in 1988. However, linewatch hours—the most direct measure of INS effort—were up about 37 percent. This evidence, then, suggests hardly any increase in flow. For the first three months of 1990 (January to March of FY 1990), however, apprehensions were 52 percent higher than one year earlier, while INS effort was up only 17 percent. The majority of the increase in apprehensions was accounted for by a 73 percent increase in apprehensions in the San Diego sector, which had a roughly constant number of enforcement hours (Michael Hoefer, personal communication, May 1990). The level of apprehensions per linewatch hour during the first nine months of calendar year 1990 is higher than during the previous year, but below the levels attained in corresponding quarters of 1986–1988. Thus, there may have been a turnaround in the flow beginning in early 1990.

This tentative indication of a turnaround suggests some difficulties for IRCA in the future. Additional research with data from the 1990s is clearly needed to report on the direction and size of the flow of undocumented immigration.

It is important to continue to assess IRCA's effects on illegal immigration and the U.S. labor force. Data from the 1990 Census should shed additional light on some of these issues by providing the first detailed look at the foreign-born population since the enactment of IRCA. As the legalized aliens progress through the process of attaining permanent resident status and, eventually, citizenship, more information on their settlement patterns and adaptation to American society will become available. Such information has been particularly lacking on the SAW population to this point. As IRCA continues to be implemented and its employer sanctions enforced, its success

Table 7.1 BORDER PATROL APPREHENSIONS: OCTOBER 1985–SEPTEMBER 1990, SOUTHERN AND WESTERN REGIONS

Period	Fiscal Year					Ratio to Previous Year*				Ratio to FY 1986*			
	1986	1987	1988	1989	1990	1987	1988	1989	1990	1987	1988	1989	1990
Linewatch Apprehensions (000s)													
Oct–Dec	160	168	117	91	129	105	69	79	140	105	73	57	80
Jan–Mar	256	201	207	118	180	78	103	57	152	78	81	46	70
Apr–Jun	275	172	149	149	168	62	87	100	113	62	54	54	61
Jul–Sep	256	215	141	163	192	84	66	116	118	84	55	64	75
FY Total	947	755	614	522	668	80	81	85	128	80	65	55	71
Linewatch Hours (000s)													
Oct–Dec	554	650	560	476	654	117	86	85	137	117	101	86	118
Jan–Mar	598	685	523	564	654	115	76	108	116	115	88	94	109
Apr–Jun	643	635	505	702	619	99	80	139	88	99	79	109	96
Jul–Sep	607	597	477	695	622	98	80	146	89	98	79	114	102
FY Total	2,402	2,566	2,065	2,437	2,549	107	80	118	105	107	86	101	106
Line Apprehensions per 1,000 Linewatch Hours													
Oct–Dec	290	258	208	192	197	89	81	92	102	89	72	66	68
Jan–Mar	428	293	396	209	275	68	135	53	131	68	93	49	64
Apr–Jun	428	271	295	213	272	63	109	72	128	63	69	50	64
Jul–Sep	421	360	295	234	308	85	82	79	131	85	70	56	73
FY Total	394	294	297	214	262	75	101	72	122	75	75	54	66

*Ratio is per 100.
Source: Unpublished INS tabulations.

or failure at reducing the stock and flow of undocumented immigrants should become more measurable. At this point, however, we can conclude that although IRCA *has* had an impact, this was due to a large extent to the legalization of a large proportion of the formerly undocumented population. Whether the effects will persist can only be answered with the passage of time.

References

Bean, Frank D., Barry Edmonston, and Jeffrey S. Passel. 1990. "Introduction." In *Undocumented Migration to the United States: IRCA and the Experience of the 1980s*, Frank D. Bean, Jeffrey S. Passel, and Barry Edmonston, eds. Washington, D.C.: Urban Institute Press.

Bean, Frank D., Thomas J. Espenshade, Michael J. White, and Robert Dymowski. 1990. "Post-IRCA Changes in the Volume and Composition of Undocumented Migration to the United States." In *Undocumented Migration to the United States: IRCA and the Experience of the 1980s*, Frank D. Bean, Jeffrey S. Passel, and Barry Edmonston, eds. Washington, D.C.: Urban Institute Press.

Bean, Frank D., Georges Vernez, and Charles B. Keely. 1989. *Opening and Closing the Doors: Evaluating Immigration Reform and Control*. Santa Monica, Ca., and Washington, D.C.: The RAND Corporation and The Urban Institute Press.

Bean, Frank D., and Teresa Sullivan. 1985. "Immigration and Its Consequences: Confronting the Problem." *Society* 22 (May/June): 67–73.

Bean, Frank D., Edward Telles, and Lindsay Lowell. 1987. "Undocumented Migration to the United States: Perception and Evidence." *Population and Development Review* 13, no. 4 (December): 671–690.

Bustamante, Jorge A. 1990. "Undocumented Migration from Mexico to the United States: Preliminary Findings of the Zapata Canyon Project." In *Undocumented Migration to the United States: IRCA and the Experience of the 1980s*, Frank D. Bean, Jeffrey S. Passel, and Barry Edmonston, eds. Washington, D.C.: Urban Institute Press.

Chavez, Leo. 1988. "Settlers and Sojourners: The Case of Mexicans in the United States." *Human Organization* 47, no. 2 (Summer): 95–107.

Crane, Keith, Beth J. Asch, Joanna Zorn Heilbron, and Danielle C. Cullinane. 1990. *The Effect of Employer Sanctions on the Flow of Undocumented Immigrants to the United States*. Program for Research on Immigration Policy JRI-03, Urban Institute Report 90-8, Washington, D.C., and Santa Monica, Ca.

Cornelius, Wayne. 1990. "Impacts of the 1986 U.S. Immigration Law on

Emigration from Rural Mexican Sending Communities." In *Undocumented Migration to the United States: IRCA and the Experience of the 1980s*, Frank D. Bean, Jeffrey S. Passel, and Barry Edmonston, eds. Washington, D.C.: Urban Institute Press.

Cornelius, Wayne. 1989. "Impacts of the 1986 U.S. Immigration Law on Emigration from Rural Mexican Sending Communities." *Population and Development Review* 15, no. 4 (December): 689–706.

Espenshade, Thomas J. 1990. "Undocumented Migration to the United States: Evidence from a Repeated Trials Model." In *Undocumented Migration to the United States: IRCA and the Experience of the 1980s*, Frank D. Bean, Jeffrey S. Passel, and Barry Edmonston, eds. Washington, D.C.: Urban Institute Press.

Espenshade, Thomas J., Michael J. White, and Frank D. Bean. 1990. "Patterns of Recent Illegal Migration to the United States," in *Future Demographic Trends in Europe and North America*, ed. W. Lutz. Laxenberg, Austria: International Institute for Applied Systems Analysis.

Fix, Michael, and Paul Hill. 1990. *Enforcing Employer Sanctions: Challenges and Strategies*. Program for Research on Immigration Policy JRI-04, Urban Institute Report 90-6, Washington, D.C.: Urban Institute Press.

González Baker, Susan. 1990. *The Cautious Welcome: The Legalization Programs of the Immigration Reform and Control Act*. Program for Research on Immigration Policy JRI-05, Urban Institute Report 90-9, Washington, D.C.: Urban Institute Press.

González Baker, Susan and Frank D. Bean. 1990. "The Legalization Programs of the 1986 Immigration Reform and Control Act: Moving Beyond the First Phase." In *In Defense of the Alien*, ed. L. Tomasi, New York: Center for Migration Studies.

INS (U.S. Immigration and Naturalization Service). 1989. *Annual Report of the Immigration and Naturalization Service: 1988*. Washington, D.C.: U.S. Government Printing Office, April.

Martin, Philip L. and J. Edward Taylor. 1990. "SAWs, RAWs, and U.S. Agriculture." Paper presented at the Annual Meetings of the American Statistical Association, Anaheim, California, August.

Massey, Douglas S., Rafael Alarcon, Jorge Durand, and Humberto Gonzales. 1987. *Return to Aztlan: The Social Process of International Migration from Western Mexico*. Berkeley, Ca.: University of California Press.

Massey, Douglas S., Katharine M. Donato, and Zai Liang. 1990. "Effects of the Immigration Reform and Control Act of 1986: Preliminary Data from Mexico." In *Undocumented Migration to the United States: IRCA and the Experience of the 1980s*, Frank D. Bean, Jeffrey S. Passel, and Barry Edmonston, eds. Washington, D.C.: Urban Institute Press.

Muller, Thomas and Thomas J. Espenshade. 1985. *The Fourth Wave: Cali-*

fornia's Newest Immigrants. Washington, D.C.: The Urban Institute Press.

Passel, Jeffrey. 1986. "Undocumented Immigration." *The Annals* 487 (September): 181–200.

Passel, Jeffrey S., Frank D. Bean, and Barry Edmonston. 1990. "Undocumented Migration Since IRCA: An Overall Assessment." In *Undocumented Migration to the United States: IRCA and the Experience of the 1980s,* Frank D. Bean, Jeffrey S. Passel, and Barry Edmonston, eds. Washington, D.C.: Urban Institute Press.

Portes, Alejandro and Robert Bach. 1985. *Latin Journey: Cuban and Mexican Immigrants in the United States.* Berkeley, Ca.: University of California Press.

U.S. Select Commission on Immigration and Refugee Policy. 1981. *U.S. Immigration Policy and the National Interest: The Staff Report of The Select Commission on Immigration and Refugee Policy.* Washington, D.C.: U.S. Government Printing Office.

Warren, Robert. 1990. "Annual Estimates of Nonimmigrant Overstayers in the United States: 1985 to 1988." In *Undocumented Migration to the United States: IRCA and the Experience of the 1980s,* Frank D. Bean, Jeffrey S. Passel, and Barry Edmonston, eds. Washington, D.C.: Urban Institute Press.

Warren, Robert, and Jeffrey Passel. 1987. "A Count of the Uncountable: Estimates of Undocumented Aliens Counted in the 1980 U.S. Census." *Demography* 24, no. 3 (August): 375–396.

Warren, Robert and Ellen Percy Kraly. 1985. *The Elusive Exodus: Emigration from the United States.* Population Trends and Public Policy Occasional Paper No. 8. Washington, D.C.: Population Reference Bureau.

White, Michael J., Frank D. Bean, and Thomas J. Espenshade. 1990. "The U.S. 1986 Immigration Reform and Control Act and Undocumented Migration to the United States." *Population Research and Policy Review* 9, no. 2: 93–116.

Woodrow, Karen A., and Jeffrey S. Passel. 1990. "Post-IRCA Undocumented Immigrants to the United States: An Assessment Based on the June 1988 CPS." In *Undocumented Migration to the United States: IRCA and the Experience of the 1980s,* Frank D. Bean, Jeffrey S. Passel, and Barry Edmonston, eds. Washington, D.C.: Urban Institute Press.

Chapter Eight

EMPLOYER SANCTIONS: EXPECTATIONS AND EARLY OUTCOMES

Demetrios A. Papademetriou, B. Lindsay Lowell,
and Deborah A. Cobb-Clark

The 1986 Immigration Reform and Control Act became law after a lengthy and emotional debate that focused primarily on how best to control illegal migration. The effectiveness of the law's centerpiece—employer sanctions—is the topic of this chapter. In assessing the effectiveness of sanctions about one year after full implementation we have encountered numerous obstacles. These revolved around issues of data quality and availability, difficulties in isolating the effects of employer sanctions from those of IRCA's other major provisions and, most fundamentally, questions of whether sufficient time since IRCA's passage has lapsed for substantial—and hence readily perceptible—changes in hiring practices to occur.

This chapter first evaluates the "success" of IRCA's employer sanctions provision by juxtaposing its effects against the expectations of the law's architects. Employer sanctions were expected to be the principal tool for reducing the flow of unauthorized workers into the United States. In many quarters, the marked decrease in the number of illegal aliens apprehended since IRCA's passage is offered as prima facie evidence that the law has had the intended effect. We assess the validity of this premise by evaluating the relative contribution of IRCA's two major provisions—legalization and sanctions—on the decline in apprehensions. We also use evidence from the INS, the Census Bureau, and the relevant field research to assess further the law's overall effect on the flow of unauthorized migrants. Finally, we review and draw lessons from the European experience with employer sanctions enforcement in an attempt to provide some guidelines for the future. In the conclusions we offer some tentative observations on the intersection between policies of immigration control and those of labor force standards.

EXPECTATIONS VERSUS REALITY
IN THE PASSAGE OF IRCA

The principal reason for the 1979 impaneling of the Select Commission on Immigration and Refugee Policy (SCIRP), as well as the focus of the debate following the release of the Commission's 1981 report, was the need to address what was perceived to be the most crucial immigration challenge facing the nation at the time: controlling illegal immigration. Academic and policy discussions had arrived at what amounted to a near consensus: "push" factors aside, the "magnet" that attracted illegal aliens to the United States was their relatively unhampered access to the U.S. labor market.[1] As a result, much of the Select Commission's work addressed what it called the " . . . ambiguous position of espousing respect for the law as a cornerstone of society, while refusing to make the enforcement of its immigration laws a priority" (SCIRP, 1981b, p. 560).

Employer sanctions had been considered as a possible deterrent to illegal immigration even before the 1952 enactment of the Immigration and Nationality Act. In 1951, the Truman Commission on Migratory Labor recommended adopting sanctions as a response to illegal immigration from Mexico.[2] However, the relatively low levels of illegal immigration during the second half of the 1950s and the first half of the 1960s, often attributed to the existence of the "bracero" program (Congressional Research Service, 1979), pushed employer sanctions to the policy back burner until the early 1970s. Beginning in 1971, a succession of legislative[3] and executive branch[4] initiatives attempted to prohibit the employment of illegal aliens and thus shift some of the legal risk associated with this practice to employers. But it was not until 1986, with the passage of IRCA, that this effort was successful.

The authors of IRCA envisioned a concerted enforcement effort resting on a triad of major initiatives to be undertaken simultaneously. The first initiative was a legalization program. Legalization was intended to "bring out of the shadows" long-term illegal aliens who had been contributing to society and had developed significant social and economic "equities" in the process. The case for legalization rested on both humanitarian and economic grounds. The humanitarian argument made the case that conflicting signals resulted from a combination of what the Select Commission had called the "conspicuous legal loophole of the Texas proviso" and an equally inconsistent and largely ineffective border control policy. Such conflicting signals, according to the argument, had in fact encouraged illegal immigration. The economic argument responded to the concern that the new immigration law should not disrupt the economy. The legislation's second initiative was improved U.S.-Mexico border security. This was to be accomplished by providing the Border Patrol with additional resources—an ongoing priority for successive administrations in the 1970s and 1980s.[5]

Although legalization and stricter border enforcement were both critical elements in the strategy to curtail illegal immigration, they were not expected to accomplish that goal by themselves. During the lengthy consideration of the issues leading to the passage of IRCA, witness after witness had argued in favor of the additional initiative of employer sanctions. The Reagan administration's own 1981 Immigration Task Force had strongly endorsed sanctions in repeated testimony. And despite a spirited campaign against employer sanctions led by representatives of employer groups and ethnic communities, it was eventually agreed that a successful policy of immigration control should have as its centerpiece the statutory prohibition of the employment of aliens who were not authorized to work in the United States. As a result, although sanctions were only one of three concurrent major IRCA initiatives, they gradually came to be viewed as the ". . . only credible deterrent to the flow of ambitious men and women who will spend a lifetime of earnings and take great personal risks to find work in the United States . . ." (SCIRP, 1981b, p. 565.)

For sanctions to be effective, employers would have to be convinced that the employment of aliens without appropriate work authorization would no longer be risk-free. The determined and consistent enforcement of IRCA would send a message to the ethnic communities in the United States, and through them to the immigrant-sending communities abroad, that illegal aliens could no longer expect to find jobs readily in the U.S., nor would they be able to act as free agents in the U.S. labor market. Three years after IRCA became law this goal remains extremely elusive.

UNAUTHORIZED EMPLOYMENT AFTER IRCA: AN EARLY ASSESSMENT

Apprehensions of illegal entrants to the United States, a rough indicator of the growing supply of unauthorized workers, increased over 300 percent between 1970 and 1978 (North, 1981, p. 277). The years just prior to the passage of IRCA witnessed a further intensification of this trend. Border Patrol apprehensions of deportable aliens, which had stabilized at approximately 800,000 in each fiscal year from the mid-1970s through 1982, more than doubled to a total of 1.7 million by fiscal year 1986.[6]

In a reversal of this trend, however, recorded apprehensions show a drop in the post-IRCA period (see figure 8.1). In FY 1987, the first year after the passage of IRCA, apprehensions fell by 29 percent, to 1.2 million. During FYs 1988 and 1989, apprehensions declined an additional 27 percent below the 1987 level—to 891,000. While this is a dramatic decline in apprehensions, two questions remain: a) How much of the change is associated with the enforcement of the employer sanction provisions? And b) Does a recent upturn in apprehensions during the latter half of 1989 and early 1990 indicate that illegal aliens, after an initial uncertainty, now view IRCA as little threat to obtaining a job in the U.S.?

Apprehensions may have fallen for any or all of the following reasons:

☐ Unauthorized workers may now find it difficult to find work in the U.S. as a result of employer sanctions. As anticipated by the framers of the law, sanctions would inhibit the magnet (demand) for unauthorized labor. Both first-time and experienced migrants may stay home.
☐ Over three million persons have been legalized under IRCA and, thus, their border crossings no longer result in any apprehensions. Given generally high rates of mobility, these newly legal individuals may account for much of the decline.
☐ As a result of job uncertainties caused by IRCA, residual unauthorized persons may be less likely to circulate between the U.S. and their home countries. Similarly, early legalization applicants may have been less likely to travel back-and-forth, thus resulting in fewer persons exposed to possible apprehension.[7]
☐ Increases in INS border enforcement effort might actually increase the number of (or rate of) apprehensions. This might well discourage potential entries. If border enforcement was lax this might lead to fewer apprehensions and less of a long-term deterrent effect.
☐ Changes in methods or locations of illegal entry may have led to the successful evasion of INS apprehension, thus leading to fewer recorded apprehensions.
☐ Changes in Mexican-U.S. economic conditions that affect incen-

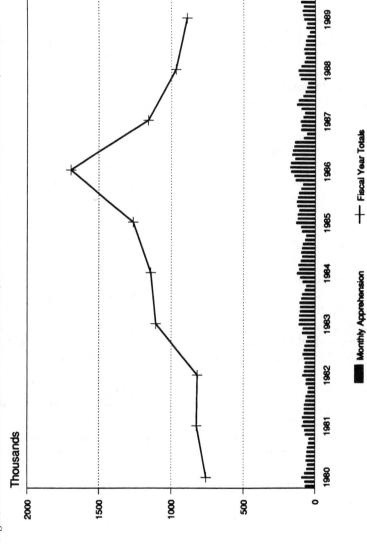

Figure 8.1 DEPORTABLE ALIENS APPREHENDED, FISCAL YEAR TOTALS AND MONTHLY, 1/80–9/89

tives to migrate may change the numbers of those crossing the border.[8]

Two of IRCA's provisions attempt to control directly the number of illegal entries: increased border enforcement efforts, and employer sanctions.[9] Because employer sanctions did not become fully implemented until December 1988, they are unlikely to have accounted directly for the sharp decline in apprehensions noted during FYs 1987 and 1988.

Full implementation, i.e., the commencing of routine sanctions and fines of U.S. employers, first began on June 1, 1988.[10] As a result of this phased-in implementation, many observers are skeptical of claims that the sharp decline in apprehensions implies that employer sanctions have been meeting the objective of significantly reducing the flow of illegals. As an alternative explanation, they point to the three million newly legalized persons as the predominant cause for the decline in apprehensions (Bustamante, 1990, pp. 3, 16; Cornelius, 1989b, p. 6; Massey et al., 1989, p. 10; North and Portz, 1988).

Legalization and the Decline in Apprehensions

How many apprehensions would the newly legalized individuals have accounted for in 1987–1988 had they not been legalized? In attempting to answer this question, we offer one way for deriving plausible lower and upper boundaries on the number of apprehensions averted by the legalization program. This range estimate is then evaluated within the context of the available research on illegal entries.

Our estimate of apprehensions averted by IRCA's legalization program requires information on three basic parameters (White et al., 1989; Massey et al., 1989, p. 9): 1. the size of the population no longer at risk of making an illegal crossing of the U.S. border; 2. the proportion of this population that would have circulated between Latin America and the U.S. in any given period;[11] and 3. the probability that those attempting to cross the border illegally are actually apprehended.

Using these three basic parameters, figure 8.2 presents the process by which apprehensions take place. The first parameter is known: IRCA legalized three million persons under the general (I-687) and agricultural (I-700) programs. Some portion of this population—the second parameter—would actually have been "at risk" of attempting to cross back into the U.S. The third parameter is reflected in the

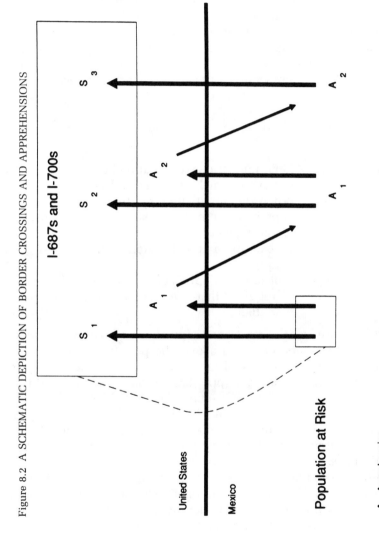

Figure 8.2 A SCHEMATIC DEPICTION OF BORDER CROSSINGS AND APPREHENSIONS

arrows representing cross-border moves that may have resulted in either a successful/unapprehended crossing (S_1) or an apprehension (A_1). We assume that individuals who are apprehended will attempt to cross the border again, resulting in either success (S_2) or yet another apprehension (A_2), and so on. In calculating the number of apprehensions averted, we must account for differences in circulation and the risk of apprehension characteristics between general legalization applicants and agricultural legalization applicants.

The factors represented in the figure can be incorporated into a model of the total number of apprehensions averted by legalization. In particular:

$$A = [N \times r(c) \times p(A_1)] + [N \times r(c) \times p(A_1) \times p(A_2|A_1)]$$

where,

A	=	total number of averted apprehensions,
N	=	number of newly legalized individuals,
r(c)	=	proportion circulating into the U.S. or at risk of apprehension in the 2-year period following the passage of IRCA,
$p(A_1)$	=	probability of apprehension on the first attempt,
$p(A_2|A_1)$	=	probability of apprehension on the second attempt given that one was apprehended on the first attempt.

The first term on the right-hand side of the equation represents the three parameters discussed above: the population of legalized persons (N) actually at risk of crossing the border (r(c)) who are apprehended on a first attempt $(p(A_1))$. Our model assumes that these individuals then try again to re-enter the United States. Of these unsuccessful entrants, a portion $p(A_2|A_1)$, will be reapprehended. Thus, the second term on the right-hand side shows the number of individuals apprehended on their second attempt to re-enter the United States.[12]

In order to calculate the number of apprehensions averted, the first parameter for which we need information is the number of those individuals who were legalized under IRCA. Only the legalized population from Latin America needs to be considered, as it accounts for practically all of those individuals apprehended (INS, 1989a; Bjerke and Hess, 1987).[13]

We also need information on the rate of circulation of illegal migrants between the U.S. and Latin America. Because no firm data exist, we make certain assumptions about the rate with which these persons had circulated between Latin America and the U.S. We assume that at least 5 percent, but no more than 25 percent, of those legalized under the general legalization program would have crossed the U.S. border between 1986 and 1988.[14] The population of Special Agricultural Worker (SAW) applicants can be assumed to be much more mobile and we assume that at least 50 percent, but no more than 75 percent, would have crossed the border during the relevant two-year period in the absence of IRCA.[15]

The probability of apprehension is the third parameter for which information is required. The overall number of apprehensions includes both first and subsequent apprehensions of the same person(s). We assume that the probability of subsequent apprehension increases because apprehension is relatively "painless," and reapprehension data reflect a selectivity for persons who have knowingly chosen a "risky" entry strategy. Fortunately, our sources of information on apprehension rates are somewhat better than those for circulation, and support this latter assumption. A national survey of general legalization applicants permits us to estimate their average rate of apprehension: the first-time apprehension rate for general legalization applicants is placed at 0.25 in accordance with that survey, and we assume a subsequent rate of 0.33.[16] As an upper boundary estimate for SAWs, we use data from a large sample of Mexican males that suggest that the probability of reapprehension is sharply higher than the first-time probability (Kossoudji, 1989).[17]

Apprehensions averted during the period of FYs 1987 to 1988 are considered to be an appropriate base against which to evaluate the effects of legalization. By assuming that in lieu of IRCA apprehensions would have remained at 1986 levels, there was a cumulative total of 1,260,000 fewer apprehensions during both fiscal years (INS, 1989b, table 73).[18] Calculations for apprehensions averted are given in table 8.1. Consideration of both legalization programs suggests that the apprehensions averted by IRCA's legalization programs account for somewhere between 16 and 53 percent of the overall decline in apprehensions. Because the model is sensitive to assumptions for which no firm data exist, we have opted against attempting to narrow this range further.

One other attempt to disentangle statistically the determinants of declining apprehensions likewise implies that legalization accounts for a substantial portion of the decline. It also suggests a cautious evaluation of the role of employer sanctions and the continuing efficacy of thier deterrent effect. In a study released by The Urban

Table 8.1 APPREHENSIONS AVERTED

		Low estimate		High estimate	
		p	n	p	n
General Legalization: I-687					
Legalized Persons	N		1,378		1,378
Active Migrants	r(c)	.05	69	.25	345
1st Apprehension	$p(A_1)$	.25	17	.25	86
2nd Apprehension	$p(A_2|A_1)$	.33	6	.33	28
3rd Apprehension	$p(A_3|A_2,A_1)$	—	—	.33	9
General: Apprehensions Averted			23		124
Seasonal Agricultural Workers: I-700					
Legalized Persons	N		1,116		1,116
Active Migrants	r(c)	.50	558	.75	837
1st Apprehension	$p(A_1)$	.25	140	.30	251
2nd Apprehension	$p(A_2|A_1)$	.33	46	.66	166
3rd Apprehension	$p(A_3|A_2,A_1)$	—	—	.75	124
SAW: Apprehensions Averted			186		541
TOTAL APPREHENSIONS AVERTED			208		665

Institute, Bean et al. (1990) developed a monthly time-series model for the level of linewatch apprehensions and non-linewatch apprehensions from FYs 1977 through 1989. A regression equation is used to estimate the association between several factors associated with changes in apprehensions. The SAW legalization program accounts for a simple majority (52%) of the change in apprehensions not associated with INS border enforcement effort. The remaining decrease (48%) in apprehensions is associated with an IRCA deterrent effect that includes employer sanctions, but that deterrent effect appears to have seriously weakened recently (Espenshade et al., 1990).

The regression estimate is very different from that derived from the simple mathematical model used here. Regression estimates are "net" of other differences and temporal effects. They measure most directly the relationship between monthly SAW applications and the monthly decline in apprehension rates. The regression model might not fully capture certain elements of IRCA's legalization programs, for instance, it does not consider the general legalization program.[19] If applicants had actually entered in months prior to their actual processing by the INS in order to secure jobs and prepare documents (i.e., if declines in apprehensions lag application data), the regression model might underestimate the role played by the legalization programs. Such factors may be implicit in the "gross" estimates derived from our cruder mathematical model.

Additional Information on Illegal Migration

Additional research also implies that, to date, there has been relatively little reduction in illegal entries. This research falls into two categories: micro-level surveys of individuals primarily in Mexico, and macro-level estimates derived from aggregated, national-level data. If IRCA is having a substantial effect in stemming the flow of illegal immigration, this effect might be observed by narrower and more intensive studies. If aggregate data systems imply relatively small changes in the flow of illegal migrants, this would further support the notion that the control elements of IRCA have been only marginally effective so far.[20]

There have been few intensive investigations of changes in migration, and those that exist focus on Mexican migrants, the dominant group of illegal migrants. One such study has monitored the flow of illegal migrants across the U.S.-Mexico border in Tijuana since August 1986 (Bustamante, 1990). The Zapata Canyon project photographs persons in the act of crossing a particular part of the border at the same three times each day. The photo counts, which document the predictable monthly fluctuations, show no substantial change in the annual flow since the enactment of IRCA.

Another type of study focuses not on the point of crossing, but on surveys of individual migrants within the interior of Mexico. A survey (Cornelius, 1989a) of 585 household-heads and migrants in three rural communities in the Mexican states of Jalisco, Michoacan, and Zacateca found that few potential migrants expressed fears about employment problems associated with IRCA and few thought it was more difficult to cross the border. Among the experienced illegal migrants who had considered going to the U.S. in the 1987–1988 period, 33 percent had actually done so. A study of the migration histories of 200 individuals from a community in the state of Guanajuato, a primary sending region for migrants to the U.S. (North and Houstoun, 1976), found no post-IRCA change in the probability of migration to the U.S. (Massey et al., 1989).

Aggregate measures of the stock and flow of illegal migrants offer an additional way to assess IRCA's effect on the entry of illegal immigrants into the United States. The Census Bureau's Current Population Survey (CPS) permits the estimation of the net numbers

of additions to the illegally resident population as an indirect indicator of IRCA's impact. The INS's records of the nonimmigrant
visa system produce numerical estimates of the flow of illegal immigrants that overlap those derived from the CPS, making up a sub-
component of total illegal entries.

Data on persons overstaying the legal period specified on their
nonimmigrant visa suggest only a small decline in the number of
illegal overstays in 1987; by 1988 that number had basically returned
to pre-IRCA levels (Warren, 1989). And updates of CPS estimates of
the flow of illegals imply that there has been an unchanged number
of net additions to the illegal stock. On average, the net number of
illegal migrant entries was about 200,000 each year between 1986
and 1988 (Woodrow and Passel, 1989, table 6).

Despite the seemingly stable **number** of illegal entries, the aggregate estimates point to a small change in the mobility patterns of the
long-term, resident population of illegal immigrants. Considered
against the growing populations of the countries of origin and the
much larger numbers of visitors to the U.S., these estimates suggest
a marginal decrease in the **rate** of illegal migration in the immediate
post-IRCA period.[21] Thus, there is some indication that an incremental decline in illegal entries may be occurring in the aftermath
of IRCA's passage. However, the results of both the micro-level and
aggregate-level studies generally indicate that employer sanctions
have probably had only a marginal effect in reducing illegal migration
thus far.

WESTERN EUROPE'S EXPERIENCE: THE CASE
FOR PATIENCE

Our review of the available research evidence leads us to conclude
that, so far, IRCA's principal goal of reducing appreciably the entry
of illegal aliens still eludes us. Our review of the literature on the
effectiveness of employer sanctions in Europe makes a strong case
for being patient in our expectations about measurable progress, and
for being willing to revisit, rethink, and fine-tune the program.

The Western European countries have a much longer history than
the U.S. of protecting their workers by controlling access to their
labor markets by unauthorized aliens. Although France adopted employer sanctions as early as 1926, and again in 1946 (Miller, 1987b,
p.1), most other advanced industrial European countries instituted

similar provisions in the early to mid-1970s.[22] As in the U.S., most of these countries adopted sanctions only after considerable debate concerning uncertainties regarding such programs' administrative feasibility, the degree to which they would be aggressively enforced (especially by judicial agencies), and the nature and magnitude of their expected impact (Miller, 1987a, 1987b; GAO, 1982).

Europe's underlying rationale for adopting employer sanctions differed substantially from that in the United States.[23] Europeans adopted sanctions primarily as an employment standard.[24] Sanctions are used as a mechanism for preventing unfair labor practices and controlling the exploitation of "clandestine" or illegal immigrants, thus stemming the spread of the "black" or underground economy in such sectors as construction, agriculture, and the food industry.[25] In contrast, the U.S. adopted sanctions primarily as an immigration control measure—with improved conditions in secondary labor markets as an ancillary benefit. Thus, because the main motive behind the relevant statutes gives rise to different expectations in each case, relevant measures of "effectiveness" may also differ.

Comparisons of the history of European experience with the brief U.S. experience suggest that it takes time to establish what amounts to a new employment standard—legal immigration status for all employees. Employer sanctions entail a change in the culture of work that includes a rather fundamental transformation in the employment practices of certain economic sectors. And while a significant level of unauthorized immigration is a relatively new phenomenon for most European countries (France being a major exception, see Miller, 1981), illegal workers in the U.S. have been employed routinely for several decades and through the formative years of certain industries.

This historical and special role of illegal workers in the U.S. demands particularly effective responses and takes a somewhat longer period to resolve. It is clear that the long-term solution to our illegal immigration dilemma rests in simultaneously undertaking responses to all major factors that fuel illegal immigration. An emphasis on single approaches to enforcement, and policies that make detection and substantial penalties even more unlikely, risk lengthening the transition period.

The European experience also encourages the broadening and refinement of the available tools for the control of unauthorized employment, while making it clear that it is important to set modest goals and engage in a sustained enforcement effort within that framework. Such effort is likely to prove more effective if it focuses simultaneously on clarifying and simplifying both the law and its implementation. That effort must incorporate a sustained educational effort directed to employers and the public, and it must systematically reinforce the perception that the government attaches high priority to enforcing the law.

Violations must thus be pursued aggressively—and lead to substantial fines and prosecutions. In France, for instance, the "administrative fine," often the largest component of the monetary penalties, is automatic and non-negotiable. This approach is thought to have a large deterrent effect, although some critics think that it makes the government reluctant to prosecute some cases. In fact, the French implementation effort is beginning to focus more on persuading judicial authorities to pursue prosecutions more aggressively, and on the possible creation of an independent prosecutor's office.[26]

The primary European motive for employer sanctions—that is the desire to improve employment standards for all workers—suggests that employer sanctions must also be part of a larger effort to enforce all immigration and labor laws. By themselves, sanctions will neither significantly deter illegal immigration nor curb the growth in the underground economy. Significant gains in the pursuit of both objectives thus require a sustained and comprehensive effort that includes not only border controls and employer sanctions, but the determined enforcement of all labor laws.

Those in the U.S. who, like their European counterparts, argue for a more aggressive enforcement of labor laws as a means of controlling unauthorized employment and exploitation should continue to advocate a broad-based approach. However, only by reducing the economic incentives at the heart of the exploitative employment of workers can enforcing labor laws prove an effective strategy for controlling the spread of the underground economy.

Finally, our review of the experiences of advanced European democracies makes it clear that virtually no policy will eliminate pressures for illegal immigration as long as few gains are made in parallel efforts to reduce domestic social and political conflict in immigrant-sending societies. Economic disparities between countries—and particularly between contiguous countries that share extensive historical migration relationships—must be addressed as part of a broad-based solution to international mobility.[27] Therein lie the roots of unauthorized population movements. Absent the improvement of international inequalities, even Draconian control measures cannot eradicate and would likely be only partially successful in reducing illegal immigration.[28]

CONCLUSIONS

Our assessment leads us to question the wisdom of relying on what has in effect been a single-element control strategy in which employer sanctions are the sole additional deterrent to new illegal immigration. Particularly short-sighted appear to be expectations that, in the short time since their full implementation on December 1, 1988, employer sanctions could have altered the hiring process while making measurable progress toward reforming the culture of work in industries that have long relied on a ready supply of illegal aliens.

Recent research in traditional immigrant-sending communities suggests that potential illegal migrants do not fear a change in the culture of work in the United States. As has been argued elsewhere (Papademetriou, 1986, p. 789), given the severe communication overloads attendant to living in a complex society, and considering our history of policy and enforcement ambivalence on immigration, ambiguous or conflicting signals will be ". . . taken as a sign of equivocation and weakness." As a result, deviations from a consistent and determined implementation of the immigration law run the risk of failing to persuade ethnic communities and, through them, failing to dissuade prospective illegal immigrants from undertaking the journey to the United States.

Sanctions, however, represent more than a pivotal tool in the nation's overall strategy against illegal immigration. They provide the U.S. government with an enforcement tool that can be used to combat exploitative workplace practices and to eliminate the competitive advantage of firms that employ illegal aliens. While focusing on the rationalization and enforcement of U.S. immigration laws, then, IRCA has in fact created and provided the statutory mechanism for the enforcement of a new employment standard: U.S. work authorization.

While some employment practices do appear to be changing as a result of employer sanctions, legal status has not yet become an employment standard for which employers expect to be held fully accountable. This, despite evidence that the law appears to be contributing to a more hostile work environment for the residual illegal alien population (i.e., those unable to benefit from IRCA's various legalization programs) and for those illegal immigrants arriving in the U.S. since the passage of IRCA (Bach and Brill, 1989; DeWind, 1989; California Fair Employment and Housing Commission, 1990; Committee on Immigration and Nationality Law of the Association of the Bar of the City of New York, 1989; New York State, 1988; MALDEF/ACLU, 1989). While the available research apparently cannot make comparisons with pre-IRCA levels of discrimination, it does strongly indicate that sanctions actually increase the potential for the erosion of standards in the workplace.

Within certain parameters, the effectiveness of the effort to stem illegal immigration hinges on this nation's ability to devote sufficient resources to enforce all of the law's provisions. Otherwise, as the Select Commission argued (SCIRP, 1981b, p. 560), "illegal migration will continue to undermine the most valued ideals of this nation—the integrity of the law and the fundamental dignity of the individual."

Notes

This chapter was presented at The Urban Institute conference on the implementation of the Immigration Reform and Control Act of 1986, Washington, D.C., December 1989. The authors are with the Bureau for International Labor Affairs, U.S. Department of Labor. The conference was carried out under the auspices of the Program for Research on Immigration Policy, a program of public policy research and assessment in the area of immigration involving The Urban Institute and the RAND Corporation. Core support for the program is provided by the Ford Foundation. Conclusions or opinions expressed in this chapter are those of the authors and do not necessarily reflect the views of the other staff members, officers, trustees of The Urban Institute, the RAND Corporation, or any organizations that provide financial support to the Program, or the U.S. Department of Labor. The authors express appreciation to Frank D. Bean, Thomas J. Espenshade, Michael D. Hoefer, Sherry A. Kossoudji, and Michael J. White for their comments on earlier drafts of this chapter.

1. The 1952 Immigration and Nationality Act (INA) had codified a legal anomaly (known as the "Texas Proviso") that, in the words of the Select Commission, had amounted to a "... 'half-open door' policy" (SCIRP, 1981b: p. 560) that prevented the effective enforcement of U.S. immigration laws. While the INA forbade illegal entry (Section 274 of the INA prohibited the "willful importation, transportation, or harboring" of illegal aliens), it exempted employers of illegal aliens from legal liability by stating that the employment of illegal aliens did not constitute harboring. A notable exception in this regard was a prohibition against the knowing hiring of unauthorized aliens by farm labor contractors or farmers under the Farm Labor Contractor Registration Act.

2. Employer sanctions were not adopted at that time because Congress perceived a ready demand for labor. The "bracero" program with Mexico was instituted in 1942 in response to war-induced labor shortages in the U.S. agricultural sector, and was formally reauthorized in 1952. It was terminated in 1964 (see Congressional Research Service, 1979; Briggs, 1984).

3. Legislation actually passed the House twice in the early 1970s (92nd and 93rd Congresses), but made lesser progress in the next two Congresses. The initiatives

usually began in the House of Representatives but failed to make progress in the Senate (SCIRP, 1981b, p. 630).

4. All three administrations in the 1970s engaged in the review of the issue that led to recommendations favoring sanctions. These included the 1973 Nixon administration's Crampton Report, the Ford administration's Domestic Council Committee Report on Illegal Aliens, and two initiatives under the Carter administration: the proposed 1977 Alien Employment Act and the impaneling of the Select Commission in 1979.

5. As an integral part of the INS's overall border control strategy, enforcement resources were concentrated on the few areas of the border where the large majority of illegal entries were attempted. That strategy was implemented in the early 1980s and is still in place today (chapter 11, this volume).

6. Data are from INS (1989b, table 73, and special tabulations by the agency's Statistical Analysis Division). Border Patrol apprehension data do not include interior apprehensions by the INS Investigations staff. In 1986, 86 percent of all aliens apprehended had been in the U.S. less than 72 hours (Bjerke and Hess, 1987).

7. If IRCA has made crossing the border even a little more difficult and increased the difficulty for illegals to obtain new jobs, the frequency of circulation—and hence apprehensions—could be expected to be substantially lower than in the pre-IRCA period.

8. The relative economic position of Mexico vis-à-vis the U.S. has not changed substantially in the post-IRCA period. Thus, it is unlikely that the large decline in apprehensions can be attributed to this factor.

9. Increased border enforcements have not yet been fully implemented. Congress was supposed to have made three annual appropriations to the INS that would have increased the size of the Border Patrol by as much as 50 percent over pre-IRCA levels. However, the additional funds were allocated only for FY 1988—a year during which a significant share of Border Patrol resources was diverted to such non-border control activities as employer education, drug interdiction and education, and the investigation of criminal aliens (chapter 11, this volume; Interpreter Releases, 1989).

10. Full implementation was somewhat later for the agricultural sector. In that sector, the education phase lasted until November 30, 1988. Nevertheless, it is possible that although fines were not being issued, the extensive publicity efforts by the INS regarding employer sanctions may have had a deterrent effect on apprehensions.

11. "Circulation" is a migratory pattern in which individuals make recurrent trips back and forth between Mexico and the U.S. for social visits, to check on property, to earn supplemental income, etc. Such migratory patterns are common throughout third world populations (see, for example, Goldstein, 1978).

12. The model can be extended to multiple attempts at entry.

13. Specifically included are the populations of "Entries Without Inspection" from Mexico, Central America, and South America (Hoefer, 1989, table 3).

14. The lower boundary is implied by the date-at-last-entry question reported by general legalization applicants (Hoefer, 1989, table 5). This is a lower boundary because in any given year an unknown number of persons not reporting a "final entry" would have entered. The upper boundary is arbitrarily set at 25 percent (rather than a higher proportion) to reflect the generally permanent nature of that population and the cost and disruption of home visits.

15. Kossoudji's (1989, table 1) analysis of the CENIET 1978–79 survey in Mexico of male agricultural migrants suggests a high rate of 1.3 entries over a 2-year period. We assume that many U.S. SAWs moved much less frequently. For example, 18 percent of a small sample of SAW applicants in California were part of family units with settled residence patterns (Kissam and Intili, 1989). Also, it is likely that the majority

of SAW applicants were "target earners" who made infrequent trips to the U.S. In a sample of traditional Mexican sending communities, the majority of temporary, mostly undocumented migrants had made only two trips to the U.S. by the age of 35 (Massey et al., 1989, 185).

16. This rate is based on unpublished tabulations from the first survey of general legalization applicants undertaken by Weststat for INS (calculations made by Michael Hoefer, INS Statistical Division). This is consistent with what for many years has been a widely accepted assumption among Border Patrol personnel that two or three illegal aliens "get away" for every single apprehension. This implies that apprehensions rates are between 0.25 and 0.33 (White et al., 1989; Massey et al., 1989).

17. The 1978–79 CENIET study was undertaken by the Mexican government and surveyed persons who are most like the mobile SAW population. Furthermore, the apprehension rates shown in table 8.1 are for males only (and are weighted to the overall sample; see Kossoudji, 1989, tables 1 and 2). It is encouraging to note that the first-time SAW rate extrapolated from this sample (0.28) is similar to that derived from the sample of general legalization applicants discussed in the previous footnote.

18. These two fiscal years correspond with an appropriate "lead in" and "lag period" against which to evaluate the drop in apprehensions due to legalization. The start of FY 1987 closely corresponds to the signing of IRCA into law. It is also about seven months prior to the start of the legalization programs. During this period individuals may have reduced their circulation (e.g., as a result of feeling locked into their current jobs) in anticipation of applying for legalization. Thus a portion of the early drop in apprehensions may have been due to "legalization," despite the fact that the formal program had not yet begun. Because we endeavor to account for all legalized persons inside U.S. borders, this model does not deal with those who are discouraged and drop out after one apprehension. Clearly, all legalized persons were successful in entering the U.S. legally.

19. Applications under the general legalization program were not found to play a statistically significant role by Urban Institute researchers. Yet our estimates suggest that this program may have had a measurable role in decreasing apprehensions.

20. Note, however, that small changes in total (aggregate) illegal migration might not be visible in intensive studies of traditional sending communities or points of entry that are less easily affected than communities with less "invested" in migrant networks.

21. The overall rate of visa overstay relative to nonimmigrant visa-entries dropped in New York, California, New Jersey, Illinois, Texas. The national rate declined from 2.4 percent in FYs 1985–1986 to 1.9 percent in both 1987 and 1988 (Warren, 1989). Similarly, the CPS estimates imply a small decline in the rate of illegal entry relative to populations at the origin and destination communities. The decline in the rate of outmigration measured against the origin Mexican population is from 2.5 to 2.4 per 1,000 (Bureau of the Census, 1987, table 1379).

22. France decreed employer sanctions again in 1976; Great Britain adopted legislation prohibiting the harboring of illegal aliens—though not their employment (out of fear of fueling discrimination)—in 1971. Switzerland has had similar anti-harboring statutes since 1931 and adopted an explicit statute aimed at the employment of illegal aliens in 1984. The Federal Republic of Germany first prohibited the employment of clandestine aliens in 1975, as have The Netherlands (1974), Austria (1981), Italy, Spain, and Belgium (see Miller, 1987b; GAO, 1982).

23. France may be the only partial exception to this statement in that, like the U.S., it too places the accent more on sanctions than other control measures that it perceives as "impractical." See Miller (1987b, p. 35); also an interview by Demetrios G. Papademetriou with Madame Cervaise Hue, director, Mission de Lutte Contre le Travail

Clandestin, l'Emploi Non Déclaré et les Trafics de Main-d'Oeuvre, Paris, February 12, 1989.

24. Immigration control per se remained the responsibility of border controls and an intricate system of residence and work permits (see Papademetriou, 1988).

25. See the reports of the Ministère des Affaires Social et de l'Emploi, 1988, and the Mission de Liaison Interministerielle pour la Lutte Contre les Trafics de Main-d'Oeuvre, 1987 and 1988; see also Mission de Lutte Contre le Travail Clandestin, 1987; Conseil Fédéral Suisse, 1987; and Bundesministerium fuer Arbeit und Sozialordnung, 1987.

26. It should be kept in mind that the European system's heavy social safety net sets employer payroll taxes and related overhead costs at levels much higher than they are in the U.S. This provides an additional incentive to employ unauthorized aliens. While the European fine structure may thus need to be much more substantial than our own, the entrenched history of unauthorized employment in the U.S. may just as well require even more substantial fines. For example, some simple economic calculations suggest that, for employer sanctions to be effective, at least one-quarter of employers who hire illegal aliens would have to be assessed the maximum fine of $2,000 per unauthorized worker (Todaro and Maruszko, 1987).

27. See the discussion of the special U.S.-Mexico immigration relationship presented in a report by the U.S. Department of Labor (DOL, 1989, chapter 1). Similar relationships have developed between several European nations following the "guestworker" programs of the late 1950s and 1960s (Miller, 1981; Miller and Papademetriou, 1983).

28. It is important to note that both IRCA and the Select Commission recognized that concurrent initiatives in such areas as trade and investment, aid, and economic, social, and political reforms are crucial adjuncts to unilateral immigration control measures. IRCA impaneled the Commission on International Migration and Cooperative Economic Development, which issued its report to Congress in summer 1990. And the Select Commission gave prominent space in its recommendations to addressing the nexus between conditions in sending countries and illegal immigration to the United States (see SCIRP, 1981a, Recommendations I.A–D).

References

Bach, Robert, and Howard Brill. 1989. "Shifting the Burden: The Impacts of IRCA on U.S. Labor Markets." Unpublished interim report to the Division of Immigration Policy and Research, U.S. Department of Labor, November.

Bean, Frank D., Thomas J. Espenshade, Michael J. White, and Robert F. Dymowski. 1990. "Post-IRCA Changes in the Volume and Composition of Undocumented Migration to the United States: An Assessment Based on Apprehensions Data." In *Undocumented Migration to the United States: IRCA and the Experience of the 1980s*, eds. Frank D. Bean, Barry Edmonston and Jeffrey S. Passel, Washington, D.C.: Urban Institute Press.

Bjerke, John A., and Karen K. Hess. 1987. "Selected Characteristics of Illegal Aliens Apprehended by the U.S. Border Patrol." Unpublished paper, Statistical Analysis Division, U.S. Immigration and Naturalization Service, Washington, D.C.

Briggs Jr., Vernon M. 1984. *Immigration Policy and the American Labor Force*. Baltimore: John Hopkins University Press.

Bundesminister fuer Arbeit und Sozialordnung. 1987. *Illegale Beschaeftigung und Schwarzarbeit Schaden uns Allen*. Bonn: Der Bundesminister fuer Arbeit und Sozialordnung.

Bustamante, Jorge A. 1990. "Undocumented Migration from Mexico to the United States: Preliminary Findings of the Zapata Canyon Project." In *Undocumented Migration to the United States: IRCA and the Experience of the 1980s*, eds. Frank D. Bean, Barry Edmonston, and Jeffrey S. Passel. Washington, D.C.: Urban Institute Press.

California Fair Employment and Housing Commission. 1990. "Public Hearings on the Impact and Effectiveness in California of the Employer Sanctions and Antidiscrimination Provisions of the Immigration Reform and Control Act of 1986: Report and Recommendations." San Francisco: California Fair Employment and Housing Commission.

Committee on Immigration and Nationality Law of the Association of the Bar of the City of New York. 1989. "Methodology, Legal Definitions and Interpretations in Documenting the Employer Sanctions and Anti-Discrimination Provisions of IRCA." Report by the Association of the Bar of the City of New York, August.

Congressional Research Service. 1979. "Temporary Worker Programs: Background and Issues." Senate Judiciary Committee, 96th Congress, 2nd Session, Washington, D.C.: U.S. Government Printing Office.

Cornelius, Wayne A. 1989a. "Impacts of the 1986 U.S. Immigration Law on Emigration from Rural Mexican Sending Communities." Paper presented at the 15th International Congress of the Latin American Studies Association, Miami, December.

―――――. 1989b. "Presentation to the Ninth Annual Briefing Session for Journalists." Center for U.S.-Mexican Studies and Foundation for American Communications, La Jolla, California, June.

Conseil Fédéral Suisse. 1987. "Ordonnance Limitant le Nombre des Etrangers (OLE), Modification du 5 Octobre 1987." Séjour et Etablissement des Etrangers, Switzerland.

DeWind, Josh. 1989. "Employment Obstacles Experienced by Foreign-Born Workers in New York City Because of the Employer Sanctions Provisions of the Immigration Reform and Control Act of 1986." Paper prepared for the Division of Immigration Policy and Research, Department of Labor, Washington, D.C., September.

DOL (U.S. Department of Labor). 1989. "The Effects of Immigration on the U.S. Economy and Labor Market" (Report 1). Washington, D.C.: U.S. Department of Labor, Bureau of International Labor Affairs.

Espenshade, Thomas J., Michael J. White, and Frank D. Bean. 1990. "Patterns of Recent Illegal Migration to the United States." In *Future De-mographic Trends in Europe and North America*, ed. W. Lutz. Lax-enburg, Austria: International Institute for Applied Systems Analysis.

GAO (U.S. General Accounting Office). 1982. "Information on the Enforce-ment of Laws Regarding Employment of Aliens in Selected Coun-tries." GAO/GGD-82-86, Washington, D.C.: U.S. General Accounting Office.

Goldstein, Sidney. 1978. "Circulation in the Context of Total Mobility in South-east Asia." Papers of the East-West Population Institute, No. 53.

Hoefer, Michael. 1989. "Characteristics of Aliens Legalizing under IRCA." Paper presented to the annual meeting of the Population Associa-tion of America, Baltimore, March.

INS (U.S. Immigration and Naturalization Service). 1989a. "Provisional Le-galization Application Statistics." Statistics Division, July 20.

————. 1989b. *1988 Statistical Yearbook of the Immigration and Natu-ralization Service*. PB 89-193932, Washington, D.C.: U.S. Govern-ment Printing Office.

Interpreter Releases. 1989. "Former General Counsel Blasts INS as 'Totally Disorganized.'" *Interpreter Releases* 66, no. 41, pp. 1169–1171.

Kissam, Edward, and Jo Ann Intili. 1989. "Legalized Farmworkers and Their Families: Program and Policy Implications." California Human De-velopment Corporation, Santa Rosa, CA.

Kossoudji, Sherry A. 1989. "Playing Cat and Mouse at the Border: Does the INS Alien Apprehension Strategy Alter the Aggregate Supply of Illegal Labor?" Unpublished paper, Department of Economics, Uni-versity of Michigan.

MALDEF/ACLU (Mexican-American Legal Defense and Educational Fund and American Civil Liberties Union). 1989. "The Human Costs of Employer Sanctions: Recommendations for GAO's Third Report to Congress under the Immigration Reform and Control Act of 1986." Washington, D.C.: Mexican-American Legal Defense and Educa-tional Fund.

Massey, Douglas S., Rafael Alarcon, Jorge Durand, and Humberto González. 1987. *Return to Aztlán: The Social Process of International Migra-tion From Western Mexico*. Berkeley: University of California Press.

Massey, Douglas S., Katherine M. Donato, and Liang Zai. 1989. "Effects of the Immigration Reform and Control Act of 1986: Preliminary Data from Mexico." In *Undocumented Migration to the United States: IRCA and the Experience of the 1980s*, eds. Frank D. Bean, Barry Edmonston, and Jeffrey S. Passel. Washington, D.C.: Urban Institute Press.

Meissner, Doris. 1989. "IRCA in Context: A Recent History of the I.N.S." Paper presented at the Urban Institute conference on the Imple-mentation of the Immigration Reform and Control Act of 1986, Washington, D.C., December.

Miller, Mark J. 1987a. "Employer Sanctions in Europe: Deterrence Without Discrimination." Center for Immigration Studies, Paper Number 3, Washington, D.C.

————. 1987b. "Employer Sanctions in Western Europe." CMS Occasional Paper No. 7. Staten Island: Center for Migration Studies of New York, Inc.

————. 1981. *Foreign Workers in Western Europe: An Emerging Political Force.* New York: Praeger Publishers.

Miller, Mark J. and Demetrios G. Papademetriou. 1983. "Immigration Reform: The United States and Western Europe Compared." In *The Unavoidable Issue: U.S. Immigration Policy in the 1980s,* eds. Demetrios G. Papademetriou and Mark J. Miller. Philadelphia: Institute for the Study of Human Issues.

Ministère des Affaires Sociales et de l'Emploi. 1988. *1986–1987: Le Point sur l'Immigration et la Présence Etrangere en France* (Documents Affaires Sociales). Paris: La Documentation Française.

Mission de Liaison Interministerielle pour la Lutte contre les Trafics de Main-D'Oeuvre. 1988. "La Lutte contre les Trafics de Main-d'Oeuvre en 1986–87: Elargissement du Dispositif et Nouvelles Formes Illégales d'Emploi." Rapport au Ministre du Travail, de l'Emploi et de la Formation Professionnelle. Paris: La Documentation Française.

————. 1987. "La Lutte Contre les Trafics de Main-d'Oeuvre en 1982–1986: Objectif Prioritaire, le Travail Clandestin." Rapport au Ministre des Affaires Sociales et de l'Emploi. Paris: La Documentation Française.

Mission de Lutte contre le Travail Clandestin. 1987. *Mission de Lutte contre le Travail Clandestin, l'Emploi Non Déclaré, et les Trafics de Main-d'Oeuvre.* Cahier No. 1. Paris: Gervaise HUE.

New York State. 1988. "Workplace Discrimination under the Immigration Reform and Control Act of 1986: A Study of Impacts on New Yorkers." Inter-Agency Task Force on Immigration Affairs, New York, November 4.

North, David C. 1981. "Enforcing the Immigration Law: A Review of the Options." In *U.S. Immigration Policy and the National Interest.* Staff Report: Appendix E, Ed. SCIRP (Select Commission on Immigration and Refugee Policy), Washington, D.C.: U.S. Government Printing Office.

North, David S., and Marion Houstoun. 1976. *The Characteristics and Role of Illegal Aliens in the U.S. Labor Market: An Exploratory Study.* Washington, D.C.: Linton and Company, Inc.

North, David S., and Anna M. Portz. 1988. *Through the Maze: An Interim Report on the Alien Legalization Program.* Washington, D.C.: TransCentury Development Associates.

Papademetriou, Demetrios G. 1988. "International Migration in North America and Western Europe." In *International Migration Today,* Volume 1, ed. R. Appelyard. Paris: UNESCO Press and the University of Western Australia Press.

————. 1986. "The Foreign Policy Context of U.S. Immigration Reform: A Forgotten Dimension." In *Policy Studies Review Annual,* ed. R. Rist. New Brunswick: Transaction Books.

SCIRP (Select Commission on Immigration and Refugee Policy). 1981a. *U.S. Immigration Policy and the National Interest.* Final Report. Washington, D.C.: U.S. Government Printing Office.

————. 1981b. *U.S. Immigration Policy and the National Interest.* Staff Report. Washington, D.C.: U.S. Government Printing Office.

Todaro, Michael P., and Lydia Maruszko. 1987. "Illegal Migration and U.S. Immigration Reform: A Conceptual Framework." *Population and Development Review* 13, no. 1, pp. 101–114.

U.S. Bureau of the Census. 1987. *Statistical Abstract of the United States: 1988.* Washington, D.C.: U.S. Government Printing Office.

Warren, Robert. 1990. "Annual Estimates of Nonimmigrant Overstays in the United States: 1985–1988." In *Undocumented Migration to the United States: IRCA and the Experience of the 1980s,* eds. Frank D. Bean, Barry Edmonston, and Jeffrey S. Passel. Washington, D.C.: Urban Institute Press.

White, Michael J., Frank D. Bean, and Thomas J. Espenshade. 1989. "The U.S. Immigration Reform and Control Act and Undocumented Migration to the United States." Urban Institute Working Paper PRIP-UI-5. Washington, D.C., July.

Woodrow, Karen A., and Jeffrey S. Passel. 1989. "Post-IRCA Undocumented Immigration to the United States: An Assessment Based on the June 1988 CPS." In *Undocumented Migration to the United States: IRCA and the Experience of the 1980s,* eds. Frank D. Bean, Barry Edmonston, and Jeffrey S. Passel. Washington, D.C.: Urban Institute Press.

Chapter Nine

IMMIGRATION REFORM AND FARM LABOR CONTRACTING IN CALIFORNIA

Philip L. Martin and J. Edward Taylor

Employer sanctions under the 1986 Immigration Reform and Control Act (IRCA) were intended to encourage farmers to adjust their production and hiring practices to the smaller and more legal workforce expected to result from IRCA. Agriculture was considered a "special case" under IRCA. Farmers argued that they had become dependent on unauthorized immigrant workers because the U.S. government had not prohibited them from hiring such workers in the past. As a result, special provisions were included in IRCA to provide farmers with additional time to adjust to a more legal workforce.

INTRODUCTION

In 1989 we conducted a survey of California farm employers to assess the initial impacts of IRCA on agriculture in California (Martin and Taylor, 1990a and 1990b). The survey findings indicated that farm employers were not yet adjusting to 1986 immigration reforms. Employers reported that nearly half of all seasonal workers on California farms in 1988—the year covered by the survey—were illegal aliens in 1985–1986 who had applied for legal status under the Special Agricultural Worker (SAW) program. In anticipation of employer sanctions, employers reported making little effort to retain newly legalized SAWs through changes in wages, benefits, or personnel practices. Instead, farmers reported that they expected to hire more workers through farm labor contractors (FLCs) if the seasonal workforce shrinks in the 1990s.

Farm Labor Contractors

Farm labor contractors are the middlemen who, for a fee, recruit and supervise perhaps half of the workers employed in California agriculture. They are a wild card in assessing the effectiveness of IRCA in agriculture. There is evidence that they have been a major first employer of unauthorized immigrant workers in the past. Many farmers appear to perceive FLCs as a buffer between themselves and immigration and labor laws that regulate the employment of farmworkers. Most relevent to the discussion of IRCA's effects, FLCs are poised to absorb many of the risks and costs associated with hiring illegal immigrant workers. Using labor market intermediaries can be an effective means of shifting the risks and liabilities related to employer sanctions from growers to FLCs. However, the ways in which FLCs avoid the same costs and risks associated with hiring unauthorized workers has not been well understood.

Labor contractors could in theory help to provide farmworkers with more stable employment despite the tremendous seasonality of labor demand that characterizes fruit and vegetable farming. Average wages for farmworkers (about $5.50 hourly in California) are generally competitive with wages for low-skilled workers in other sectors, and they are far higher than wages in rural Mexico, where most of the California farm workforce originates (Taylor & Espenshade, 1987). However, most seasonal workers, though available to work 40- to 50-hour weeks or 2,000 hours per year, find only about 1,000 hours of employment, giving them average annual earnings of only $4,000 to $7,000. This lack of stable employment is undoubtedly one of the key reasons why agriculture is unable to retain most of its workforce, losing large numbers of workers each year to other sectors. In theory, crews of workers employed by a contractor can be moved from farm to farm to satisfy a series of short-term labor demands on individual farms, allowing seasonal workers to benefit from relatively stable work under an FLC. FLCs can play employment-stretching roles similar to hiring halls or labor exchanges, reducing unemployment spells for workers between seasonal jobs. If IRCA succeeds, the FLC would be called on to manage such a workforce in the face of highly seasonal labor demands. This, in turn, would result in a smaller, more legal workforce in agriculture.

If IRCA does not succeed in forcing California agriculture to adjust to a smaller, more legal workforce, FLCs will maintain their present comparative advantage—the ability to recruit new workers from abroad. Traditionally, labor contractors have reached across a porous U.S.-Mexico border to channel large numbers of new, mostly unauthorized, immigrant workers into short-term farm jobs. FLCs have been characterized not by their ability to offer stable employment to farmworkers, but by their revolving door employment: they have the highest worker turnover rates of all employers in California agriculture. The comparative advantage of FLCs has been their ability to tap into migrant "networks" that extend from the fields of California to villages in remote corners of Mexico.

Considering the size of FLC employment and the potential role of FLCs as buffers between farmers and immigration and labor laws, trends in FLC activity are a key indicator of the effectiveness of IRCA and employer sanctions in forcing California agriculture to adjust to a more legal workforce.

This chapter presents the findings of a 1990 study of trends in FLC activity and of characteristics of FLCs, based on an intensive analysis of secondary data and in-depth interviews with FLCs in two farm regions of California. The first section examines FLC activity in the 1980s, prior to IRCA, and the second section draws from secondary data to examine the growth and pattern of FLC operations subsequent to the implementation of employer sanctions. Our statistical findings offer evidence that IRCA has not succeeded in encouraging California agriculture to adjust to a more legal workforce. FLC activity appears to have grown substantially since employer sanctions took effect in agriculture, and the characteristics of this growth are consistent with the hypothesis that IRCA has not reduced the flow of new, low-skill immigrant workers into seasonal farm jobs. That is, the comparative advantage of labor contractors continues to be their ability to recruit new immigrant labor for short-term jobs, rather than their ability to manage the smaller, more stable farm workforce envisioned by IRCA. Our conclusion summarizes the findings and presents their policy implications.

LABOR CONTRACTORS AND CALIFORNIA AGRICULTURE IN THE 1980s

Thirty years ago, Ernesto Galarza wrote *Merchants of Labor: The Bracero Story* to chronicle how the U.S. government and farm employers used temporary Mexican farmworkers—Braceros—to expand labor-intensive fruit and vegetable agriculture in the southwestern states. Today, labor-intensive agriculture is once again expanding in the southwestern states with the help of recent immigrants from Mexico, but today's handmaidens of expansion are farm labor contractors (FLCs).

History and Role of Farm Labor Contractors

Farm labor contractors are formally defined as individuals who, for a fee or salary, recruit, transport, and supervise farmworkers. In California agriculture, FLCs employ over one-third of the 900,000 seasonal or year-round workers who have farm jobs during a typical year and over half of the 600,000 workers with seasonal farm jobs.

FLCs perform labor market functions that are normally handled directly by employers and workers. They are found throughout California agriculture, but they are especially pervasive in California's inland areas. For example, FLCs play a major role in seasonal grape harvesting in Fresno County, the U.S. county with the most farm sales. The table, raisin, and wine grape vineyards around Fresno employ about five times as many workers in September as they do in April, and FLCs are responsible for assembling almost 25,000 workers into crews of 20 to 30 workers each for Fresno's September harvests. Since few workers are employed by FLCs for the whole year, this means that FLCs assemble over 1,000 25-worker crews in September for Fresno farmers and move them from farm to farm as needed. FLCs must know where to recruit workers for several weeks of work and where to find jobs for these workers, and they must ensure that the work done by these seasonal workers meets minimum quality standards.

Most FLCs are Hispanic ex-farmworkers who are very familiar with the circumstances of the workers they employ—where they come from, what their U.S. job options are, and what services such as housing and transportation they need in addition to jobs. At the turn of the century the U.S. Industrial Commission explained that labor contractors who recruited newly arrived immigrants in the early 1900s could "drive the hardest kind of bargain" with them because they live among the workers they employ and "know their circumstances" (Fisher, 1953, p. 43).

FLCs are more than employers: they often recruit, transport, house, feed, and train new arrivals. The price they exact for providing employment and social services is measured in lower wages and poorer working conditions than offered by other farm employers. They also often charge excessive fees for the settlement services needed by immigrant farmworkers.

Farm labor contractors first emerged in California as worker advocates and bilingual intermediaries who enabled Chinese and Japanese workers to find seasonal farm jobs. However, since the 1920s, when Hispanics became the major ethnic group in the farm labor market, FLCs have acquired a reputation for abusing workers by profiting from the gap between what farmers pay to have a job done and what workers get. FLCs are widely seen today as an undesirable feature of farm labor markets. Farmers usually consider FLCs a necessary evil to bring some order and certainty to a labor market that matches recent immigrant workers with seasonal jobs. Farmworker advocates consider the presence and persistence of FLCs as evidence that the farm labor market remains isolated from mainstream American society.

FLCs as Risk-Absorbers

Rather than shoulder the risks and costs of hiring illegal immigrant workers directly, farmers may effectively shift them onto FLCs: it is exceedingly difficult to demonstrate that a farmer has knowingly hired illegal immigrants *through* labor contractors. The FLC offers a mechanism through which farmers can "comply" with employer sanctions without significantly reducing their reliance on unauthorized immigrant workers. Under IRCA (unlike under the California Agricultural Labor Relations Act), a farm labor contractor can be and usually is an employer in his own right. Therefore, the contractor—not the client farmer—has responsibility for complying with employee verification procedures.

The Staying Power of FLCs

Given their importance in the farm labor market, FLCs are little studied. There are dozens of books and articles about Cesar Chavez and the United Farm Workers (UFW) union, even though the UFW never matched more than 10 percent of California's seasonal workers with jobs. One reason why FLCs are so little studied is because they have been widely expected to disappear as labor law reforms took effect. Union hiring halls were expected to displace FLCs in the 1970s, and immigration reforms were expected to dry up their supply of recent immigrant workers in the 1980s. But instead of being relegated to a footnote of history, more FLCs are matching workers and jobs than ever before, and there is evidence that FLC activity is on the rise.

Recurrent objections on the part of union hiring halls, the public Employment Service, and employer hiring cooperatives to FLCs taking a fee for job-matching in the low-wage farm labor market have produced an extensive set of federal and state regulations governing

FLCs. These regulations should make it as expensive or more expensive for farmers to hire workers through FLCs who comply with the law than to hire workers directly. The high cost of conforming to FLC regulations and a federal ban on knowingly hiring illegal alien workers were expected to encourage farmers to hire workers directly or with the assistance of union hiring halls, the Employment Service, or employer cooperatives. Without a constant influx of vulnerable immigrant workers, and with both tough regulation and the availability of alternative job-matching intermediaries, FLCs were expected to wither away in the 1980s.

But instead of withering away, FLCs have increased their market share. FLCs matched about one-third of California's seasonal workers with jobs in the early 1980s, and the evidence presented below indicates that this share is rising. There are several reasons for this unexpected FLC expansion, but they all have a common thread: FLCs are better at employing new immigrants and evading labor market regulation than farmers and other job matchers. As legal and regulatory changes increase the gap between labor standards and labor market realities, FLCs play a more important role in the labor market. For example, before IRCA, 20 to 40 percent of California's seasonal farmworkers were probably illegal aliens, and most who worked illegally in the mid-1980s were legalized under the SAW program (Mines and Martin, 1986; Taylor and Espenshade, 1987). Since IRCA, there has been a continued influx of illegal aliens, so that 20 to 40 percent of the seasonal workers are once again illegal aliens (Huerta, 1990). Today's illegal aliens have "documents" that permit them to work legally in the United States, although most of these documents were not issued by government authorities. FLCs are willing to assume the risk of fines for employing such "documented illegals" (Martin and Luce, 1988; Rosenberg and Perloff, 1988). As a result, more farmers turn to FLCs to perform, at no cost, a new regulatory duty imposed by IRCA. Without the services of the FLC, farmers would have to buy a photocopy machine or hire a clerk to comply with IRCA's I-9 requirements. FLCs do incur costs to comply, but they recoup these costs through various means. For example, they sell documents to new immigrants who need them, or simply require all newly hired workers to provide their own copies of documents so that the FLCs can comply with the law at no cost to themselves.

The expansion of FLC activity after IRCA suggests that illegal immigration has increased rather than decreased since the mid-1980s. But there would probably be FLCs even without illegal immigrants, even though their role would be different. If FLCs complied with IRCA's ban on hiring new illegal immigrants, they would be fewer in number and larger in size. In this sense, the level and pattern of FLC activities are indicators of the success of IRCA in seasonal agriculture. The expansion of FLCs with high turnover rates since the mid-1980s suggests that IRCA has failed to reduce the influx of illegal alien workers into seasonal agriculture.

IMMIGRATION REFORMS AND FARM LABOR CONTRACTING IN CALIFORNIA

Although FLCs offer the potential to provide stable employment for a crew of workers despite the seasonal demand for labor, in practice the range of roles FLCs play is defined by two extremes that are closely linked to U.S. immigration policy. At one extreme, FLCs may play a *destabilizing employment role*, channeling a continuing stream of new and unskilled immigrants into low-paying farm jobs that are characterized by a high degree of employment turnover. Recent illegal immigrants were disproportionately represented in the FLC workforce in the early 1980s, just prior to the passage of IRCA (Vandemann, 1990). Once new immigrants become more established and tied into labor market information networks in the U.S., these workers' mobility increases. They leave FLC jobs for more stable and higher paying jobs, which are more likely to be offered directly by farmers or by employers outside of agriculture. In this model, the FLC is a conduit for new immigrant labor, a vital link in the migrant networks extending to villages in rural Mexico.

The immigration policy context that is most conducive to this high turnover model is one of loose border and interior enforcement. The FLC as a conduit of new alien labor presupposes a ready supply of low-skill labor from abroad. As long as such labor is available, FLCs stand to benefit from their ability to tap into migrant networks and to obtain workers more cheaply than farmers could if they hired workers directly.

At the other extreme, FLCs can play the role of *stabilizer of employment* for an existing farm workforce. This could happen in an opposite environment—one of tight border and interior enforcement and labor scarcity, where FLCs' comparative advantage is more likely to be in managing a smaller farm labor force than in recruiting new immigrants. Thus, FLCs can have two very different effects, depending on the environment in which they operate. In a surplus immigrant labor-supply environment, the proliferation of FLCs in agriculture is likely to be accompanied by little improvement—or even deterioration—in employment and earnings stability for farm-workers. In an environment of labor shortage, the expansion of FLC activity should imply the reverse.

Hypotheses

The role of farm labor contractors in California agriculture and the effect of IRCA on FLC activity in the future are empirical questions. The analysis above suggests a number of possibilities, each with distinct implications for the structure and functioning of the farm labor market. The future role of FLCs in California agriculture will be closely tied to, and should reflect, IRCA's effectiveness in elim-inating the use of illegal alien labor in farm jobs.

The following testable hypotheses were explored and tested using data from a 1989 employer survey and California unemployment insurance (UI) records.

1. In the environment of an abundant immigrant labor supply that characterized California agriculture just prior to IRCA, FLC work-ers had a high degree of labor turnover. Specifically, controlling for region, crop, and employer characteristics, worker retention from year-to-year and quarter-to-quarter was significantly lower for FLCs than for other farm employers.
2. The use of FLCs is greatest in operations where labor demand is most seasonal (e.g., the harvesting of perishable commodities with short seasons). Larger growers have more of an incentive to hire workers directly, since they can spread fixed recruitment costs over more workers.
3. IRCA increases recruitment and hiring costs and risks to farm employers. This should result in an increase in growers' use of farm labor contractors as a means of reducing recruitment costs and/or as a buffer against new hiring costs and risks created by IRCA. Growers with longer mean employment periods (i.e., lower seasonality) will be induced to fill all or part of their labor needs through FLCs.
4. Successful enforcement of IRCA should weaken the advantage of FLCs as recruiters of new immigrant labor. However, it will strengthen the potential role of FLCs as recruiters and managers of a smaller and more legal workforce. It should lead to fewer

and larger FLCs with less seasonal operations and lower worker turnover.

5. If IRCA is not effective in eliminating the use of illegal immigrant workers, one would expect a) a greater proliferation of FLCs, b) a fragmentation of existing FLCs into multiple small operations, and c) perhaps, paradoxically, increasing hourly earnings together with stable piece-rate wages, as employers screen tightly for the most productive workers from a large pool of immigrant labor.

Data Sources

Below is a description of our 1989 employer survey and the California unemployment insurance records used to test the hypotheses.

THE 1989 FARM EMPLOYER SURVEY

The Farm Employer Survey, conducted in early 1989, was designed to provide data on California employment, wages, and production practices in 1988. This period is critical to assessing the impacts of immigration reform on the California farm labor market because it precedes the December 1, 1988 imposition of employer sanctions against employers who knowingly hire illegal immigrant workers in perishable agriculture. A second purpose of the survey was to explore the initial impacts of IRCA on recruitment patterns and to solicit farmers' perceptions of the likely impacts of IRCA on their future operations. Findings of this survey are reported in detail in Martin and Taylor (1990a and 1990b).

The data gathered in the survey are intended to paint a picture of the structure and functioning of the California farm labor market in 1988, before employer sanctions took full effect. Full implementation of employer sanctions in agriculture was delayed until December, 1988 in order to provide farm employers with extra time to adjust to IRCA. The findings we describe below do not support the hypothesis that employers, including FLCs, took steps to retain legal farm workers, or that IRCA succeeded in reducing the influx of new immigrants into agriculture by the end of the adjustment period.

The survey questionnaire covered a wide range of farm employment issues relevant to U.S. immigration policy and agriculture. The first part gathered information about each farmer's workforce, including total payroll, employee benefits and payroll taxes, turnover, and employment from 1986 to 1988. The second part focused on the farmer's major commodity, i.e., the one in which the farmer had the highest dollar sales in 1988. This part of the survey obtained detailed data for 1988 on recruitment practices, wages, seasonality, the immigration status of workers, and production practices. The last part of the questionnaire asked how immigration reforms were affecting or would affect farm operations. This part included questions about how farmers had adjusted or planned to adjust their hiring, recruitment, and production practices.

The employer survey data were used to test for differences in FLC use across types of employers.

California UI Data

California unemployment insurance laws require employers who pay $100 or more in wages during a calendar quarter to report the names, social security numbers, and earnings of their employees and to pay a tax of 3 to 6 percent on the first $7,000 of each employee's earnings. We obtained 5 percent random samples of all workers who were reported at least once by a crop, livestock, or agricultural services employer in each of 1985–1989. Of the 1.2 million workers reported on average each year, 906,000 were employed on crop or livestock farms or by "farm" agricultural service firms. The others worked for pet or landscape services or multi-establishment employers, such as retailers who also own farms.

The UI information is the best available "census" of people employed on farms, but it has several shortcomings. First, not all of the employees reported by farms have farmworker occupations. About a third of the unemployed workers claiming UI benefits on the basis of work on farms are in non-farm occupations such as clerk or mechanic. Second, the UI worker analysis is based on social security numbers. If a substantial proportion of farmworkers use several numbers, the UI figures inflate the numbers of farmworkers and lower the average earnings and weeks worked. Conversely, if several workers share the same social security numbers, the size of the workforce will be understated and average earnings and weeks worked will be exaggerated. Finally, some employers may not report all of their workers, and wages and weeks worked in the UI data are not verified unless workers file UI benefit claims.

The annual UI farmworker files are used in the present study to track changes in the total number of FLCs and in the share of employment controlled by FLCs in California from 1985 to 1989. A longitudinal farmworker data file was also created covering a random sample of farmworkers in each of five years (1985–1989) drawn from the annual UI files. It consists of five progressively smaller "waves" of sampling across the years, 200 workers in year one, 180 in year two, 160 in year three, and so on. For each worker drawn in year one, information on *all* jobs held by that worker during the year—both inside and outside of agriculture—was placed in the worker record.

For each job the worker held during the year, the UI data include an employer identification number. This identification number was used to assemble data on characteristics of the worker's employer in each job from the UI employer file. For each job in which the worker was observed, characteristics of the employer were woven into the worker's data record. The augmented worker record makes it possible to track the worker's movements across regions and commodities as well as across "types" of employers. It also provides information on worker/employer combinations, including the worker's earnings with the employer and number of quarters working with the employer since the start of the data series in 1985.

Each worker drawn in year one was also tracked through time. All jobs in other years in which the worker was observed in at least one California farm job were folded into the worker's record. A large number of workers in the year-one sample exit from farm jobs in one of the four subsequent years. With the five-year time series it is possible to estimate exit rates for different workers and different combinations of commodities, regions, and employer types.

The longitudinal UI worker file is used to test the hypothesis that worker turnover rates are higher for FLCs than for other employers, and that turnover rates have decreased since the implementation of employer sanctions under IRCA.

Findings

Below we discuss the findings from the 1989 employer survey and our review of California UI records.

THE IRONY OF POST-IRCA EXPANSION OF FLC ACTIVITY

California UI data suggest that FLCs have increased rather than decreased since the implementation of IRCA. Between 1985 and 1989, the number of FLCs who paid UI taxes rose 1 percent, their wages paid rose 43 percent, and their average annual employment rose 36 percent. The number of large FLCs rose 9 percent (from 42 to 46), but the wages paid by these largest FLCs and their employment increased only 11 percent, indicating that most of the growth in FLC wages and employment during the mid-1980s occurred among the

FLCs that had annual wage bills of $500,000 or less. The number of FLCs reporting the equivalent of at least a 50-person year-round crew jumped 32 percent, from 385 to 508, and their employment rose 80 percent in the mid-1980s.

Although federal and state legislation from the mid-1960s to the mid-1980s was expected to extirpate farm labor contractors, regulatory legislation has had just the opposite result: instead of fewer and more lawful FLCs, there are more FLCs today than in 1960. Furthermore, the U.S. Department of Labor finds that over two-thirds of all the FLCs it investigates are violating at least one labor law.

One explanation for the apparent paradox of more regulation resulting in more FLCs is that the FLC workforce is changing. Rather than consisting of workers with a legal right to work in the U.S., as during the 1960s and 1970s, the FLC workforce of the 1980s was comprised increasingly of unauthorized or illegal aliens (Martin, 1988). FLCs appear to be a door of entry into the U.S. labor market for the newest and least sophisticated unauthorized aliens, and they employ a more vulnerable workforce in order to offset increased regulation (Vaupel and Martin, 1987).

VARIATIONS IN FLC USE AMONG EMPLOYERS

Nearly one-third of all employers responding to the 1989 farm employment survey reported hiring labor through FLCs or custom harvesters in 1988, usually to harvest crops or to prune trees and vines. In the San Joaquin Valley, 42 percent of the respondents used labor market middlemen, while in the Inland Southern California region, only 9 percent did. About two-thirds of the citrus farms hired labor through contractors, but none of the berry or livestock farms or nurseries did.

Most of the commodities produced on responding farms were characterized by a high degree of seasonality in labor use and by a labor-intensive production process. The exceptions are tree nuts, the harvest of which is mechanized; nurseries, which usually produce flowers and plants year-round in controlled greenhouse environments; and livestock products, which require employees year-round. Most fruits and vegetables, on the other hand, are labor-intensive and have seasonal labor demands.

Probit findings reported in Martin and Taylor (1990a) confirm the hypothesis that FLC use is greatest where production is both labor-intensive and seasonal. The probability of FLC use on grape, tree fruit, field fruit, and vegetable farms, other things being equal, is significantly higher than on nut farms (the reference category). In these commodities, characterized by a high degree of employment seasonality, there is an incentive to avoid the sunk costs of recruitment by using indirect recruitment methods. By contrast, in commodities where workers are needed year-round (e.g., cut flowers grown in controlled greenhouse environments),[1] growers may find it feasible to incur the sunk cost to recruit their own labor in order to ensure direct control over the hiring process. Dummy variables for nursery and livestock operations could not be included in the probit equation because none of these operations reported using FLCs in 1988.

The probit estimates do not support the hypothesis that larger employers have less incentive to hire labor through FLCs. Controlling for region and commodity, the probability of FLC use decreases with payroll size, but this relationship is not statistically significant. This finding suggests that considerations other than minimizing fixed recruitment costs—such as efforts by farmers to buffer themselves from immigration and labor laws—may play an important role in farmers' recruitment practices. Alternatively, spreading fixed recruitment costs over a large number of workers may not result in significant recruitment cost savings.

There is little variation in FLC use across regions, with the exception of the San Joaquin Valley, where the probability of FLC use is far higher than in the desert region (the reference category). Past studies find that the San Joaquin Valley also had the largest number

Table 9.1 CALIFORNIA LABOR CONTRACTORS BY SIZE IN 1987

FLC size[a]	Reporting units[b]	Percent of FLC wages	Percent of FLC employment
Small	23	1	2
Medium	50	22	30
Large	27	77	68
Total	845	$398 million	61,547

a. Small FLCs paid less than $50,000 in annual wages; medium FLCs paid $50,000 to $500,000, and large FLCs paid more than $500,000.

b. Reporting units may include more than one FLC, e.g., an FLC who has three crew leaders would be registered as four FLCs.

Source: California Employment Development Unemployment Insurance data for 1987.

of illegal immigrants prior to IRCA, suggesting that there is a high correlation between FLC activity and use of illegal immigrant labor (Mines and Martin, 1986).

FLCs AND WORKER TURNOVER

Econometric analysis of the longitudinal UI worker file indicates that farmworker turnover rates not only are higher for FLCs than for all other employers, but are increasing over time. This pattern contradicts the argument that IRCA has forced farm employers to adjust to a smaller, more stable workforce. It suggests that since IRCA was enacted, FLCs have continued to be short-term employers of new immigrants, maintaining their comparative advantage as recruiters of new labor from abroad.

Our econometric analysis is based on the assumption that workers choose employers to maximize expected earnings and utility from non-pecuniary aspects of jobs, and that farm workers' labor market information and options improve as they acquire experience in farm jobs. This means that, although workers may initially work for employers offering low wages, unstable employment, or poor working conditions, over time these workers tend to gravitate away from these employers and toward "better" employers. The probability that workers will switch employers at a given point in time (for example, at time t + 1) depends on their earnings under their employer in the last time period (time t), together with other variables reflecting their expected utility from staying with their time-t employer versus their utility from changing to a new employer at t + 1.

This expected utility differential reflects workers' expected next-period earnings with their current employers—as reflected by current earnings, opportunities for mobility in the current job, and assurances of stable employment in the next period. The expected utility differential also reflects non-earnings characteristics of jobs—for example, the financial, transportation, and housing services provided by FLCs to new immigrant workers. The demand for these "non-pecuniary" aspects of employment may decrease as workers' information and labor market options increase. This is certainly likely to be the case for the services typically offered by FLCs, usually at non-competitive prices. As workers acquire experience, they should begin to shift toward employers who bring them the highest longer-term utility. The employers they systematically leave behind, other things equal, should be an indication of which employers offer the least competitive employment packages, and should be those employers that have the highest worker turnover rates.

We would expect turnover rates for FLCs to be significantly higher than for other seasonal agricultural employers for several reasons:[2] first, FLCs' easy access to vulnerable, inexperienced workers discourages FLCs from offering non-pecuniary incentives to retain workers; second, the low wages and limited job security FLCs offer; and third, workers' diminishing need for FLC services as they acquire experience in farm work.

If IRCA's employer sanctions have been ineffective in "closing the doors" to new immigrant workers in agriculture, we would expect to find an increase (or at least, no decline) in farmworker turnover rates over time in addition to higher turnover for FLC workers.

The "IRCA/FLC/Farmworker Turnover" Hypothesis. This hypothesis was tested by using a probit to estimate differences in turnover rates across employers and over time, controlling for other variables. The units of observation are individual workers (social security numbers) at different points in time (quarters) between 1985 and 1989. The (dependent) worker turnover variable (MOVE) is defined as:

$$MOVE_{i,\,t+1} = \begin{cases} 1 \text{ if worker i changed principal employers} \\ \quad \text{between quarters t and t} + 1 \\ 0 \text{ otherwise} \end{cases}$$

The probability of a move is modeled as

$$\text{Prob}(MOVE_{i,\,t+1}) = \Phi(Z'_{i,\,t+1}\beta)$$

where $\Phi(.)$ is the normal density function, $Z_{i,\,t+1}$ is a vector of explanatory variables, and β is a vector of parameters reflecting the effect of explanatory variables on the transitional probability.

The explanatory variables in Z include a time trend to capture changes in worker turnover over time; dummy variables for workers' region of principal employment at time t, covering five major agricultural regions in California (the default region is inland Southern California, which includes the Imperial Valley); a dummy variable equal to one if workers' time-t employer was a farm labor contractor, and zero otherwise; dummy variables for crop (SIC codes) of workers' time-t employment; time-t earnings with the principal employer; workers' quarters of experience with the same employer, in the same region, and in the same type of work since the beginning of our series in 1985; and characteristics of workers' time-t employer, including total payroll size and three-month trend in total employment in quarter t.

The estimation and econometric findings are reported in detail in Taylor and Thilmany (1991). Here we summarize these findings and then focus on FLC turnover and changes in overall turnover over time.

The Probit Findings. The probit findings support the hypothesis that FLCs provide unstable employment to a transitory workforce. The coefficient on the FLC dummy is positive and significant at well below the 0.01 level; it indicates that workers employed by FLCs are substantially more likely to change employers, other things being equal, than workers in the default category. (The default category in this probit primarily includes multi-establishment employers.) It is particularly striking that FLCs are the *only* employer group with significantly *higher* turnover rates than the default category. Vegetable growers have lower turnover than the default group (and by implication, far lower turnover than FLCs), while for the others turnover is not significantly different than for the default group.

A second striking finding is that, controlling for other explanatory variables, there is a significant, increasing trend in farmworker turnover over time. This contradicts the hypothesis that farmers are having to adjust to a smaller, more stable workforce.

Not surprisingly, workers' earnings with their principal time-t employer are inversely related to their probability of changing primary employers at time t + 1. Employment changes are also discouraged by consecutive years of experience with the same employer and by experience in the same region, although not by experience in the same type of work or unemployment. Large employers are associated with significantly lower worker turnover than smaller employers. Employers' month-to-month employment trends, which primarily reflect seasonality of employment, are inversely related to turnover.

In theory, it could be argued that the increasing trend in farm turnover is caused by high exit rates of SAWs from agriculture or by a reshuffling of jobs within agriculture by SAWs in search of more desirable employment. However, the available evidence to date does not support either of these explanations. There is no evidence of high exit rates for SAWs from agriculture. The only comprehensive data available on farmworkers by legal status since IRCA is the Department of Labor's National Agricultural Worker Survey (NAWS). Just under half of all workers in this survey are reported to be SAWs, but the exit rate for these workers is low (below 10 percent). This finding was instrumental in the decision by the secretaries of Agriculture and Labor not to authorize any Replenishment Agricultural Workers (RAWs) for 1990. High turnover could be caused by SAWs seeking better jobs within agriculture; however, there appears to be less, not more, mobility among legal workers than among illegal workers in California agriculture after IRCA. Mobility of legal workers who are employed is discouraged by a preference among employers to hire "undocumented illegals" over legal workers.[3]

Figure 9.1 illustrates the difference in worker turnover between FLCs and other employers over the 1984–88 period. Average turnover is high for all workers in the longitudinal sample—41 percent. However, the average turnover rate is 65 percent for FLCs.

Figure 9.2 shows the rising trends in predicted probabilities of employer change for FLC workers and for other workers over the five years covered by the sample. The difference in transition probabilities between FLCs and other employers in this figure is larger than that indicated by the coefficient on FLC in the probit reported in Taylor and Thilmany (1991). This is because the probability of changing employers is affected by other variables (e.g., earnings), which are different for the two employer groups. In general, variables that are negatively related to worker turnover have lower averages for FLCs than for other employers; the reverse is true for variables that are positively related to turnover. For example, average earnings are substantially lower for FLC workers—74 percent below the average earnings of other workers. Low earnings, in turn, significantly increase the probability of employer change.

CONCLUSIONS

FLCs are the intermediaries in farm labor markets whose livelihood depends on the difference between what an employer pays to have a farm job done and what a worker gets. FLCs originally emerged in California as necessary go-betweens for Chinese and Japanese speaking workers and English-speaking farmers, but they soon acquired an independent interest in maximizing the gap between farmer costs and worker pay.

FLCs have a slightly shady reputation. Farmers consider them a necessary evil. FLCs can assume the task of recruiting and supervising a seasonal harvest workforce at about the same costs that farmers themselves would incur. Farmworker advocates and unions

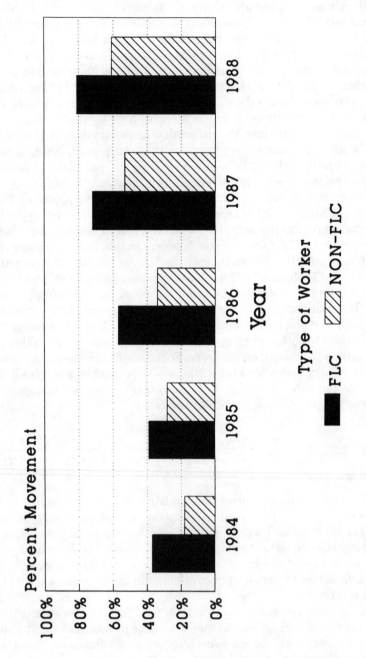

Figure 9.1 OBSERVED SHARE OF WORKERS CHANGING PRINCIPAL EMPLOYERS: FLC AND NON-FLC WORKERS

Source: Tabulations of California Unemployment Insurance Longitudinal Data California Employment Development Dept.

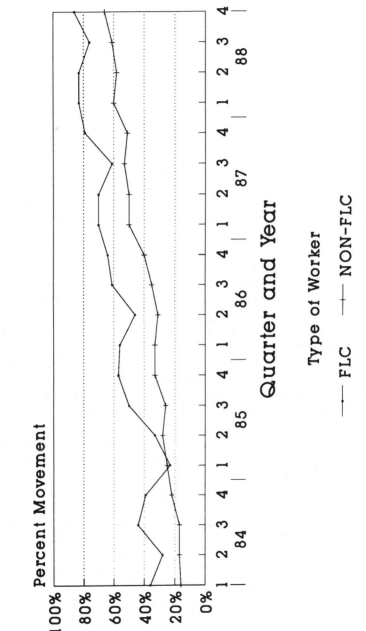

Figure 9.2 EXPECTED PROBABILITIES OF CHANGING PRINCIPAL EMPLOYERS: FLC AND NON-FLC WORKERS

Source: Econometric estimate using Unemployment Insurance Longitudinal Data California Employment Development Dept.

bemoan the 10 to 30 percent that FLCs pocket for their services, arguing that free Employment Service offices or union hiring halls could provide these intermediary services and leave low-wage farmworkers with higher pay. Public policies permit FLCs to operate, but attempt to regulate FLCs so that they do not undermine labor standards. Federal and state FLC public policies rest on registration and a requirement that if an FLC offers a service such as housing to workers, it must satisfy minimum standards.

The Proliferation of Farm Labor Contractors

By all accounts, efforts to regulate FLCs have failed. Since the mid-1960s, federal and state regulations were designed to produce fewer and better FLCs, but their changing character and limited enforcement of the regulations generated more FLCs and more violations of labor laws.

There is disagreement over whether supply or demand factors are responsible for the proliferation of FLCs. Unions and some farmworker advocates argue that farmers encourage FLC activities to undermine unions, for example, encouraging "independent growers" to have FLCs harvest crops instead of unionized farmworkers. Unions agree that FLCs tend to hire recent and vulnerable immigrants, but they put less emphasis on the increased availability of such workers to explain the rise of labor contracting. Others argue that the availability of vulnerable immigrant workers is the major factor encouraging the spread of FLCs; such workers need the services provided by FLCs, they argue, so it is only natural that FLCs emerge to organize them for seasonal farm work.

If IRCA were effective at decreasing new immigration and discouraging the use of unauthorized immigrant labor, we should have seen certain trends emerge in the late 1980s. These trends include a greater use of FLCs for seasonal work, as employer sanctions raise the costs and risks of hiring seasonal workers directly; a change in the role of FLCs toward managing a more stable and legal workforce; and greater stability in the farm labor market, where stability means less worker turnover and more regular employment for more workers.

However, our statistical analysis of farm employment in California does not reveal such trends. Use of FLCs is increasing in the wake of IRCA. Farmworker turnover is also increasing, not decreasing, as both FLCs and other seasonal agricultural employers are offering less stable employment opportunities to workers over time. This analysis paints a picture of a farm labor market that is still being fed by streams of new and vulnerable immigrants. In addition, FLCs appear to be fragmenting into smaller operations. This may be a response to IRCA: many small operations increase the cost of immigration and labor law enforcement, and FLCs may be fragmenting with the *intent* of making immigration and labor law enforcement more costly and difficult. In the wake of IRCA, the role of FLCs in California's farm labor market promises to increase.

The Elusive Nature of FLCs

Who are these FLCs? Our field interviews have constructed a portrait of the "typical" FLC and his operation. FLCs are principally Mexican men with little schooling and sometimes limited English skills. They operate on oral contracts and have slim profit margins—so slim that it can be said they are engaged in "destructive competition"—a proliferation of FLCs undercutting one another to win farmer contracts. Their total payrolls are large enough to classify them as large employers by U.S. Department of Commerce criteria, but their average per-worker payrolls are small. Because of the large number of workers they employ, their accounting and record-keeping burdens are substantial, but their ability to deal with them is limited. Significant shares of FLCs and FLC employment do not appear to be captured by state and federal agencies, despite the fact that FLCs are regulated by such agencies and are required to register with them. Thus, the recent growth in FLC activity, phenomenal as it has been, may be understated by official data. This new and unprepared group of employers is bearing an increasing burden in managing California's single largest workforce.

The Future

What does the future portend? Our analysis indicates that employer sanctions are not stopping the demand for immigrant workers or illegal immigrants in U.S. agriculture.[4] The forms of these workers' employment are changing, but not the fact of their employment. The seasonal demand for agricultural workers remains high, and all indications are that new and vulnerable immigrant workers continue to be drawn into seasonal farm work, largely through the recruitment activities of FLCs. If farmers continue to turn hiring over to FLCs, and FLCs continue to be recruiters and first employers of new immigrants, the welfare problems of illegal immigrants, if anything, will be greater than before. Further growth in FLC employment and intense competition among many FLCs may mean low wages, unstable employment, and poor working conditions for a large and growing share of the California farm workforce.

Notes

1. In the case of cut flowers, in the past a high degree of seasonality was attributable to market demand, i.e., peaks in demand at key holiday periods. Market-related seasonality has declined markedly in recent years, however, as more stable, year-round demand for cut flowers has emerged.

2. Citrus is a commodity that has traditionally relied on FLCs to provide two-thirds or more of its seasonal workers. In the aftermath of a December 1990 freeze that eliminated about 12,000 jobs, surveys revealed that about one-third of the workers were post-IRCA illegal aliens, and 50 percent were SAWs. If, in December, citrus has such a high proportion of illegals in its workforce, when presumably more seasonal illegal aliens have returned to Mexico, then the FLC link with illegals seems firmly established in California.

3. Statement of Dolores Huerta to the Commission on Agricultural Workers, Coachella Hearing, December 5–7, 1990. More illegal workers are allegedly coming to the U.S. and saving their pay stubs and receipts in the hope of a second amnesty; it has been asserted that the SAW program has convinced rural aliens from Mexico that they must be in the U.S. if they wish to obtain U.S. immigrant status. Over 90 percent of the almost 700,000 illegal aliens who applied for RAW visas gave U.S. addresses.

4. There are several reasons why enforcement has failed in agriculture. Before IRCA, Border Patrol enforcement usually involved driving vans into fields and apprehending workers who ran away. IRCA required the INS to obtain search warrants before raiding "open fields" for aliens, so post-IRCA enforcement has been converted from an alien chase to a paper chase. The INS has been shifting enforcement personnel from its interior stations to the border, so that, in the 18 months ending in December 1990, there were only 122 agricultural employer visits in California.

References

Fisher, Lloyd. 1953. *The Harvest Labor Market in California.* Cambridge: Harvard University Press.

Gabbard, Susan. 1991. "The Impact of Immigration Reform on Salinas Farmworkers." Berkeley: California Policy Seminar, University of California (forthcoming).

Huerta, Dolores. 1990. Testimony to Commission on Agricultural Workers (CAW) in Visalia and Coachella, CA., August and December.

Martin, Philip. 1988. "Network Recruitment and Labor Displacement." In *U.S. Immigration in the 1980s: Reappraisal and Reform*, ed. D. Simcox. Boulder, CO: Westview Press.

Martin, Philip L., and Stephanie Luce. 1988. "IRCA's Effect on Large Farms." *California Agriculture* 43, no. 3, pp. 26–28.

Martin, Philip L., and J. Edward Taylor. 1990a. "The Initial Effects of Immigration Reform on Farm Labor in California." *Population Research and Policy Review* 9, no. 3 (Sept.): pp. 255–283.

———. 1990b. "Immigration Reform and California Agriculture: A Year Later." *California Agriculture* 44, no. 1 (Jan.-Feb.): pp. 24-27.

Mines, R., and P. L. Martin. 1986. "California Farmworkers-Survey Results of the UC-EDD Survey of 1983." Mimeo. Department of Agricultural Economics, University of California, Davis.

Rosenberg, Howard, and Jeffrey M. Perloff. 1988. "Initial Effects of the New Immigration Law on California Agriculture." *California Agriculture* 43, no. 3 (May-June): pp. 28–29.

Taylor, J. Edward, and Thomas Espenshade. 1987. "Foreign and Undocumented Workers in California Agriculture." *Population Research and Policy Review* 6, no. 3 (Sept.): pp. 223–239.

Taylor, J. Edward, and Dawn Thilmany. 1991. "Farm Labor Contractors, Turnover and the Impact of IRCA on the Farm Labor Market." Mimeo. Department of Agricultural Economics, University of California, Davis.

Vandemann, Anne. 1990. *Labor Contracting in California Agriculture.* Ph.D. Thesis, University of California, Berkeley.

Vaupel, Suzanne, and Philip L. Martin. 1987. "Evaluating Employer Sanctions: Farm Labor Contractor Experience." *Industrial Relations* 26, no. 3 (Fall): pp. 304–313.

Part Three

REFORM OPTIONS

Chapter Ten

IRCA-RELATED DISCRIMINATION: WHAT DO WE KNOW AND WHAT SHOULD WE DO?

Michael Fix

In March 1990 the U.S. General Accounting Office (GAO) submitted its third and final mandated report on the impact and implementation of the 1986 Immigration Reform and Control Act (IRCA). Its conclusion was that the law had given rise to "widespread discrimination" against foreign-sounding and looking job applicants. This result had been anticipated during the two-decade debate over IRCA by opponents of the law's principal policy innovation, employer sanctions. Sanctions were intended to right an asymmetry in American law that made it illegal for undocumented aliens to enter and work in the United States but imposed no penalties on employers who hired them. Righting this asymmetry involved the largest expansion of labor-related regulation since 1970, as well as the broadest regulatory expansion to take place during the fiercely anti-regulatory Reagan administration. By deputizing employers as "junior immigration officers" (Roberts and Loehr, 1987), sanctions for the first time brought the hitherto obscure and little-encountered world of immigration law and immigration law enforcement to the nation's workplace. (And indeed, because sanctions govern all hiring transactions, in theory, to the homes of the nation's citizens.)

BACKGROUND

The battle for sanctions was a long and arduous one that forced its proponents to consent to a series of major political trade-offs. Among other things, it led to the enactment of the two largest legalization programs in recent history (one for aliens who had been in the U.S. since 1982, the other for agricultural workers with only minimal recent farm-work history); a $4 billion intergovernmental grant program to appease states that feared their services would be overrun by recently legalized aliens; and a series of new civil rights protections that responded to fears that IRCA would generate new discrimination.

Five rights-related protective provisions are embodied in the law. First, IRCA banned national-origin discrimination in the *hiring* or *terminating* of employees in firms with four or more employees, thereby extending partial coverage of Title VII of the 1964 C vil Rights Act from 13 to 48 percent of the nation's employers.[1] Second, the law introduced a legislative bar against discrimination in hiring or termination on the basis of citizenship or alienage (i.e., immigration status). Third, the law established a new bureaucracy to help enforce these new rights: the Office of Special Counsel within the Department of Justice. Fourth, it provided for the "sunset" of employer sanctions—essentially a premature "exit" from the political bargain struck by IRCA's architects—should the GAO find that the law had given rise to "widespread discrimination." And fifth, as a correlate of this sunset, the law mandated that GAO undertake what were, in effect, a series of discrimination-impact studies.

The GAO report has fueled two predictable types of political debates. One focuses on the policy implications of the report: Should we sunset sanctions? If we retain sanctions, what types of remedial measures need to be taken? What further analysis and monitoring is required? The other debate has focused on the merits of the report itself. Senator Alan Simpson (R.-WY) has been especially critical of the report's methods and findings, making public an internal GAO critique of a draft of the report. In this paper I review and characterize the two major elements of the GAO study (the employer survey and an hiring audit), note some of the criticisms lodged against each, and conclude with what I view to be some of the policy implications of the report.

THE EVIDENCE OF IRCA-RELATED DISCRIMINATION

The results of the two waves of GAO studies of IRCA-related discrimination, when viewed alongside the hiring audit and the studies of other state and local organizations in this area, present an unusually detailed picture of the kind and extent of discrimination encountered by foreign-looking and sounding job applicants. The results of these studies suggest that policymakers concerned with remedying discrimination against foreign-appearing individuals confront not one, but three types of discrimination:

☐ *Confusion discrimination* stemming from incomplete understanding of IRCA's requirements, not from antagonism toward any ethnic group;
☐ *Bias-based discrimination* against Hispanics or other foreign-appearing people, at least some of which occurs independently of IRCA; and
☐ *Opportunistic discrimination* stemming from a fear of sanctions enforcement and a belief that knowingly discriminatory practices reduce the employer's total regulatory burden.

The distinction between the three is important because they drive different policy responses, which we will turn to in the final section of this chapter.

The GAO Survey

The GAO's third report on IRCA-related discrimination (GAO, 1990) drew on a survey of over 9,000 employers who were asked what actions they had taken "as a result of the 1986 immigration law." Two kinds of IRCA-related discrimination were reported. In terms of *national origin* discrimination;

☐ An estimated five percent of employers reported that as a result of IRCA they began a practice of not hiring persons because of their foreign appearance or accent; and
☐ An estimated eight percent of employers surveyed reported that as a result of IRCA they applied the law's verification system only to foreign-looking or foreign-appearing or sounding persons.

With regard to *citizenship or alienage* discrimination, an estimated 14 percent of employers reported that they began a practice (a) of hiring only persons born in the United States or (b) of not hiring persons with temporary work eligibility documents.

Critics of the survey and of the GAO's overall findings have made much of an internal GAO memorandum written by Eleanor Chelimsky, the Assistant Comptroller General for Program Evaluation and Methodology (Chelimsky, 1990). The memo advances several criticisms of the GAO employer survey and its results, two of which are central to her skepticism regarding the report's findings.

First, Chelimsky notes that the survey results might have exaggerated reported levels of discrimination because employers might have falsely claimed to be noncomplying in order to build a case for repealing sanctions. The trouble with this "ulterior motive critique" is that it not only assumes a perfect understanding of IRCA on the part of employers, it also assumes that employers understood the possibility that their responses to the survey might cause the repeal of the sanctions provision. Field research conducted by The Urban Institute and the RAND Corporation suggests that these assumptions are unrealistic.[2] Indeed, it is far more likely that employers would intentionally *overstate* compliance when responding to a government questionnaire in order to avoid possible enforcement actions.

Second, Chelimsky points to the fact that the GAO study was not able to marshall any evidence other than employers' statements to indicate that there had been a rise in national origin discrimination following IRCA. She notes the absence of any baseline data and the failure of other enforcement measures to reveal a rise in discrimination (for example, a rise in complaints regarding national origin discrimination filed with the Equal Employment Opportunity Commission). She argues that these deficiencies make it difficult to claim that there had been such an increase, much less to tie it solely to IRCA.

The absence of any baseline data must be taken seriously. No "before and after" data exist that would allow us to state with great confidence that the discrimination measured by the GAO did *not* exist before IRCA. Thus the main evidence we have linking IRCA to increased discrimination is employers' statements that they introduced a series of discriminatory practices as a result of the legislation. The issue, then, becomes how confident we can be in relying on those responses. It should be noted that our confidence in those responses is substantially reinforced by an earlier survey of a different sample of 6,000 employers conducted by the GAO that revealed that one in six employers had initiated discriminatory practices following IRCA's enactment.[3] The degree to which employer responses obtained by these two studies point to similar conclusions—as do the responses from studies conducted by a substantial number of public and private organizations—has gone largely unnoticed (The City of New York Commission on Human Rights, 1989; San Francisco State University and the Coalition for Immigrant and Refugee Rights and Services, 1989; and New York State Inter-Agency Task Force on Immigration Affairs, 1988.) Furthermore, as I note in the final chapter in this volume, no evidence has been advanced demonstrating that sanctions did *not* give rise to increased discrimination.

The fact that complaints about national origin discrimination have not risen proves little, I would argue. In fact, it would have been surprising if the number of complaints filed by victims of discrimination had substantially increased in the wake of IRCA. Over time, IRCA's discriminatory impact on foreign-appearing job candidates will be increasingly likely to take place at the point of hire. Debriefings of Urban Institute auditors over the course of two major studies of hiring discrimination revealed that job applicants are rarely given reason to think that their rejections were the result of discrimination. This means that persons subjected to such discrimination would be less likely to file official complaints than persons already on a job whose promotion might be affected by more readily discerned discrimination. Furthermore, the population protected by IRCA's anti-discrimination provision remains one that is in general more suspicious of government institutions and one that is less litigious than other groups in society.

The Urban Institute Hiring Audit

In the summer of 1989 The Urban Institute conducted 360 hiring audits in two cities, San Diego and Chicago. Matched pairs of Anglo and Hispanic testers applied for the same entry-level jobs, documenting differences in subsequent treatment (Cross et. al, 1990). The hiring audit confirmed in part the results of the GAO study, revealing high levels of differential treatment that favored Anglos over their Hispanic counterparts. Had the audit revealed little or no discrimination, they would not have validated the results of the GAO employer survey in the way they did.

The audit results, which in the larger scheme of things may carry the most significant and far-reaching of all the findings reported in the GAO report, include the following:

☐ Hispanic testers received unfavorable treatment from three of every ten employers (i.e., were denied an application, interview, or job when one was offered to their Anglo counterpart);

☐ Anglo testers achieved more favorable outcomes in 33 percent of the audits, while their Hispanic counterparts fared better in 11 percent of the audits;

☐ Anglos received 33 percent more interviews than did Hispanics; and

☐ Anglos received 52 percent more job offers than did Hispanics.

While the audit confirmed the existence of extensive discrimination against foreign-appearing job candidates, it did not link differential treatment to IRCA. This linkage might have been made *if* the Hispanic candidates had been systematically subjected to more rigorous documentation requirements than their Anglo counterparts. But they were not; they simply fared worse in terms of outcomes.[4] Moreover, the limited data generated by the study afforded no qualitative evidence that would suggest that these outcomes were tied to sanctions. Indeed, in those cases where the Hispanic auditors were steered into lower level jobs or the Anglos into higher level jobs, IRCA-related factors were not driving the outcome. In general, the audit's results suggest that stereotypes and bias rather than confusion were responsible for at least a significant share of the different outcomes observed.

But again we confront the question of how confident we can be in the methodology and results of the study. After having viewed a brief videotape of the eight auditors, one critic of the study's results wrote that he was "struck by the number of instances in which the Anglo testers attended more selective universities and displayed more self-assurance than their Hispanic counterparts. Indeed, the Anglos generally appeared to have a social class advantage over the Hispanics which would explain much of the discrimination encountered by the latter" (Skerry, 1990).

There is a problem here. This observer views the candidates in light of their actual, revealed biographies, while the employer would view them through the lens of their identical, fictional credentials. Beyond this problem, though, the differences in the actual credentials of the testers have been exaggerated, as there was no meaningful difference in the relative "selectivity" of the universities attended. The exaggeration of these distinctions between the testers raises questions about the degree to which the other relative qualities ascribed to the Anglo auditors by this viewer ("articulateness, self-assurance") were similarly overstated, and, in turn, whether the testers' ethnic traits ultimately determined their attractiveness ("the social class advantage") to this viewer.

In the final analysis the audit's results tend to call into question the degree to which discrimination is absent from the lives of foreign-born, if not native born, Hispanics, and suggests that the experience of at least foreign-born Hispanics may be more analogous to that of blacks than some observers have thought.[5]

POLICY RESPONSES

Soon after the submission of the GAO report, a bipartisan bill was introduced by Senators Kennedy (D-MA) and Hatch (R-UT) in the Senate calling for the repeal of employer sanctions and a substantial increase in the size of the Border Patrol.[6] But one year later the political prospects of repeal remain low despite endorsement by such important civil rights groups as the National Association for the Advancement of Colored People, formerly a powerful proponent of sanctions.

With sanctions' repeal off the political table, four intermediate strategies for remedying IRCA-related discrimination make sense: 1. increasing employers' awareness of the law and its requirements; 2. simplifying employer compliance by reducing the number of documents that non-citizens can present or by introducing some form of national identifier; 3. increasing the protections available to those who have been discriminated against; and 4. continuing to monitor IRCA-related discrimination, again linking the results to the repeal of sanctions.

If it is the case that IRCA-related discrimination is driven more by confusion than animus, then education and simplification should prove to be the most effective remedial strategies. Furthermore, where discrimination is driven by an effort to comply with, rather than evade, the law, we may find that substantial progress can be made without undertaking heroic, expensive, and intrusive measures.

Discrimination Based on Lack of Knowledge or Confusion

On the basis of Urban Institute research and a close reading of the GAO report, I believe that the impetus to discriminate appears to derive from several different kinds of misunderstanding. First, it appears that a share of employers are *only* aware of IRCA's sanctions provisions, not its ban on discrimination. These employers believe that they are acting lawfully when they shun foreign-appearing job applicants. Presumably, they are inclined toward law abiding behavior, and simply informing them of the law will be enough to change their behavior.

Second, many employers appear unaware of their limited exposure to liability under IRCA. They believe that there is, in effect, strict liability for hiring an illegal alien. These fears are no doubt compounded by a perception that unauthorized workers are likely to present counterfeit or fraudulent documents. A logical response is to discriminate against foreign-appearing job candidates. Presumably some employers would abandon these practices if they knew that they need only determine if the documents presented by a job applicant seem reasonably genuine upon their face. Thus, increasing employers' understanding of this "affirmative defense" and their limited obligations under IRCA would eliminate some discrimination.[7]

Third, some employers may be violating the law because its requirements are so complex or ambiguous that they genuinely do not know how to comply. Respondents to the GAO survey and our own employer interviews indicated that they had difficulty understanding the combination of documents that were acceptable (and unacceptable) under the law. Furthermore, employers often did not understand at what stage in the application process they should ask for documents or whether the verification process applied to all applicants.

REMEDIES TO REDUCE CONFUSION DISCRIMINATION

There are several possible responses to these types of *confusion* discrimination:

Revise the I-9. We know from separate research by the GAO, the Department of Labor and The Urban Institute/Rand IRCA project that substantial numbers of employers are aware of IRCA and are verifying work eligibility. As a result, one way to counteract some of these misconceptions in a cost-effective manner would be to embed in the I-9 form instructions that could eliminate much of the inadvertent "confusion" discrimination that appears to be taking place. The objective would be to more closely link the process of complying with the law's employer sanctions and anti-discrimination provisions. The form might instruct the employer that:

☐ The employer must ask all applicants for documents; he or she cannot single out those applicants who look or sound foreign;
☐ The employer has satisfied the law if the documents he receives reasonably appear on their face to be genuine;
☐ All applicants requested to produce documents must be asked to do so at the same stage of the hiring process;
☐ The applicant and not the employer should determine which authorized documents will be presented to establish work eligibility;
☐ The applicant has three work days to comply following a request to produce proper documentation; and

□ Violation of the antidiscrimination provisions, like violation of sanctions, subjects employers to fines and possible damages.

The regulations could further reduce employer discretion and the potential for discrimination by mandating that employers ask for documents of work eligibility only *after* a bona fide offer has been extended.

But here I must introduce a *caveat*. Recent developments in employer sanctions law, driven by the INS, may reduce the effectiveness of simply informing employers of their obligations under the law. This is especially true of the limits on employer liability afforded by the "affirmative defense" referred to above.

The changes, first announced in case law and later by interim regulation, redefine the term "knowing" as it relates to the knowing hiring of undocumented aliens to include not only actual knowledge but also knowledge that can "fairly be inferred" from "certain facts and circumstances" (*Federal Register* 55. June 25, 1990; and Schmidt, 1990). This means that employers can now be prosecuted for a substantive, knowing violation under IRCA for constructive knowledge (i.e., what the employer *should have known*) when actual knowledge (what the employer *did know*) cannot be established. The shift in policy moves the legal standard for a prosecutable offense closer to one of negligence and away from the specific intent standard contemplated by Congress. The change should force employers to become more vigilant in policing their work forces, with the result that they are likely to discriminate more in hiring decisions. And it reflects the fundamental tensions that exist between the INS's goals of effectively enforcing the law and eliminating sanctions-induced discrimination.

Educate Employers. Further employer education is clearly in order. The Urban Institute/Rand implementation study revealed that employer education regarding discrimination was "crowded out" by agency efforts to simultaneously educate employers about sanctions and inform the undocumented population about legalization. Our field studies also suggest that it may not make sense to rely heavily on the already overcommitted field enforcement staffs of the INS and the Department of Labor to carry out this education assignment.

Because IRCA enlists all employers, large and small, in enforcing the immigration laws, it is unrealistic to expect that this vast and changing community will be systematically reached by any means other than the mass media. As a result, carefully designed public information spots should be run, perhaps in "prime time," in those urban media markets with especially high concentrations of the foreign-born. After all, it is in these locations that the GAO reported the highest levels of discriminatory behavior.

The campaign should be designed by experts at the Department of Justice's Office of the Special Counsel, working with media consultants. Research will have to be conducted into effective public information campaigns that attempt to convey complex requirements simply. Policy analysts have found that federal regulators have much to learn from the techniques used by "commercial compliance" professionals such as fund raisers, lobbyists and the like who operate without the benefit of legal sanctions (Cialdini, 1988).

Reduce the Number of Work Authorization Documents. Because IRCA assigns responsibility for enforcing the nation's immigration laws to non-professionals (i.e., employers), their responsibilities should be as simple to execute and permit as little discretion as possible. Analysts in the area of tax policy have found that complexity increases the costs of compliance and in so doing reduces levels of compliance (Nagin, 1990).

Currently, 17 documents can be used to satisfy IRCA's verification requirements. The generous purpose served by allowing applicants the freedom to present so many different documents was to limit the burden the law imposes on job applicants and in so doing to reduce the labor market impact of the law on employers. (It was also driven by the wide variety of work authorization documents that the INS has historically issued to non-citizens.) The unintended result of permitting so many documents to satisfy regulatory requirements has been to complicate the policing function played by employers.

Reducing the number of work authorization cards issued to non-citizens to two—one for permanent resident aliens, one for all other work-authorized non-citizens—would eliminate the most confusing and complex aspect of complying with IRCA's documentation requirements. Further reducing the number of employment documents to two would simplify employer compliance, if for no other reason than because the entire field of acceptable documents could be easily listed on the face of the I-9, making compliance appear less complicated.

One drawback of this approach is that it shifts the burden of compliance to the nation's immigrants, some of whom will have to apply for, and be issued, new documents. Shifting the burden in this manner raises equity issues, suggesting that the costs of this transition (i.e., issuance of new cards) should be borne by the government and not passed on to this generally low-income population in the form of user fees.

The clear advantages of this approach are that it is relatively cheap, administratively feasible, and already underway. But it needs to be congressionally reinforced and expedited.

To simplify the employer's responsibilities and to defeat the kind of document fraud that currently appears rampant, many thoughtful observers have called for the introduction of a national identification card, supplemented by a telephone verification system (GAO, 1990; Briggs, 1991; chapter 11 of this volume). Such a system would be modeled on the Systematic Alien Verification for Entitlement Program (SAVE)—an electronic verification system used to determine the eligibility for public benefits of foreign-appearing persons. The studies of SAVE suggest that an expansion of the system would involve a host of costs that include:

□ Creation of a universal database;
□ Constant manual updating of the database;
□ The issue and periodic reissue of social security/work authorization documents to the nation's population (unlike the current social security card, photo ID's need to be periodically updated);
□ Manual record searches when electronic searches fail;
□ Employer purchase of point-of-sale or other devices required to get access to and read information from the central database; and
□ The operating costs of charges to the employer for each verification undertaken.

Interviews with staff of the INS indicate that 15 percent of the verifications that have been conducted under the SAVE system require manual searches because computerized searches fail to accurately verify the applicant's identity. This ratio of "hits" to "misses" would generate high costs if translated to the operation of a national employment system. Beyond such operational concerns are those related to the privacy issues that have frequently been raised by opponents of such a system (see chapter 5 of this volume).

FURTHER RECOMMENDATIONS

The above three recommendations are intended to remedy discrimination based on confusion. Below are two general recommendations aimed at better dealing with IRCA-related discrimination more broadly.

Increase Protections to Victims of Discrimination. Efforts to increase awareness and simplify compliance are primarily intended to pre- vent discrimination. Increasing the protections available to victims is intended to redress the damage caused by discriminatory acts. To the extent that discrimination against foreign-looking job candidates has its roots in ethnic or racial stereotypes and not confusion, then education and simplification are likely to have little effect.[8] This bias-based discrimination, which may occur independently of IRCA, requires new or expanded protections and enforcement. Anti-dis- crimination norms have been better established in the area of race rather than national-origin or citizenship discrimination. It could be the case that discrimination against Hispanics or other ethnic mi- norities may be far more common than is generally assumed. This suggests that enforcement of both IRCA-related and bias-driven dis- crimination against the foreign-appearing, especially Hispanics, be expanded.

Continue Monitoring. There are a number of strong reasons to con- tinue monitoring IRCA and its impact on discrimination. First, the period of study, like all start-up phases, was artificial. Our own field studies indicate that sanctions enforcement through the spring of 1989 was limited in its reach and power. This was because of the law's novelty, because of a congressionally mandated transition phase that focused on education rather than enforcement, and because the INS did not have a strong incumbent commissioner during much of this period. Second, as we indicate above, the attention paid to dis- crimination education has been extremely limited to date. Third, one unnoticed dimension of the larger policy experiment that IRCA rep- resented was the development of new analytic tools to measure the extent and character of discrimination. These tools have been im- proved as the law has matured. Fourth, with two GAO surveys and the Urban Institute employment audit, we now have an unusually rich database on the extent of discriminatory practices attributed to IRCA and of the differential treatment accorded Hispanic-appearing job candidates. Taken together, they represent a baseline of discrim- inatory behavior that can be used to determine if discrimination against foreign-looking and sounding persons is increasing. Survey results can again help link changes in the extent of discrimination to employer sanctions. Indeed, it may make sense to monitor dis- crimination in employment more systematically as is done by the federal government in the area of housing.

Finally, IRCA should be placed within the context of many other laws enacted during this regulatory reform era, with further monitoring linked to possible sunset should the law's costs clearly outweigh its benefits. These sunset provisions focus legislative attention on the underlying need for the regulatory program and oblige their advocates to make an affirmative case for their continuation (Commission on Law and The Economy, 1979). IRCA should be brought in line with those laws, with a full review to be conducted by Congress six years following enactment.

Notes

1. Significantly, IRCA did not extend its protections to the "terms, conditions and privileges of employment" as Title VII does. 42 USC Section 2000-2(a)(1982).

2. In 1988 and 1989 The Urban Institute and the RAND Corporation undertook a large study of the implementation of employer sanctions as well as other major provisions of IRCA. In the course of those studies we interviewed approximately 200 employers in immigrant-dependent industries in eight cities as well as representatives of major trade associations. See Fix and Hill, 1990.

3. See GAO, 1988. Specifically the survey revealed that one in six employers who were aware of the law had begun or increased the practice of 1) asking only foreign-looking persons for work authorization documents or 2) hiring only U.S. citizens.

4. The study design itself may be in part responsible for the results, since the profile of the testers called for them to assume the biography of U.S. citizens. Thus, when the testers were asked early in the process whether they were U.S. citizens—as happened in one third of the audits—they responded "yes" and in so doing possibly removed a potential concern of the employer early on. In most cases the question was asked on job application forms that both auditors filled out.

5. The audit's results are consistent with the few other studies that have directly tested discrimination against Hispanics. See Hakker, 1979.

The results of this audit of the sale and rental of housing units in Dallas, Texas, revealed that 42% of dark-skinned Mexican Americans, and 16% of light-skinned Mexican Americans encountered unfavorable, differential treatment. See also James et al., 1984, finding discriminatory treatment in sales and rental of housing against Hispanic auditors in Denver, Colorado.

6. See S. 2797, introduced June 27, 1990, 101st Cong. 2d Sess.

7. At the same time, though, it may subvert the goal of restricting the employment of undocumented aliens by reducing the effectiveness of workplace screening that occurs. Indeed, law enforcement objectives may be better served if employers are not fully aware of how limited their liability is under the law. This tension between the conflicting objectives of stopping illegal immigration and limiting the regulatory burden placed on employers broadly characterizes IRCA and its implementation to date.

8. Along the same lines, to the extent that sanctions give rise to opportunistic discrimination, i.e., discriminating to reduce total regulatory outlays but with the knowledge that it is proscribed, education and simplification will not be effective remedies.

References

Bach, Robert L., and Doris Meissner. 1990. *Employment and Immigration Reform: Employer Sanctions Four Years Later.* The Carnegie Endowment for International Peace, September.

Briggs, Vernon M., Jr. 1990. "Employer Sanctions and the Question of Discrimination: The GAO Study in Perspective." *The International Migration Review* 24, no. 4, p. 803.

Chelimsky, Eleanor. 1990. Memorandum, accompanied by letter of Charles A. Bowsher, Controller General of the United States. To Senator Alan K. Simpson (R-WY), June 26.

Cialdini, R.B. 1988. "Social Motivation to Comply: Norms, Values and Principles." In *Paying Taxes: An Agenda for Compliance Research,* vol. 2, eds. J.T. Sholtz, T.A. Roth, and A.D. Witte. Philadelphia: University of Pennsylvania Press.

The City of New York Commission on Human Rights. 1989. *Tarnishing the Golden Door: A Report on the Widespread Discrimination Against Immigrants and Persons Perceived as Immigrants Which Has Resulted From the Immigration Reform and Control Act of 1986.* The City of New York Commission on Human Rights, August.

Commission on Law and the Economy. 1979. "Federal Regulation: Roads to Reform." The American Bar Association.

Cross, Harry, Genevieve Kenney, Jane Mell, and Wendy Zimmermann. 1990. *Employer Hiring Practices: Differential Treatment of Hispanic and Anglo Job Seekers,* Urban Institute Report 90-4. Washington, D.C.: Urban Institute Press.

Fix, Michael, and Paul Hill. 1990. *Enforcing Employer Sanctions: Challenges and Strategies.* Washington, D.C.: Urban Institute Press.

GAO (United States General Accounting Office). 1990. "Immigration Reform, Employer Sanctions and The Question of Discrimination," GAO/GGD 90-62, March.

————. 1988. "Immigration Reform: Status of Implementing Employer Sanctions after Second Year," GAO/GGD-89-16, November.

Hakker, Jon. 1979. "Discrimination against Chicanos in the Dallas Rental Housing Market: An Experimental Extension of the Housing Market Practice Survey." Washington, D.C.: U.S. Department of Housing and Urban Development.

James, Franklin, Betty McCummings, and Eileen Tynan. 1984. *Minorities in the Sunbelt.* New Brunswick, NJ: Center for Urban Policy Research.

Nagin, Daniel. 1990. "Policy Options for Combatting Tax Noncompliance," *Journal of Policy Analysis and Management,* Winter, pp. 15–16.

New York State Inter-Agency Task Force on Immigration Affairs. 1988. *Workplace Discrimination Under the Immigration Reform and Control Act of 1986: A Study of Impacts on New Yorkers.* New York State Inter-Agency Task Force on Immigration Affairs, November.

Roberts, M., and S. Yale Loehr. 1987. "Employers as Junior Immigration

Inspectors: The Impact of the 1986 Immigration Reform and Control Act." *The International Lawyer* 21, no. 1013.

San Francisco State University Public Research Institute and the Coalition for Immigrant and Refugee Rights and Services. 1989. *Employment and Hiring Practices under the Immigration Reform and Control Act of 1986: A Survey of San Francisco Businesses.* Conducted by the San Francisco State University Public Research Institute and the Coalition for Immigrant and Refugee Rights and Services. San Francisco, Sept.

Schmidt, Paul. 1990. "INS Employer Sanctions Interim Regulations." *Interpreter Releases* 67, p. 1057, September 24.

Skerry, Peter. 1990. "Hispanic Job Discrimination Exaggerated." *The Wall Street Journal*, April 27.

Chapter Eleven

EMPLOYMENT AND IMMIGRATION REFORM: EMPLOYER SANCTIONS FOUR YEARS LATER

Robert Bach and Doris Meissner

IMMIGRATION CONTROL AND EMPLOYER SANCTIONS

In March 1990 the GAO delivered a report to Congress finding widespread discrimination against foreign-looking and sounding citizens and legal aliens in the wake of IRCA. The report labeled the discrimination "serious but not pervasive," and attributed a "substantial amount" of it to sanctions (GAO, 1990). With this finding, Congress could have repealed sanctions by adopting a joint resolution within 30 days after the report. Appropriate resolutions were offered, but Congress failed to act. Several other bills that modify or repeal sanctions have now been introduced and will be considered in the normal course.[1]

Thus, the fundamental debate that culminated in IRCA's enactment four years ago is still alive. If the measure of a free society is what it bans, revisiting employer sanctions and legalization should involve nothing less than a review of our commitment to basic national principles and how best to reconcile them in specific policy arenas.

The nation has long sought to prevent unauthorized employment of immigrants by holding employers responsible for explicit and implied work contracts. By repealing the "Texas Proviso,"[2] employer sanctions returned to a tradition established in 1885 with enactment of the Alien Contract Labor Law (Calavita, 1984; Erickson, 1957; Brill, 1991). Through these and other means, Congress has sought to protect and improve working conditions and living standards for all workers in the United States.

Equally important has been the struggle to include immigration reform as an aspect of extending civil rights protections (U.S. Commission on Civil Rights, 1980). Father Theodore Hesburgh, chair of the Select Commission on Immigration and Refugee Policy, repeatedly pointed to the elimination of discriminatory practices from immigration law as having been the primary motive behind immigration reform measures in recent decades.

Our analysis selects the central principles of seeming agreement from the IRCA debate as the framework for discussion. We then outline future directions for reform. Our goal is not to replay prior debates or to provide an overall grade for IRCA's achievements or failures. As with most significant public policy initiatives, enactment, implementation, evaluation, and reform are phases in a process that resists summary judgment. We offer this analysis to help guide future discussions of IRCA and as a framework for formulating immigration policy more generally.

PRINCIPLES OF AGREEMENT

". . . to improve our border control; to expedite, consistent with fair procedures and our Constitution, return of those coming here illegally; to strengthen enforcement of our fair labor standards and law; and to penalize those who would knowingly encourage violations of our laws. The steps we take to further these objectives . . . must also be consistent with our values of individual privacy and freedom."
(President Reagan, 1981)

Assuring Legal Status

A pervasive concern about a continuing flow of illegal immigrants is the creation of a "subclass" of people who contribute to the economy and participate in the society but whose futures are not guaranteed the equality of freedom and opportunity upon which the nation's destiny rests. Conditions that tolerate or reproduce illegal status, for whatever reasons, contradict elemental American commitments to civil and human rights.

Assuring a legal status for all participants in U.S. society is a broadly shared value. IRCA provides powerful evidence of its importance. The legalization experience across the nation demonstrates a transformation of people's economic, social, and personal lives when they become eligible to participate fully in society. They begin to stand up to exploitative work conditions and prepare for economic advancement. They enroll in, attend, and value English language classes. They begin to participate in broader social arenas, including community organizations, which previously intimidated them. They even gain some of the personal confidence that marks a sense of national membership (Rodriguez and Hagan, 1990). Whatever the disagreement over strategies, one common goal should be clear: Everyone should have a legal status. The sacredness of this goal permeates the discussion surrounding sanctions today. Senator Alan K. Simpson (R-WY), a leading sponsor of IRCA and ardent supporter of employer sanctions, recently declared that

> [t]he purpose of the bill for me was to avoid exploitation of human beings. It was not a jobs bill; I didn't care about numbers. I cared about the fact that if people were coming to the United States, go to work like dogs, that they ought to have a legal status so that they would not be exploited by their fellow man. That was my purpose, and the great pleasure of the bill. . . . (Simpson, 1990)

Some proponents of legalization also had a very practical objective in mind. They acted on the premise that future enforcement of U.S. immigration law, particularly employer sanctions, would be made more efficient and effective if a large, resident illegal population became transformed into a legal population.

However, by establishing a cut-off date of 1982 for eligibility for legalization, Congress severely hampered IRCA's capacity to achieve either its humanitarian or practical goals. With its grant of status to almost 3 million formerly undocumented immigrants, legalization was a success by almost every measure. Still, because legalization was incomplete, perhaps as many as 1.5 to 2 million people were ineligible to apply, having arrived after January 1, 1982. Many of them have remained in the country without a legal status.

Within this group, Central Americans have been particularly affected. Most were ineligible to apply for legalization because the migration of hundreds of thousands who fled in response to general political, social, and economic disintegration peaked in the mid-1980s, after the legalization cut-off date. Thus, employer sanctions hurt Central American immigrant communities because of their limited access to legalization.

Employer sanctions assume that work is the primary motive for coming to the United States illegally; if job-seekers cannot find employment, they can go home. But the illegal immigrant population is not homogeneous. To the extent that migrants arrive seeking not only jobs or better wages but safety from political violence and persecution, they may be barred from legal employment but unable to return home (Hernandez and Hesburgh, 1982).

Legalization created another problem for the implementation of employer sanctions. It added to a diverse set of statuses and rules that, according to several recent studies, have confused employers and complicated the hiring process. While some employers have used these new complexities to ignore and to mask well-established but illegal practices, many have genuinely attempted to comply with difficult distinctions (New York State Interagency Task Force, 1983). Difficulties include unfair employment practices toward "grandfathered" workers and "intending citizens," and punitive actions toward newly legalized workers regarding seniority and retirement pay (Mexican-American Legal Defense Fund and the ACLU, 1989).

Implementation of sanctions never enjoyed a point at which the slate was relatively clean, giving the government, employers, and immigrant communities the chance to establish new relationships and behaviors. Though the flow seemed to have slowed dramatically during the early months of passage, it did not stop. It has gradually climbed again, and today apprehension rates are almost at the level experienced before passage of IRCA.

Albeit doing so imperfectly, legalization extended legal status to millions and may, in the end, constitute IRCA's most important achievement. In revisiting the law and moving the debate toward new remedies, the principle of assuring legal status for the largest possible share of the population remains of paramount policy importance. Assuring legal status should continue to command policy attention as the resident illegal population grows and remains beyond the reach of fundamental rights and protections.

Establishing a New Employment Standard

Neither legalization nor employer sanctions was designed to have a direct impact on the flow of workers across the border. Rather, each was intended to change the labor market conditions for authorized and unauthorized workers in order to remove the "magnet" of employment that sustains the illegal flow.

Employer sanctions repealed the anomalous Texas Proviso by holding employers responsible for hiring only legal workers. The goal was straightforward: to make the legal status of workers a new employment standard. Holding employers and individual aliens responsible for enforcement objectives was to become the primary mechanism to reduce the magnet for illegal immigration and to protect U.S. workers from the unfair and exploitative conditions that arise when employers hire undocumented aliens.

Broad consensus exists on the role of employment standards as the most effective means of controlling undocumented immigration. Many believe that wider and stricter enforcement of established labor laws and health and safety protections would achieve the same result as sanctions. For instance, Senator Edward M. Kennedy has argued that

> [b]efore moving to sanctions, we must intensify enforcement of existing laws—including minimum wage, OSHA, Fair Labor Standards, SSI, unemployment insurance, and Title VII of the Civil Rights Act— to reduce the incentive for employers to hire undocumented workers and to protect against their exploitation. It will also protect the American labor market in ways which employer sanctions simply cannot. (Kennedy, 1981)

Others believe that, while enforcement of existing standards should precede new efforts, legal status represents an additional, distinct employment standard. Malcolm Lovell, Jr., former Under Secretary of Labor, has added that greater enforcement of existing wage and hour laws would not be adequate to cope with the problem of illegal immigrants because the majority of illegal workers are in positions that already pay at or above the minimum wage (Lovell, 1981).

The problem with undocumented workers, after all, is not that they are immigrants, but that they work here illegally. An ultimate measure of the effectiveness of IRCA, then, is the extent to which it lives up to the goal of becoming an employment standard. This criterion for evaluating its effectiveness has not been carefully explored in the public debate.

IRCA reinforced the idea that labor market protections and immigration regulations are closely intertwined. Employers who hire illegal aliens benefit just as do those who offer subminimum wages and poor working conditions. IRCA addressed the same issues of responsibility, burden sharing, competitiveness, and productivity that are inherent in any workplace-oriented legislation. Accordingly, employer sanctions attempted to redefine the employer/employee relationship on the basis of legal immigration status. They also sought to distribute certain immigration-related burdens more equally between employers and workers. IRCA tries to distribute the social responsibility among those who share in the process of attracting and employing these workers.

Studies of labor market impacts show that the law produced little change in local labor markets or within industrial sectors that have traditionally used large numbers of undocumented workers. Although these labor markets are undergoing significant reorganization and restructuring, implementation of IRCA has had little effect on fundamental economic conditions. The moving of firms offshore to gain access to cheaper labor or an epidemic of plant closings have not materialized. There has been no significant effect on employment levels among authorized workers, and no evidence that employers have tried to search more extensively or in new ways for alternative supplies of labor, especially among authorized workers (Cornelius, 1991; Bach and Brill, 1990). Few reports of labor shortages can be attributed to employer sanctions' removing a necessary local labor supply (Bach and Brill, 1990).

One reason is the effects of legalization. Many legalized workers have remained in their previous or similar jobs, obscuring the labor market impact of employer sanctions by relieving employers of the need to search for authorized workers. Another reason is the availability and use of fraudulent documents. Various recent studies, including the GAO study, have reported that compliance is not burdensome for employers because of the availability to the worker of fraudulent papers. Most employers comply, but it is with the letter, not the spirit of the law. As a result, the law has not yet made legal status an employment standard that changes the behavior of employers. Failing this, the law has not achieved the immigration enforcement objective of diminishing the magnet of available employment in the United States (see chapter 7 of this volume).

What has happened to labor markets was probably predictable. The burden of immigration enforcement has disproportionately remained on individual aliens, their families, and the communities in which they reside. As a result, immigrants have pooled wages to help support kin unable to locate work, undocumented workers share jobs with or work as subcontractors to the newly legalized, day labor sites have flowered in cities like Los Angeles, sweatshop working conditions are reportedly on the rise, and many illegals have located appropriate-looking documentation. Employers, on the other hand, have not largely changed their hiring practices, and many are prepared to risk illegal practices.

Despite widespread agreement on the desirability of the link between employment and legal status, there is little evidence that employer sanctions have achieved this goal. Part of the problem is enforcement. Knowledge of the law and paperwork compliance are not enough. The historical evidence of enforcement of other employment standards supports this conclusion. Despite an equally contentious public debate over minimum wage legislation and continuous problems with compliance, only sustained enforcement over time has made wage and hour provisions an accepted, functioning standard for the nation's businesses.

Placing the Burden on Employers

> "GAO also found that there was widespread discrimination. But was there discrimination as a result of IRCA? That is the key question Congress directed GAO to answer. GAO's answer is yes." (GAO, 1990, p. 3)

Understandably, controversy over employer sanctions has concentrated on discrimination because of its social significance and role as a trigger for congressional re-evaluation of the law.

In the long run, one of the fundamental issues underlying employer sanctions is social responsibility and burden sharing. If everyone should have a legal status and workplace standards should support broader regulation, the question becomes who should bear the burden of achieving these goals.

Employer sanctions are an element of a larger contemporary debate about burden sharing. The business sector sees itself as embattled by efforts to remain competitive in the international marketplace and to bear an increasing share of the costs of the nation's social problems. "It is a war," one journalist writes, "a war against the nation's social problems, and American business, with personnel executives shoring up the front, has been drafted to eliminate the problems" (Halcrow, 1987). Immigration reform, he says, has joined minimum wage, minimum health benefits for all workers, and family and parental leave as the primary threats to productive enterprise.

Involving business in solutions to social problems, including immigration, has a long, familiar history. The record is one of concern about competitiveness, productivity, and loss of jobs as a result of raising the U.S. employment standards. Opposing minimum wage legislation in the 1930s, one Congressman argued as follows:[3]

> would we rather have the employers in business and have the people . . . earning something or be out of employment and have the employers also go out of business? . . . That is the main trouble now. We have been passing laws that have forced hundreds, and even thousands of employers to go out of business and when they closed shop it left millions of employees without jobs.

Testifying in the 1980s against passage of employer sanctions, one Senator echoed these fears:

[the law] will cause economic chaos for thousands of American businessmen, small businessmen in particular, many of which will be forced into bankruptcy because they will not be able to find sufficient American labor willing to take these low-skilled jobs.

Similar arguments for reducing the responsibility and burden on employers of maintaining employment standards were made during the initial debates on the establishment of a minimum wage and against passage of the Fair Labor Standards Act in the 1930s. George Sutherland, associate justice of the Supreme Court, for instance, argued against the minimum wage on the following grounds:

The law [minimum wage legislation] takes account of necessities of only one party of the contract. Within the limits of the minimum sum, he [the employer] is precluded, under penalty of fine and imprisonment, from adjusting compensation to the differing merits of his employees. . . . [I]t amounts to a compulsory exaction from the employer for the support of a partially indigent person, for whose condition there rests upon him no peculiar responsibility, and therefore, in effect, arbitrarily shifts to his shoulders a burden which, if it belongs to anybody, belongs to society as a whole.

Today, business does not universally oppose regulation of the workplace as a legitimate means of apportioning responsibility for larger societal problems. For example, Robert L. Crandall, chairman and president of American Airlines, has argued that "in our free enterprise system, the privilege of participation carries with it a social responsibility" (Halcrow, 1987, p. 61).

Where employer sanctions are concerned, as a practical matter, there may not be many policy choices. Elliot L. Richardson, former U.S. Attorney General, has argued that it is simply not feasible to secure observance of our immigration laws without placing responsibility for enforcement upon the employer.

Current evidence suggests that employers have not shouldered an unacceptable burden. The GAO report states that seven percent of employers in their study who expressed an interest in hiring someone during 1988 were unable to because the applicant could not present a work authorization document. It also reports that "the burden that employer sanctions place on employers, though viewed as cumbersome by some employers, cannot be considered unnecessary." Even concerns about potential harassment of employers because of IRCA's special anti-discrimination provisions did not present a problem. They neither led to employer harassment nor to an unreasonable burden on employers (GAO, 1990).

In current discussions, business community representatives freely state that their opposition to sanctions based on burdensome paperwork requirements was misplaced; there has not been an outcry from employers demanding that the law be rolled back. Business is also not in the forefront of repeal efforts and has even declined in important cases to testify against sanctions or announce a position on the question. Repeal of sanctions is not a priority because there is minimal demand for aggressive advocacy by employers themselves.

At the same time, however, business does, as a matter of principle, object to employers' being required to carry out "police" functions. Accordingly, some business groups have joined in a business-civil rights coalition supporting politicians who are sponsoring repeal legislation (S. 2797). Described by Raul Yzaguirre, president of the National Council of La Raza, as "the transcendent civil rights issue of our time," repeal is being supported by politicians who denounce discrimination but also stress the need to, in Senator Dennis De-Concini's words, "lift this burden off the business communities" (DeConcini, 1990).

Preventing Discrimination

The business community's tepid support of repeal makes the political coalition with civil rights groups particularly problematic. Civil rights concerns, specifically discrimination, and immigration policy have been linked for some time. The last major reform of the Immigration and Nationality Act in 1965 was an expression of the Kennedy/Johnson administration's frontal assault on the laws that institutionalized discrimination in society. Abolishing the national origin quotas that guided immigrant selection was a natural extension of the social agenda. It was a platform, though, that sought to increase rather than decrease social responsibility and burden sharing.

The struggle to bring immigration policy and practice into conformance with civil rights imperatives continues with IRCA. According to the GAO, widespread discrimination exists against U.S. ethnic minorities in the labor markets where undocumented workers concentrate, and employer sanctions bear some of the responsibility (GAO, 1990). Representatives of ethnic community-based organizations have long expressed the fear that employer sanctions would facilitate if not increase discrimination against authorized minority workers, including both native-born U.S. citizens and permanent resident aliens.

The GAO's determination that IRCA has resulted in widespread discrimination has reignited a longstanding political and empirical controversy. For opponents of sanctions, GAO's finding has provided proof for their policy admonitions. They have voiced surprise and a sense of betrayal that the Congress and the public have not reacted with greater vigor. Accusing the responsible committee of "delay and subterfuge," Congressman Bill Richardson, a member of the House Hispanic Caucus, reprimanded his colleagues for a "breach of the pact reached by Congress with the Hispanic community" when IRCA was passed (Richardson, 1990). The importance some groups attach to the issue has led to strains within the traditional civil rights coalition, where labor unions continue to support the necessity of sanctions and Hispanic organizations have demanded support for repeal as testimony to the needs and political agenda of their community.

Sanctions' supporters have been no less concerned with GAO's findings but have attacked the validity of the discrimination conclusion. Senator Simpson has angrily recalled that the legislation required the GAO to determine whether a finding of widespread discrimination could be linked "solely" with IRCA. Under the circumstances, research was probably incapable of definitively linking discriminatory acts to one piece of legislation. The GAO carefully attended to the technical difficulty of the task given it by Congress and the reasons for the conclusions it reached. Although GAO stands by its findings, the underlying issues remain unsettled and the subject of sharp political disagreement.

The intensity of the political debate has threatened the coherence of national principles underlying immigration reform. In a democratic society, legal status, employment safeguards, and equal opportunity share the goal of providing protections to individuals. Antidiscrimination measures in the workplace, whether growing out of immigration reforms or changes in other labor and social measures, are clear attempts to protect workers from unfair hiring and promotion practices. These protections include ensuring equal opportunity for all in the labor market. They hold employers and the government responsible for developing strategies and standards for compliance that need not and should not become an either/or proposition. The conflict that some see between employer sanctions and reducing employment discrimination is primarily a matter of overlapping approaches to labor standards enforcement. The goal of both standards would be mutually reinforcing if effective enforcement were achieved.

FUTURE DIRECTIONS

When enacted, employer sanctions were perceived as labor-related immigration law. In retrospect, it is increasingly clear that they are, and should be treated as, immigration-related labor law.[4] The distinction is important because it suggests the timeframe and methods that are realistic to achieve effectiveness.

Our own national experience with comparable kinds of workplace regulation teaches us that as much as a decade or more has been required before new employment standards transform workplace behavior, conditions, and practices. Europe's experience with employer sanctions, dating from the early 1970s, is similar. The lesson in both cases is that changes like those employer sanctions imply only come with a sustained effort over a period of years and a willingness to adjust law and practice to reflect experience.

Just as the 1982 legalization date was arbitrary, so is the three-year GAO review. We do not know whether sanctions have reduced illegal immigration, although it may have slowed the rate of increase of the flow. This would not be an insubstantial achievement, given the economic pressures to migrate. Nevertheless, the deterrence that IRCA contemplated has not yet really been tested because jobs remain available, albeit perhaps more difficult and costly to get, for substantial numbers of illegal workers.

The policy question is whether we have a sufficient basis to conclude that sanctions are an ineffective tool to address illegal immigration. The answer is that it is too early to make that judgment, but that we have sufficient information on a number of key points to call for some substantial adjustments. Making the adjustments is particularly important as we look to the future. The 1990s will be a decade of continuing high levels of immigration and pressures for illegal immigration. Reform of the immigrant selection system is actively being debated in Congress and deserves legislative attention. A generous, evolving immigration policy cannot sustain public support in the absence of effective deterrents to illegal immigration.

The GAO found discrimination linked to IRCA. The Urban Institute's hiring audit reports national-origin discrimination of a more general nature. The Congress and the executive branch should acknowledge the problem as one that is real and legitimate, and that merits serious attention.

Solutions proposed by the GAO and pending legislation that do not seek repeal fall into two areas: *education* and *documents issues*. To them we add a third, *enforcement issues*, which we believe deserve particular attention and priority at this time. If actions to address this triad are taken, there is the chance that IRCA can effectively deter increased illegal immigration while also assuring legal status, establishing a new employment standard, and preventing discrimination. Without changes, we will have compliance as a paperwork exercise, where employers and workers learn to abide by the letter of the law alone, and where discrimination is heightened. With repeal of employer sanctions, we may legitimize work environments where exploitation based on legal status flourishes, and risk public disapproval for failing to control illegal immigration.

It is generally accepted that a tamper-proof, photo social security card is the best mechanism for verifying employment eligibility and ending a sanctions-induced basis for discrimination. This or a similar regime should now be seriously explored. The exploration must include a careful examination of civil liberties questions so that the national debate it requires, which extends well beyond the issue of immigration, begins to take place.

To that end, Congress should hold comprehensive hearings to consider the current state of knowledge about technology, organizational arrangements, and costs for achieving a single identification regime to support sanctions. The hearings should result in a timetable for the executive branch to meet in moving toward an acceptable identification system. The timetable should include systematic reporting, such as IRCA already requires on other implementation issues, and annual oversight hearings to focus legislative attention on these issues at regular intervals.

At the same time, we already know that the costs of a system that resolves the document verification problem through a single identifier are substantial and probably prohibitive, particularly in today's fiscal climate. Looking to this ultimate answer is important as a long-term analytic and planning proposition. But it is also a shield that can absolve us from responsibility for taking steps that can improve the picture now. Interim, realistic initiatives must also be taken in the near term. To them, we devote the remainder of our discussion.

Policy should proceed from agreement by Congress to charge the GAO with preparing a follow-up evaluation of the effectiveness of

IRCA, to be delivered in 1995.[5] The evaluation should answer three questions: Have employer sanctions continued to cause discrimination? Do they function effectively as an employment standard? Have they led to deterrence of increased illegal immigration?

Recommendations for Improving the Efficacy of Employer Sanctions

For the next GAO evaluation to be useful, Congress and the executive branch must begin now to make adjustments that increase education, improve documents, and result in more enforcement.

EDUCATION

GAO's findings on discrimination identified confusion among employers as the primary reason for discriminatory practices. This confusion discrimination included incomplete understanding of both how to comply with the law and prohibitions against hiring only citizens or other presumed non-foreign workers. Mobilizing the resources and commitment required to eliminate the confusion that surrounds employer sanctions should be a priority task for the government that would significantly reduce discrimination linked to IRCA. A comprehensive education initiative should include the following elements:

Revise the I-9 Form. The I-9 form constitutes the paperwork required of all employers to comply with employer sanctions. In the previous chapter, Michael Fix suggested that the best way to counteract some of the confusion surrounding sanctions would be to embed in the I-9 form instructions that walk employers through compliance and anti-discrimination requirements as part of completing the form. INS is reportedly revising the I-9 at this time; revisions should be designed with this objective in mind.

Focus on New Employers. Special efforts should be made to systematically advise new employers of their responsibilities regarding employer sanctions. During the six-month sanctions education period provided by IRCA to precede actual enforcement, INS worked closely and effectively with the Internal Revenue Service—the federal agency that is regularly involved with all employers through receipt of withholding and social security tax payments—to conduct its education campaign regarding the new law. This relationship should be ongoing, and new employers, in particular, should receive a complete set of appropriate materials, including a hotline or similar resource for answering questions, as part of their indoctrination regarding federal compliance requirements.

Create Office of Special Counsel Field Offices. Proposed legislation calls for the Department of Justice to establish field offices of the Office of Special Counsel (OSC) to broaden the government's outreach capability and provide a federal presence in areas with high concentrations of foreign-born residents. OSC's work has been guided by an acting director for some time. The appointment of a permanent head is reportedly to be made after delivery of the Attorney General's joint task force recommendations responding to the GAO report. This appointment should be made quickly and be accompanied by the creation of field offices to receive anti-discrimination complaints and educate employers, workers, and the public about sanctions requirements. This is a step that would not require legislative authority.

Better Coordinate Roles and Responsibilities. The INS will always have a primary role in the public education arena because it works with employers on a daily basis to verify sanctions compliance, as do Department of Labor inspectors. An important element of their activities is instructing employers about their responsibilities and correcting misunderstandings and improper practices. This is an essential part of the sanctions enforcement mission. However, additional, broader-based efforts are also required. These should not be the responsibility of the line enforcement agencies, which already carry the burdens of burgeoning workloads and whose focus, properly, should be on law enforcement.

The Interagency Task Force, established by the Attorney General more than a year ago and chaired by the OSC, is an appropriate vehicle for lead responsibility and interagency coordination where general education efforts are concerned. It should work closely with all affected agencies as well as with local authorities and constituent groups to determine how and where to direct public education initiatives. These are the efforts that require particular priority at this time, especially in urban areas with high concentrations of foreign-born workers. Field researchers tracking the effects of sanctions enforcement in communities report, for example, that radio advertisements generated by the OSC in target cities have been effective in increasing awareness of anti-discrimination requirements, but that a great deal more of this kind of effort is required to make workers aware of their rights.

Increase Legislation. At least two pieces of proposed legislation provide considerable increases in funding for education.[6] Resources along the lines these bills describe should be provided.

In addition, the penalty for discrimination infractions should be made the same as the penalty for noncompliance with verification procedures. This would eliminate any possibility of incentives to err on the side of discrimination in an effort to avoid the stiffer punishment of failure to comply with verification requirements.

DOCUMENTS

Improvements in documents are fundamental to the ability of employers, the government, and workers to comply with sanctions requirements. The number and range in quality of valid documents create complexity in implementing this law that must be diminished. Doing so would reduce the system's vulnerability to the use of fraudulent documents as well as the potential for discrimination.

Both funding and legislation are required. Even then, improvements will be largely prospective since it is unlikely that sufficient resources or capacity would ever be available to recall the millions of documents that have already been issued, imperfect though they may be. Instead, future and replacement documents must be the fulcrum of concern. Government agencies and the Congress must be prepared to deal with the issues in a sustained fashion over the long term. There are several things that should be done:

Reduce the Number. Sanctions regulations list 17 documents that may be presented to employers to establish eligibility to work. The large number reflects the range of immigration statuses, each with accompanying documents of varied age and quality, that carry with them authorization to work. Categories of legal status have proliferated over the years as more and more types of immigration situations have arisen and demanded resolution, generally encompassing the right to work. Congress wanted inclusiveness to guide enforcement officials in implementing the law, because one of IRCA's early compromises was to avoid the issue of a new or single document in connection with sanctions legislation.

Experience has shown this sentiment to be impractical. The Congress is open to executive branch leadership for a more manageable scheme. Because the INS issues 10 of the 17 documents, its actions are critical in this area. For some time, it has had plans to collapse to 2—1 card for nonimmigrants, 1 (the "green card," which is pink) for permanent residents—from the 10 identifying documents it presently issues. Its program in this regard is workable, already underway, and needed. But its timetable is slow because of insufficient funding.

The administration and Congress should allocate resource increases for the INS document issuance effort and the INS itself should raise the priority and funding allocation devoted to this activity.

Test Telephone Verification. IRCA provided authorization for the President to request the Attorney General to test telephone verification as an alternative to physically presenting documents to employers during hiring transactions. Telephone verification is the most promising technology presently available to streamline work eligibility requirements. Patterned after credit card systems, it would enable employers to transmit electronically a number, perhaps the social security number, to receive verification of work eligibility. If workable, this method could reduce discrimination and be highly fraud-resistant. Moreover, it would bypass the need to develop a new identifier, which is an expensive, controversial, and elusive solution.

The INS has proposed pilot study plans but presidential approval has not been given because of Department of Justice opposition to national uses for government databases (Buraff Publications, Inc., 1990). INS's current proposal for a test and approach to telephone verification is relatively inexpensive and uses a combination of existing databases, avoiding the time and cost involved in creating new data sources.

There are many legitimate questions and issues raised by telephone verification and some observers view it as more problematic than a national identifier. Nevertheless, it holds great promise for effective compliance and deserves to be tested now.

If the administration does not quickly change its position on testing telephone verification methods and technology, Congress should mandate testing.[7] Among the corollary tasks telephone verification would entail would be the need for the INS to upgrade dramatically the attention and professionalism accorded its record-keeping systems. Records responsibilities have been chronically neglected by the agency, and records security is often haphazard. A 1989 audit showed about 17 percent of the data from its central alien information repository to be missing or incorrect (Buraff Publications, Inc., 1990). Such levels of error should not be tolerated and would make a national system virtually unworkable.

Pursue Use of Drivers' Licenses for Verification. In its IRCA-mandated report regarding social security number validation systems, the Secretary of Health and Human Services proposed looking to state drivers' licenses as a method of validating employment eligibility. The report observes that 29 states issue licenses showing the social security number (SSN). Some states request verification of the number from the Social Security Administration at the time of issuance. In these states, license holders are prevalidated for work purposes, as it were, because the photo on the license links the SSN to the job applicant when presented to an employer. In states where the number is not validated, the federal government could seek states' agreement to do so (U.S. Department of Health and Human Services, 1988).

Proceeding on this track would allow a potentially sizeable population of employers and workers to meet work eligibility verification requirements in a simple, straightforward fashion with the most widely used identification document in use today. The GAO advocates this idea; federal officials should pursue it and test it in a demonstration project as outlined in the enforcement section below.

In states where drivers' licenses do not carry SSNs, arrangements should be encouraged whereby state employment agencies review documents and certify work eligibility of prospective employees. This is presently done in Texas, and should be established more widely. Similar efforts have been fostered by discrete employer groups and should also be encouraged.

ENFORCEMENT

The need for increased education and improved documents has been widely acknowledged. Far less attention has been directed to an equally important aspect of an effective sanctions program, enforcement. Sanctions enforcement represented a major new mission for immigration officials, one that the INS had advocated and worked diligently to win for more than a decade. With it came a significant infusion of new resources with which it recruited personnel who brought a broad range of new skills and professional experiences to the operations of the agency.

The INS devoted considerable analytic effort to developing implementation plans that mirrored the enforcement approaches of the IRS, widely viewed as the agency that most successfully achieves high rates of citizen compliance with the law it administers. The INS's well-publicized education visits to two million employers earned praise and good will.

Nevertheless, because of the deliberately gradual timetable established in IRCA for sanctions enforcement, full enforcement has been underway for just over two years. To its credit, the INS has been acutely aware of the importance of the GAO three-year review and has placed a high priority on shaping its activities to protect the viability of sanctions as an enforcement tool. To this end, it recognized the need to work closely with employers to elicit compliance, not confrontation; belatedly, it began to underscore anti-discrimination responsibilities as well.

The time has come for the INS to be more aggressive in its approach; to insist on greater internal consistency and coordination of sanctions policy; to evaluate its work in border enforcement, records management, and document issuance priorities in light of the sanctions mission; and to experiment with new ideas in anticipation of continuing innovations in the program. The time has also come for the administration to use the limited resources available for workplace enforcement more effectively where sanctions are concerned.

Increase Level of Effort. Evidence is building that the early effort among employers to comply in response to publicity about the new law and wide-ranging INS contacts is dissolving into complacency as employers experience the low probability of an actual INS visit. This is understandable, to an extent, but it is also a response to declining and unpredictable shifts in the priority directed at sanctions enforcement in key metropolitan areas by local INS offices.

In the Urban Institute/RAND Corporation study of eight large cities, sanctions were the priority enforcement activity in only two. The INS has several important interior enforcement missions that legitimately deserve attention. Nevertheless, the INS must establish a consistent level of effort for sanctions enforcement and pursue a strategy of fines and methods that are carefully observed in operations around the country. Employer behavior is very sensitive to the signals sent by enforcement levels of effort. Compliance can only be assured over the long run if the enforcement threat is credible.

One area that requires particular attention is the role of the Border Patrol. In several cities in the Southwest, Border Patrol units enforce sanctions, generally using very different approaches from Investigations personnel. Coordination among these two arms of the agency is poor. Moreover, border enforcement levels of effort have fluctuated considerably since IRCA was enacted. Congress and the executive branch have always held that the best deterrent to illegal immigration remains prevention of entry, thus explaining the significant increases in Border Patrol resources by IRCA. Border Patrol activity should not be directed at other purposes.

Such issues must be resolved if the INS hopes to capitalize on the able start it made in managing the difficult new tasks assigned by IRCA.

Enhance the Department of Labor Role. Most observers are not even aware that the Department of Labor (DOL) is involved in sanctions enforcement. In fact, both the INS and the DOL are charged with sanctions responsibilities. The DOL inspects employer records for I-9 compliance, in the course of its ongoing workplace review of other labor law compliance and refers suspected irregularities to the INS. The INS inspects for compliance and also investigates irregular practices, levying fines upon employers and criminal penalties in "pattern and practice" circumstances.

Together, they are equipped to cover less than 1.5 percent of employers each year. And far fewer are realistically subject to actual penalties because the INS follows up on only one in five DOL leads, and conducts one-third the number of inspections that DOL conducts. The government's modest level of resources for sanctions could be leveraged more effectively if DOL inspectors had enforcement authority similar to that of the INS. This could be accomplished by cross-designating DOL inspectors, as has been done for immigration and customs officers at ports of entry for years.

Cross-designation is not without problems, the most important of which is organizational resistance, generally by both parties. INS staff tend to believe no one else has the expertise and interest to carry out "their" laws properly. And it is frequently the case that government programs suffer when they require effort from organizations whose primary duties lie elsewhere.

In the case of the INS and the DOL, this takes the form of the former's authority not only to levy fines against employers but to determine a person's alienage, which can result in the arrest of undocumented workers for deportation purposes. The INS is protective of this authority and uses it regularly in the course of sanctions enforcement activities. The DOL levies fines against employers as part of its non-sanctions labor law compliance work, and could surely be entrusted with carrying out the same function where sanctions are concerned. Yet, the DOL would resist any responsibilities involving arrest or deportation because it sees them as conflicting with its broader role of worker advocacy. Such difficulties can be managed, but only through close coordination, careful delineation of appropriate roles, and strong direction from responsible senior officials.

We know that employers who violate one labor law are likely to violate others. From the standpoint of federal policy, enforcement is undermined when one arm of government inspects employer records and notes potential irregularities that are not pursued. Moreover, sanctions have introduced a new employment standard. Institutionalizing this standard is likely to occur more quickly and fully if the agency identified with labor standards enforcement is a full partner in the enforcement enterprise.

Develop Demonstration Projects. Demonstration projects of at least two kinds should be developed to test more effective enforcement approaches for the future. One project should target for special enforcement priority an industrial sector, such as construction, which has relied heavily on illegal workers. The demonstration should test the level of resources, enforcement approaches, labor market conditions, and anti-discrimination provisions required to transform hiring practices so that employment of legal workers truly functions as a new employment standard. Singling out particular sectors of the labor market for special treatment is done regularly in areas such as garments and agriculture, for example. To do it with the purpose of determining "what it takes" to achieve IRCA's enforcement objectives would be very useful for operational agencies and decision makers alike.

Another demonstration should test the use of a single, secure identifier. This could be done on a state-wide basis in a state that issues secure driver's licenses. The results of such a demonstration would contribute importantly to the knowledge and experience needed to proceed with the longer term planning required to resolve the document verification problems that create confusion and give rise to discriminatory practices. In both cases, the results of the demonstration efforts would provide valuable guidance for the future.

Notes

1. These proposals include S.2797, S.2446, and H.R. 4421. Proposed S.2797 is cosponsored by Senators Orrin G. Hatch (R-UT), Edward M. Kennedy (D-MA), Dennis DeConcini (D-AZ), Jeff Bingaman (D-NM), and Alan Cranston (D-CA) and by Representative Edward R. Roybal (D-CA) in the House of Representatives. It repeals employer sanctions and doubles the size of the Border Patrol to 6,600; adds 250 positions to the Wage and Hour division of the Department of Labor for enforcement of wage laws against illegal immigrants; adds 21 assistant U.S. Attorneys to prosecute alien smugglers; and increases the penalties for smuggling. Proposed S.2446, sponsored by

Senator Alan K. Simpson (R-WY), provides funds for an outreach program regarding antidiscrimination measures of IRCA; issues new tamper-proof social security cards that include photos to all who qualify; and calls for demonstration projects to test telephone verification. Proposed H.R. 4421, sponsored by Representative John Bryant (D-TX), also allocates additional funds to educate employers; establishes regional offices of the Office of the Special Counsel, Department of Justice, to receive and decide sanctions discrimination complaints; and extends GAO's study mandate for two more years.

2. The Texas proviso is the provision of immigration law enacted in 1952 that imposed fines and imprisonment for furthering unlawful entry or residence in the U.S. but stated that "the usual and normal practices incident to employment shall not be deemed to constitute harboring" (Hutchinson, 1981).

3. The following quotes appear in Bach and Brill, 1990, pp. 33–34.

4. For this insight, we are indebted to Judge Marvin H. Morse, Administrative Hearing Officer, Executive Office for Immigration Review, U.S. Department of Justice.

5. Because Congress is unlikely to legislate in this area until 1991, another three-year review would span mid-1991 through mid-1994. Sufficient time thereafter to analyze data, write a report, and get past the 1994 election season leads to early 1995 as the earliest practical reporting date.

6. See S.2446, Employer Sanctions Improvement Amendments of 1990, and H.R. 4421, IRCA Anti-Discrimination Amendments of 1990.

7. S.2446, the Employer Sanctions Improvement Admendments of 1990, contains a provision instructing the administration to conduct demonstration projects on telephone verification.

References

Bach, Robert, and Howard Brill. 1990. "Shifting the Burden: The Impact of IRCA on Local Labor Markets." Report to the U.S. Department of Labor.

Brill, Howard. 1991. "America's First Employer Sanctions Law: The Alien Control Labor Law, 1885–1952." In *State, Labor Markets, and Immigration*, eds. Robert L. Bach and Howard Brill. Binghamton, N.Y.: Institute for Research on Multiculturalism and International Labor, State University of New York.

Buraff Publications, Inc. 1990. *Immigration Policy and Law*, vol. 4, no. 6: p. 5.

Calavita, Kitty. 1984. *U.S. Immigration Law and the Control of Labor: 1820–1924*. London: Academic Press.

Cornelius, Wayne. 1991. "Mexican Immigrants in California Today." In *California Immigrants in World Perspective*, eds. Ivan Light and Parminder Bhachu. Forthcoming.

DeConcini, Dennis. 1990. Transcript of Sen. DeConcini's Press Conference of June 27 announcing introduction of S.2797, the Employer Sanctions Repeal Act of 1990.

Erickson, Charlotte. 1957. *American Industry and the European Immigrant, 1860–1885*. Cambridge: Harvard University Press.

GAO (U.S. General Accounting Office). 1990. *Immigration Reform: Employer*

Sanctions and the Question of Discrimination. GAO/GGD-90-62, March.

Hernandez, Antonio, and Reverend Theodore Hesburgh. 1982. Statements before U.S. Congress, House and Senate Subcommittee on Immigration, Refugees and International Law, and Subcommittee on Immigration and Refugee Policy of the Committees on the Judiciary, April 1 and 20.

Halcrow, Allan. 1987. "Should Business Alone Pay for Social Progress?" *Personnel Journal,* 66, no. 9, September pp. 58–73.

Hutchinson, E.P. 1981. *Legislative History of American Immigration Policy 1798–1965.* University of Pennsylvania Press, Philadelphia.

Kennedy, Edward. 1981. Opening Statement before U.S. Senate Subcommittee on Immigration and Refugee Policy of the Committee on the Judiciary, September 30.

Lovell, Malcolm Jr. 1981. Statement before U.S. Senate Subcommittee on Immigration and Refugee Policy of the Committee on the Judiciary, September 30.

Mexican American Legal Defense and Educational Fund and the American Civil Liberties Union. 1989. *The Human Costs of Employer Sanctions.* November.

New York State Interagency Task Force on Immigration Affairs. 1983. "Immigration in New York State: Impacts and Issues." Albany, New York, February 23.

Richardson, William. 1990. Statement before U.S. House of Representatives Subcommittee on Immigration Refugees and International Law of the Committee on the Judiciary. As reported in *Immigration Policy and Law,* 4, no. 10, June 28.

Rodriguez, Nestor, and Jacqueline Hagan. 1990. "The Impact of IRCA on Houston's Labor Markets." Unpublished paper. Binghamton, N.Y.: Institute for Research on Multiculturalism and International Labor, State University of New York, June.

Simpson, Alan K. Transcript of Press Conference on General Accounting Office, *Immigration Reform: Employer Sanctions and the Question of Discrimination.* Senate Radio-Television Gallery, March 29.

U.S. Commission on Civil Rights. 1980. *The Tarnished Golden Door: Civil Rights Issues in Immigration.* Washington, D.C.: U.S. Government Printing Office, September.

U.S. Department of Health and Human Services, Social Security Administration. 1988. "A Social Security Number Validation System: Feasibility, Costs, and Privacy Considerations." A report pursuant to Section 101(e) of P.L. 99-603, The Immigration Reform and Control Act of 1986. Washington, D.C., November.

Chapter Twelve

TOWARD AN UNCERTAIN FUTURE: THE REPEAL OR REFORM OF SANCTIONS IN THE 1990s

Michael Fix

As the 102d Congress convened in January 1991, there appeared little interest in, or inclination to push further reform of the nation's immigration policies. Not only was the arduous process of enacting IRCA complete, so also was the bruising effort to reform the nation's legal immigration policy—a reform codified in the 1990 Immigration Act. Indeed, the Chairman of the House Judiciary Committee, Jack Brooks, took the opportunity to rename the subcommittee that had traditionally dealt with immigration matters, subordinating the word "immigration" in its title to reflect his waning interest in the issue.[1]

There remained, however, some outstanding business. The issue of employer sanctions would probably be revisited and the issue of their repeal deliberated. The repeal issue remained alive because it was broadly believed that the experiment with employer sanctions had not been a success. Representative Howard Berman (D-CA) stated the matter simply: "It would appear that employer sanctions have not done what proponents said they would do, and it is clear to me that they can cause well-intentioned employers to commit discrimination" (Berman, 1991).

In general, it appears that Congressman Berman is correct when he states that sanctions have not had the impact that their framers intended. Flows of undocumented migrants across the southern border appear to have revived after a two-year decline. Agriculture appears to have remained a magnet for undocumented migrants, as worker turnover is increasing rather than decreasing. At the same time, sanctions do appear to have contributed—at least marginally and perhaps substantially—to increased citizenship and national-origin discrimination. Finally, the difficulties inherent in simultaneously enforcing sanctions and reducing discrimination have led policymakers to toughen both regimes of regulation in a way that will increase employers' compliance burden. This tightening is due at least in part to the declining political viability of efforts to develop what might be a workable national identity card and verification system.

Although these results suggest that the employer sanctions provisions of IRCA have fallen short of the hopes of their framers, they do not necessarily lead to the conclusion that sanctions should be repealed. Some scholars argue that sanctions' legitimacy rests on the moral and cultural values they help to sustain. Sanctions represent an important, if perhaps largely symbolic, policy that seeks to define the limits of membership in society and to create the perception that the nation has control of its borders and destiny. Sanctions, then, can be viewed as playing an important role in reinforcing the national ideal that American society has the power to "choose whom it wants, exclude those whom it does not want, and sanction those who violate its rules" (Schuck, 1990). In so doing, sanctions may help politicians and bureaucrats continue the essentially liberal, expansionist immigration policy that we have had in place since the mid-1960s. This liberal, inclusive policy is nowhere more evident than in the 1990 Immigration Act, which increased legal admissions to the United States by 40 percent (Fix and Passel, 1991).

I begin this chapter by sketching a number of recent legislative, administrative, and legal developments that bear on the enforcement of employer sanctions and the potential success of the nation's efforts to control illegal immigration in the 1990s. My purposes are to update the volume through February 1991 and to anticipate how these recent developments may influence efforts to control illegal immigration.

In the first section I take up the substantial reforms introduced by the Immigration Act of 1990—a law that is closely identified with legal immigration policy, but one that also includes important IRCA-related reforms. I then describe developments in the INS's implementation of employer sanctions as well as recent efforts by the agency's leadership to restructure the INS. I follow this with a brief review of changes in federal administrative and judicial case law that are likely to influence sanctions policy. I end the chapter by re-examining the evidence developed in earlier chapters on sanctions' impacts, implementation, and potential reforms in light of the ongoing debate over whether employer sanctions should be retained and reformed, or repealed.

THE 1990 IMMIGRATION ACT

The unexpected passage of the Immigration Act of 1990 (IA 90) brought to a close a remarkable decade in immigration reform. The decade opened with the enactment of the Refugee Act of 1980, which revamped the rules pertaining to *humanitarian immigration* to the United States. The Immigration Reform and Control Act of 1986, which, as this volume has exhaustively documented, dealt with reform of our procedures for controlling *illegal immigration*, represented the next major step toward reform of the nation's immigration policies. And the decade closed with the IA 90, whose principal thrust was to reform *legal immigration* (i.e., the family and employment grounds for permanent and temporary entry). But while legal immigration reform may have been the impetus for the IA 90, the bill was an omnibus piece of legislation that addressed at least four areas of policy that are directly relevant to employer sanctions and the nation's efforts to control illegal immigration. In this regard, the 1990 Immigration Act 1) expanded IRCA's anti-discrimination protections; 2) made it easier for the INS to prosecute those who make and use fraudulent documents; 3) sustained the mismatch between enforcement resources and responsibilities within the INS; and 4) made possible a substantial reduction in the size of the undocumented population in the United States.

Anti-discrimination

The IA 90 introduced a number of reforms intended to counteract the discrimination that appeared to be arising as a result of employer sanctions. (See chapter 10 of this volume).[2] The reforms included:

□ Expanding employer and employee education regarding citizenship and national-origin discrimination;[3]
□ Expanding the reach of IRCA's anti-discrimination protections to include Special Agricultural Workers;[4]
□ Eliminating the requirement that an alien filing a claim of discrimination under IRCA have previously filed a declaration of intent to become a citizen;[5]
□ Increasing the penalties for violating IRCA's discrimination provisions so they parallel violations of employer sanctions;[6] and
□ Banning employers from requiring more or different documents from job applicants than are set out in the law and its implementing regulations,[7] coupled with a special penalty providing for fines ranging from $100 to $1,000 for each individual discriminated against in this way.[8]

The last two provisions may have the most far-reaching impact for employers and victims of discrimination, as they make it an action-able offense for employers to commit two common errors in attempting to comply with sanctions. First, they bar employers from asking job applicants for documents other than those specified by law or regulation in order to prove eligibility for employment. Second, they prohibit employers from specifying that they will accept only certain documents (a driver's license or a social security card) to prove work eligibility. The law makes these forms of "document abuse" subject to fine whether or not they are applied to *all* job applicants and whether or not the applicant eventually receives the job for which he or she applies. By introducing a special penalty provision for these violations, the law creates an additional cause of action that can be invoked by the government or by those who claim to have been victims of discrimination. Even in cases in which no harm can be identified (where the applicant got the job) or where the harm is fully compensated (through lost pay), this cause of action for a separate money penalty limits the extent to which enforcement authorities can or will mitigate fines.

The document abuse provisions suggest a general trend—reflected in subsequent regulations and court decisions—toward expanding employers' exposure to liability under IRCA.

Document Fraud

The prevalence of fraudulent documents has, if anything, proved even more of an obstacle to the enforcement of sanctions than anticipated (Cornelius, 1990). A comparatively little noted provision in the IA 90 makes it possible for the INS to bring *civil* prosecutions against manufacturers and users of fraudulent documents. The provision will make it easier for the INS to set and collect fines, as the agency can proceed administratively instead of criminally, thereby reducing the standard of proof that has to be met and permitting the agency to prosecute violators using its own attorneys. Cases can be tried before an administrative law judge and result in fines of up to $5,000 for each document *used* or *received*. Here again, the potential liability to which employers are exposed for immigration-related violations has been effectively expanded. Criminal prosecutions for actions like document fraud are problematic because they can only be brought by U.S. Attorneys, who rarely can find time to prosecute cases that are not politically visible or have little potential impact on public safety.

Continuing Mismatch between Enforcement Responsibilities and Resources

The IA 90, like IRCA,[9] substantially increases the INS Investigations division's workload. It does so by expanding the agency's powers to deport criminal aliens and by granting agents authority to carry firearms and make arrests for any federal offense committed in their presence.[10] The workload also increased with the agency's new powers to bring civil actions against manufacturers and users of fraudulent documents. Lead responsibility in both instances will fall to the INS's Investigations branch, where these areas of expanded authority will compete for time and resources against ongoing efforts to enforce employer sanctions and the Anti-Drug Abuse Amendments of 1986 and 1988. Despite these changes, the only provision for increased staffing made by the IA 90 is an authorization for 1,000 additional positions for the Border Patrol,[11] which is less likely than other parts of the INS to bear the brunt of the agency's additional workload.

Reducing the Size of the Undocumented Population

One of the most powerful impacts of the IA 90 will be the way it reduces the size of the undocumented population in the United States: a development that could influence the scope and targeting of enforcement. First, the IA 90 codified and liberalized the INS's administrative policy of "family fairness" by granting a temporary stay of deportation and work authorization to the spouses and unmarried children of aliens legalizing under IRCA's amnesty provisions.[12] To be eligible, these family members had to have been continuously present in the United States since May 5, 1988. According to the Congressional Budget Office, 300,000 spouses and 380,000 children of newly legalized aliens could be eligible for legal status under this provision.[13]

Second, the law grants temporary protected status, or the equivalent of "safe haven," to undocumented Salvadorans in the United States since September 19, 1990. The size of this population is estimated to be roughly 500,000 (Ruggles and Fix, 1985). The conditions of the grant are rather exacting, as applications must be filed by June 30, 1991, and the grant lasts for only 18 months and must be renewed every six months.[14]

Third, the IA 90 provides roughly 65,000 visas to undocumented Irish in the United States.[15]

In theory, then, the family fairness provisions, the grant of temporary protected status, and the Irish amnesty could reduce the size of the undocumented population by a million persons.

Congress has not been alone in setting policy that will reduce the size of the nation's undocumented population. In February 1991 the Supreme Court handed down a major decision holding that IRCA permits class action suits challenging the INS's procedures for determining eligibility for legalization under IRCA. The decision could open the door for challenges on behalf of well over 100,000 undocumented claimants.[16]

The IA 90 may also ease some of the flow of illegal immigration from major sending countries (Mexico, the Philippines, and the Dominican Republic) by making it easier for immediate family members of permanent residents from these countries to get visas.[17] Prior to passage of the law, immediate family members of Mexican permanent residents could expect to wait nine years to obtain a visa to rejoin their family—a situation that many believed induced illegal immigration.

Employment-Based Immigration

The rhetoric of immigration reform emphasized the shift that the new law represents from family-based to employment-based criteria for admission. It would be logical to assume that a major shift in this direction could generate increased illegal migration as unskilled immigrants with relatives in the United States would be denied visas. In reality, though, this aspect of the new law is unlikely to increase illegal migration to the United States. While the number of employment-based admissions will rise sharply from 40,000 to 140,000, the rise will not come at the expense of family-based admissions. Indeed, family-based admissions themselves will rise slightly under the new law. The law does reflect a new emphasis on skilled rather than unskilled workers (admissions of the unskilled are halved), but the absolute numbers are so small that the impact will be negligible.[18]

The Immigration Act of 1990 and Employment Verification

Finally, the IA 90 is significant both for what it did and did not do vis à vis the control of illegal immigration. The bill that was considered by a House-Senate conference committee authorized a pilot project to test the use of drivers' licenses as a national identity card. The project, which was proposed by Senator Alan K. Simpson (R-

WY), would have coded biometric data (finger prints) onto the licenses. The applicant's identity would be validated before the license was issued and the license could then be used to establish both employment authorization and identity under IRCA. (Drivers licenses with photos can now be used only to establish identity.)[19]

The proposal touched off a firestorm of opposition among Hispanic legislators led by Congressman Edward Roybal (D-CA) that threatened to kill the bill, a bill that otherwise had the legislators' strong support. Pressure from the White House led Simpson to delete the proposal and the bill survived (Kirschten, 1990). But the lesson of the revolt was clear: prospects for any form of national identification system were politically dead for the forseeable future. As Congressman Howard Berman recently stated: "The possibility of a national identifier is over and gone—it won't happen in this decade" (Berman, 1991).

In sum, the IA 90 only deepens the problems that employers face in meeting the pressures and counterpressures of sanctions and antidiscrimination. On the one hand, a misstep could expose employers to substantial new financial liability under the IA 90's document fraud provisions. On the other hand, defensive efforts that go too far could lead to violations of the law's new anti-discrimination provisions. As the editors of *Interpreter Releases*, the most respected digest of immigration law and policy in the field, have written,

> Since 1986 employers have had to walk a tightrope between IRCA's employer sanctions and antidiscrimination provisions. . . . It can be argued that the 1990 Act removes employers' tightrope and makes them walk in thin air. . . . In sum, the 1990 Act's discrimination provisions, combined with the current problems in employer sanctions enforcement, may make the INA [Immigration and Nationality Act] unworkable for employers.[20]

At the same time, the IA 90 offered thousands of undocumented immigrants an opportunity to gain legal status and escape the strictures of employer sanctions. Finally, debate over the law marked another setback for a national identity card.

IMPLEMENTING SANCTIONS AT THE INS: MOTION WITHOUT MOVEMENT

While Congress was enacting major shifts in immigration policy, significant administrative changes were slow to emerge at the agency level, despite the efforts and intentions of the new INS Commissioner, Eugene McNary. Soon after taking the job, McNary made it clear that he was interested in attacking some of the institutional problems facing the INS's enforcement divisions. These included the overlapping jurisdiction of the Investigations and Border Patrol branches and the autonomy with which the agency's regional, district, and Border Patrol sector offices operated, an autonomy reflected in widely varying enforcement practices and outcomes across the country.[21] The principal vehicle chosen for agency reform was a major reorganization plan that McNary submitted to Attorney General Richard Thornburgh in June 1990. The plan would have:

□ Reduced significantly the power of the four regional commissioners who would be renamed regional administrators;
□ Abolished the regions' role in enforcement;
□ Closed several Border Patrol sectors located away from the border; and
□ Ended the use of Border Patrol agents in the enforcement of employer sanctions.[22]

One year later a plan has been approved by the Justice Department that would implement some of these changes and would centralize much of the INS's operations in Washington, D.C. For the past year it was widely reported that the leadership of the INS is locked in a running feud with senior officials at the Justice Department over a range of matters large and small (*The Washington Times*, 1991).

At the same time, the level of sanctions-related penalties appears to be declining (see table 12.1). For INS activity as a whole, the number of notices of intent to fine (NIF) fell 31 percent, from 3,547 to 2,460, between FY 1989 and FY 1990, while the number of final orders issued during the same period fell by 19 percent, from 1,616

Table 12.1 INS EMPLOYER SANCTIONS ACTIVITY
(Includes both Investigations and Border Patrol)

	FY 1988	FY 1989	FY 1990	FY 1991 (projected)*
Warnings	3,061	2,108	2,099	2,640
NIFs	1,648	3,547	2,460	2,130
Final Orders	N/A	1,616	1,310	1,068

Source, Immigration and Naturalization Service.
*Projected totals based on reported figures from October and November 1990.

to 1,310. Activity levels in early FY 1991 indicate that further reductions are likely.

For the Investigations branch the trends are slightly different (see table 12.2). A downward trend in NIFs is noticeable here, too. The trend in warnings is less clear, however, with warnings increasing substantially in the Southern region and staying relatively constant in the Eastern and Western regions. The ratio of warnings to NIFs increased in three of the five regions.

INS officials offer a number of explanations for the decline in sanctions-related enforcement activity. First, they point to a January 1990 policy statement issued by Commissioner McNary barring agents from fining employers for paperwork-only violations where no education visit has been made. Following this order the number of paperwork-only fines fell dramatically.[23]

Second, there has been a continuing diversion of enforcement resources to other INS and congressional priorities, principally the criminal alien removal provisions of the Immigration Act of 1990. Under these provisions, INS agents can execute warrants in non-immigration cases, are granted general arrest authority for all offenses committed in their presence, and are authorized to carry firearms.

Third, agency officials note that successful actions have declined as use of fraudulent documents has proliferated, making cases more difficult and increasing the time they take to investigate and prosecute. They also note that the downturn in the economy has generally led to reduced hiring.

This reduced level of activity does not characterize sanctions enforcement alone. Despite the Congress's announced interest in expanding employer education in the area of anti-discrimination, it appears that the INS's employer education arm, the Employer Labor Relations (ELR) division, has atrophied significantly. The division,

Table 12.2 EMPLOYER SANCTIONS ACTIVITY (INVESTIGATIONS BRANCH ONLY)

	Warnings			NIFs		
	1988	1989	1990	1988	1989	1990
INS	1,425	1,199	1,375	1,092	1,700	1,278
N. Reg.	318	436	321	309	310	233
S. Reg.	177	133	432	437	706	339
E. Reg.	603	341	327	148	289	261
W. Reg.	327	289	295	198	395	445

Source, Immigration and Naturalization Service.

which agency officials believed would assume the lead in its anti-discrimination education campaign, appears to have been a victim of the proposed reorganization, which would have phased out the office.[24] Not surprisingly, the announcement of the proposed reorganization led ELR staff to seek positions elsewhere, and little capacity remains, at least within the central office. This leaves only the relatively small staff of attorneys in the Department of Justice's Office of Special Counsel (OSC) to carry out the anti-discrimination education mandated by the IA 90. These developments suggest little promise that a systematic campaign to educate employers and employees about their rights and obligations under IRCA and Title VII's anti-discrimination provisions will take place.

DEVELOPMENTS IN CASE LAW AND REGULATIONS: THE REGULATORY RATCHET MOVES UP

IRCA represented a major expansion of federal regulation in an anti-regulatory era. Because its framers were sensitive to the compliance burden that the new law would impose on employers, the law includes a number of protections that are unusual by federal regulatory standards. These protections include an 18-month transition period to full enforcement of sanctions, mandatory employer education, and the creation of an affirmative defense against prosecution for knowingly hiring an undocumented alien once the law's verification requirements (i.e., filling out the I-9) have been satisfied. These protections were accompanied by frequently stated congressional assurances that employers would not have to become forensic experts to determine the validity of documents presented by job applicants.

However, recent developments in case law and INS regulations seem to be eroding the safeguards extended to employers. The most significant of these pertain to what constitutes the "knowing" hiring (or "continuing to hire") of an undocumented alien. Here, the clear direction of both case law and regulation has been away from a strict intent standard requiring proof of actual knowledge toward a negligence standard of constructive or imputed knowledge. That is, the employer is now liable for what he or she *should have known*, not what what he or she actually *did know*.

Regulations issued by the INS in summer 1990 offered a comparatively expansive definition of the term "knowing" that reaches:

not only actual knowledge but also knowledge which may fairly be inferred through notice of certain facts and circumstances which would lead a person, through the exercise of reasonable care, to know about a certain condition.[25]

The standard's breadth was criticized by the American Immigration Lawyers Association (AILA), which expressed concerns that it would lead to sanctioning employers for negligent rather than intentional acts. AILA suggested that the agency use instead a narrower "conscious avoidance" standard (often used in criminal law), which ascribes knowledge only to those who act with a "conscious purpose to avoid learning the truth" (Schmidt, 1990).

A recent decision by an administrative law judge in an employer sanctions case, *United States of America v. Collins Foods International*,[26] now on appeal to the federal courts, provides an insight into the potential reach of this interpretation of the knowledge standard.

In *Collins*, an administrative law judge found the owner of a Sizzler Steak House in Arizona guilty of the knowing hiring of an undocumented alien. The manager of the steak house had promised a job over the telephone to the brother of a former colleague whom he had known in Mexico. When the brother appeared, the manager checked his driver's license and then, some time later (how much later remained in dispute throughout the trial), his social security card.

The judge's subsequent discussion of the inadequacy of the restaurant manager's inspection of the social security card suggests the standard of care to which employers may now be held in inspecting documents under IRCA:

> At a glance the face of the card might not appear to be false. Both the genuine (social security card) and the false card have large letters reading "SOCIAL SECURITY" across the top, drawings of columns at the sides, a circle in the center, and a signature across the bottom.
>
> Nonetheless, more than a glance is required by the legislation. The card must appear reasonably to be valid. Had Soto taken the time to make a comparison, he would have found that the printing on the reverse side of the card did not contain all of the language found on the Social Security card example provided in the INS Handbook. He further would have found that every Social Security card is considered void if laminated. . . .
>
> Finally, Soto would have found that Rodriguez was misspelled, and that the card presented by Rodriguez made no reference to the United States.[27]

While the judge's decision stops short of mandating that Mr. Soto become a forensic expert, it does appear to require a rather careful inspection of documents to determine their authenticity.

This constructive knowledge standard should be viewed alongside employers' increased liability under IRCA's anti-discrimination provisions, and the way in which INS prosecutions of employers for receiving fraudulent documents has been made easier. Taken together, these developments make it clear that employers enjoy fewer and fewer degrees of freedom in meeting the regulatory requirements of IRCA. At the same time, their exposure to civil and criminal liability continues to expand, even as enforcement declines.

SHOULD EMPLOYER SANCTIONS BE REPEALED?

In this final section I examine the arguments for and against the repeal of sanctions, viewing them in light of the evidence presented by the papers in this volume. I begin with a brief survey of sanctions' impacts.

The Impacts of Employer Sanctions

Below is a brief summary of sanctions' impacts as presented by the analysts in this volume.

FLOWS OF ILLEGAL IMMIGRANTS

The analyses of flows based on apprehensions along the southern border indicate that illegal immigration has declined since IRCA's enactment in late 1986. But the comparatively steep decline evident through FY 89 reversed itself sharply in FY 1990, as the number of apprehensions per linewatch hour rose 22 percent. While the level of apprehensions in 1990 remained fully one-third lower than the level attained in 1986, the reversal since 1989 tends to reinforce the conclusion that flows have been moving upwards toward their pre-IRCA levels (see chapter 7 of this volume).

IMPACT ON FARM LABOR STABILITY

Another indicator of the effectiveness of employer sanctions is trends in the farm labor employment. Martin and Taylor argue in chapter 9 that if sanctions were having their intended effect there would have been less worker turnover and more regular employment of authorized workers in California agriculture. Their analysis reveals this not to be the case. Instead, farmworker turnover is increasing, and "all indications are that new and vulnerable immigrant workers continue to be drawn into seasonal farm work, largely through the recruitment of farm labor contractors."

NATIONAL ORIGIN AND CITIZENSHIP DISCRIMINATION

The evidence that sanctions have led to increased discrimination in hiring against ethnic minorities derives primarily from the two studies conducted by the GAO in 1988 and 1989. The studies rely on the self-reported retrospective answers of employers, a significant share of whom revealed that since 1986 they had introduced discriminatory practices on the basis of their understanding of the 1986 immigration law. Specifically, five percent of respondents reported that as a result of IRCA they began a practice of not hiring persons because of their foreign appearance or accent. Eight percent reported that as a result of IRCA they applied the law's employment verification system only to foreign-looking and sounding persons. Fourteen percent responded that they began a practice to hire only persons born in the United States or not hire persons with temporary work eligibility because of IRCA (GAO, 1990). These results were validated by an Urban Institute audit of hiring practices, which revealed that Hispanic testers were three times as likely to encounter unfavorable treatment when applying for jobs as were closely matched Anglo auditors.

Unlike data on sanctions' impact on flows, the basic findings of the GAO have been severely criticized by some scholars and politicians who claim the results carry little weight because no pre-IRCA baseline of discriminatory behavior exists. They claim that because we have no baseline there is insufficient evidence on which to base a judgment that employer sanctions *caused* additional discrimination (Teitelbaum, 1990).

While this argument has merit, it goes too far. Given the way in which GAO studies in 1988 and 1989 strongly cross-validate one another, and given the supporting evidence provided by The Urban Institute's hiring audit and the numerous studies of sanctions-related discrimination conducted by other public and private agencies, it is reasonable to conclude that some new discrimination can be tied to IRCA. That the findings of so many studies conducted by so many different institutions using different methods converge around the same results increases confidence in GAO's survey results.

Further, while critics may contend that the substantial evidence indicating that sanctions have led to increased discrimination is largely circumstantial and flawed, no evidence has been advanced that demonstrates that employer sanctions did not give rise to increased discrimination.[28] Given the vital interests at stake, such as the right to work and all that flows from it, policymakers may need some affirmative evidence indicating that sanctions are not linked to increased discrimination before they dismiss the results of the GAO and others.

Put simply, it appears that over the first few years of implementation, sanctions appear to have had a limited effect in curbing illegal immigration, have not succeeded in making California's agricultural workforce more stable, and have led to increased discrimination.

The Case for Repeal

The evidence arrayed above suggests that at least in the short run sanctions are not working as designed. It could be argued, though, that no statute works exactly as the framers intend, and few congressional actions—especially those with broad societal implications like IRCA—can show positive effects by the end of their second full year of implementation. Indeed, had the nation's environmental or occupational safety and health laws been subjected to comparable cost-benefit analyses so early, it is unlikely they would remain on the books today.

But in some ways the case of IRCA and employer sanctions is unique. No major federal law enacted in recent years has been demonstrated to have the unintentional effect of significantly increasing discrimination against minority citizens. Because one of the strongest thrusts of public policy over the past 25 years has been to eliminate discrimination against the nation's ethnic and racial minorities, the possibility that sanctions might have increased discrimination strikes an especially sensitive nerve that makes waiting for better evidence or more complete compliance difficult.

CAN WE REDUCE DISCRIMINATION?

This in turn raises the question: is it likely (versus possible) that the Congress and administration can respond to this discrimination in a manner that will significantly reduce, if not eliminate, it short of sanctions' repeal? Are there practicable reforms that could reduce discrimination that are within political and fiscal reach?

The GAO reports that much of the discrimination detected was based on confusion about IRCA's employer requirements. Indeed, employers with high percentages of Hispanic or Asian employees were more likely to report discriminatory practices than were employers with lower percentages (Task Force on IRCA-Related Discrimination, 1990). This finding suggests two reforms: substantial simplification of the document verification process, and increased employer and employee education. Are such changes politically likely? The answer appears to be no. The prospects of a single national identity card are low to nil. The idea has a few avid proponents and a substantially larger number of fervent opponents, as the revolt led by Democratic Congressman Edward Roybal (D-CA) against using state drivers' licenses as identity documents makes clear.

At the same time, prospects for the kind of massive, energetic employer education campaign needed to reverse the discriminatory practices uncovered by the GAO appear to be waning. The principal institutional vehicle for this campaign, the Employer Labor Relations branch of the INS, has atrophied in the wake of its proposed elimination, and responsibility for carrying out such a campaign remains a bureaucratic orphan.

The trend in sanctions case law and regulations toward a negligence standard and away from a strict intent standard (i.e., holding an employer liable for what he should have known, not what he actually knew) should also provide a greater incentive to discriminate against foreign-looking and sounding job applicants. If employers, as in the *Collins* case cited above, are held accountable for not knowing that a laminated social security card is fake, or that the words "United States of America" always appear on the card, many will subject "strangers" to a kind of exacting scrutiny not contemplated by IRCA's framers. This defensive scrutiny can only war against anti-discrimination objectives.

Finally, it could be the case that lawmakers have underestimated the prevalence of discrimination against Hispanics. The employment audit conducted by The Urban Institute provided dismaying findings about the degree to which Hispanics were treated unfavorably compared to their Anglo counterparts. The study's results are, in turn, confirmed by a recent survey conducted by the National Opinion Research Center (NORC) at the University of Chicago (Smith, 1990). The NORC survey found extremely negative stereotypes or images of Hispanics broadly held among respondents. A *majority* of the respondents questioned believed that Hispanics were more inclined than whites to prefer welfare and to be lazier, more prone to violence, less intelligent, and less patriotic. If it is the case that national-origin discrimination is a larger social problem than lawmakers might have guessed, the compounding effects of IRCA could, in turn, be greater than anticipated.

CAN WE INCREASE SANCTIONS' EFFECTIVENESS?

If discrimination can be viewed as the "costs" side of the sanctions equation, reduced illegal immigration and the resulting shifts in the labor market toward greater stability, increased wages, and improved working conditions can be viewed as the "benefits" side of the equation. What can be done to increase the benefits associated with effective immigration controls? Are sanctions likely to be altered in a way that will lead to a significant reduction in undocumented migration to the United States? Here again it is hard to be sanguine.

By authorizing 1,000 new Border Patrol officers and no new staff for the Investigations branch of the INS, the IA 90 sustained a mismatch between resources and responsibilities within the agency. But as we have seen, the new law increased the powers and responsibilities of Investigations in overseeing the highly visible and politically appealing criminal alien removal program. The result is likely to be a further decline in the priority assigned sanctions enforcement, a decline reflected in recent enforcement statistics.

Furthermore, the adaptations seen in the illegal immigrant and employer communities seem likely to erode sanctions' effectiveness. The use of fraudulent documents has grown increasingly common, until it is functionally defeating enforcement of the law according to some observers (see chapter 4 of this volume). And, at least in agriculture, employer "compliance" has led to increased reliance on intermediaries, or farm labor contractors (FLCs). As Martin and Taylor note in chapter 9, these FLCs appear to be proliferating and to be recruiting new, vulnerable, and presumably illegal workers into California agriculture.

At the same time, legislative, regulatory, and judicial adjustments to problems encountered in enforcing sanctions have effectively increased employer liability to both government and private enforcement actions. Taken together, these and other policy changes remove the flexibility employers might have enjoyed in complying with the broad new regimes of labor and civil rights regulation announced by IRCA. In so doing, they may marginally increase compliance costs for law-abiding employers. At the same time, the decline in INS enforcement activity may diminish the compliance costs of employers unwilling to obey IRCA's requirements. Thus, in markets where law-abiding and law-evading firms compete with one another, the latter may come to enjoy an increased cost advantage as these programs evolve.

THE LIMITED LESSONS OF THE EUROPEAN EXPERIENCE

Early proponents of employer sanctions as well as some current observers urge a close examination of the European experience for both the historical and policy lessons that it holds (see chapters 8 and 11). They claim that sanctions in Europe have proved far less controversial, are comparatively more effective in controlling illegal immigration, and do not generate the kind of discrimination seen so far in the United States. The lesson of Europe for American lawmakers, they argue, is the need for patience and a willingness to make incremental changes.

But the European experience may hold less promise than some believe. Recent research reveals substantial differences between European and U.S. political and legal culture (Martin, 1990; Miller, 1990). Despite these differences, which favor the use of sanctions in Europe over their use in the United States, sanctions' recent history in Europe seems increasingly to parallel the frustrations of the U.S. experience. That is, to the extent that they can be ascertained, the results of sanctions enforcement in Europe since the mid-1970s are, in Miller's words, "mixed and still tentative." He writes:

> The phenomenon of illegal alien residency and employment in Western Europe has proven durable and resistant to governmental efforts to curb it. Enforcement of employer sanctions in Western Europe therefore increasingly is perceived in Sisyphean terms, as necessary but insufficient. (Miller, 1990, pp. 3–4)

The differences in legal and political cultures between Western Europe and the United States can be seen in the greater tolerance for high civil and criminal penalties in Europe. In Germany, employers can be fined up to $60,000 per *illegal alien hired* and have the profits that they earned by hiring illegal aliens confiscated (Martin, 1990, p. 3). In France, Parisian courts condemned over half of the violators appearing before them to prison (Martin, 1990, p. 19). Such draconian measures create incentives to compliance that are not politically feasible in the United States. The penalties levied in Europe reflect in part the persistence of unemployment in Europe from the mid-1970s, when sanctions were introduced, through the mid-1980s, and may explain why illegal immigration could be broadly viewed as a comparatively serious crime. By contrast, sanctions were introduced in the U.S. at a time of strong economic growth, low unemployment, and labor shortages.

A second distinction between Europe and the U.S. is the well-developed work and resident permit systems that are found in Europe. These appear crucial to the limited success that controls are thought to have achieved. No such system exists in the U.S. and, as we have seen, the political prospects of introducing even the most rudimentary version of such a system are small. Another important, related difference is that undocumented immigrants appear to have less access to fraudulent documents in Europe than in the United States (Martin, 1990, p. 5).

Third, the system of border controls in place in Europe is far more developed than what is feasible given the long land borders between the U.S. and Mexico. Moreover, until recent developments in Eastern Europe, the economic disparities that have existed between European nations have borne no resemblance to those between the U.S. and Mexico. Sanctions enforcement in Europe, unlike the United States, represents a third line of defense against the flow of undocumented migrants that includes border controls and established systems of work and residence permits. In the United States, for all practical purposes, sanctions operate as a stand-alone system of controls.

Sanctions' proponents often point to the fact that sanctions-related discrimination is not an issue in Europe. But it is hard to know what to make of this claim. In the first place, we have no empirical evidence that this is so. Second, as Miller notes, there is broad agreement that the North African and other immigrant communities in France encounter widespread discrimination, which may mask whatever effects sanctions might cause. To the extent that there is less *confusion-based* discrimination against immigrants in Europe, it is likely that this owes to the resident and work permit systems in place, systems that appear to be beyond political reach in the U.S.

The discussion of discrimination points to what appears to be another relevant difference between Europe and the United States. On this issue, at least, it seems that European officials are more willing to take on faith the fact that sanctions are "working" and that the size of the undocumented population would be higher without them. Our more contentious public policy debate has been cast in terms of quantitative evidence that sanctions do or do not reduce illegal immigration or cause discrimination. In short, the notion that sanctions "work" in Europe may be the product of a broad political consensus around the need for controls, rather than objective evidence that they reduce immigration and have no negative, unin-tended effects.

Finally, from an institutional perspective, it appears that enforce-ment of sanctions in Europe is typically assigned to inspectors charged with enforcing other labor-related laws and to agencies often housed in departments responsible for matching jobs with workers (Martin, 1990, p. 5). This placement *may* contribute to more effective en-forcement than do existing institutional arrangements in the U.S., where labor-related inspections are, for all intents and purposes, carried out separately from inspections to detect immigration-related employment violations. It is here that the European experience may offer its most valuable lesson to U.S. lawmakers.

Despite these differences and the advantages they provide Euro-pean governments, sanctions' recent history in Europe in many ways resembles recent U.S. experience. In France, there is sharp variation in the levels of enforcement between the Paris region and the rest of the country. As Fix and Hill point out in chapter 3, similar regional variation also characterizes sanctions' enforcement in the U.S. In Germany, the number of sanctions cases brought between 1977 and 1989 has dropped steadily, with the number of fines imposed for violations falling by two-thirds. In Germany and Switzerland, Miller notes, the political will to control illegal immigration has fallen off sharply as policies to deregulate labor markets have been introduced (Miller, 1990, p. 37).

CONCLUSION

In sum, the European experience, so often held out by sanctions' proponents as exemplary, offers few concrete lessons in terms of policy guidance, and in the end does not tell a very promising story for sanctions' eventual success in the United States. Furthermore, if we array the evidence of sanctions' limited success in reducing un-documented immigration, stabilizing turnover in low wage indus-tries like California agriculture, and avoiding the unintended costs of additional discrimination, the case for sanctions is not strong. That case is made even weaker by the recent developments in reg-ulatory policy, which should increase the burden borne by law-abiding employers, and by the limited prospects for meaningful re-form.

But the inquiry need not stop here, as other issues are also relevant to the debate over sanctions' repeal.

The Case against Repealing Employer Sanctions

The problems that have dogged sanctions' early enforcement—their limited impacts, the discrimination that has surfaced, and the political and cultural constraints under which they operate—do not close the case on sanctions' repeal. Few U.S. residents believe in open borders: public opinion polls have consistently revealed that popular opinion favors decreasing the number of immigrants who are admitted to the U.S. (Simon, 1987, p. 47). Peter Schuck, a self-professed expansionist when it comes to immigration, notes what he perceives to be an emerging political consensus favoring some growth in immigration levels along with increased use of labor-oriented criteria in determining admissions. He contends that this liberalization of immigration policy is implicitly "coupled with a demand for stepped up enforcement against illegal aliens" (Schuck, 1990). His observations are consistent with the Select Commission for Immigration and Refugee Policy's (SCIRP) vision of immigration policy of "closing the back door while keeping the front door open" (Fuchs, 1990).

In this view, an essential goal of immigration policy, and hence of employer sanctions, is to create a symbol and perception of commitment to controlling membership within the society.

Americans' demand for limits, I believe, springs from a deeper anxiety than the ones discussed earlier. The master theme of immigration politics is the fear that we are losing control of our way of life. We seek to relieve this anxiety by focusing on things, like immigration, we think we can control. Virtually all participants in the long debates about the 1986 reforms managed to agree on one slogan, continually recited as if it were an incantation: "We must regain control of our borders." This slogan was intended to conjure up a memory of a past golden age when we actually exercised control, an age that of course never existed. It also exalted a compelling ideal according to which the nation deliberately chooses whom it wants, excludes those whom it does not want, and sanctions those who violate its rules. The Border Patrol's recent growth testifies to the ideal's evocative force.

Expansionists should not dismiss this popular demand for border enforcement as a macho fantasy about decisive government, impregnable territory, and firm control. Individuals, families and tribes define and defend their turf, not just nations. They may believe, with Frost, that good fences make good neighbors but Michael Walzer stresses a more potent motive: the same fence that keeps most people out is necessary to enable those within to think of themselves as co-venturers and to flourish as a community.

> Immigration threatens Americans' sense of control by seeming to jeopardize three fundamental values: national autonomy, economic security, and the "social contract" that secures the welfare state. Because each of these concerns has some basis in fact, public demands for tougher laws limiting who can enter, work, and claim welfare benefits seem plausible. Past reforms have not succeeded in allaying the public's anxiety. (Schuck, 1990)

At the time of IRCA's enactment it remained unclear whether the law would usher in a new restrictive phase in American immigration policy. Now, in the wake of the Immigration Act of 1990, it seems clear that it did not. Hence, IRCA and sanctions may reflect a consensus—at least among lawmakers—that tolerates increased admissions as long as the perception of control remains in place. In short, sanctions are part of a tacit political bargain that makes it possible to sustain the nation's essentially liberal immigration policies.

Sanctions may also have a related, positive effect on immigration policy that goes beyond providing political "cover" for liberalizing our immigration laws. Sanctions may be impelling us to rationalize of government policy on granting legal status to immigrants with strong claims to community membership. Prior to the enactment of sanctions, the "tax" for being undocumented was comparatively low. While deportation and exploitation were always a threat, work was not prohibited. This permitted the government to selectively ignore the presence of groups whose claims for inclusion were arguably strong but whose cases raised political and other concerns that made deliberate action difficult (e.g., selected asylum applicants with strong humanitarian claims or other undocumented immigrants classified as permanent residents under color of law, or PRUCOL). The punishing aspect of sanctions—described by some as a slowly tightening noose—could partially account for the several legalization programs of large undocumented populations embedded in the Immigration Act of 1990. Sanctions may have also played a role in the INS's willingness to settle the *American Baptist Churches* case (see note 14).

Whatever the causal relationship, the introduction of the temporary protected status or safe haven principle,[29] the INS's willingness to readjudicate cases where asylum has been denied in the past, and the publication after 10 years of new, liberalized asylum regulations should help disentangle the conceptually distinct issues of sanctions' merits and whether Central Americans should be permitted to enter and reside in the United States on humanitarian grounds.

Finally, despite the slow and in some ways troubling start of sanctions' implementation, it could be that there is no good policy alternative to sanctions and that they are a necessary part of any overall, long-term strategy to control illegal immigration. Shifting the focus of enforcement from employers to undocumented immigrants is too inefficient.[30] Besides, even if the nation chose to sanction illegal entry more severely, we do not have the prison space available for detention or the courtrooms available for adjudication, and the migrants themselves are unlikely to be able to pay even modest fines.

Eliminating sanctions and enforcing existing labor regulations (e.g., minimum wage, child labor, workplace safety) in their place, as some have advocated, may do too little to eliminate the job magnet. Indeed, studies have found that most undocumented immigrants are receiving at least the minimum wage. Relying on increased border patrolling and interdiction could also be portrayed as unrealistic given the length of the border, the incentive for undocumented border-crossers to keep trying to enter until they finally succeed, and the large share of undocumented immigrants who enter the country legally and overstay their temporary visas.

PRACTICAL REFORMS

Moreover, it could be argued that a series of reforms is possible (if not imminent) that could make enforcement more fair and effective and generate less discrimination. Among such reforms (each of which is described elsewhere in this volume) are the following:

□ Substantially increased resources dedicated to employer education regarding discrimination (Fix, chapter 10; Bach and Meissner, chapter 11);
□ A federally funded follow-up survey of sanctions-related discrimination, using both audits and surveys (Fix, chapter 10);
□ More systematic oversight of sanctions practices and penalties, coupled with the expedited development of a national database that permits enforcement officials to track implementation for fairness and consistency (Fix and Hill, chapter 3);
□ Rapid transition to two identification documents for immigrants (Fix, chapter 10; Bach and Meissner, chapter 11); and
□ A substantial expansion in the role assigned the Department of Labor (DOL) in enforcing employer sanctions (Bach and Meissner, chapter 11).

The most challenging and potentially far-reaching reform would be to vest substantially greater enforcement and prosecution authority for sanctions and for anti-discrimination education with the DOL. One of the lessons of the European experience is that linking sanctions to labor law enforcement may increase their effectiveness. Not only would enforcement rely on an inspection staff that is more experienced in enforcing workplace regulations, it also has the advantage of identifying those employers who violate both immigration and labor laws and coordinating their prosecution. Inspection coverage would be expanded. Also, given the fact that DOL field operations are more automated than those of the INS, more effective national oversight and management might be possible. At the same time, shifting increased responsibility to the DOL would have the derivative benefit of allowing the Inspections division of the INS to focus on the drug, criminal alien, and document fraud missions that have dominated the agency's recent law enforcement efforts. In short, over time, immigration-related regulatory responsibilities would continue to migrate to the DOL, a regulatory agency, while immigration-related criminal law enforcement functions would be emphasized within the INS.

Bolstering the DOL's institutional role in administering IRCA may also make sense given the fact that it already administers a major civil rights program through the Office of Federal Contract Compliance (OFCCP). This capability could prove invaluable in linking administration of employer sanctions with the conduct of a broad and effective employer education campaign under IRCA and Title VII's anti-discrimination mandates.

Notes

1. The name of the subcommittee was changed from the House Subcommittee for Immigration, Refugees and International Law to the House Subcommittee for International Law, Immigration and Refugees. *Immigration Policy and Law* 4, February 7.

2. Many of these reforms had been suggested in a report developed by a legislatively designated task force composed of the Attorney General and the Chairmen of the U.S. Civil Rights Commission and the Equal Employment Opportunity Commission, "Report and Recommendations of the Task Force on IRCA-Related Discrimination, September 1990." The reforms were subsequently incorporated in legislation proposed by Congressman John Bryant (D-TX), i.e., the IRCA Antidiscrimination Amendments of 1990, H.R. 5572.

3. Section 531, IA 90.

4. Section 532, IA 90.

5. Section 533, IA 90.

6. Section 536, IA 90.

7. Section 535, IA 90.

8. Section 536(a)(IV), IA 90.

9. 8 USC 1101(b)(2), or the Moorhead Amendment, mandates that a sufficient share of the funds authorized for increased enforcement under IRCA be provided to increase the number of Border Patrol personnel by 50 percent over the level in 1986.

10. Section 501, 503, IA 90.

11. Section 541, IA 90.

12. Section 301, IA 90.

13. See "The Immigration Act of 1990 Analyzed: Part 2—Family-Sponsored Immigrants." *Interpreter Releases* 67, p. 1398 (Dec. 10, 1990).

14. Section 302, IA 90. Shortly after (and perhaps stimulated by) the passage of the IA 90 the government settled a major case, *American Baptist Churches vs. Thornburgh*, involving undocumented Salvadorans and Guatemalans. U.S. District Court, N. Dist. CA. Civ. No. C-85-3255 RFP, December 1990. Under the terms of the settlement, Salvadorans and Guatemalans who have been in the United States since fall 1990 and who register with the INS will have their claims for asylum adjudicated *de novo* and will be granted a stay of deportation and work authorization for the period during which their cases are pending.

15. Section 132, IA 90. This controversial provision cloaks this targeted amnesty by stating that 40 percent of the visas granted under this provision "go to the country that received the most visas under section 314 of IRCA." That country was Ireland.

16. See *McNary v. Haitian Refugee Center*, No. 89-1332, U.S. S. Ct. February 21, 1991, noted in "High Court Rules Aliens Can Sue over Procedures in Amnesty Law." *The New York Times*, February 21, 1991, p. A1.

17. Immediate family members are defined as spouses and minor children. The law accomplished this by allowing visas granted under this provision to exceed the 25,000 annual cap on all family and employment visas extended to individual nations.

18. Visas for unskilled workers fall from 18,000 to 10,000. Section 121, IA 1990.

19. S.358, Sec. 322. 1990.

20. "The Immigration Act of 1990 Analyzed: Part 11—Employer Sanctions, Antidiscrimination and Document Fraud." *Interpreter Releases* 68, pp. 245–246 (March 4, 1991).

21. See, generally, "Immigration Control: Bordering on the Impossible." Government Executive 22, September 1990, pp. 32–39. See also Memorandum to Regional Commissioners et al. of January 9, 1990, from the Office of Commissioner Eugene McNary, cautioning against placing "undue emphasis . . . on the act of fining alone, or on maximizing the amounts of fines imposed." The memo also bars the use of quotas for fines in setting employee performance standards. See also chapter 3 of this volume.

22. See "McNary Proposes Massive INS Reorganization." *Interpreter Releases* 67, p. 605 (May 25, 1990).

23. While agency officials claim that the ratio of paperwork-only to knowing, substantive violations has declined, the INS's data collection does not, as yet, permit an analysis of the accuracy of the statement. Current efforts to develop a complete case tracking system are now being worked out, according to agency officials.

24. See note 22.

25. Federal Register 25, no. 25,932 (June, 25, 1990).

26. Executive Office for Immigration Review, Office of the Chief Administrative Hearing Officer, Case No. 89100084 (January 9, 1990).

27. See note 26.

28. I owe this insight to my colleague Frank D. Bean of the University of Texas.

29. Safe haven makes possible the temporary admission of groups of individuals fleeing political turmoil, natural disaster, and the like without undergoing individual adjudication. As such, its introduction in the IA 90 is thought by many to represent a major step forward in the development of our humanitarian immigrant admissions policy.

30. Former Colorado Governor Richard Lamm has written that enforcing the immigration laws against individual immigrants rather than their employers is like prosecuting individual bettors rather than the bookies who run gambling operations (Lamm and Inhoff, 1985).

References

Berman, Howard. 1991. Comments at the Carnegie Commission for International Peace. Washington, D.C., February 1.

Berman, Howard. 1991. Comments to a seminar sponsored by the Carnegie Commission on International Peace, February 1. Reported in *Immigration Policy and Law* 4 (February 7).

Cornelius, Wayne. 1990. Quoted in "Traffic in Fake Documents Is Blamed for Rise in Illegal Immigration," by Robert Suro. *The New York Times*, November 26, p. A14.

Fix, Michael, and Jeffrey Passel. 1991. "The Door Remains Open: Recent Immigration to the United States and a Preliminary Analysis of the Immigration Act of 1990." Program for Research on Immigration Policy, PRIP-UI-14, February.

Fuchs, Lawrence H. 1990. *The American Kaleidoscope: Race, Ethnicity, and the Civic Culture.* Hanover, N.H.: Wesleyan University Press.

GAO (U.S. General Accounting Office). 1990. "Immigration Reform, Employer Sanctions and the Question of Discrimination." GAO/GGD-90-62, March, pp. 41–43.

Kirschten, Richard. 1990. "How an Immigration Bill Barely Survived." *The National Journal*, November 3, p. 2666.

Martin, Philip. "The Quest for Control: Immigration to Western Europe." Draft. The University of California, Davis, December 28.

Lamm, Richard, and Gary Inhoff. 1985. *The Immigration Time Bomb: The Fragmenting of America.* New York: E.P. Dutton.

Miller, Mark J. 1990. "Towards Understanding State Capacity to Regulate International Migration: Employer Sanctions in Western Europe." Prepared for the Southern Political Science Association meeting, Atlanta, Georgia, November.

Ruggles, Patricia, and Michael Fix. 1985. "Impacts and Potential Impacts of Central American Migrants on HHS and Related Programs of Assistance." Urban Institute Working Paper, September.

Schmidt, Paul W. 1990. "INS Employer Sanctions Interim Regulations." *Interpreter Releases* 67, p. 1057 (September 24).

Schuck, Peter. 1990. "The Great Immigration Debate." *The American Prospect* (Fall): 111.

Simon, Rita. 1987. "Immigration and American Attitudes." *Public Opinion*, July/August, p. 47.

Smith, Tom. 1990. "Ethnic Images." National Opinion Research Center, GSS Topical Report no. 19, December.

Task Force on IRCA-Related Discrimination. "Report and Recommendations of the Task Force on IRCA-Related Discrimination," September, p. 23.

Teitelbaum, Michael. 1990. Letter to Hon. John R. Dunne. In Task Force on IRCA-Related Discrimination, "Report and Recommendations of the Task Force on IRCA-Related Discrimination" (Appendix 3), September.

The Washington Times. 1991. "Justice Targets INS Chief for Ouster." *The Washington Times*, February 25, p. A3.

ABOUT THE EDITOR

Michael Fix is an attorney and Senior Research Associate at The Urban Institute, where his work focuses on the issues of immigration, regulatory policy, federalism, and civil rights. Recent works include: *Opportunities Denied, Opportunities Diminished: Racial Discrimination in Hiring* (with Margery A. Turner and Raymond J. Struyk); *Enforcing Employer Sanctions: Challenges and Strategies* (with Paul T. Hill); and *Coping with Mandates: What Are the Alternatives?* (coedited with Daphne A. Kenyon).

ABOUT THE CONTRIBUTORS

Robert Bach is Associate Professor of Sociology and director of the Institute for Research on Multiculturalism and International Labor at the State University of New York, Binghamton. He is also a research associate at the Carnegie Endowment for International Peace. Among his recent published works are *Shifting the Burden: The Impacts of Employer Sanctions on U.S. Labor Markets* (with Howard Brill) and "Hemispheric Migration in the 1990s."

Frank D. Bean is Ashbel Smith Professor of Sociology and Research Associate, Population Research Center at the University of Texas at Austin. A demographer with specializations in international migration, fertility, the demography of racial and ethnic groups, and population policy, his recent books include *Undocumented Migration to the United States: IRCA and the Experience of the 1980s* (edited with Barry Edmonston and Jeffrey S. Passel) and *The Hispanic Population of the United States* (with Marta Tienda).

Deborah A. Cobb-Clark is Assistant Professor of Economics at Illinois State University. Before that, she worked at the U.S. Department of Labor researching the impact of immigration on the U.S. labor market. She was awarded the 1991 Dorothy S. Thomas Award for her paper entitled "Migrant and Immigration Policy Selectivity: The Impact on the Wages of Married Foreign-Born Women."

Barry Edmonston is a senior research associate in the Population Studies Center of The Urban Institute. He was previously Associate Professor of Demography and Epidemiology at Cornell University's International Population Center. He has studied population change in Canada and the United States, fertility variations among immigrant groups, and demographic models of the family in recent years. Recent publications include *Population Distribution in American Cities*, and *Infant Mortality in Bangladesh*, coedited with Rahdeshyam Bairagi.

Paul T. Hill is a senior social scientist in RAND's Washington office. He directs studies of accountability in site-managed public schools, urban education, and immigration, and contributes to RAND studies on defense policy. Before joining RAND he directed the National Institute of Education's Compensatory Education Study and conducted research on housing and education for the Office of Economic Opportunity. Recent publications include *Enforcing Employer Sanctions: Challenges and Strategies* (with Michael Fix) and *High Schools with Character.*

Jason Juffras is a research associate with The Urban Institute's Changing Domestic Priorities Project. He has studied and written about a variety of budget, human resource, and immigration issues. Currently he serves as project manager for The Urban Institute's Roundtable on Children, a bipartisan effort of high-level officials, scholars, and program managers to promote better public policy for children. Recent publications include *Impact of the Immigration Reform and Control Act on the Immigration and Naturalization Service*, as well as discussion papers on child support assurance, a children's tax credit, and promising prevention programs for children.

B. Lindsay Lowell is a social demographer at the U.S. Department of Labor. He has studied migration historically and addresses development issues in the book *Scandinavian Exodus*. He also has conducted substantial research on unauthorized migration and the U.S. labor market. His most recent work includes contributions to *The President's First Triennial Report on Immigration*, and editorship of *Foreign Born Workers and the Labor Force: A Baseline Assessment of U.S. Immigration Legislation.*

Philip L. Martin is Professor of Agricultural Economics at the University of California, Davis. He was a Staff Associate at the Brookings Institute 1978, and an economist for the Select Commission on Immigration and Refugee Policy in 1979. He has conducted research on immigration and labor market issues in the U.S. and in Germany, Turkey, Egypt, and Mexico. He is a member of the Commission on Agricultural Workers established by the Immigration Reform and Control Act of 1986.

Doris Meissner is a senior associate at the Carnegie Endowment for

International Peace where she directs its Immigration Policy Project. She served in a variety of senior positions in the U.S. Department of Justice and the Immigration and Naturalization Service during the 1970s and 1980s. Recent publications include "America's Economy in the 1990s: What Role Should Immigration Play?" (with Robert Bach), and "The Legalization Countdown: A Third Quarter Assessment" (with Demetrios Papademetriou).

Demetrios G. Papademetriou is Director of Immigration Policy and Research at the Bureau for International Labor Affairs in the U.S. Department of Labor. He has taught International Policy Economy and Comparative Public Policy at the University of Maryland, Duke University, and the Graduate Faculty of the New School for Social Research. His most recent works include *The Unsettled Relationship: Migration and Development* (with Philip Martin) and *Reluctant Promised Lands: Immigration Labor in Advanced Industrial Societies.*

Jeffrey S. Passel is The Urban Institute's codirector of the Program for Research on Immigration Policy, a joint program with RAND. Over the last decade, he has written extensively on measuring illegal immigration. Prior to joining The Urban Institute, he directed the Census Bureau's program of population estimates and projections and its research on demographic methods for measuring census undercount. Recent publications include *The Coverage of Population in the 1980 Census* (with Robert Fay and J. Gregory Robinson), and "A Count of the Uncountable: Estimates of Undocumented Aliens Counted in the 1980 United States Census" (with Robert Warren).

Abby Robyn is deputy director of the Education and Human Resources Program at RAND. She is currently directing a study of adult immigrants' vocational education needs. Her primary research focus is education implementation issues.

Elizabeth Rolph is a political scientist in the Social Policy Department of RAND. She has conducted and collaborated on numerous research efforts primarily in the areas of implementation analysis, program evaluation, and program design. In addition to her work on the implementation of IRCA, she is currently engaged in research on design and implementation problems in compensation systems and on alternative health care delivery systems.

Martina Shea is an economic statistician in the Poverty and Wealth Branch, Housing and Household Economic Statistics Division, U.S. Bureau of the Census. While working at the U.S. Department of Labor, she coauthored *The President's First Report on the Implementation and Impact of Employer Sanctions.*

Shirley J. Smith is a labor economist in the Division of Immigration Policy and Research, Bureau of International Labor Affairs, U.S. Department of Labor. She coauthored "The Effects of Immigration on the U.S. Economy" which is part of *The President's First Comprehensive Triennial Report on Immigration,* as well as *The President's First and Second Reports on the Implementation and Impact of Employer Sanctions.*

J. Edward Taylor is Assistant Professor of Agricultural Economics at the University of California, Davis. He is a developmental and labor economist and an applied econometrician. He has conducted village household surveys in rural Mexico and farm employer surveys in California. He has been a Research Associate at The Urban Institute and a visiting scholar in the Harvard University Migration and Development Program. His Ph.D. thesis on migration from rural Mexico won the Outstanding Thesis Award from the American Agricultural Economics Association.

Wendy Zimmermann is a research associate at The Urban Institute. She has a master's degree in Latin American Studies from Stanford University. Since she began working at the Urban Institute in 1989, she has conducted research primarily on immigration policy and employment discrimination. Most recently she has been researching immigrant policy in Europe and in the United States.